This is a Parragon Book
This edition published in 2002

Parragon
Queen Street House
4 Queen Street
Bath BA1 1HE,UK

ISBN 0-75258-441-3

Produced for Parragon by
Foundry Design & Production
Cover design by Design Principals, Warminster

Thanks to: Sonya Newland, Claire Dashwood and Ian Powling.

A copy of the CIP data for this book is available from the British Library.

Printed in China

ILLUSTRATED GUIDE TO BRITISH HISTORY

David Boyle, Alan Brown, Malcolm Chandler,
David Harding, Brenda Ralph Lewis and Jon Sutherland

GENERAL EDITOR:
Professor E. J. Evans

Contents

HOW TO USE THIS BOOK

The entries in this encyclopedia are organised into seven thematic chapters, each with an introductory synopsis, including a timeline and details of some of the key events covered.

- To find information on a particular era or year, use the Chronological List of Entries on pages 6–13.
- To follow a particular sub-theme within a chapter, use the key and the cross-references indicated next to the entry heading.
- To find information on a specific event, person or subject, use the Index on pages 262–272.
- Events that have had a particularly significant impact on history can be traced through the 'Triumphs & Tragedies' theme recurring throughout the book.
- Each spread contains a 'Distant Voices' quotation, offering a contemporary insight into subjects and events.

Chronological List of Entries

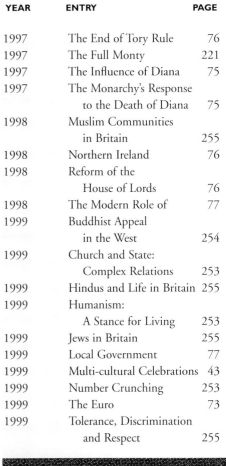

Introduction

NO AREA OF COMPARABLE SIZE has had such a varied and distinguished history as have the British Isles. During the past 2,000 years, most of Britain was first occupied as part of the Roman Empire, then became the site of frequent conflict between Celts, Angles, Jutes, Saxons and Danes. The Norman Conquest of 1066 established a new type of leadership of England, and it stuck. Since 1066, no successful invasion of England has taken place, and the political stability which has been such a pronounced feature of the country's development owes much to the long thread of continuity which has been woven in a nation whose borders have not been breached.

The themes of integration and diversity are crucial to understanding British history. Out of the frequently warring groups which struggled for supremacy after the retreat of the Roman armies early in the fifth century emerged four significant states: England, Scotland, Wales and Ireland. All had their separate histories, but they have been closely interconnected throughout the last millennium. Whereas historians outside Scotland, Wales and Ireland used to write 'the history of Britain' as if it were basically the history of England, the story of these islands is now more frequently (and more appropriately) understood as a genuinely British one. It reflects conflict at least as much as co-operation. Actual political unification is surprisingly late in coming. England and Scotland, who fought over border territory almost incessantly during the Middle Ages, shared one ruler (usually a member of the Scottish house of Stuart) from the death of Queen Elizabeth I in 1603, but the nations did not become politically united until 1707. Even then, Scotland retained its own legal and educational systems. English power, under the Plantagenet monarch Edward I, had established a position of dominance over Wales from the end of the thirteenth century but administrative unification did not come until the first half of the sixteenth century during the reign of Henry VIII.

The area of the British Isles which sustained most conflict over the last millennium has been Ireland, which has endured a succession of religious and political struggles for supremacy. The history of a largely Catholic Ireland cannot be written without understanding the influence, and frequently the social and cultural dominance, of both the Scottish and English Protestant settlers from the sixteenth century. The Catholic Stuart monarch James II tried, and failed, to win back the English and Scottish crowns from Ireland in 1690 when he was defeated by a Dutchman who was the Protestant King of England. Throughout the later seventeenth and eighteenth centuries, English interests and concerns greatly influenced Irish development before fear both of revolution and French invasion forced the British government to offer political union to Ireland in 1800, on terms which its Protestant elite were unlikely to refuse. The troubled history of relations between Britain and Ireland in the so-called 'United Kingdom of Great Britain and Northern Ireland' has been a prominent feature of

British history during the last two centuries. It has been characterised by a succession of searches for a mutually acceptable settlement both between Britain and Ireland and between the Protestant and Catholic communities within Ireland; the threat of bloodshed and violence has been almost constant. For a significant period, bloodshed has been a bitter reality.

This encyclopedia reflects national diversity and integration as one of its key themes. It shows also what a vital role has been played by the immigration and emigration of minority groups. Its construction also reflects another crucial element in the proper understanding of national development. History is not made only by monarchs and by political leaders. The book gives due weight to the role of both ordinary folk and of those who helped forge its rich culture. Knowing how power is exercised, and by which political and social groups, is crucial to understanding the context in which the lives of ordinary people were lived. Those ordinary people also made their own history in the villages, towns and (later on) the great industrial conurbations of Britain. As this book shows, history works 'bottom up' as well as 'top down'.

Inevitably, though, much attention is paid to the three areas in which Britain can claim to be unique. The encyclopedia charts the development of representative political institutions. It shows how the powers of the monarchs became limited and how, though this was not for the most part the intention of the rulers, Britain emerged as a democracy. It is important to understand how the influence of Britain's middle classes grew, how working people struggled for direct representation and how women demonstrated that they should not be seen as second-class citizens either in terms of political representation or of their social roles. Britain was also one of the few European nations to manage the transition to democracy in the nineteenth and twentieth centuries without political revolution.

The second British claim to uniqueness lies in its industry. Britain was the first nation in the world to undergo that most

thoroughgoing of all transformations, an industrial revolution. How that happened, and with what consequences both for the lives of its citizens and for its role in the world, is one of the central features of this book. It is also closely linked with the third unique element in Britain's history: the development of the British Empire and Britain's world role. By the early twentieth century, Britain ruled over an empire larger than any in recorded history: 'the empire on which the sun never sets'. Though most of the territory which became the 'British Empire' was acquired relatively late, during the eighteenth and nineteenth centuries, Britain was always unusual among European powers in that its main concern over defence was with its coastline rather than with land borders. Britain became the world's leading maritime nation before it became the world's biggest empire and the two factors are closely linked. The success of Britain's industrial revolution depended to a large extent upon the success of its trading overseas. The process of becoming the world's leading trading nation, the 'workshop of the world' and also the world's most substantial imperial power were all closely linked. This encyclopedia shows how the empire was acquired and how that empire confirmed Britain's status as the world's leading power in the nineteenth century. It also shows how, and with what consequences, both empire and world status went into retreat as the twentieth century developed.

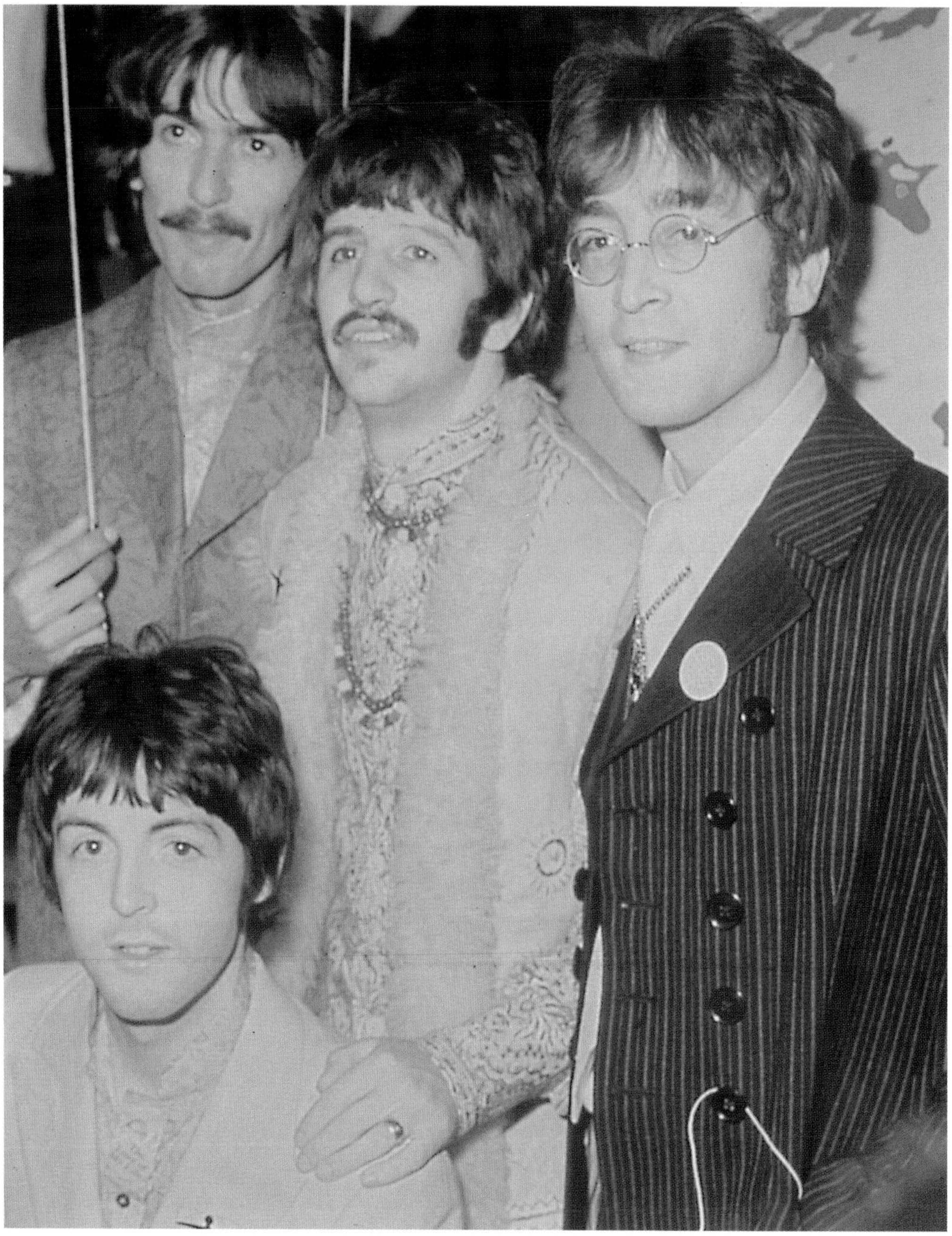

The organisation of this encyclopedia allows the reader to follow all of these themes through the centuries. You will find chapters on the peoples of Britain, on politics and power, on the ordinary lives of British people through the ages, on industry and invention, culture and the arts, the changing face of religion and Britain's role in the world. Britain's story is rich and fascinating, complex and important. This book helps to make sense of it all. With luck it should also kindle your enthusiasm to find out more!

Professor E. J. Evans

The Peoples of Britain

BRITISH SOCIETY WAS originally formed by wave upon wave of invaders and, later on, by immigrants. The island country has been formally conquered twice, first by the Romans in AD 43, later by the Normans after 1066. Other invaders – the Celts, the Anglo-Saxons and the Vikings – settled and infiltrated rather than conquered and though Britain first knew the last two invaders as terrifying raiders, eventually they returned to make the country their home. Britain was well worth the move, with its fertile land and space, rich grazing for animals and large supply of raw materials. In time, the cultural and other differences between the early invaders were softened by centuries of living together. Britain eventually emerged as a society distinctly different from mainland Europe, where all the invaders had their origins. In time, too, Destination Britain came to have a new meaning: as a haven from persecution or poverty and a place to start a new and better life. One or other – or both – of these accounted for the arrival of later immigrants – Huguenots, Jews, African, West Indians, Asians and smaller communities of Poles or Czechs – whose contribution to the British mix have made it the multi-cultural, multi-racial society it is today.

KEY THEMES

- LIFESTYLE
- RELIGION
- SOCIETY
- CONFLICT
- CULTURE
- INVASION
- INDUSTRY

KEY EVENTS

1 900 BC
THE CELTS

The Celts were extremely talented people. Though warlike, they were also creative and artistic. Their technology, especially in farming and the use of metals, was far in advance of peoples who came to Britain before them. Even the Roman army, the best in the ancient world, was wary of them.

2 AD 426
ANGLES, JUTES AND SAXONS

The Angles, Jutes and Saxons, known collectively as Anglo-Saxons, came to Britain first as terrifying raiders, then as settlers and, ultimately, as the rulers of powerful kingdoms and purveyors of the ideas of government and law that persist today. Although Britain was invaded many times, the Anglo-Saxons were the most influential.

3 AD 793
THE VIKINGS

Tough, hardy, warlike, merciless and greedy for plunder, the Vikings, like the Anglo-Saxons, first raided, then settled in Britain, mainly along the east coast. Their daring as seafarers had enabled them to cross the North Sea from their native Scandinavia, a feat no one in Britain had thought possible.

4 1066
THE COMING OF THE NORMANS

The Normans, the last successful invaders of Britain, came as conquerors and imposed their rule with horrific brutality. The existing population was largely dispossessed, as the Normans took for themselves all the titles, lands, offices and much of the wealth of Britain.

5 1572
FAITHS COLLIDE

The persecuted Calvinist Huguenots from France were the first true immigrants to Britain, between 1572 and 1685, when they joined a long-established community. They brought many talents to their new home and worked hard to earn their well-deserved place in British society. One Huguenot innovation was white paper.

6 1655
JEWS RETURN

The Jews were twice invited into Britain – in 1070 and 1655 – to lend rulers their experience in the courts of Europe and their financial expertise. Thrown out in 1290, they returned to stay in 1655. Though never a large community, the Jews have made considerable contributions to British life.

7 1940
ASYLUM SEEKERS AND REFUGEES

Britain has long been a safe haven for asylum seekers and refugees who have valued the freer society, better life and greater security that the island country has to offer. Its shelter benefited fugitives from Nazi Germany before the Second World War, and those fleeing from wartime Europe, particularly from Poland and Czechoslovakia.

8 1952
MOTHER COUNTRY OF THE EMPIRE

For two or three centuries, the vast British Empire overseas made Britain the focus of hope and opportunity for many colonial peoples. This led Indians, Pakistanis, West Indians and Hong Kong Chinese to bring their families to Britain to start new lives. Unfortunately, the pressure of immigration created its own problems.

TIMELINE

2000 BC Beaker people
1550 BC Walls built to delimit fields; organised farming communities established
1450 BC Bronze, copper and tin used in early industries
1 **900 BC** Arrival of the Celts
300 BC Celts develop early mills for grinding grain, and early metal tools
100 BC Trade between Romans, Gauls and Celts leads to use of gold coins
AD 77 Gnaius Julius Agricola introduces benefits of Roman life to Britons
AD 313 Christianity comes to Britain
AD 352 Britannia under attack from the Picts, Pirates and Scots
2 **AD 426** Arrival of the Angles, Saxons and Jutes
AD 490 St Patrick converts the Irish and founds monasteries
AD 570 Time of legendary 'King' Arthur
AD 597 Christian missionaries sent from Rome by Pope Gregory I
AD 789 Offa's Dyke constructed
3 **AD 793** Viking raids
AD 825 Vikings kill the monk Blathmac
AD 865 'Great Army' of Vikings lands in East Anglia
AD 900 Danelaw established
AD 991 Vikings vessels raid the Thames Estuary
4 **1066** Arrival of the Normans
1070 Vikings and Saxons join forces to attack the North
1144 Jews confined to ghettos
5 **1572** Huguenot refugees arrive in Britain
1598 Edict of Nantes
6 **1655** Jews ask Oliver Cromwell for permission to live in Britian
1686 Huguenots exiled in England
1829 Emancipation of the Jewish communities
1881 Persecuted Jews flock to London's East End from Russia
7 **1940** Refugees flock to Britain as Germany advances through Europe
8 **1952** Influx of West Indian immigrants into London
1958 Racial tensions erupt in riots in Notting Hill, London
1960 Wales and Scotland begin campaign of independence
1969 Indians, forced out of Uganda and Kenya, move to Britain
1975 Britain takes in refugees from Vietnam
1993 Murder of Stephen Lawrence
1999 Devolution comes into effect for Wales and Scotland

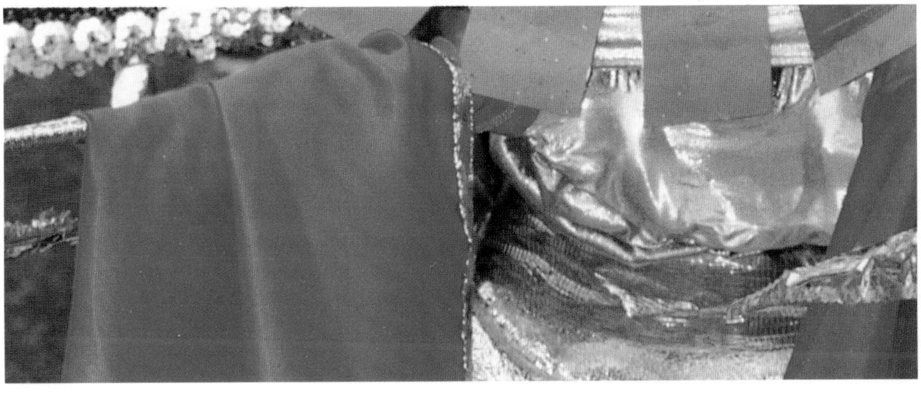

Earliest Britain

11,000–900 BC

UNTIL THE YEAR 1066, Britain was probably the most invaded territory in the world. The invasions began far back in prehistory, when people who lived by hunting and gathering for food wandered across the marshy land bridge which, before 5000 BC, joined Britain to Europe. This process continued after the waters of what we now call the English Channel supervened and Britain became an island. At this stage, there were no large numbers of people involved. Britain's population probably numbered only a few hundred until, in about 1900 BC, the first primitive Britons were joined by a much more sophisticated culture. Archeologists, who later uncovered the drinking vessels they used, called them the Beaker folk.

▲ *People began to develop increasingly effective tools to enable them to hunt more efficiently.*

11,000 BC
BRITAIN AS THE BEAKER FOLK FOUND IT

The prehistoric lifestyle was about survival, nothing else. In the very earliest times, when its climate was drier than it later became, the grasslands and woodlands of Britain provided relatively easy hunting. The animals provided everything – not just food, but clothing made from their hides and fur, implements made from their bones and oil for simple lamps from their body-fat. Then, between 11,000 BC and 8000 BC, the Ice Age gradually came to an end, rainfall increased and with that the environment changed. Alder and oak forests sprang up, harbouring wild boar, wolves or brown bears. This made life much more dangerous and humans found themselves largely confined to the chalk and limestone hills where forests could not grow easily.

◀ *Early man survived by hunting and gathering their food, using animal skins for clothing.*

☏ ▶ p. 26

4000 BC
FARMS AND FARM ANIMALS

Farming, which enabled people to replace the nomadic hunter-gatherer life in favour of settling in one place, had filtered slowly into Europe from Asia by *c.* 4000 BC. This was a fundamental change in lifestyle and farming practice, as it developed, probably explains the 193 km (120 miles) of thick stone walls about a metre (two to three feet) high which have been uncovered by archeologists at Grimspound, on Dartmoor in Devon. The purpose of these walls, archeologists believe, was to separate the crop fields from lands grazed by cattle and sheep. Working with large stone structures was already an established skill for those who built the walls. Not far away, whole villages have been found with up to 15 houses, each equipped with substantial stone foundations.

▶ p. 23

4000 BC
FARMING LIFE IN PREHISTORIC TIMES

As farming edged out, though did not entirely replace, hunting and gathering of food, village communities sprang up close to the fields and pastures which provided their livelihood. The work was hard and continuous and the land had to be used wisely. Fields that produced crops one year, were allowed to lie fallow, or rest, the next year. Everything, of course, had to be done by hand, but basic technology was there to help the work along. Ploughing teams were assembled, using bronze implements. Other tools were employed, too, for tilling the fields. There were cattle and sheep to be tended and guarded. It was a lifestyle which emphasised close family life and links of kinship as communities worked together to make a living.

2000 BC
BRONZE PRODUCTION IN PREHISTORIC WALES

Even in prehistoric times, Britain had its exports, including bronze products made in Wales. Goods were traded to present-day

Brittany, the Netherlands and possibly Ireland. The industrial centres in Wales were located around Snowdonia and at Great Orme where miners, working up to 12 m (40 ft) underground, dug out copper and tin for smelting and later for fashioning into axeheads, other weapons and tools. Archeologists have uncovered large bronze moulds that could be used to cast up to 50 axes or more before fresh ones had to be made.

1900 BC
USERS OF METAL

Before the Beaker folk came, technology in Britain was largely based on flint and wood. Chipping one stone against another produced weapons for hunting, knives for cutting or axeheads for wooden spears. Bronze, gold and copper were not unknown, but the Beaker folk were the ones who put metals to regular use. Beautiful gold Beaker necklaces have been found in Cornwall and Ireland. The wealthy were buried with copper and flint daggers, metal bracelets and the carefully shaped and intricately decorated beakers that gave these metal-users their name. Despite its artistry, this was a warrior society that differentiated between men and women even in their burial rites. Men were buried with their heads pointing north, women with their heads pointing south.

▶ p. 25

1900 BC
SPIRITUAL LIFE IN BEAKER TIMES

Stone circles and 'standing stones' probably connected with Britain's early sun-, moon- and earth-worshipping religions, date back over a thousand years before the Beaker folk arrived. The most famous of these mysterious stone structures, Stonehenge on Salisbury Plain in present-day Wiltshire, seems to have had some spiritual significance for the Beaker people, who are believed to have widened the existing entrance and provided an avenue a mile long running down to the River Avon. In addition, a double inner circle of 82 blue dolerite stones, each weighing some five tonnes, was added to the existing structure. Previously, Stonehenge was aligned with the rising of the sun in midsummer. Now, though, the alignment was changed in favour of the midsummer moon.

1150 BC
DISASTER AT SEA

In about 1150 BC, the English Channel, always a dangerous and volatile waterway, claimed as victim a French sailing ship bringing a cargo of varied bronzeware from northern France to southern England. The vessel probably got into difficulties because of strong winds and adverse tides near present-day Dover. Driven shorewards, she was wrecked off the cliffs: one of the first ships – but certainly not the last – to meet such a fate. The Channel waters kept this secret until underwater archeologists discovered the unfortunate vessel, together with its cargo of axes, spearheads, daggers and chisels which never reached the buyers waiting for them in southern England. The sombre find does, however, provide tangible evidence of regular trade taking place across the Channel in prehistoric times.

900 BC
THE CLIMATE CHANGES

Farming has always been vulnerable to the vagaries of the weather, and in about 900 BC, Britain was undergoing serious climatic change. The amount of rainfall increased, accompanied by higher winds than previously experienced. The pressure exerted by these changes shortened the length of the growing season, especially for farmers living in upland areas. Fields were waterlogged and, their fertility gone, they became unusable. Around Dartmoor in Devon and in Wales, treacherous bogs were forming. Floods swept many lower-lying settlements and their hapless inhabitants were forced to move to higher ground and start again. Then, just as these challenges were taxing the Britons, new warlike invaders appeared, possessing skills, both artistic and technological, that outmatched those of the existing population. They were the Celts.

▼ *Much can be learnt about early lifestyles from flint tools recovered during archeological digs.*

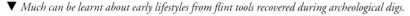

Distant Voices ▶ p. 23

Man is a creature adapted for life under circumstances which are very narrowly limited. A few degrees of temperature more or less, a slight variation in the composition of air, the precise suitability of food, make all the difference between health and sickness, between life and death.

Sir Robert S. Ball, *The Story of the Heavens* (1885)

The Celts

900–55 BC

THE CELTS, who first invaded in about 900 BC – and kept on coming after that – seem to have been warlike, artistic, individualistic, tribal, creative and emotional peoples, and they soon proved a powerful new force in Britain. With their superior technological skills, they propelled their new homeland to greater efficiency in farming, and also brought to it a poetic, imaginative standard of art and literature which is still greatly admired today. The names of Celtic tribes echo down history – the Iceni, the Parisii, the Belgae. There was, however, a strain of ferocity about the Celts which at first disrupted the established tenor of life in Britain and ultimately, many centuries later, helped persuade the great Julius Caesar that the island country indeed would be hard to conquer.

900 BC
WHO WERE THE CELTS?

The Celts, or *keltoi* as ancient Greek geographers termed them, first attracted attention as a widespread 'barbarian' people in the Alpine regions of southern Europe and in present-day Spain and Portugal. Britain, however, was not the last port of call for the migratory Celts: long after they settled there, the Celts penetrated Turkey, Italy and Germany. The Greek and Roman writers who were the chief sources of information about the Celts found them unusually tall, muscular and fair, though in fact shorter, darker Celts were not unknown. Their energy and ferocity, demonstrated by naked combat and the decapitation of enemies, made them a truly formidable force, even to the Romans, whose army was the best in the then-known world.

▶ p. 29

900 BC
THE CELTIC HIERARCHY

Early observers of the Celts gained the impression that this doughty and vivacious people were not capable of concerted action for long, if at all. The apparent wildness this suggests did not, however, extend to their social organisation. Though highly individualistic, the Celts had a well-established hierarchy or class system that formed, as it were, the matrix of their society. At the pinnacle, there was the king or chieftain and below him an aristocracy whose main business was war. Next came the freemen farmers, who were important in their own right, since the Celtic economy relied heavily on mixed farming. The aristocratic families provided the priests known as Druids, who directed Celtic religious life and performed its often semi-magic ceremonies.

▲ *A Druid priest and priestess.*

900 BC
THE CELTIC FAMILY

Family and kinship were of great importance to the Celts, providing both the cohesion that was valuable during their migrations, and demarcation of their land ownership and individual rights and duties. As was to be expected of a warrior society, their family system was patriarchal, though women were no cyphers. A tough society like the Celts had no room for passengers, whether male or female. Neither sex had much fondness for elaborate self-adornment. Both usually wore coarse linen or wool which was often brightly coloured – short tunics for the men, long tunics for the women. Both sexes wore cloaks, and the men sometimes covered their legs with trousers – a curiosity to the Romans, who thought trousers were barbaric.

▶ p. 29

500 BC
COMMUNITIES IN CONFLICT

The Celtic invasion of Britain was not a single event, but the start of a series of incursions continuing for centuries, which ultimately brought about fierce conflict with the established population. As competition for land and resources increased, the inevitable result was war. Evidence of the fighting that ensued can be found all over Britain in the remains of hill-forts which, archeologists have found, were strongly equipped to withstand sieges and massed attacks. Some forts were effectively armed villages, with living quarters and stores capable of supporting 200 people or more. Mighty as they were, however, some hill-forts were unable to resist assaults against them and the debris of battle all too often included corpses and severed heads and limbs.

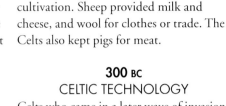

500 BC
THE CELTIC FARMS

The Celts brought something of an agricultural revolution to Britain. Ever the individuals, most Celtic farmers lived in a single homestead and cultivated their own fields; the efficiency of their methods did much to overcome any shortage of labour this might have implied. Their ploughs, drawn by a pair of oxen, used an iron tip to break the ground, not just turn it, enabling them to grow more barley and wheat. Herds of sheep were useful in increasing, through their manure, the fertility of the land, so laying it open to yet more cultivation. Sheep provided milk and cheese, and wool for clothes or trade. The Celts also kept pigs for meat.

▲ *A replica of the style of early pottery kilns introduced to Britain by the Roman invaders.*

300 BC
CELTIC TECHNOLOGY

Celts who came in a later wave of invasion, *c.* 500 BC, introduced Britain to the uses of iron, but their technological expertise did not end there. The ingenious Celtic mind was able to devise new purposes for almost any material and, in about 300 BC, they found a new role for large pivoted stones – grinding large quantities of grain into flour. With this 'rotary quern', grain was poured down the sides of the pivot, the top stone was turned and the grain emerged as flour. In addition, Celtic smiths produced specialised tools for metalworking, such as hammers and anvils, chisels and tongs and so gave everyday objects such as buckets, cauldrons and domestic implements a new and higher quality.

▶ p. 33

100 BC
THE ROMANS APPROACH

The Celts in Britain had long been aware of the Romans – their power, their conquests and their thirst for more victories – and while they were willing to trade with them, they regarded them warily, as potentially dangerous enemies. Fortunately, the Celts had numerous relatives in Europe, and were especially close, both physically and through kinship, to the Gauls in France where the Romans already had great influence in the south by about 100 BC. Cultural and trade exchanges with the Gauls brought gold coinage and beautiful pottery to Britain. However, more valuable was the stream of information that reached across the Channel, informing the Celts that the Romans, who believed Britain was rich in gold and minerals, were interested in their island.

▲ *Ancient gold coins from the Roman era in Britain.*

55 BC
BRITAIN AND THE ROMANS

Caesar had heard much about Britain as he prepared to invade in 55 BC – the inhabitants' curious habit of dyeing their bodies blue with woad, the supernatural aura which, the Romans believed, hung over the land they called *Isola Sacra*, the Sacred Isle. However, the warriors who lined the cliffs when Caesar's fleet arrived off the south coast were no longer Celts, or the descendants either of the Beaker folk or any of their predecessors. The natural melding of immigrants over time had made them Britons. And these Britons meant to fight for their homeland and their freedom.

p. 21 ◀ **Distant Voices** ▶ p. 25

I myself, with the leading ships, reached Britain about 9 a.m. We could see the enemy's armed forces lined up all along the cliffs. At this point there was a narrow beach with high hills behind it, so that it was possible to hurl weapons down from the higher ground.... After moving on about eight miles, we ran the ships ashore on an open, evenly-shelved beach.... As soon as our forces had gained a firm footing on the shore ... they charged and put the enemy to flight.

From *War Commentaries*, by Julius Caesar (*c.* 55 BC)

The Coming of the Romans

AD 43–426

THE ROMANS WERE different from any of the invaders Britain had known before. Where the Celts and their predecessors came to settle and make new homes, the Romans came to conquer and rule. Conquest did not come in 54 BC, when Caesar visited Britain again. He was prevented from adding Britain to the Roman Empire by the inhabitants' guerrilla tactics, the British weather which wrecked his ships and his quest for personal power in Rome, which ended in his assassination. Nevertheless, the Romans came to conquer in the end, in AD 43, and so began nearly four centuries of the province they called Britannia, which they tried – but did not entirely manage – to remake in their own 'civilised' image.

▶ p. 26

AD 43 CONQUEST

The Roman army, the most powerful military machine of its time, may have lost battles, but it never lost a war. Even so, the Roman conquest of Britain was by no means an easy matter, and it was never complete. There were always Britons prepared to defy the foreign invaders, even after the conquest was over. Before the Romans prevailed, the Britons' resistance was ferocious, with its damaging chariot warfare, guerrilla tactics and clever use of forest cover. But the might of Rome could not be thwarted easily and ultimately, submission was the only option. When the surrender took place at Colchester in the late summer of AD 43, the Roman emperor, Claudius, was there in person to preside at the ceremony.

▶ p. 25

AD 77 SUBVERTING THE BRITONS

From the first, Britannia proved a difficult province to control, but Gnaius Julius Agricola, Roman governor between AD 77 and 84, is credited with devising a very subtle method of reconciling the Britons to Roman rule. He romanised the province, and so offered Britons the advantages of Roman life: towns, water supplies, roads, imported luxuries, homes and villas heated by hypocausts (a form of central heating), public baths, theatres and Roman entertainments, such as gladiatorial combat. The contrast between this comparatively pampered existence and the rough, hard and often uncomfortable life they had led before this time appealed to many Britons who came to live in the towns, wear Roman togas, eat Roman food and educate their children in Roman schools.

◀ *Stone carving showing the submission of a barbarian to a group of Roman soldiers.*

Triumphs & Tragedies ▶ p. 28

AD 60 BOUDICCA'S REVOLT

With conquest came humiliation. Caractacus of the Catuvallauni, who had led the fight against the Romans, was betrayed by Queen Cartimandua of the Brigantes in AD 51. He was taken to Rome and paraded through the streets in chains. Boudicca, queen of the Iceni, was a woman of much more fearsome mettle. In AD 60, she was flogged, her daughters were raped and Colchester was plundered, after the Iceni defied a Roman official. In response, Boudicca gathered an army, some 120,000 strong, which smashed part of the 9th Roman Legion and then set Colchester on fire. She swept down on London, where she and her troops rampaged through the city, burning, looting and killing. The revolt was eventually crushed, however, and Boudicca committed suicide.

▼ *Classical art showing the public baths frequented by both men and women in Roman times.*

AD 195
STILL FIGHTING THE ROMANS

Roman Britannia was a dangerous place, requiring strong fortifications – such as the stone walls built round the rich trading port of London in AD 195 – to keep out bands of marauding rebels. Already, in 142, Hadrian's Wall, named after Emperor Hadrian and manned by nearly 12,000 soldiers, had been built between Arbeia (South Shields) and the Solway Firth to keep the Selgovae, Novantae and other Scots tribes at bay. Only three years later another defence line, the Antonine Wall, was constructed even further north. Nevertheless, there were always new uprisings and as late as 210, the ailing Emperor, Septimius Severus, was obliged to lead a punitive campaign beyond the Antonine Wall as far as Aberdeen.

▶ p. 26

AD 313
CHRISTIANITY COMES TO BRITAIN

In AD 313, Constantine I, the Roman emperor, was converted to Christianity and with that, this formerly relatively obscure faith took over the Roman Empire. Christianity had been a minority religion – and a persecuted one – among tribes in Scotland as early as 205. There had been vicious oppression, together with the torture and martyrdom in 208 of a Verulamium (present-day St Albans) man, Albanus, who had sheltered a Christian priest. This time, though, the Christian faith was official. Now, it was the pagans who were hounded. They faced execution if caught performing pagan rites and, although the old beliefs persisted in some areas, all forms of pagan ritual and worship were outlawed in 391. Pagan temples were smashed and idols destroyed.

AD 365
BRITANNIA UNDER ATTACK

The dangers faced by Roman Britannia became more frequent and more serious with time. Pirates plundered the coasts. Picts from the north staged raids deep into Roman-held territory. In response, in AD 352, the defensive walls of London, Chichester and other cities were reinforced by a series of towers to enable defenders to fire down on attackers from above. In 365, Britannia was assaulted by Picts, Scots and Attacotti in the concerted campaign which the Romans had always dreaded. Bands of 'barbarians' roamed south-east Britannia, burning, looting, terrorising and slaughtering at will. The Romans managed to push them back, but the emergency was so great that, to gain extra manpower, army deserters were pardoned and reinstalled in the ranks.

AD 410
THE DEPARTURE OF THE ROMANS

By the early fifth century AD, Rome, once so great and powerful, was in terminal decline. This weakness was forcibly brought home in AD 410 when Rome was sacked by the Visigoths. Even before that, in 401, the 'barbarian' danger had been so great that troops were withdrawn from Britannia to defend Rome, the heart of the empire. As time went on, the withdrawals continued until by about 426, Britannia had been abandoned. Already, in 410, Emperor Honorius had told the Britons, themselves beleaguered by raiders from Germany, that they must now defend themselves. In 446, the Britons made the last of many appeals for help from Rome. However, it seems they never received a reply, and the Romans never returned.

▶ p. 27

AD 426
ROME'S LEGACY

The Romans left comparatively little of their culture in Britain but the few marks of their presence are distinct even so. Except for motorways, Britain's road system still runs along the routes the Romans selected. Aspects of Roman law remain in the British legal system; there are many Latin words in the English language; Roman villas, public baths and defensive walls provide archeologists with valuable clues to the Roman way of life. Town names like Manchester or Colchester stand on the sites of Roman military camps. If this seems little to show for 400 years, one reason is that the Romans' successors, the Anglo-Saxons, had their own well-founded culture and a very different way of life from that of Rome.

▲ *Roman roads such as this testify to the great skill and ingenuity of the engineers of the time.*

p. 23◀ **Distant Voices** ▶p. 27

Some of you may have been duped by the tempting promises of the Romans. Now, you have learned the difference between foreign tyranny and the free life of your ancestors. Have we not suffered every shame and humiliation?... I fight not for my kingdom or for booty, but for my lost freedom, my bruised body, my outraged daughters. We will win this battle or perish! That is what I, a woman, will do; men may live in slavery!

Queen Boudicca of the Iceni, to her army (AD 60)

Angles, Jutes and Saxons

AD 426–789

THE ANGLO-SAXONS, as the Germanic Angles, Jutes and Saxons are normally termed, had been raiding Britain in small groups since the third century, when it was still under Roman rule. After that rule ended, the island country was even more open to exploitation by these determined and, for the Britons, terrifying invaders. Yet the Anglo-Saxons were not simply cruel and rampaging brutes. They developed the basis for concepts of community and government which remain influential in Britain to this day – for instance, the civic responsibilities of citizens, the importance of family or the function of law in maintaining peace and discipline, and the requirement that monarchs should rule with advisers, an arrangement meant to avoid the abuse of power.

AD 426
BRITAIN FACES DISASTER

The departure of the Romans brought anarchy; Roman rule had meant law and order. Now, law and order broke down as the British found themselves helpless before the fury of Anglo-Saxon raiders and marauders from the north. With the comparatively healthy Roman way of life now gone, disease asserted itself. Food supplies became endangered and new crop fields were ploughed within the apparent safety of town walls. Richer Britons took to burying their valuables, always a sure sign of fear and insecurity. The panic was such that in about AD 430, one British leader, Vortigern of Dyfed, made the grave mistake of recruiting Saxon mercenaries for protection, a move that proved virtually suicidal.

▶ p. 34

AD 426
TOUGH PEOPLE FOR A TOUGH LIFE

The Anglo-Saxons were tough people leading a tough life. Their primitive 'wattle and daub' homes were built from the wood and mud of the forests near or surrounding their villages. They wore simple, roughly made tunics. Shoes were sometimes made of leather, or might consist of thick pieces of woollen material wrapped round the feet and tied round the ankles with leather straps or cloth. The men, who might at any time be called out to fight off unfriendly neighbours or raiders, could easily convert everyday clothing into fighting outfits, by adding leather or chain-mail jerkins over their tunics, and leather belts to hold swords and daggers.

▲ *St Patrick (right) attracted many would-be monks to the monasteries he established throughout the British Isles.*

AD 565
THE GREAT DAYS OF IRISH CHRISTIANITY

Ireland, traditionally converted to Christianity by St Patrick, once a slave seized by pirates, was enjoying an exciting age of faith by about AD 565. Would-be monks, it seems, flocked to the monasteries that Patrick had introduced, and willingly embraced the particularly strict and ascetic rules of the new monastic orders. Here, in retreats separated from the rest of the population, they gave their lives over to prayer and abstinence. Before long, the Irish were expressing their new faith in superb works of art, which reached their highest form of expression in beautiful and colourful illuminated prayer books. Irish missionaries also took their enthusiasm to Europe, where they travelled long distances and endured many hardships to bring more converts to the Christian faith.

▶ p. 28

AD 570
ARTHUR, THE LEGENDARY BRITISH WARRIOR

As the Anglo-Saxons penetrated deeper and deeper into Britain, the Britons were pushed eastwards, leaving their lands to be settled by the invaders. Vortigern's mercenaries were among them. The Britons fought back as best they could and found a Romano-British leader, who was later romanticised into the legendary 'King' Arthur. It is believed that Arthur used Roman cavalry tactics in guerrilla strikes against the inexorable advance of the Anglo-Saxons, but the advance continued nevertheless. By about AD 570 small estates, usually belonging to one man, his family and his followers, had begun to take shape. Eventually, these were consolidated into Anglo-Saxon kingdoms such as Mercia (eastern and southern England), Northumbria (north-east England and south-east Scotland) and Wessex (south and south-west England).

▶ p. 36

AD 600
THE ANGLO-SAXONS BECOME CHRISTIANS

Thus far, the Anglo-Saxons had been pagans – but that was soon to change. In AD 597, a group of Christian missionaries, sent from Rome by Pope Gregory I and led by St Augustine, landed in Kent; their initial aim was to convert the king, Athelbert. Athelbert became a Christian in about 600 and over the ensuing years, Christianity spread throughout Britain. It was, however, no speedy or simple task, even though Augustine did not demand that the Anglo-Saxons give up all their existing gods and practices. Instead, they were encouraged to bring some pagan beliefs into the new faith. Meanwhile, more conversions were being achieved by St Dyfed in Wales and St Columba among the Picts in Scotland.

▶ p. 34

AD 625
BURIED LIKE A KING

The glory that could be attained by Anglo-Saxon monarchs was stunningly illustrated in 1939 when the burial ship of King Radwald was excavated at Sutton Hoo, Norfolk. The ship, some 27 m (30 yd) long, was full of splendid grave artefacts, including a Byzantine silver dish, bottles with silver mounts and golden ornaments encrusted with garnets. In addition, archeologists found a lyre and Radwald's personal weapons: sword, shield, helmet, axe-hammer and a large whetstone carved with faces and decorated with bronze. As this splendid show of riches suggests, Radwald was a powerful 'over-king', controlling all the Anglo-Saxon realms south of the River Humber. He had been converted to Christianity while at the court of King Athelbert of Kent, but reverted to paganism on returning home to East Anglia.

AD 658
THE FIRST CHRISTIAN POET IN BRITAIN

Some time between AD 658 and 679, Caedmon, a north Yorkshire cowherd, became the first Christian poet in Britain, after he dreamt he was commanded by God to set down the story of the Creation. The illiterate Caedmon was apparently given some of the verses and the poetic talent to write more. At first, Caedmon's claims were sceptically received at nearby Whitby Abbey. However, the cowherd proved to the monks' satisfaction that he had, indeed, received a heavenly gift when he wrote down several verses within a few hours. Later, Caedmon became a monk at Whitby Abbey. The source for Caedmon's story, told some 50 years later, was the Venerable Bede, a famous Anglo-Saxon historian.

AD 789
OFFA'S DYKE

Christianity did not turn Britain into a land of peace. There were vicious rivalries between the Anglo-Saxon kings which led to civil war and anarchy. One of the most ambitious of these monarchs was Offa, who seized power in Mercia in about AD 757 and afterwards made his realm supreme south of the River Humber. In about 789, Offa built a huge 257-km (160-mile) long earthwork, later known as Offa's Dyke, to protect his territory from attack. The dyke was 2 m (6 ft) deep, with a 7.6-m (25-ft) earth rampart, strengthened by timber palisades and a stone wall. However, only four years later, new invaders appeared in the east who were far more dangerous and terrifying than any home-grown enemies – the Vikings from Scandinavia.

▲ *Offa's Dyke, a magnificent earthwork built around AD 789 by Offa, king of Mercia, to protect his territory.*

p. 25◀ **Distant Voices** ▶p. 29

Then all the councillors, together with that proud tyrant Guthrigern [Vortigern] ... were so blinded that, as a protection to their country, they sealed its doom by inviting in among them, like wolves into a sheep-fold, the fierce and impious Saxons, a race hateful both to God and men.... Nothing was ever so pernicious to our country, nothing was ever so unlucky. What palpable darkness must have enveloped their minds – darkness desperate and cruel! Those very people whom, when absent, they dreaded more than death itself, were invited to reside, as one may say, under the selfsame roof.

St Gildas, in *De Excidio Britanniae* (*c.* AD 540)

The Vikings

AD 793–1014

IN AD 793 NEW invaders, the Vikings, arrived in Britain from across the North Sea, so driving the Anglo-Saxons into a new situation – as desperate defenders of their land. They soon learned well enough to dread the appearance out at sea of the long, slim Viking warships heading for shore. However, like the Anglo-Saxons before them, the Vikings were not simply fighting machines intent on robbery, pillage and destruction. They were people of extraordinary skills, not least their ability to sail the seas for long distances unexplored as yet by any other Europeans. The Vikings were also a people who had a vibrant spiritual life, with their myths of great hero-gods and the rewards that awaited valiant warriors in Valhalla.

▶ p. 30

AD 793
THE VIKINGS COME RAIDING

On 8 June AD 793, Vikings from Scandinavia suddenly appeared off the Isle of Lindisfarne, stormed ashore, killed or captured the monks, ravaged the monastery and just as suddenly departed. The news produced fear and trepidation throughout Britain. Not only were these new invaders utterly terrifying, but no one had believed their voyage from Scandinavia was possible. It became possible many times over, as the Vikings proved nowhere was safe if their longships could reach it. They twice attacked the island of Iona, in 795 and 806, ravaged Lambay near Dublin in Ireland, and spread similar destruction through western Europe. No wonder then that a special prayer was written into the Christian Litany: 'Save us, O Lord, from the fury of the Northmen.'

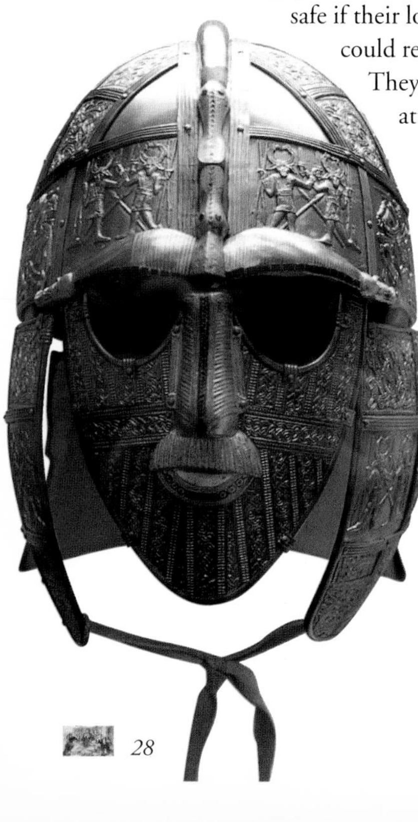

AD 800S
WHO WERE THE VIKINGS?

The ice-bound, mist-wrapped, rugged lands of Viking Scandinavia, required plenty of stamina, courage and self-reliance. Vikings worked hard at farming, hunting, and fishing or harpooning whales. Every summer, in Norway, the Vikings climbed the mountains to fell trees for making charcoal. Metalworkers camped by mountain bogs and spent weeks there smelting iron ore to forge into weapons, household utensils and other objects. The Vikings' great love was the sea, which they called 'the silver necklace of Earth'. They developed clinker-built longships and the ability to sail by the stars and reckon latitude by the shadow of a notched stick, which accounted for their ability – virtually unique in its time – to navigate while out of sight of land.

◀ *The Vikings used their metal-working skills to produce protective armour as well as weapons; this helmet was discovered at Sutton Hoo.*

AD 802
THE RISING POWER OF WESSEX

Saxon Wessex, which was eventually to bring the Vikings under control, grew vastly in power in the early ninth century. King Egbert, who seized the throne of Wessex in ad 802, spread his territory into Cornwall (AD 815), overpowered his chief rival, King Beornwulf of Mercia (AD 825) and then moved to control Kent, East Anglia and Northumbria. This expansionist policy was not without its setbacks. In 836, Egbert suffered defeat at the hands of the Vikings. Within two years, however, he returned to defeat them in battle at Hingston Down, Cornwall. The king died in the following year, 839, but he left behind a strong, well-organised realm which proved its worth when, at length, the Vikings turned from raiding Britain to settling there.

AD 865
THE VIKINGS COME TO CONQUER

The Vikings were not long content with small-scale, hit-and-run raids. In AD 865, the 'Great Army', a mighty force of Danish,

p. 24◀ **Triumphs & Tragedies** ▶p. 31

AD 825
THE MONK WHO DEFIED THE VIKINGS

When Viking raiders returned to Iona in AD 825, they were confronted by a lone, unarmed Irish monk called Blathmac who headed all that was left of the community after the depredations of 19 years before. The Vikings, suspecting that the shrine of St Columba – who had founded the Iona monastery in 563 – contained valuable booty, demanded that Blathmac tell them where to find it. Although he realised he faced martyrdom, Blathmac refused and despite terrifying threats, went on refusing. This, perhaps, surprised the pagan Vikings for whom Christianity represented the humility and love of peace which they, as warriors, despised. Ultimately, the Vikings lost patience, and in their fury seized the hapless monk and literally tore him to pieces.

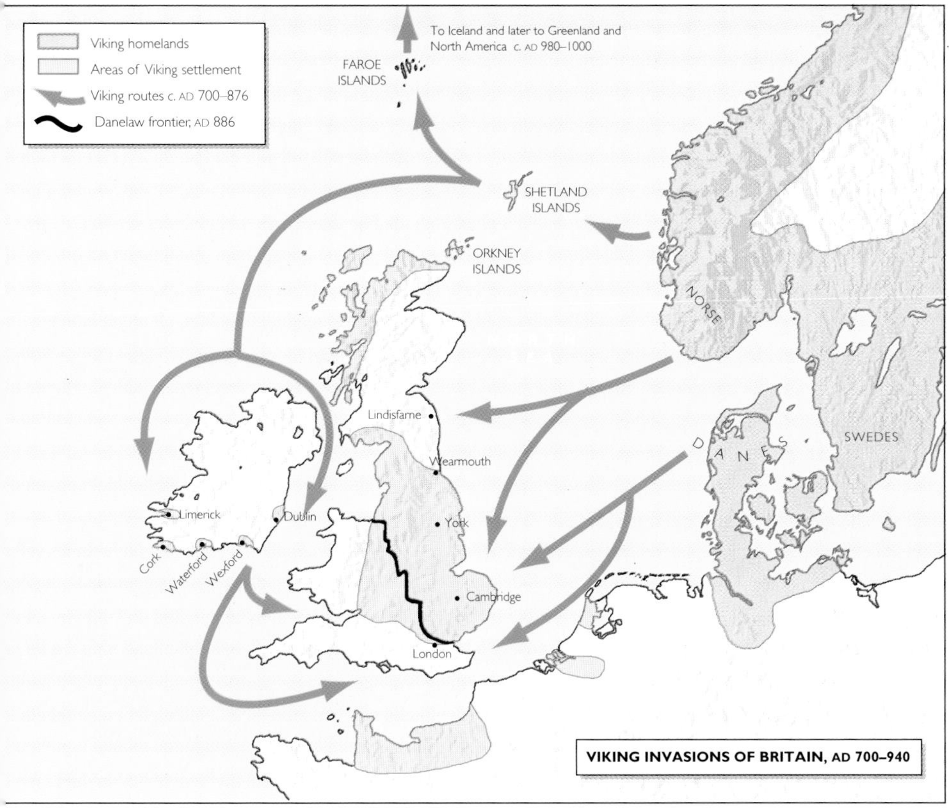

VIKING INVASIONS OF BRITAIN, AD 700–940

Norwegian and Swedish Vikings landed in East Anglia. They captured York and London and then moved south, only to suffer a bloody defeat, at Ashdown, near Reading, from an army headed by Alfred of Wessex, only 22 years old but already an inspirational leader. Alfred, who became king the same year, 871, knew he had earned only a breathing space, but by the time the Vikings came back, he was ready for them with a stronger, better-equipped army. In 878, Alfred defeated the Vikings at Edington, Wiltshire and forced their king, Guthrum, to make peace.

▶ p. 30

AD 886
ALFRED'S REVIVAL OF LEARNING

Despite his successes against the Vikings, Alfred was eventually obliged to share England with them, agreeing in AD 886 that they should occupy lands in the north, central and eastern parts of England, later known as the Danelaw. This at least allowed Alfred to concentrate on a task much dearer to him than war: a revival of learning, not just for the privileged few but for all his people. He encouraged literacy, and codified new laws designed to make the law courts, rather than private vengeance, the proper way to settle disputes. Treason was made a punishable crime for the first time, and other laws set levels of compensation in cases of accident. A devout Christian, Alfred made crimes committed on Sundays liable to double punishment.

AD 900s
THE DANELAW

By the early tenth century, it was a fact of life that the Vikings had come to stay in Britain, and that at least half of England, the Danelaw, was subject to their laws and their dominance. Sadly, but naturally, the Saxons were ousted from places within the Danelaw, which stretched from the River Tyne to just north of London. Inside the Danelaw, the Saxons lost out to the newcomers especially heavily in Mercia and Northumbria. It was not an arrange-ment which could avoid resentment and enmity from the established population, as they saw those they considered unwelcome foreigners taking over land and farming it for their own benefit. Even the Anglo-Saxon nobles had to yield to their Viking counterparts.

▶ p. 30

AD 918
MORE VIKING RAIDS

By AD 918, after prolonged warfare, King Edward, Alfred's son, retrieved most of the Danelaw for the kingdom of Wessex. This, though, did not solve the Viking problem. The terrifying Viking raids were renewed. In 991, a fleet of over 90 Viking vessels sailed up the Thames estuary, ravaging and pillaging at will. London itself was attacked in 994. The 'fury of the Northmen', it seemed, was unabated and in 1014 a further force from Scandinavia not only invaded but seized the crown, making King Cnut sovereign of all England two years later. Britain, however, was not yet finished with foreign incursions. There was one more to come – the invasion led by William the Conqueror of Normandy.

▲ *The Vikings travelled from Scandinavia in their crafts known as 'long-boats'.*

p. 27◀ **Distant Voices** ▶p. 31

Guthrum, king of the pagans [Danish Vikings] called Aller near Athelney. And Alfred received him as his son by adoption, raising him from the sacred font of baptism; and his chrism-loosing on the eighth day was in the royal vill called Wedmore. After he was baptised, he stayed with the king twelve nights, and to him and all his men with him, the king generously gave many valuable gifts.

From *The Life of King Alfred*, by Asser, Bishop of Sherbourne (d. AD 909)

The Coming of the Normans

1000–87

IN 1066, THE LAST successful invasion from outside the British Isles took place, when the duke of Normandy arrived to claim the crown he believed to be his. What followed was the most thoroughgoing takeover of power Britain had yet known. For the Normans were not only conquerors and rulers, they arrogated to themselves all the land, all the noble titles, church offices and other places of dominance. Over the centuries, the melting-pot syndrome had turned Celts, Saxons, Vikings and their predecessors into a single nation whose warriors faced the Normans together at Hastings on 14 October 1066. The superior warfare tactics of the Normans prevailed and with that the established population of Britain found themselves second-class citizens, or worse, in their own country.

1000s

WHO WERE THE NORMANS?

Exchange Norman for Northmen, from which it evolved and it is evident who the new invaders were. Britain had not been the only territory raided and ravaged by the Vikings; France, too, had suffered their depredations and after about AD 911, a group of Norwegians had first attacked, then settled in the north of France. The Normans who invaded England were their descendants, although in some ways changed from their restless pagan ancestors. The Normans were Christian, strictly disciplined – even ascetic – in nature, skilful rather than rampaging warriors and they no longer itched to roam the seas. However, they were still very Viking in their love of power and riches and, as the Britons were soon to discover, in their ruthlessness, too.

▶ p. 32

1066

A CROWN IN DISPUTE

The Norman conquest of Britain came about because both Harold Godwinson, brother-in-law of King Edward the Confessor, and William of Normandy, Edward's distant cousin, believed they had been promised the throne. In an attempt to pre-empt his rival, Harold seized the crown when the Confessor died on 6 January 1066. Nine months later, however, William prepared to invade and enforce his own right to be king. Harold, meanwhile, had other troubles – an invasion by King Harald Hardrada of Norway, backed up by his brother Tostig. Harold prevailed, but had to force-march his soldiers south from Yorkshire when he learned that William's fleet was approaching. Consequently, an utterly exhausted army lined up to confront the Normans.

▶ p. 39

1066

IMPOSING NORMAN RULE

William was crowned King William I at Westminster Abbey on Christmas Day, 1066, but by then the Normans had already proved their resolve to rule with an iron fist. Within six weeks of the Battle of Hastings, they had ravaged south-east England, laying waste to vast areas of countryside, and sacking both

▲ *The events of the Norman conquest were recorded in the Bayeux Tapestry, much of which still survives.*

p. 28◀ **Triumphs & Tragedies** ▶p. 32

1066
THE BATTLE OF HASTINGS

When Harold Godwinson and William of Normandy met at Hastings on 14 October 1066, the contest was painfully uneven. The Normans were experts at a form of warfare – fighting on horseback – as yet unfamiliar in Britain. Harold's forces were drawn up in traditional fashion, shoulder to shoulder and hoping in this way to form a wall that would stand against the Norman onslaughts. They were mistaken. The nimble, speedy Norman cavalry pushed in amongst them, swords slicing down from above, while the Norman archers poured down a storm of arrows. The result for the English troops was carnage, and among the dead was King Harold himself, killed by an arrow in the eye.

Romney and Dover to quench support for another claimant to the throne, Edgar the Atheling, and secure the surrender of London. It was blackmail by terror – and it worked. As the Normans crossed the River Thames to threaten Wallingford, the royal council gave in, and offered William the crown. Only then did the depredations cease, but not, as it soon turned out, for long.

▶ p. 33

1067
BRITAIN BECOMES A FEUDAL SOCIETY

The Normans changed the face of British society when they introduced the feudal system soon after their victory at Hastings. Feudalism, an interconnecting network of duties and obligations, had evolved in Europe as a defence against attack in dangerous, troubled times. It also served to control the population by enforcing a hierarchy in which nobles swore fealty to the king, and ordinary people swore to the nobles. These oaths had religious overtones and were a powerful motivation in a deeply superstitious age. The system served, too, to give nobles enormous power over their vassals, who were tied to their overlords' lands and, where necessary, had to fight in the armies that the lords were duty bound to provide for the king.

1068
NORMAN RETRIBUTION

Despite the ferocity with which they imposed their rule, the Normans faced continuing resistance in Wales and the north, while in England furious resentment followed the shutting off of the New Forest near Winchester as a hunting preserve for the king and his nobles. Losing access to the forest was a serious matter for the local people. They relied on it for firewood and game. The Normans dealt with Wales by building grim, imposing castles, like the fortress of Chepstow, which were designed to keep the people subdued. The fullest weight of Norman retribution fell, however, on northern England, which was virtually laid waste, its villages burned, crops destroyed, cattle slaughtered and the people left to starve.

1077
A RECORD OF VICTORY

In Norman times, literacy was usually restricted to the clergy. William the Conqueror himself was illiterate and signed state documents with a cross. Pictures, however, could be readily understood by everyone and to make the victory at Hastings widely known, a tapestry, 70 m (230 ft) long and 50 cm (20 in) high, was created at Canterbury. Today, nearly 1,000 years later, the tapestry can still be seen on display at Bayeux in northern France. The Bayeux Tapestry tells the story of Harold's rise to power, then moves on to the Norman ships crossing the Channel and an almost blow by blow account of the fighting at Hastings. For those who could read, short Latin captions were provided, identifying the main players in the drama.

1087
THE *DOMESDAY* FINDINGS

In 1087, King William ordered that a finely detailed record be made of the land, people and wealth of his realm. The result was the *Domesday Book*, a remarkable document which noted everything down to the last plough, sheep and acre. The book recorded, too, how very thoroughly the Normans had come to dominate the country. Of the land acreage, the largest portion, some 48.5 per cent, was owned by the Norman nobility, the next largest, 26.5 per cent by the Church, 17 per cent by the king and last, and very much the least, a mere 5.5 per cent by native landowners. Due to the orgy of destruction nearly 20 years earlier, large areas in Yorkshire and other northern counties were designated as 'waste'.

p. 29◀ **Distant Voices** ▶p. 33

The king and his head men loved much, and overmuch, covetousness in gold and in silver; and recked not how sinfully it was got.... The king let his land at as high a rate as he possibly could; then came some other person, and bade more than the former one gave ... and the king let it to the men that bade him most of all; and he recked not how very sinfully the stewards got it of wretched men, nor how many unlawful deeds they did....

From *The Anglo-Saxon Chronicle* (1087)

Saxons vs Normans

1070–87

RESISTANCE TO THE Normans in Wales and the north of England in the first years after the conquest was not the end of the story. If the conquerors believed they had cowed the populace by wreaking death and destruction in the north, they were wrong. They faced trouble from across the border in Scotland and from the Vikings in Denmark. The legendary Saxon patriot Hereward the Wake was active in the fenlands near Ely, Cambridgeshire, and several personal vendettas were carried out in violence and blood. All this served to make Norman reactions increasingly savage and retributive, but until the day William the Conqueror died, in 1087, there were still Saxons determined never to acknowledge his right to rule.

► p. 38

1070
TROUBLE FROM SCOTLAND

Edgar the Atheling, 15, was a closer relative to Edward the Confessor than William the Conqueror, and believed he had a better right to the throne. He found a willing supporter for his claim in his brother-in-law, the Scots king Malcolm III who, in 1070, sent an army to ravage northern England. Two years later, Malcolm struck again in an apparent attempt to annexe Northumbria to his own realm. William struck back with full, retributive force and on 15 August 1072, when the two kings met at Abernethy on Tayside, Malcolm was obliged to submit and hand over his son Duncan as hostage. When Malcolm also agreed to eject Edgar from his court, the boy fled across the English Channel to Flanders.

◄ *Malcolm III, king of Scotland, who led a failed attempt to capture Northumbria and extend the borders of his realm.*

1070
VIKINGS AND SAXONS COMBINE

In 1070, a once-unlikely combination of Danes and Saxons came together to mount a ferocious attack on Peterborough Abbey in Cambridgeshire. The Danish fleet had arrived at the Wash, and landed troops who made their base on the Isle of Ely. It seemed a good moment to mount an attack, since King William was preoccupied with assaults on his lands in Normandy. Together with a force of Saxon rebels, who included the *thegn* (a land-holder from the king) called Hereward, the Danes marched on the Abbey and on 2 June, set about plundering it of its gold and silver crucifixes, money, books and everything else of value. The local military commander, Abbot Turold, with only 160 men at his disposal, was helpless in the face of such an attack.

p. 31◄ Triumphs & Tragedies ►p. 35

1080
MURDER AT DURHAM

The hatred of Saxon for Norman did not only manifest itself in uprisings and battles. Savage personal vendettas shadowed these bigger set-piece events. One of the most horrific acts of vengeance occurred on 14 May 1080, when Walcher, the Norman bishop of Durham, and one of his relatives, Gilbert, took refuge in a church to escape a furious mob, who were convinced that the bishop had murdered a Saxon thegn. Walcher, in fact, had tried his best to calm the arrogant behaviour of Norman knights under his command, but this counted for nothing as the mob set the church on fire, forcing Walcher and Gilbert out into the street. As they and their followers emerged, they were seized and summarily killed.

1071
HEREWARD THE WAKE

The year after he took part in the looting of Peterborough Abbey, Thegn Hereward, known as Hereward the Wake, staged an uprising of his own in the treacherous, marshy fenlands near Ely. This time, the

▼ *Hereward the Wake, who staged an unsuccessful uprising against the Normans in the fenlands near Ely.*

▲ *William I ordered an abbey to be built on the spot his enemy, Harold, died.*

Normans came in force to deal with him, and although Hereward and his men held out for months against assaults from both land and sea, their cause was ultimately doomed. Cunningly, the Normans confiscated lands belonging to monks near Ely, precipitating their surrender and with that Hereward's resistance was critically weakened. Inevitably, his own men were obliged to follow suit, but Hereward himself managed to escape. Nothing definite is known about him after this, but legends about this great hero-patriot from Lincolnshire proliferated long after he was dead.

▶ p. 36

1072
PAYING FOR NORMAN DEATHS

Using military might to suppress revolts against their rule did not suffice for the Normans. They also used the law at its most vengeful to bring the Saxons to heel. In 1072, King William decreed that murdering a Norman would cost the killer dear, and his lord and community with him. Lords were duty bound to hand the miscreant over to the authorities within five days, or pay a very heavy fine – 46 marks of silver (about £30). If the lord could not afford this sum, it had to be made up by local people. However, as later events proved only too well, fines did little to deter a people who hated the Normans as much as the Saxons did.

1074
EDGAR THE ATHELING SURRENDERS

In 1074, once the immediate danger to his safety had passed, Edgar the Atheling returned to Scotland from Flanders, where Malcolm III gave him a great welcome. King Philip I of France was also interested in the youthful pretender to the English throne and offered him a castle near Dieppe, on the north coast of France. This could have served as an ideal base for launching attacks on England, but Edgar never reached France to claim it. His fleet was wrecked in a storm and he had to return to Scotland. It was the end of his quest; on Malcolm's advice, Edgar surrendered to King William. He was well treated, but his role as a thorn in the Normans' side was over and he died in obscurity in about 1125.

▶ p. 37

1080
BUSINESS AS USUAL

Despite the upheavals that marked the first decades of Norman rule, some aspects of everyday life continued as usual. In towns, manors and villages, industries still produced their goods; fairs and markets still took place. The rivers and some of the better-preserved Roman roads were still in regular use for transport. At ironworks close to mines in the Forest of Dean, the forges made horseshoes, picks, shovels and nails. Salt, so vital for preserving meat and other perishables for the winter, was produced in Worcestershire and Cheshire. Lead was mined in Northumbria and Cumbria. In London, trading ships from Norway, the Rhine, Flanders, Normandy and from as far away as the Mediterranean arrived, loaded or unloaded cargo and departed.

1087
WILLIAM THE CONQUEROR DIES

For all the terrible things he and the Normans did in Britain, for all his greed and cruelty, King William I was a devout Christian, very mindful of the accounting he would have to make in the next world. It was, therefore, a much more contrite William who, in 1070, ordered an abbey to be built on the spot where his rival, Harold, fell at Hastings. After William died in his turn and was buried at Caen, Normandy on 12 Sep-tember 1087, his will revealed a concern for the ordinary people of Britain that he had never shown in life. Part of the considerable treasure he had amassed during his 20-year reign was set aside for the relief of the poor.

p. 31◀ **Distant Voices** ▶p. 35

King William gave Earl Robert the earldom over Northumberland, but the landsmen attacked him in the town of Durham and slew him.... Soon afterwards, Edgar Etheling came with all the Northumbrians to York; and the townsmen made treaty with him: but King William came from the south unawares on them with a large army, and put them to flight, and slew on the spot those who could not escape; which were many hundred men: and plundered the town. St Peter's minster he made a profanation, and all other places also he despoiled and trampled upon.

From *The Anglo-Saxon Chronicle* (1068)

The Jews in Britain

1070–1881

JEWS ARE THE most experienced migrants in the world. For well over 2,000 years, *diasporas* (dispersions) of Jews have lived in many different countries, often unwelcome, often at risk from persecution. The first substantial Jewish community in Britain was invited in by King William I in 1070. After some 200 years – in 1290 – they were expelled and although individuals are known to have lived in Britain in Tudor times, Jews did not return to stay until Oliver Cromwell was persuaded to re-admit them in 1655. Jews have lived in England ever since, never a very large community but, like the Huguenots whose situation was similar, a community which has in many ways proved an asset to their British hosts.

▲ *A Jewish rabbi; the religion, customs and lifestyle of the Jews were alien to the people of Britain.*

1070
WILLIAM I HIRES JEWISH EXPERTISE

King William I, like numerous other European monarchs, employed Jews to handle his financial and diplomatic affairs. It was not only that Jews were permitted to lend money where Christians were forbidden. They had well-established links with Europe and were thoroughly experienced in handling the funds that would enable William to expand trade, and build castles and monasteries. The Jews who arrived in Britain in 1070 came from Rouen, in William's duchy of Normandy, and they came and stayed under his protection. The king was not giving them a special privilege; if they were to be of any use to him, the Jews had to have some defence against his subjects, who hated them from the start.

1655
CROMWELL'S INVITATION

Late in 1655, Manasseh ben Israel, a rabbi from Amsterdam, presented a 'Humble Address' to the Lord Protector of England, Oliver Cromwell, asking him to permit Jews to live in Britain once again. Memories of previous Jewish settlement, in medieval times, were painful, but fortunately Cromwell, a religious man, was willing to listen as ben Israel told him that if the Jews were re-admitted, this would serve as a signal for the coming of the Messiah. Cromwell's council was more hard-headed. They believed the Jews could bring economic benefits with them; they were shrewd financiers and diplomats, accustomed to dealing with European monarchs and their ministers. The new English Republic, although regarded with contempt in Europe, had a great deal of use for such people.

▲ *Lord Protector of England, Oliver Cromwell, readmitted Jewish settlers to England.*

▶ p. 39

1655
AN ANCIENT BUT ALIEN CULTURE

The Jews were the first settlers in Britain to come from a very ancient culture which had long ago worked out its own customs, traditions and laws, all predating those of Europe. They were the first, too, to bring to Britain a different faith which had none of the links that Protestants and Catholics, despite their mutual enmity, possessed. They were different in dress and looks from the established population and they were barred from British citizenship. Most of the Jews who arrived in 1655 were either Spanish or Portuguese. It was, therefore, extremely problematic for the Jews to settle down in Britain, for at the start, they were very much the strangers in a strange land.

▶ p. 40

1700s
STILL HELPING OUT THE KING

Britain was now a very different country from the one medieval Jews had known. Anti-Semitism was still present, but less violently expressed and Jewish family life and worship could proceed with less risk. It was also possible, with limitations, for Jews to advance in British society. For instance, the army contractor who supplied John Churchill, Duke of Marlborough, for his campaigns in Europe was Solomon de Medina who, as a reward, became the first Jew to receive a knighthood. Later in the eighteenth century, Sampson Gideon organised financial help from the Jewish community to aid King George II after the Jacobite Rebellion of 1745, and Michael Abulafia was musical director to the Duke of Cambridge, one of George III's many sons.

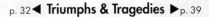

1800s
TOWARDS EMANCIPATION

Despite their respectable family life and their willingness to advance by hard work and dedication, the Jews still lacked rights of citizenship well into the nineteenth century. In 1753, a proposal to offer Jews citizenship created such a furore in Parliament that it had to be dropped. In the event, Jews had to wait until 1858, almost 30 years longer than the equally disadvantaged Catholics, to see their discrimination removed. Discrimination, however, did not affect their ambitions or their resolve, especially strong in Jews, to see their children advance themselves. They certainly advanced; there was a Jewish sheriff of London in 1835, a Jewish baronet in 1841 and in 1855, David Salomans – a Jew – became Lord Mayor of London.

1800s
LEAVING BRITAIN

The Huguenots and the Jews welcomed and valued the opportunities Britain gave them, but there were others whose only thought was to leave the country and start afresh far from its shores. The Highland Clearances, which saw thousands of Scots ejected from their homes, prompted many of them to emigrate to Canada and Australia between 1763 and 1775. The terrible Irish famine of 1845–47, led to around one million deaths after the failure of the potato crop, the staple diet on which the Irish depended. Starvation, deprivation, destitution and a deep hatred of the British who, the Irish believed, had done far too little to relieve their sufferings, gave the impetus to mass emigration, mainly to the United States, but also to Australia.

1881
JEWS FLOCK TO BRITAIN

The Russian Jews were no strangers to murderous pogroms. Nothing compared, however, to the systematic persecution they suffered after Alexander III became tsar in 1881. The result was an immense surge of emigration. The Russian Jews who poured into Britain at this time were poor, with few resources. Many settled in the East End of London, but despite their squalid surroundings, long hours of work in poor conditions and a daily struggle to survive, their vibrant Yiddish culture with its characteristic humour, music and literature added a new dimension to British life.

▲ *Many Jewish families worked in harsh conditions in the sweatshops of England.*

p. 32◀ **Triumphs & Tragedies** ▶p. 39

1144
JEWS ACCUSED OF RITUAL MURDER

Despite popular enmity and the isolation in which they lived, the Jews successfully established themselves and some moved out from London to towns like Norwich and York. There, far from the royal purview, they were crucially exposed and in 1144, they were accused of killing a Norwich boy by 'ritual murder'. The accusation of ritual murder was repeated in 1255, but long before then Jews were confined o ghettoes, and from 1218 were forced to wear distinguishing badges. At the accession of Richard I in 1189, Jews were massacred in London. This was repeated in York in 1190 when 150 Jews were slaughtered in York Castle. A century later, their use to the king at an end, the Jews were ordered to leave.

p. 33◀ **Distant Voices** ▶p. 37

When I was in the synagogue, I counted about or above a hundred right Jews ... they were all gentme(mhts). I saw not one mechanic person of them; most of them rich in apparel, diverse with jewels glittering (for they are the richest jewellry), they are all generally black, so as they may be distinguished from Spaniards or native Greeks, for the Jews hair hath a deeper tincture of a more perfect raven black, they have a quick piercing eye, and look as if of strong intellectuals; several of them are comely gallant, proper gentlemen.

From a letter written by John Greenhalgh (22 April 1662)

Faiths Collide

1572–1727

WHERE RIVAL RELIGIONS, or rivals within one religion, contest a monopoly of faith, there are always victims for whom emigration is often the only rescue. This is how the Huguenots, Calvinist refugees from Catholic France, came to be among the peoples of Britain after 1572. However, when they arrived, they were only the latest in a long line of fugitives to experience the battle of beliefs. As far back as 1095, when Pope Gregory VII preached the First Crusade to rescue the Holy Land from the Muslims, he set off a train of enmity which is still not resolved today. After the Reformation began in 1517, Protestants killed Catholics and Catholics burned Protestants, each convinced that theirs was the only proper Christian way.

1572
MASSACRE IN PARIS

As a Protestant minority in a strongly Catholic France, the Huguenots had long been vulnerable. Nothing, however, compared to the horrors that overtook them in Paris on 24 August 1572. On the orders of King Charles IX, Huguenot homes were attacked and pillaged and their inhabitants brutally murdered. Huguenot shops were looted and destroyed. On 25 August, the government ordered a halt, but the killing went on, turning towns like Rouen and Toulouse into scenes of carnage. The mobs stormed into prisons where Huguenots had been confined for their own safety, hauled them out and slaughtered them. By the time the massacre finally subsided in October, it is reckoned that 40,000 Huguenots had been slaughtered.

1572
FLEEING PERSECUTION

It is no small matter to leave home and an established way of life for another, different country. Especially hard when, as happened to the Huguenots, the land they once called home had turned against them and become a hostile place. At first, all such migrants seem to have gained is physical safety. For the rest, they must start again and struggle to survive. Earlier migrants, such as the Celts or Anglo-Saxons, arrived when Britain was still forming as a country and there was space for added variety. The Huguenots, on the other hand, were the first to arrive as foreigners in a country with a long-established identity and way of life. Their job was to fit in and gain acceptance.

▶ p. 38

1572
THE HUGUENOTS IN BRITAIN

Many people in England were shocked and appalled when news of the massacre arrived, together with the first Huguenot refugees who landed at Rye in Sussex, on 27 August 1572. Human sympathy soon gave way to curiosity and then to a certain amount of wariness as the Huguenots turned out to be different Protestants from the majority in Britain, whose faith the newcomers regarded as papist. The Huguenots were much more ascetic, dressed far more plainly, as their strict Calvinism required and seemed, at first, to want little to do with the general population. In fact, one of the first things the Huguenots did was accept invitations to already established French Protestant churches in London, Canterbury and Norwich.

▲ *The massacre of the Protestant Huguenots in France, an event that led to their flight to seek refuge in England.*

1598
THE EDICT OF NANTES

The Huguenots' initial diffidence came partly from their belief that Britain was a temporary stopping place and that one day, they would be able to return to France. However, another 26 years passed before any hope of an end to their exile emerged, when King Henri IV of France published the Edict of Nantes in 1598, giving Huguenots freedom of worship. Those Huguenots who did not take this as evidence of a new start for their faith in France proved wise. By 1685, opinion had once more

▶ *The expulsion of the Huguenots from Toulouse in France.*

swung against them as King Louis XIV revoked the Edict and turned what had for some years been a steady trickle of migrants into a mass-exodus, which brought an estimated total of 50,000 Huguenots to Britain.

1685
DROWNED FOR FAITH

In 1685, two Scotswomen, the elderly Margaret McLauchlan and Margaret Wilson, aged 18, were sentenced to death by a court in Dumfries for refusing to deny their Catholic beliefs. On 11 May, they were tied to stakes set up on the beach at Wigtown. The tide came in and began to swirl around their feet. The waters gradually rose until they closed over McLauchlan's head. Margaret Wilson, further up the beach, survived for a moment longer and the crowd of locals and soldiers watching hoped that, having seen her companion's fate, she would recant and so be saved. But the girl refused to do so and at length, one of the soldiers pushed her head beneath the water with his halberd.

1686
THE HUGUENOTS COME TO STAY

Although, in 1686, the circumstances were less dramatic than in 1572, when England received refugees from a bloodbath, the English greeted the new influx of Huguenots with practical sympathy. Churches collected money from their congregants for the relief of the Huguenots who, according to one minister had been 'cruelly, barbarously and inhumanly suppressed'. The government, however, stood apart from such emotionally driven charity, since King James II of England was a zealous Catholic. News that might have thrown light on what had happened in France was suppressed, and rumours abounded that a book about the mistreatment of the Huguenots by their Catholic countrymen had been burned. As for the Huguenots, they knew that, this time, there was no chance of them returning home.

▲ *The Huguenots brought many new skills to Britain, including an expertise in silk-weaving.*

▶ p. 42

1711
SETTLING DOWN IN BRITAIN

Many Huguenots were well equipped to rebuild their lives in Britain, for they were hardworking and had brought their skills and knowledge with them. Most settled in London, such as the silk traders in the area round Spitalfields and those in the professions in Leicester Fields, but they soon spread out to East Anglia, and south-west England and 10,000 are reckoned to have set up home in Edinburgh. As minorities will, the Huguenots lived in tight-knit, somewhat exclusive, communities. Though this arrangement altered with time as they mixed in with the general population, in the early days the success of the newcomers aroused resentment. In 1711, for instance, Huguenot silver- and gold-smiths were accused of deliberately undercutting British craftsmen by employing cheap labour.

1727
THE HUGUENOT INFLUENCE

The Huguenots sought to earn their place in British life by making a distinct contribution to it. Their contribution was considerable, and it did not take a long time to become apparent. They excelled in law, banking, insurance, education, the arts and sciences, and glassware and cabinet manufacture. Huguenots introduced white paper into Britain. David Garrick (1717–79), one of Britain's most famous and admired actors, was of Huguenot descent. In Ireland, Huguenots established silk and poplin industries, and introduced glove- and lace-making and silk-weaving. Their horticultural skills influenced the layout of what is now regarded as the typical English garden. However, to them this was probably a little bit of home from home, as they imported their seeds and bulbs from France.

p. 35◀ **Distant Voices** ▶p. 39

Flight is lawful, when one flies from tyrants.

Racine, *Phaedra* (1677)

Asylum Seekers and Refugees

1931–67

BRITAIN HAS LONG proved a haven for refugees from war and persecution. Political dissidents, asylum seekers and many others have sought and found in Britain a better life and greater security than they had before. The British proved a generally tolerant people and there was a freedom of expression and a lack of violent political upheaval which all too often scarred the lands from which refugees fled. During the Second World War, when Britain was the only combatant in western Europe to remain unconquered by Nazi Germany, thousands crossed the English Channel to safety. Some, such as Poles and Czechs, who had no desire to live under communist rule at home, stayed on to make a new life for themselves.

1931
THE DRIFT TO LONDON

The 'big city', with its promise of work, fun and, hopefully, riches, has been a powerful lure for a very long time. In the days of the Roman Empire, the city of Rome exerted this seductive attraction and in more recent times London did exactly the same. So much so that 'colonies' of London Scots, London Welsh and London Irish grew up and people, mostly young, left cities such as Manchester, Liverpool or Birmingham resolved to 'seek their fortune' in the capital. The drift southwards, as it was called, was already evident when a census in 1931 revealed that London's population had grown by about 10 per cent in the previous 10 years, reaching a total of eight million.

✶ ▶ p. 41

1933
GERMANY BECOMES A DANGEROUS PLACE

When Nazi *führer* ('leader') Adolf Hitler became chancellor of Germany in 1933, this signalled fearful danger for socialists, trades unionists, Jews, homosexuals, the physically or mentally disabled, gypsies and anyone else the Nazis thought 'inferior' or undesirable. As the 1930s progressed and the nightmares of Nazi persecution came true, all who were able to left Germany. A major destination for them was Britain. Many arrived practically penniless, but they soon discovered that the British were not to be cowed by Nazism. In 1934, for example, when the fascist leader Sir Oswald Mosley held a rally at Olympia in London, his opponents tried to break up the meeting and fighting broke out. In 1936, the police were granted additional powers to deal with the fascists.

1940
THE EVACUEES

Britain had its native refugees of a sort: the 1.3 million children and their mothers from city areas vulnerable to air raids who were sent to the countryside or to provincial towns. There they were taken in by local families, many of whom were horrified to discover what city slum life meant for the evacuees. Some children had no idea how to use knives and forks or operate a toilet. Some mothers, weighed down by poverty, were barely able to look after them. There were, in fact, two Britains: comfortable, secure middle-class Britain, and a critically disadvantaged Britain. This mixing of the two greatly influenced the concept of the Welfare State which came into force after the War.

▼ *For many children, evacuation provided better nutrition, support and education as well as safety.*

▲ *Adolf Hitler, leader of the fascist Nazi Party, being greeted by his supporters.*

1940
THE ENEMY ALIENS

As a country at war, Britain could not afford to let enemy aliens – German or Italian citizens – have complete freedom to move about and mix with the general population. There was a chance they might be spies, or become spies, even if they were also refugees or had lived in Britain for years and had British husbands or wives. About 50,000 aliens, including many who had fled from Nazi Germany, were therefore rounded up and placed in detention camps, most of which were on racecourses on the Isle of Man. Some were sent to America, but not all of them arrived. Ships carrying enemy aliens were torpedoed and sunk in the Atlantic by Nazi submarines, resulting in heavy loss of life.

1940
THE REFUGEES WHO REMAINED

Many refugees who came to Britain lived in hope of ultimately returning home. This, though, proved impossible for many Poles and Czechs. Both nationalities fought for Britain – for instance, Polish pilots participated in the Battle of Britain in 1940 – but post-war communist takeovers precluded their return home. Instead, many remained in Britain, married British wives and brought up British families. They never forgot their lost homelands, though. They formed clubs to enjoy the company of their countrymen. Many collected their countries' postage stamps to maintain a link, however tenuous. And although the end of communism in Europe after 1990 allowed some to go home after nearly 50 years, many found their British lives were too deep-rooted to make the return permanent.

▶ p. 40

1941
THE GIs COME TO BRITAIN

Shortly after the United States entered the War in 1941, American GIs began arriving in Britain. They were only visitors, due to return home once the war was over, but even so, they had a profound influence on the population. GIs were breezy, self-confident, liberated and well supplied with money and goods. They knew nothing of the class divisions in Britain, nor, it seemed, did they accept, as many British people did, that there were limits to ambition based on class. By the time the GIs left for the invasion of France in 1944, many British people had glimpsed a new world, one in which opportunities and success were there for everyone who could attain them, no matter what their class.

▲ *Air strikes during the Second World War brought destruction to cities across Britain and Europe.*

1960s
AIMING FOR INDEPENDENCE

In the 1960s, determined moves were made in Wales and Scotland for a measure of independence from England. The Irish, too, resolved to detach Northern Ireland from English dominance and in 1969 there was a renewal of terrorism aimed at forcing English agreement. The Welsh and the Scots proceeded differently. Their main method was political, though some Welsh nationalists destroyed English holiday homes in Wales to make their point. The first MP to sit for Plaid Cymru, the Welsh nationalist party, was elected in 1966 and the first Scottish National Party MP in 1967. Another 30 years would pass, however, before the Welsh and Scots were given the chance to vote for devolution and their own assemblies separate from Parliament in London.

p. 35◀ **Triumphs & Tragedies** ▶p. 49

1939
BRITAIN IN WARTIME

The refugees from Germany were joined by thousands more after the Second World War broke out in 1939 and the Nazis invaded western Europe in 1940. Terrible carnage took place on the roads of France, as families struggled to escape the Nazi advance, only to be machine-gunned from the air. Those who managed to survive crossed the Channel to Britain in anything that would float. Many refugees reached Britain stunned and terrified, among them young mothers who knew nothing about the fate of their husbands. The monarchs of invaded Norway and the Netherlands joined them. Polish airmen lucky enough to be out of Poland when the Nazis struck in 1939 came to Britain to enlist in the Royal Air Force.

p. 37◀ **Distant Voices** ▶p. 41

As soon as news of the invasion of Holland (10 May) was received in England, a number of destroyers were dispatched to Dutch ports with a view to taking off refugees.... One British naval officer became 'Commissionaire for the Hook of Holland' as he himself called it. 'My job as to assist evacuees,' he said 'but ... every time we moved, we were bombed. It was like partridges with a hawk. Refugees were everywhere. Some arrived in motor coaches, and we bunged them into ships and sent them to England.

The War Illustrated (31 May 1940)

Britain: Mother Country of the Empire

1750–1968

BRITAIN WAS THE natural hub of the British Empire, which at its greatest extent covered one quarter of the Earth's land surface and contained one quarter of its population. It became and remained – even after colonial independence – a place of better opportunities and especially a place where children could obtain better education. A certain admiration for the British way of life also persisted among former colonial peoples, making Indians, Pakistanis, Hong Kong Chinese and West Indians uproot themselves to settle and forge new lives in Britain. However, as the numbers of immigrants increased, their presence was not universally welcomed among the established population of Britain and the advantages the newcomers hoped to find were soon tempered by problems.

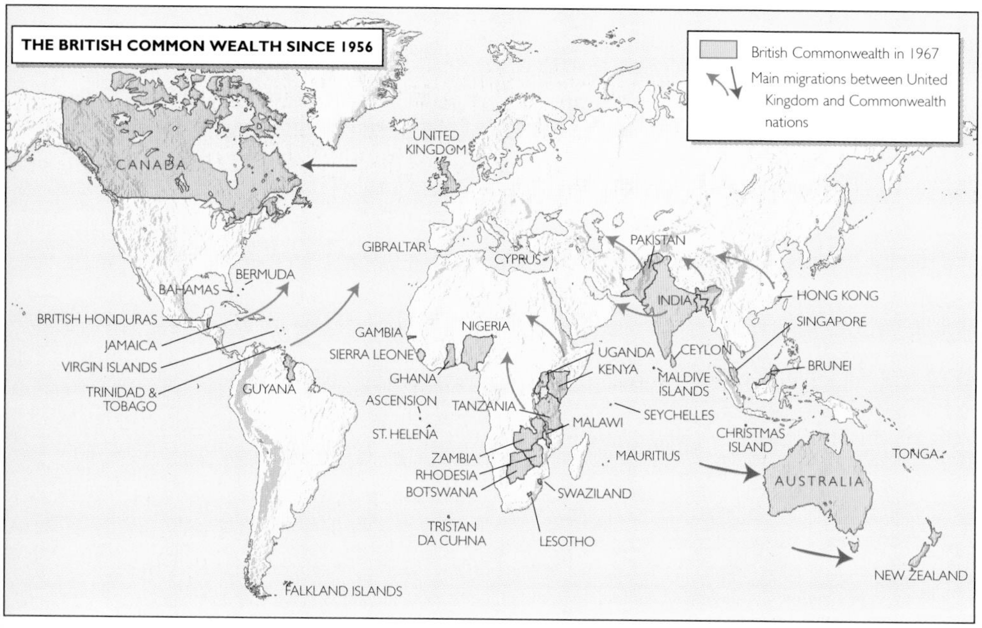

1750s
THE NABOBS

Although later Britons in colonial service in India disdained such displays, wealthy eighteenth-century factors (merchants) of the British East India Company, returned to Britain to commission portraits of themselves dressed as the phenomenally rich Indian princes, the nawabs, from whom their own nickname 'Nabobs' was derived. They wore splendid brocades, jewelled turbans and gem-encrusted footwear, and were attended by small boys, also richly dressed, whom they had brought from India as servants. For many Britons at home, glimpsing these boys on top of the Nabobs' coaches as they drove through the streets was a first chance to see an Indian in the flesh. Similarly, planters in the West Indies brought home black servants and sometimes black nannies for their children.

1800s
THE BRITISH WAY

In the nineteenth century, men and women who left Britain to live and work in one or other of the territories of the British Empire naturally took their way of life with them. Though many unfortunately evinced a disdain for native cultures and adopted an arrogant or patronising approach to colonial peoples, the latter did gain certain benefits from the imperial presence. The British introduced railways, impressive new architecture, strong, well-organised government and also offered educational and professional opportunities to people who otherwise had no real hope of them. Many Indians – for example, Mohandas Karamchand Gandhi, the future Mahatma, (1869–1948) – qualified as lawyers in London, while others trained and practised as doctors, land surveyors or teachers.

1952
INFLUX FROM THE INDIES

Before 1952, the British were not unfamiliar with blacks or Indians. There had, in fact, been a large contingent of African-Americans among the GIs in wartime Britain and Indian students were frequently seen in London. However, the increasing number of immigrants who arrived from the West Indies, with British passports and automatic rights to settle, suggested a new, more permanent situation. The West Indians came for jobs, some of which, such as work with London Transport, had been advertised in their homelands as a means of overcoming the labour shortage. But finding a place to live proved more difficult for many of them; before long, houseowners with rooms to let were putting up notices saying 'No Blacks'.

▶ p. 43

1952
SETTLING DOWN IN BRITAIN

The West Indians, some of whom solved their accommodation problems by buying and letting houses themselves, settled in London and also further afield, in Yorkshire and the West Midlands. By this time, the Jews whose culture had so enlivened the East End of London, had largely moved on

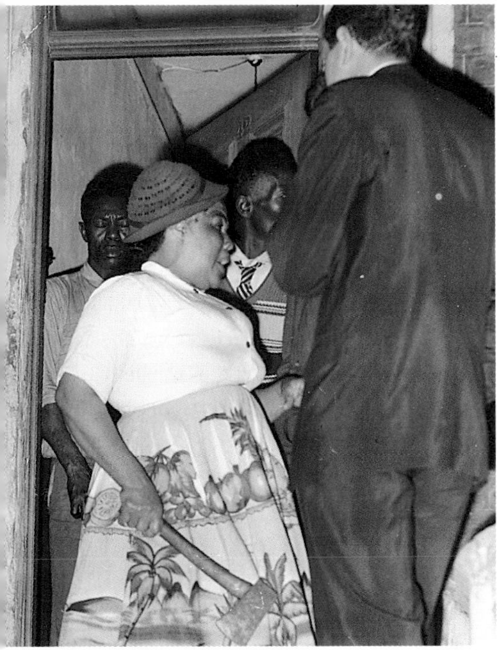

▲ *A woman, armed with an axe for protection, stands in her doorway in Notting Hill, during the race riots.*

and the West Indians began to replace them. The East End and other London suburbs, such as Cricklewood or Kilburn, took on a whole new atmosphere. The West Indians brought with them their lively, rhythmic music, their own choice of foods, their colourful style of dress and, in time, their extended families, who were forced to live in crowded conditions in small houses and flats never designed to hold so many people.

1958
RACE RIOTS

Although the West Indian newcomers settled peacefully, racial tensions began to build up and in 1958, in Notting Hill, London, they erupted. On 9 September, a group of white youths taunted blacks living in a house in Notting Hill Gate. The blacks answered back with a hail of milk bottles and a home-made petrol bomb. A group of black men then weighed in and set about the white youths with iron bars. This, too, was answered when black men leaving a club in nearby Bayswater were attacked. The police arrived to find blacks and whites embroiled in violent fighting. Before order was restored, there were many serious injuries and 59 people were arrested and charged with using offensive weapons.

1963
CONTROLLING IMMIGRATION

Although the Notting Hill Riots had been an isolated incident at the time, it became clear before long that the resentment against blacks that had been the root of the problem was widespread. By 1963, popular concern was such that the government had to take action. New rules imposing work permits on immigrants came into action at midnight on 1 July 1963. During that day, there was a rush of people trying to beat the deadline. Jamaicans on board an aircraft delayed by bad weather nearly lost their chance after they landed at Belfast almost an hour too late. An exception was made for them and they stayed. For others, though, the new rules were strictly enforced: many Indians and Pakistanis without work permits were repatriated.

1968
RISING TENSIONS

The government action of 1963 did little to solve the problem of rising racial tensions. Race hatred and the idea that Britain was going to be 'swamped' by a tide of immigrants gained ground fast among Britons in the years that followed. On 6 May 1968, at a time when 50,000 dependents of immigrants were being admitted to Britain each year, the right-wing Conservative MP Enoch Powell gave a speech in Birmingham in which he predicted 'rivers of blood' as a result of this policy. Powell was a scholar of Classics and the allusion was a Classical one, but it nevertheless sparked off vigorous support from some 74 per cent of Britons polled on the subject, and in a protest march by London dockers.

1968
FROM THE BLACK POINT OF VIEW

The West Indians were deeply disturbed by the hatred rising against them. From their viewpoint, the country which had apparently welcomed them and allowed them to settle was becoming full of enemies. The better life they had hoped for, and the improved prospects for their British-born children, seemed to be slipping from their grasp. The first generation of West Indians in Britain were known for their politeness, their calm and even their diffidence. But the younger ones, those who would have to make their way in an increasingly hostile atmosphere, began to feel they could not afford to behave so well and that fighting for the rights they had been promised was going to prove the only way to obtain those rights.

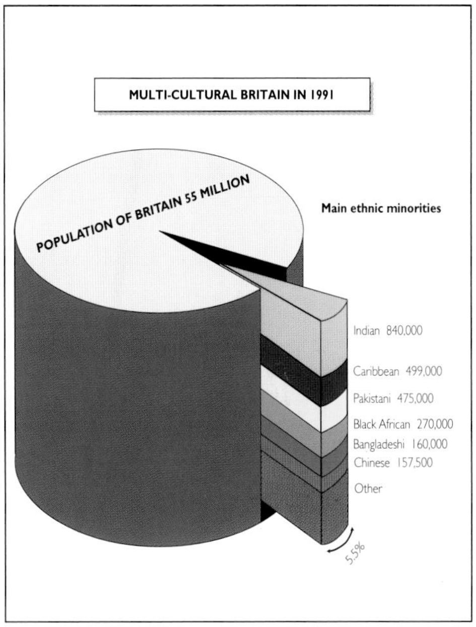

p. 39◀ **Distant Voices** ▶p. 43

As I look ahead, I am filled with foreboding. Like the Roman, I see the River Tiber foaming with much blood.' With this classical quotation, Enoch Powell, the Conservative Shadow Minister of Defence, today triggered fierce controversy over race relations. In a Birmingham speech ... he said that Britain must be 'mad, literally mad as a nation' to allow 50,000 dependents of immigrants into the country each year.... The present situation, he argued, is like a nation 'busily engaged in heaping up its own funeral pyre.

Newspaper report (21 April 1968)

Multi-cultural Britain

1969–99

TODAY, BRITAIN IS a multi-cultural society, with many distinct communities, including Americans, Australians, Italians, Cypriots and Chinese as well as Asians, Africans, West Indians and several different religions – numerous Christian faiths, Judaism, Islam, Hinduism and Buddhism. Living in such a society has not proved easy. Tensions, rivalries and prejudice, sometimes violent prejudice, remain. Despite many years of living in Britain, there is ongoing trepidation among minorities that their place in the country is not as safe as they would like it to be. This, though, has not deterred others who can benefit from the fact that Britain's doors are as open as ever they were to refugees and victims of war such as the Vietnamese, the Bosnians or the Kosovans.

1969
INDIANS FROM AFRICA

When Uganda achieved independence in 1962 and Kenya in 1963, their minority Indian populations received British passports in case, one day, they had to leave. Possibility became reality in Kenya in 1969 and in Uganda in 1972, when the rulers of these countries determined to expel the Indians, whose forebears had come to Africa in British colonial times. In Kenya, the Indians' trading licences were taken away, leaving them with no means of making a living. In Uganda, they were accused of sabotaging the economy. Some 10,000 Indians had already left Kenya in 1968 and in 1969 another 15,000 followed. In 1972, 50,000 Indians were expelled from Uganda and arrived, thanks to their passports, with an automatic right to settle in Britain.

1969
AFRICANISATION

Many Kenyan and Ugandan Asians, the victims of 'Africanisation' in the countries they left, had never seen India itself but nevertheless preserved their Indian culture and once transplanted to Britain, they went on doing so. Some people in Britain expected them to assimilate and mix with the general population, but this did not take account of the important fact that their Indian identity was vital to them. Like many previous immigrant groups, they lived largely within their own communities and followed their own customs. At least at first, their wives were not expected to appear too often in public – if at all – and their children still had their marriages arranged with husbands or wives chosen by their elders.

1969
STORES, SHOPS AND LONG HOURS

The Indians from Kenya and Uganda proved to be extremely hardworking and often engaged their whole families in their commercial business enterprises. Many of them opened shops such as grocery stores and newsagents and worked long hours, often for seven days a week. Having come from Kenya and Uganda with very little, their energy and enterprise restored the prosperity they had once known within a remarkably short time. Their extended family life encouraged education and Indian boys and girls soon began to excel at school. Before long, they were counted the cleverest group among schoolchildren as a whole. Inevitably, though, through school, the children absorbed new, less traditional ideas about relationships, dress and personal freedoms, and many began to become 'westernised'.

1981
BRITISH BLACKS GROW UP

Black youngsters born in Britain were also under racial pressures. Their image, in the eyes of many British, was an indolent and aggressive one, and they attracted a great deal of discrimination. Black dislike of the whites ran no less deep. Young blacks chafed at jobs denied them because, so they believed, of their skin colour. Blacks were convinced too, that if they committed crimes, they were dealt with far more roughly by the police than whites in the same situation. All this planted a deep distrust of the police in young black minds and in 1981, helped fuel a horrific series of violent and destructive riots in Toxteth, Liverpool and Brixton, London where shops were looted, vandalised and set on fire.

1993
STEPHEN LAWRENCE MURDERED

After the 1981 riots, which were duplicated in Hull, Reading and elsewhere, black leaders named black poverty, unemployment and the negative attitude of the police as the root cause. Despite the Race Relation Acts of 1965, 1968 and 1976, designed to reduce racial conflict, the problem remained unsolved. Police leaders had made many efforts to build bridges of understanding with the black community, but their quest for better relations was dogged by incidents such as the murder of black teenager Stephen Lawrence, who was killed in 1993. The case against five young

▶ *The murder of black teenager Stephen Lawrence sparked widespread public outrage.*

whites seemed strong, but it collapsed for legal reasons. The Lawrence family pursued the case, without success, although the police publicly admitted their failure to handle the crime properly.

1997
THE CHINESE IN BRITAIN

Chinese communities have existed in many parts of the world since the beginning of the twentieth century. Britain was only one of their destinations, though there was a special influence at work through the British presence – until 1997 – in Hong Kong. Chinese immigration into Britain and elsewhere arose from the same impetus that attracted Jews or Indians: the opportunities Britain offered for self-advancement in a stable atmosphere, where they had the freedom to preserve their own traditions quietly and without interference. The Chinese in Britain tend to mix mainly with their compatriots. Their main contact with the general population comes about through the burgeoning countrywide popularity of Chinese shops and Chinese restaurants, with their dis-tinctive oriental surroundings and exotic food.

▼ *Vietnamese refugees fled, leaving their homes and possessions, as the war continued to destroy their villages.*

1975
VIETNAM WAR

As the Vietnam War drew towards its bloodstained close in 1975, Britain was among several countries that admitted refugees. On 6 April, for example, 105 Vietnamese orphans were flown in from South Vietnam. Their need for shelter and succour was so great that, to save time, immigration arrangements were finalised on the way. Adults were also allowed in and the public mood of sympathy was overwhelming. This act of mercy was repeated during the civil war in Yugoslavia which began in 1991, when Bosnians were rescued from the widespread destruction, and again when persecuted Kurds, treated with especial brutality in Iraq, took shelter in Britain. In 1999, the Kosovan plight led to governments all over the Western World taking in refugees.

1999
MULTI-CULTURAL CELEBRATIONS

Every August Bank Holiday, the streets of Notting Hill provide the stage for colourful parades, and rhythmic Caribbean music and dancing as the West Indian community celebrates its culture in what has become, over the years, the largest carnival in Britain. Vast crowds come to watch and participate in the fun and though there is a strong police presence to prevent trouble, it has not been unknown for the police themselves to join in. The Notting Hill Carnival is part of the outward, more positive face of multicultural Britain. So are Hindu celebrations of Diwali, the festival of lights held in September and October, and the brilliantly coloured dragon that dances through the streets of London's Soho to herald the Chinese New Year each February.

▲ *Enjoying the famous Notting Hill Carnival, the largest in Britain.*

p. 41◀ **Distant Voices** ▶p. 47

Irma Hadzimuratovic, the desperately ill Bosnian child whose pitiful appearance on Britain's television screens touched the heart of the nation, was flown out of the besieged capital, Sarajevo, yesterday and rushed to the Great Ormond Street children's hospital. Irma, 5, suffered severe injuries in a mortar attack which killed her mother. She then developed meningitis and faced certain death in Sarajevo's shattered hospital, where her plight was filmed. Public outrage led prime minister John Major to intervene, and she was flown out by the RAF.... She is a frail symbol of Sarajevo's suffering. [Irma died in 1995]

Newspaper report (9 August 1993)

Politics and Power

SINCE THE ESTABLISHMENT of the Roman Republic, with its ordered system of democracy, the British Isles have seen the adoption and destruction of many great political ideals. Throughout its history, this small island has held its own against some of the greatest powers in the world, surviving invasion and war, monarchy and republic. It has witnessed the rise and fall of figures of great repute and many infamous characters. Politicians, military leaders, kings and queens, those greedy for personal power and wealth and those who have played their part in ordering the way Britain is run today. Some of Britain's best-known figures in the fields of power and politics have been women, from Boudicca to Margaret Thatcher. The country has grown from being isolated provinces to a United Kingdom, and in many respects back to individual government, with the devolution of Scotland and Wales. The history of British politics and power is the story of both success and failure. Over the centuries, the country gradually acquired an empire covering a quarter of the globe; at the turn of the millennium, its dominions may have largely dissolved, but its standing as a world leader has not decreased.

KEY THEMES

- RELIGION
- FOREIGN INFLUENCE
- INVASION
- WAR
- MONARCHS
- LEADERS
- AGREEMENTS
- PARLIAMENT
- ECONOMICS
- POLITICAL SYSTEMS

KEY EVENTS

1 55 BC
ROMAN EXPANSION IN BRITAIN

After Britain was eventually conquered it became an administrative division – a province – of the Roman Empire. The provinces were divided socially into classes: senatorial and imperial. Britain was at first one imperial province with Roman rule extending as far as the River Humber. By the third century Britain had been divided into two: a 'Britannia Superior' and 'Britannia Inferior'.

2 1066
THE BATTLE OF HASTINGS

The battle between the English army and the Norman invaders took place at Senlac Hill, five miles from Hastings. Although holding the advantage in numbers, the English were out-fought by their enemy. The battle lasted a single day, during which the English king, Harold, was killed after an arrow pierced his eye.

3 1558
ELIZABETH I

Politically and economically, Elizabeth I was one of the most cautious of England's rulers. She tried not to be drawn into wars with the great Catholic powers of France and Spain, but when this became necessary, she assured her fame by her navy's defeat of the Armada. At home she practised economic prudence.

4 1653
THE REPUBLIC

Between December 1653 and May 1659 England entered the period known historically as the Protectorate. This came into place after the failure of the 'Barebones' Parliament; Oliver Cromwell was made Lord Protector and had vast powers.

5 1707
THE ACT OF UNION

In 1707 the political independence of Scotland ended. The English and Scottish Parliaments that existed at the time became one, with the Scottish body disappearing. Scottish MPs were now to be represented in the single Parliament covering the British Isles. They did, however, manage to retain certain religious and legal freedoms.

6 1851
DISRAELI AND GLADSTONE

Dominating the political scene of the late-Victorian era were two politicians: Benjamin Disraeli, the queen's favourite, and William Gladstone, a man she came to dislike intensely. Disraeli was responsible for making Victoria Empress of India.

7 1924
THE FIRST LABOUR PARTY GOVERNMENT

The Labour Party replaced the Liberals as one of the two major political parties in Britain after the First World War. The Labour Party pulled together factions from various strands of the working-class movement. It had served in the wartime coalition government, and came to power in its own right in 1924.

8 1999
THE EURO

In February 1992, the leaders of the European Union signed the Maastricht Treaty; this set the timetable for one of the most ambitious projects in post-war Europe – the establishment of a European central bank and single currency, effective from 1999. A reluctant Britain secured an opt-out clause, freeing it from adopting the currency, known as the Euro.

TIMELINE

7000 BC The Celts arrive
2000 BC Military power develops as Iron Age takes over
1 **55 BC** Caesar's Expeditions
AD 43 Claudian Invasions
AD 60 Boudicca resists Roman invasion
AD 300 Christianity brought to Britain by the Romans
AD 440 End of Roman rule in Britain
AD 537 King Arthur
AD 886 King Alfred re-establishes Anglo-Saxon rule and culture
1016 The last of the Danish kings, including Cnut
2 **1066** William the Conqueror becomes first Norman king of England
1086 *Domesday Book*
1100 Curia Regis (early Parliament) is set up
1154 Henry II becomes first Plantagenet ruler
1314 English defeated by the Scots at the Battle of Bannockburn
1327 Edward II deposed
1376 Edward III starts 'The Good Parliament'
1455 Wars of the Roses
1485 Richard III defeated by Henry VII
1530 Henry VIII challenges the Catholic Church
1536 Wales becomes part of political union with England
3 **1558** Elizabeth I becomes queen
1603 Stuart dynasty begins with James I
1642 Civil Wars begin
1649 Charles I executed
4 **1653** Oliver Cromwell becomes Lord Protector
1689 William III and Mary accept offer of the throne; the Bill of Rights
5 **1707** Act of Union between England and Scotland
1714 House of Hanover succeeds to the throne
1783 Pitt the Younger becomes prime minister
1832 First Reform Act
1837 Queen Victoria comes to the throne
6 **1851** Disraeli and Gladstone
1867 Second Reform Acts
1917 George V changes name of royal family to Windsor
7 **1924** First Labour Party government
1926 General Strike
1931 Ramsey MacDonald heads the National Government
1940 Winston Churchill becomes prime minister
1945 Labour Party wins general election for the first time
1948 Nationalism under Clement Atlee
1952 Elizabeth II succeeds to the throne
1956 Suez Canal Crisis
1973 Britain joins EEC
1979 Margaret Thatcher becomes prime minister
1986 Single European Act
1992 Britain leaves European Monetary Union
1997 Tony Blair becomes prime minister
1998 Good Friday Agreement paves the way for peace in Northern Ireland
8 **1999** The Euro becomes effective

Pre-Roman Britain

7000 BC–AD 43

BEHIND THE STORY of modern Britain lies a complex tale stretching back over thousands of years, drawing on a vast number of different influences. The country's development takes in the history of not only the Romans, Anglo-Saxons and Normans, but is also influenced by peoples from the lowland countries of Europe, from Germany and by the Vikings. But before these came the Celtic tribes, who settled in Britain almost 10,000 years ago. Their influence was profound and can still be felt in everyday life in areas such as language, agriculture and, to a lesser extent, religion. The Celts, in various guises, were the group most responsible for the country's development before Britain was immersed into the Roman Empire in 55 BC.

◀ *The retreating Ice Age allowed settlers to begin to re-inhabit the British Isles.*

7000 BC
THE RETREATING ICE AGE

Although settlers in Britain have been traced back as far as 250,000 BC, the first roots of modern Britain can be dated to about 7000 BC when the retreating Ice Age was the signal for settlers to begin to re-inhabit the British Isles. Expedition was made easier as land bridges within the islands and between Britain and the mainland continent still existed. This was the middle phase of the Stone Age, known by historians as the Mesolithic Period. Society was still very basic, but the first signs of order, based around the practices of hunting, fishing and gathering, quickly emerged. This period, covering the first Celtic settlers, lasted for about 3,000 years, before more sophisticated methods of cultivating food were established.

7000 BC
THE CELTS

The most important prehistoric people of the British Isles were the Celts, and their influence can still be felt today. Two of their principal dialects – Goidelic and Manx and Brythonic – later evolved into Irish and Scottish Gaelic, Welsh and Cornish. Place names such as Dyfed and the Rivers Ouse and Avon are derived from the Celtic language. The Celts were ordered into tribes with settlements based on hill-forts. These forts became tribes' capitals. Central and western Europe was their homeland and in the late Stone Age the Celts were one of the most dominant groups in that area. Druidism was the major religion. Legend has it Celts were usually tall, fair and well-built, and known for their craftsmanship.

▶ p. 49

4000 BC
THE NEOLITHIC REVOLUTION

The late Stone Age, known as the Neolithic Period, marked the introduction of agriculture into the British way of life, as people moved away from the traditional hunting and gathering methods. Corn crops were grown and small dairy herds were kept, particularly in the lowlands, the midlands and south, where the population reached about 3,000. New settlers also arrived from the Mediterranean. The influence of those from the west continued with evidence that the Irish Sea was used to link different societies from what is now the north-west coast of Wales to the east coast of Ireland. Religious practices also show that people increasingly put great store in the cult of the after-life, with large stone tombs being built.

3100 BC
STONEHENGE

The Neolithic Period saw work begin on one of Europe's most remarkable, mysterious and ancient structures – Stonehenge. To this day its purpose is still not fully known, although it is commonly recognised as a site of worship connected with the summer and winter solstices.

Modern Druids still worship the coming of the summer solstice at the

▲ *The impressive monument Stonehenge continues to perplex archeologists as to its origins and purpose.*

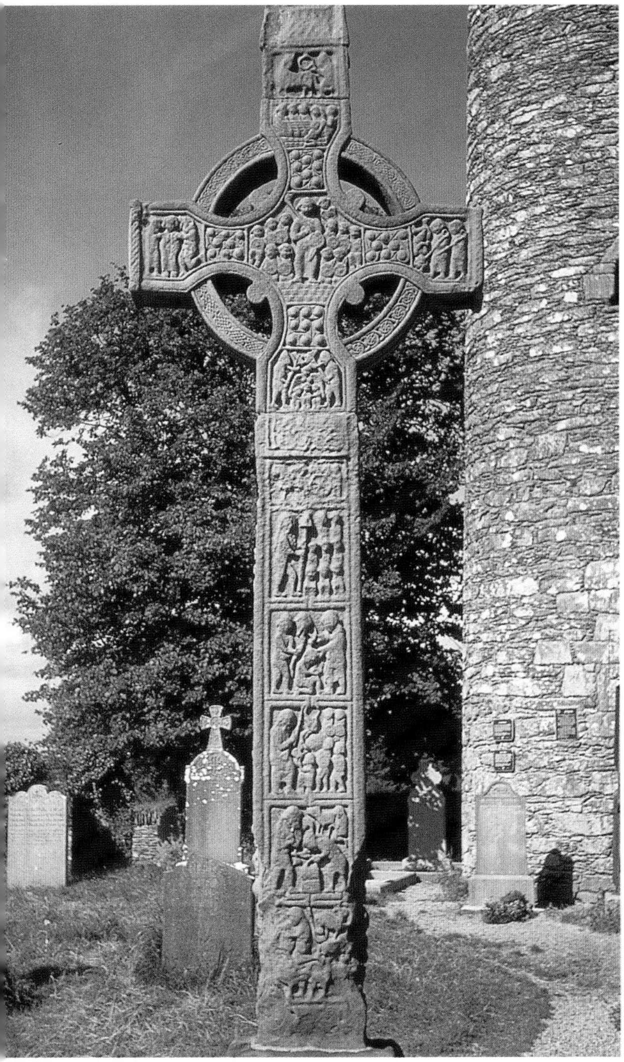

▲ *Celtic crosses can still be found scattered across the landscapes of Britain and Ireland.*

site on Salisbury Plain. Work began in about 3100 BC, but Stonehenge was re-built many times and not completed until about 1,100 years later, in 1400 BC. One estimate claims that 30 million man-hours were used up during the prolonged construction of Stonehenge. It reflects the importance of religion in prehistoric Britain and suggests ancient religious leaders played an important part in early society.

2000 BC
ECONOMICS

The Bronze Age, in the period around 2000 BC, saw a growth in trade as Britain's nascent economy began to grow. The Celts' skill in craftwork led to a flourishing metalwork industry both for home use and export. Trade in Irish copper and Cornish tin grew – the metals needed for bronze – as the economy expanded on both sides of the Irish sea. Although the tin trade was established by the Celts; its importance to the British Isles since then can be gauged by the fact that the last Cornish tin mine, South Crofty, only closed in the late 1990s. An axe industry developed later on in the Bronze Age. Later these tools would be exported to the European market as were Celtic ornaments.

500 BC
MILITARY POWER

The beginning of the Iron Age – so called because iron succeeded bronze as the basic component of tools and weaponry – saw the pre-eminence of a military ruling class in parts of prehistoric Britain, especially in the south. As hill-forts grew, ever-larger communities appear to have organised themselves into units, which generally gave political precedence to the military. These hill-forts had large populations; one in Dorset was thought to have contained 1,000 people. A large urban centre was also found on the site of modern-day Winchester. To the north and west political development took place more slowly. The Romans identified over 20 Celtic tribes, raising the possibility of political differences among the various local communities.

▶ p. 48

100 BC
THE BELGAE

One group of Celtic settlers who had a profound influence on Britain's development were the Belgae tribe, who invaded the country in the first century BC. A northern Gallic tribe, they are probably best-known for first introducing coinage into the British economy. After the relative decline of the early Iron Age, internal markets grew as numeracy and literacy grew. These earliest coins were struck in gold. The Belgae occupied large parts of southern England including Hampshire and Wiltshire and moved as far north as the River Trent. Once settled, their influence extended to those already in the country. The Belgae were among the first tribes to encounter the Romans, and they offered strong but ultimately fruitless opposition to the new invaders.

AD 43
RELIGION

The contemporary religion of Celtic Britain was Druidism. Its principal philosophy emphasised immortality and the importance of the soul. Druids were like priests and occupied a special place in Celtic society especially when it came to law and education. Entry to the priesthood took several years to achieve as prospective candidates had to prove they had understood and memorised the faith's basic principles: the Druids relied on an oral culture. The religion practised animal and some human sacrifice. Such practices appalled the Romans following their conquest in AD 43. In AD 61 Roman soldiers massacred Druids at Anglesey, an important centre for Druidism, and also destroyed sacred artefacts. After the Roman invasion Druidism largely disappeared until being revived in a modern form in the nineteenth century.

p. 43◀ **Distant Voices** ▶p. 49

Why man, he doth bestride the narrow world like a Colossus; and we petty men walk under his huge legs, and peep about to find ourselves dishonourable graves. Men at some time are masters of their fates: The fault dear Brutus is not in our stars, but in ourselves that we are underlings.

William Shakespeare, *Julius Caesar* (1599)

The Romans in Britain

55 BC–AD 420s

THE ROMANS FIRST came to Britain in 55 BC and their influence has remained ever since. For over 500 years, Britain found itself part of an empire that stretched from Portugal to Turkey and the Red Sea to the River Tyne. When Roman troops eventually withdrew, life in the British Isles, especially England and Wales, had changed irrevocably. Latin became the main language; the population grew to levels not matched again until the late-fourteenth century; literacy grew; town life flourished – many of Britain's major cities, particularly in the south, first emerged as important centres under Roman rule; the economy expanded, the currency changed; political structures fundamentally altered and the rule of law emerged. However, Roman rule was resisted most notably in Scotland (Caledonia), which the Romans never fully conquered.

▶ p. 50 **55 BC**

CAESAR'S EXPEDITIONS

Julius Caesar, emperor of Rome between 102 and 44 BC, left his mark forever on the British Isles by naming the newly conquered country incorrectly. Caesar called Rome's emerging colony Britannia in the mistaken belief that the Belgae settlers were actually from the Britanni tribe. He led his first expedition there in 55 BC following a military sortie into Gaul. This ended in failure as he was beaten back by bad weather. He returned a year later with additional troops and defeated the home army led by the Catuvellauni tribe. Adding Britain to the Roman Empire assured Caesar of great kudos back in Rome as it was considered a fabled island, separated from the continental mainland by a ferocious ocean.

▶ *Bust of the Roman emperor Julius Caesar, who first came to Britain in 55 BC.*

AD 43

THE CLAUDIAN INVASIONS

Roman rule in Britain was cemented by one of Julius Caesar's successors – Claudius – emperor between AD 41 and 54. Following political disputes in Rome, the newly-crowned Claudius turned his attention to Britain almost 100 years after Caesar. In AD 43 he assembled about 40,000 troops for a full-scale invasion of the islands. Despite fierce resistance, British troops could not match the weaponry of the Romans nor did they have sophisticated body armour like the invaders. Roman rule was confirmed when 11 British tribal kings submitted to the emperor. Claudius was present at the capture of Colchester and arrived in town complete with elephants. By AD 47 Roman forces had occupied as far north as the River Trent.

▶ p. 50 **AD 43**

ROMAN EXPANSION IN BRITAIN

After Britain was eventually conquered it became an administrative division – a province – of the Roman Empire. The provinces were divided socially into classes – senatorial and imperial. Britain was at first one imperial province with Roman rule extending as far as the River Humber. Colchester was the provincial capital. In the first and second centuries as Roman rule extended to the River Forth, London became the capital. By the third century Britain had been divided into two – a 'Britannia Superior' and 'Britannia Inferior' with York becoming another capital. By the early fourth century two provinces had become four with Cirencester and Lincoln being added as capitals. Towards the end of the century a fifth province was added taking in part of Wales.

▶ p. 50 **AD 43–300s**

GOVERNMENT IN BRITAIN

Despite sustained internal conflict during Roman rule, especially in the north, and the

▼ *Emperor Claudius overcame the resistance of the British armies with a full-scale invasion.*

THE PROVINCES OF ROMAN BRITAIN, C AD 420

division of Britain into civil and military zones – the civil zone ending at the rivers Mersey and Humber – the Romans tried to rely on a notion of rule by consent with local tribes to establish their authority. Taxes were paid by tribal kings to the Roman emperor. As well as relying on those tribes who welcomed them, they encouraged the local people in the middle ranks of society to involve themselves in local government. Law courts, civic offices and council chambers were established in town centres. However, renewed fighting, especially in the north, led to the assertion of the dominance of the military and a strengthened authoritarian outlook from the fourth century onwards.

▶ p. 52

AD 60
BRITONS FIGHT BACK

Resistance to the Romans among Britons was patchy. Some tribes fiercely resisted, others helped the invaders. Many in the south welcomed the Romans, as their arrival ended the political dominance of the local Catuvellauni tribe. The most famous resistor – in England at least – was Boudicca: Queen of the Iceni tribe in East Anglia, she led a revolt against the Romans in AD 60. On his death, the kingdom of Boudicca's husband, Prasutagas, was divided between his daughters and the Romans; however, Roman agents seized all the land. When Boudicca protested she was flogged and her daughters raped. Driven by fury, Boudicca's troops inflicted massive defeats on the Romans in Colchester, London and St Albans. After she was eventually defeated, Boudicca committed suicide.

AD 122
TROUBLE IN THE NORTH

Resistance to Roman rule was most marked in Caledonia (Scotland). Despite several attempts, the invaders never fully conquered this part of the British Isles. The border between the Romans and local tribes shifted many times from AD 78 until the end of Roman rule in Britain in 440. The Romans got as far as the Forth in the mid-second century, where soldiers constructed a 60-km (37-mile) wall to the Clyde – the Antonine Wall, similar to Hadrian's Wall – to repel attacks from the north, in 122. Agricola, governor of Britain for six years until AD 84, was the man who came closest to fully conquering Scotland, but his northern incursions were later abandoned. The Romans knew the inhabitants of the unconquered lands as Picts.

▶ p. 52

AD 300s
RELIGION UNDER ROMAN RULE

Roman culture also brought with it a new religion – Christianity. Although the extent to which Christianity became entrenched in British society during Roman times is arguable, it is now thought it was more deeply rooted than was previously believed. It appears to have been established during the later period of Roman rule. Although the influence of Christianity was patchy, it seems to have taken root among the wealthier members of ancient British society – such as in parts of Dorset and East Anglia. It was during the same period that a British monk, Pelagius, advocated his heretical views that man could be saved by the exercise of his own will rather than through divine grace – the first but by no means the last time Britain clashed with Rome on religion.

p. 39◀ **Triumphs & Tragedies** ▶p. 54

AD 410
THE END OF ROMAN RULE

The end of Roman rule came about gradually rather than because of one main event. The decline began around the middle of the fourth century. Roman forces were defeated by Picts in the north and Saxons in the south. Internal disputes among the Romans also caused instability. Roman forces in Britain were deliberately weakened as they were needed to assist in the struggle for power back in Rome. In AD 409 British forces rebelled against the rule of Constantine III. By 410 the emperor Honorius ended connections with the British part of the Roman Empire. From this time, Britain had no central government with local tribes filling the political vacuum. The Romans attempted to regain power in the late 420s, when military intervention was once again a possibility.

p. 47◀ **Distant Voices** ▶p. 51

Then none was for a party;
Then all were for the state;
The great man helped the poor,
And the poor men loved the great:
Then lands were fairly portioned;
The spoils were fairly sold;
The Romans were like brothers
In the brave days of old.

Thomas Babington (1800–59)

▲ *The Vikings were successful merchants and skilled craftsmen as well as great warriors.*

The Vikings

AD 477–1016

THE TRADITION OF invasion and the importance of foreign influences on the British Isles was strengthened between the fifth and the ninth centuries. Replacing the Romans were new invaders. First came the Germanic Anglo-Saxons who settled throughout England but largely in the south, east and west. Indeed England takes its name from a group of these settlers – the Angles. Despite fierce resistance from those already in Britain (which gave birth to one of the country's most enduring legends, Arthur), the Anglo-Saxons established strongholds throughout the country. But after settling, they in turn found themselves attempting to fight off new invaders, the Danes, during the ninth century. This gave rise to a second great historical figure – King Alfred.

▶ p. 60 **AD 477**

GERMANIC INFLUENCE

The Anglo-Saxons were a German people composed of three main groups: Angles, Saxons and Jutes. Their connection with Britain was established before AD 477 when the Saxon leader, Aelle, landed in Sussex. Trade routes between the south coast and German ports grew under the Romans. Saxons had previously led a series of pirate attacks on the south coast. When they arrived, Kent was soon conquered by the Jutes and Saxon kingdoms were established in Essex and Middlesex; Wessex and Sussex soon followed. East Anglian and Northumbrian kingdoms were also set up. Although less civilised than the Romans, kinship ties proved strong under the Anglo-Saxons. Their influence on British life can still be noticed by the amount of town names ending in -ing, -ington, or -ingham.

▶ p. 55 **AD 537**

THE ARTHURIAN LEGEND

The bloody history of Britain in the Middle Ages soon spawned its first hero – a man whose legend is well-known today, thanks to Hollywood, although how much is fact and how much fiction has not been established. Arthur – if that were his real name – was a military leader who defeated the Anglo-Saxons in 12 battles during the sixth century. He was fatally wounded in AD 537. His importance, or myth, has endured thanks to historians through the ages. Tenth-century Welsh literature eulogised Arthur. The legend of his court and Round Table emerged in the twelfth century. In 1998 a slate bearing Arthur's name was discovered in Cornwall and hailed as proof of his existence. Alas, the tales of Guinevere, Lancelot and Excalibur remain unsubstantiated myths.

▶ p. 59 **AD 600s**

KINGS AND QUEENS

The struggle for power in Britain during the seventh century remains one of the bloodiest periods in the country's history. By the time the Anglo-Saxons had asserted their dominance, Britain was ruled by a large number of different kings. One estimate claims there were dozens of English kings at this time. The Britons had largely fled to Wales, while the Anglo-Saxons controlled large parts of England. The most powerful kingdoms to emerge were Wessex, Mercia, East Anglia and Northumbria. Leaders of the larger kingdoms also ruled over smaller areas outside their own *bailiwick* (or district). The most powerful leader was known as the Bretwalda, which meant Lord of Britain. The Anglo-Saxons also developed a council – the Witan – composed of noblemen and bishops, which was designed to limit royal power.

AD 793

AN ALIEN FORCE

The late eighth century saw Britain invaded for the first time in two centuries as the Vikings began their colonisation. History used to portray them as bloodthirsty barbarians. This may be an exaggeration; though some of the battles were indeed gruesome, the Vikings' reputation as rapists and pillagers may owe as much to propaganda as fact. Evidence suggests they were also successful merchants. The areas they controlled became extremely prosperous – especially in eastern England – and trade flourished as the economy expanded. The traditional view of Vikings – the term comes from an old Saxon word for 'pirate' – may derive from their initial sorties into England, which saw the sacking of three holy sites, Lindisfarne, Jarrow and Iona between AD 793 and 795.

▶ p. 69 **AD 800s**

VIKING COLONISATION

The Vikings were successful because of their sea-power. By using longships, the Danes and Norsemen were able to conquer large areas close to the North and Irish Seas. The

Danes largely settled in England, the Norse used the Irish Sea to land in Ireland and Scotland. They brought with them a new culture, and replaced the old Saxon military aristocracy with a system based around farming; it appears to have been less authoritarian in nature. Danelaw was established in eastern, central and northern England, where the new customs and laws prevailed. The defeated Saxons also paid monies – the Danegeld – to avoid further war. Raised through taxation, the first collection in the late tenth century amounted to 20,000 pieces of silver.

✠ ▶ p. 58

AD 886
THE RISE OF WESSEX

The Viking invasions, though decisive, were not complete. They still met resistance from Saxons, the most famous of whom was King Alfred. One of England's greatest heroes, Alfred ruled the kingdom of Wessex between AD 871–899. Despite appalling odds, his army defeated the Danes at Athelney in 878 and followed this with a decisive victory in Wiltshire in the same year. In 886, he captured London and his rule was recognised by the Danish. His successes were not confined only to military victories, though. Alfred extended the use of the English language, encouraged learning, stressed the importance of widespread literacy, courted intellectuals, wrote books, translated Latin, began the *Anglo-Saxon Chronicle*, which detailed life between the ninth and twelfth centuries, and founded the Royal Navy.

◀ *An Anglo-Saxon helmet, discovered amongst many other treasures at Sutton Hoo.*

AD 900s
THE AGE OF WESSEX

Having established its rule through Alfred the Great, the kingdom of Wessex was able to consolidate this throughout the tenth century. Alfred's successors – including Edward the Elder, Aethelstan and Eadred – proved themselves to be largely competent in the face of renewed threats and further invasions from the Danes. Internal political life in the southern parts controlled by Wessex was more militaristic than that under the control of the Danes. The role of the kings also grew in importance. Instead of being only overlords, the new monarchy now presented themselves as quasi-religious figures; and monasteries received increased royal patronage. Royal authority was more keenly felt, literally, when representatives of the royal household carried out flogging on law breakers.

▼ *King Cnut, whose reign marked a renewed period of Danish dominance in England.*

1016
THE END OF THE ANGLO-SAXON ORDER

The accession of Cnut (Canute) to the throne in 1016 marked a brief period of renewed Danish dominance and the beginning of the end of Anglo-Saxon rule. Following the reign of Aethelred the Unready, who ordered the massacre of all Danes in his kingdom, the Danish launched a counter-assault on Wessex. Cnut was accepted by the Danish army and began reform of the English rulers dividing the country into four earldoms. Cnut was succeeded by his sons Harold and Harthacnut, but they were to be the last Danish rulers. The Anglo-Saxons, in the form of Edward the Confessor, returned to the throne in 1042. His successors included the last Anglo-Saxon king, Harold II, who was defeated by William the Conqueror.

p. 49◀ **Distant Voices** ▶p. 53

In this Beorthic took to wife Eadburh, daughter of King Offa. And in his days came three ships of Norwegians from Horthaland: and then the reeve rode thither and tried to compel them to go to the royal manor for he did not know what they were: and then they slew him. These were the first ships of the Danes to come to England.

Anglo-Saxon Chronicle, describing the first Danish landings in the late eighth century

The Norman Invasion

1066–1154

IF EVER ONE DAY changed the course of English history then it was 14 October 1066. Near Hastings on that day the English army was defeated by invading Norman forces. The Norman conquest has been described by historians as a 'catastrophe' and the 'greatest disaster in English history'. Even if this is an exaggeration, there is no doubt that it marked a very clear turning point in the history of the country. Although at first it represented a revolution in England only, Norman rule was to have its effect on the whole of the British Isles. As well as establishing a new political culture based around the castle, the Normans brought new legal practices, a new language and strengthened the role of the Church.

1066
WILLIAM THE CONQUEROR

William was the illegitimate son of the Duke of Normandy, who ended up marrying his cousin. When he died, he was so fat his body burst out of its stone sarcophagus, filling St Stephen's church in Caen with a foul stench. William became the first Norman king of England when he inflicted one of the most decisive defeats on an invaded power in European history after the Battle of Hastings. He also proved more than an able king. He crushed opposition, reformed the English church and created a new French political ruling class. His claim to the English throne began in 1051 when he was almost certainly offered the throne by Edward the Confessor. In 1065 Harold II promised to help William's quest for succession, but instead became king himself.

▶ p. 54

1066
THE BATTLE FOR THE ENGLISH CROWN

On 25 September 1066, Harold II defeated the king of Norway, Harald Hardraada, and his arch enemy and brother Tostig at the battle of Stamford Bridge, near York. But within days of his victory news of the Normans' arrival at Pevensey reached Harold. Mustering his forces, he marched to Sussex to meet the invaders and ultimately secure his place in history. The battle between the English army and the Normans took place at Senlac Hill, five miles from Hastings. Although holding the advantage in numbers, the English were undisciplined and out-fought by their enemy. The battle lasted a single day during which Harold was killed after an arrow pierced his eye. The victory was later commemorated by the building of Battle Abbey near the site.

▼ *The English were victorious at Stamford Bridge, but were to lose to William at Hastings.*

1066
NORMAN CONQUEST

Despite victory in battle, the Normans' grip on England was still tenuous. The Normans numbered few compared to a largely hostile English population totalled some two million. Nervous Norman guards set fire to nearby houses during William the Conqueror's coronation at Westminster Abbey on Christmas Day, fearing an attack on their leader. Between 1067 and 1071, the Normans faced a number of revolts including the taking of Hull by Danish forces. William's response was emphatic. He brutally clamped down on opposition across the country – though he also received some English support – and began the process of building castles to show off Norman power and intimidate potential enemies. A new political culture, almost certainly including the introduction of feudalism into English society, helped reinforce Norman power.

▲ *The spectacular cathedral at Ely, the main body of which was built by the Normans.*

▶ p. 57

1066
THE CHURCH UNDER THE NORMANS

One area where Norman rule changed the social landscape of Britain was religion. French religious orders and monks were brought to the newly-invaded country and were granted land to build new monasteries. At the time of the invasion in 1066 there

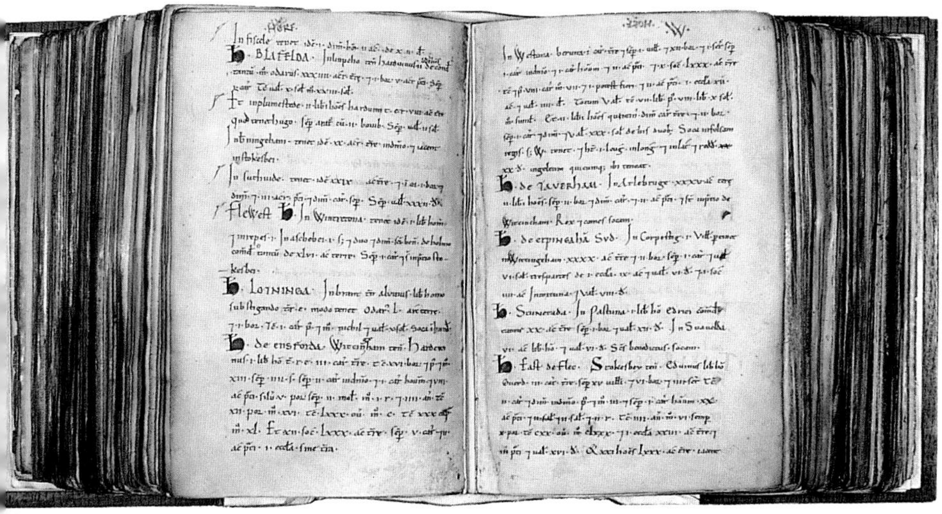

▲ *The* Domesday Book *gives an unparallelled insight into society and culture in the Middle Ages.*

were just 1,000 monks and nuns in Britain. By the early thirteenth century this figure had swollen to 13,000. Cathedrals such as Durham and Ely were also built to emphasise the new regime's religious beliefs. Catholic Christianity remained the dominant form of religion throughout this time – the religious tenets of Rome seem to have been absorbed by the population at large. Non-Christian faiths such as Judaism were rarely tolerated and in the thirteenth century all Jews were expelled from Britain.

£ ▶ p. 68

1086
SURVEY OF ENGLAND

The *Domesday Book*, today housed at the Public Record Office, was the most comprehensive record of property compiled in Europe during the Middle Ages. It was part of William the Conqueror's attempt to consolidate Norman rule by maximising as much revenue in taxes as possible. The money-raising tactics were resented, in many shires leading to rioting. Almost every English shire – only the four most northern shires and the cities of London and Winchester escaped – was visited by the king's representatives. Every village had to give details of landowners, and the size, use and value of their land. The *Domesday Book* was eventually compiled in two volumes, *Little Domesday*, dealing with East Anglia and the second with the remaining counties.

1087
WILLIAM THE CONQUEROR'S SUCCESSORS

By the time of William the Conqueror's death in 1087, the family strains that would eventually end the Norman dynasty were already beginning to show. William was succeeded in England not by his eldest son Robert, who controlled Normandy, but by his second son, William II, better known as Rufus because of his red complexion. He was once described as being 'hated by almost all his people' and almost certainly died at the hands of an assassin while hunting in the New Forest. Both William II and his successor Henry I had to establish their rule over England through war with Robert. Henry's successes as king were notable in the areas of finance, where he extended and beefed-up the role of the Exchequer, the forerunner of today's Treasury.

▶ p. 54

1100s
LAW AND ORDER IN NORMAN BRITAIN

The Norman and Angevin kings developed a new Parliament, seen now as one of the earliest forerunners of today's modern body. The Curia Regis was a legis-lative body which created and enacted new laws. It was also a court which adjudicated on matters such as land and property disputes. Its importance declined, though, when the machinery of government, especially bureaucracy, grew.

One of the departments to take on its work in the twelfth century was the Exchequer, the forerunner of today's Treasury. A further major political reform of the time was the development of the borough. Established from the Anglo-Saxons *burh*, the borough remains a political unit in Britain to this day.

1154
THE END OF NORMAN RULE

Norman rule finally ended in the twelfth century. It was usurped not by invasion but by bitter in-fighting between French dynastic houses. The Normans were eventually replaced by the Anjou (Plantagenet) dynasty, a western French house who would rule for three centuries. The last Norman ruler was Stephen between 1135 and 1154. His rule was marked by the breakdown of the rule of law. He seized the crown with the support of the Church despite Henry I's daughter, Matilda, being the rightful heir. However, his support soon crumbled, with the Scots invading England (1138) and Matilda launching her own assault (1139). Stephen was captured (1141) but was allowed back onto the throne. Matilda's son Henry II then succeeded him becoming the first Plantagenet ruler in 1154.

p. 51 ◀ **Distant Voices** ▶ p. 55

As the fire spread rapidly the people in the church were thrown into confusion and crowds of them rushed outside, some to fight the flames, others to take the chance to go looting. Only the monks, the bishops and a few clergy remained before the altar. Though they were terrified, they managed to carry on and complete the consecration of the king who was trembling violently.

A Norman monk, describing the scenes surrounding William the Conqueror's accession to the English throne (1066)

War and Politics

1295–1485

THE FOURTEENTH AND FIFTEENTH centuries were an extremely turbulent and dangerous time in the British Isles. The period was marked by great changes usually brought on by war. England found itself mired in conflicts with Scotland, France and the Low Countries. When it was not fighting other countries, its royal houses were fighting each other, most spectacularly through the 30-year-long Wars of the Roses between the houses of Lancaster and York. To add to the list there were also periods of sustained uprisings in Wales. It was the most sustained period of conflict since the Viking ages. Away from war, the Church appeared in decline and England was also ravaged by plague – in 1348 – which severely reduced the country's population.

▶ p. 58

1295
MODEL PARLIAMENT

The concept of modern Parliament owes much to the late-thirteenth-century Parliament and nineteenth-century historians who gave the body its grand title of the 'Model Parliament'. The name came about because of its political make-up, which was said to be more representative than the Parliaments which followed later. It was summoned by Edward I who occupied the throne between 1272 and 1307. Edward soon found himself clashing with Welsh armies and, later during his rule, with the Scots. He needed to convene a Parliament in order to raise revenues for his wars. The body was duly summoned in November 1295. It comprised earls and barons and members of the clergy as well as representatives from each city and borough.

▶ p. 60

1314
SCOTTISH CONQUEST

Edward I left an unpleasant legacy for his successors. His shrewdness in administrative matters was not matched in his dealings with the rest of the British Isles, and England found itself at war with both Wales and Scotland. The English army was routed in several battles with the Scots, commanded by William Wallace, most notably at Bannockburn in 1314. In 1320, a group of Scottish barons wrote to the Pope John XXII, passionately proclaiming the country's independence. The Declaration of Arbroath, as it became known, has subsequently been seen as the defining statement of Scottish independence. The English court was also concerned with its own internal warring factions which would shape the development of the country over the next two centuries.

p. 49◀ **Triumphs & Tragedies** ▶p. 56

1337
START OF THE HUNDRED YEARS' WAR

England's main overseas enemy during the fourteenth century was France. Between 1337 and 1453 the two countries embarked upon a prolonged period of conflict. At the heart of the struggle was political sovereignty and trade. France was worried by the power of the English territories in its country and was also fearful of England's growing economic influence, especially in the region of Flanders. The claim of English monarchs to the French crown was another cause for anxiety and England was troubled by France's support of Scotland. The Hundred Years' War broke out when Gascony was confiscated from the English. By the time the conflict was resolved the English, after a series of defeats led in part by Joan of Arc, retained only Calais on the French mainland.

▲ *The Hundred Years' War: a series of battles between France and England over sovereignty.*

1376
THE GOOD PARLIAMENT

The toll of the Hundred Years' War had become severe by 1376. In a period of heavy taxation and military failure – most notably at La Rochelle in 1372 when the English navy was routed – the king, Edward III, summoned what has become known as the Good Parliament. The Parliament lasted between April and July of that year. Exasperated with what it saw as the profligacy of the English court at this time, the Parliament was critical and achieved some success in changing things. The chamberlain, Lord Latimer, was successfully impeached. The practice of impeachment was begun in this era and was a process where the Commons acted as prosecutors and the Lords as judges. Another person ousted from power was Edward III's mistress, Alice Perrers.

1381
TAX REBELLIONS

Social politics during this time led to a series of uprisings collectively known as the Peasants' Revolt. Peasants and artisans rebelled against the imposition of a poll tax (a tax introduced on every person aged over 14) and the government's decision to collect arrears. Most serious of all the uprisings was in Kent, where protesters were led by Wat Tyler. Having seized Rochester Castle, Tyler led a march to London in June. Confronted eventually by the king – Richard II – the protesters dispersed but not before the chancellor and archbishop of Canterbury had been murdered by the rebels. Wat Tyler was also killed, by the Mayor of London, William Walworth.

◀ *The Peasants' Revolt: a series of uprisings protesting against taxes imposed by the government.*

✪ ▶ p. 59

1400
WELSH REBELLION

Fragile English rule in Wales in the fifteenth century was challenged by a series of uprisings. Most notable was the rebellion led by Owain Glyndwr, which began in 1400 and continued until 1415. Primarily, the uprising was a dispute about land, but it also reflected Welsh disenchantment at English attempts at the colonisation of Wales. Officials of the Church and State were largely English, promoting resentment in Wales. The fierce struggle put up by Glyndwr and his supporters led many in England to be fearful of Wales. By 1404 Owain Glydwr had proposed an independent Welsh church and separate university colleges. He also envisaged dividing the country up into several kingdoms, with himself as one of the rulers.

1455
WARS OF THE ROSES

The prize of the English crown sparked a battle between two dynastic houses in the fifteenth century – the Lancasters and the Yorks. After Edward III died (1377), both houses claimed a right to the throne. The ensuing war earned its name from the use of the red and white roses as symbols for Lancaster and York respectively. The period before 1455 was marked by weak leadership, typified by the reigns of Henry VI and Richard II. In the 1460s and 1470s after many battles including Yorkist victories at Mortimer's Cross and Lancastrian victories at Hexham, the crown swung back and forth between the two houses. During a period of relative calm under the leadership of Edward IV, war began again after his death in 1483. Peace came two years after the death of Richard III in 1485.

1485
THE DEATH OF RICHARD III

Richard III has become known, perhaps unfairly, as one of the most notorious kings ever to rule England. This may be partly to do with the history written by the Tudors, whose description of him formed Shakespeare's dramatisation. He came to the throne in 1483 after the death of his brother Edward IV. However, the manner in which he came to be king ensured his name would be remembered forever in history. As guardian of Edward IV's 12-year-old son, Edward V, Richard imprisoned him and his younger brother in the Tower of London. The brothers later disappeared, widely believed to have been killed on Richard's order. Although he had been successful in dealing with other uprisings, Richard was defeated and killed in August 1485 by Henry Tudor (Henry VII) at the Battle of Bosworth Field.

p. 53◀ **Distant Voices** ▶p. 57

But at last it attacked Gloucester, yea and Oxford and London, and finally the whole of England so violently that scarcely one in ten of either sex was left alive. As the graveyards did not suffice, fields were chosen for the burial of the dead. A countless number of common people and a host of monks and nuns and clerics as well, known to God alone, passed away.

Geoffrey le Baker, Oxfordshire cleric, on the Plague (1348)

The House of Tudor
1485–1603

HENRY VIII IS PROBABLY the most famous English monarch. His modern reputation owes more than a little to the way he has been portrayed on television and film, but largely it derives from the fact that during his reign he oversaw one of the most politically turbulent times in British history. His war on the established Church and his marrying many wives have long become well-known tales but Henry's actions had a profound effect on later developments in British life. The subsequent division of the church in England and the Reformation in Europe generally was to continue to have major implications for those rulers who followed Henry to the throne including Mary, Queen of Scots, and Elizabeth I.

▼ *Anne Boleyn, Henry VIII's second wife; she was executed after failing to bear a son.*

1485
THE RISE OF THE HOUSE OF TUDOR

The Tudor kings and queens were Henry VII, Henry VIII, Edward VI, Mary I and Elizabeth I. Elizabeth was the last Tudor; the dynasty lasted 118 years. The Tudor period was also a time of great cultural significance, giving rise to figures such as the playwrights William Shakespeare and Christopher Marlowe, and political figures like Sir Thomas More and Cardinal Wolsey. The Tudor line originated from Anglesey, north Wales. In the mid fifteenth century an ancestor, Owen, married the widow of Henry V. Their grandson – Henry VII – was to become the first Tudor king. He defeated and killed Richard III at the Battle of Bosworth Field in 1485.

1509
HENRY VIII BECOMES KING

Just 18, Henry VIII came to the throne in 1509. Guided by councillors, Henry VIII was instructed to marry Catherine of Aragon which he duly did, marking the beginning of his infamous marital life. He became heir to the throne because his elder brother Arthur had died in 1502. During his first years of rule he concerned himself largely with foreign policy, defeating both the French and the Scottish in battle in 1512 and 1513. Peace was made with France in 1514, but continued fighting, prompted by Henry's belief that war was the 'sport of kings', left England near bankruptcy in the 1520s. It was only during his later rule that Henry became obsessed with the need for a male heir.

▲ *England's most infamous king: the six-times married Henry VIII, founder of the Church of England.*

p. 55◀ **Triumphs & Tragedies** ▶p. 60

1530s
DIVORCE CRISIS

Henry VIII fell in love with Anne Boleyn while married to Catherine of Aragon. Exasperated by Catherine's failure to produce a male heir, Henry sought a divorce. Henry insisted his marriage be annulled by the English church. This was not feasible, however, the marriage had been sanctioned by Rome. He appealed to Pope Clement VII but his request was denied (the pope's political master was Catherine's nephew). To prove he could divorce Catherine, the king had to prove Rome had no dispensation over his case. This he was eventually able to do during the 1530s, installing himself as head of the English church. Anne was pregnant when she married Henry but bore him a daughter, Elizabeth I, not a son. Anne Boleyn was later executed on a trumped-up charge of adultery.

1530s
REFORMATION

Henry VIII's desire for a divorce and his subsequent war on the orthodoxy of Rome also has to be viewed with regard to the Reformation which was taking place at the same time. This resulted in the formation of Protestant churches, including those in England and Wales, which were dissatisfied with Rome during the sixteenth century. Henry's promptings for a divorce speeded up the process of reform in England and Wales. Reformers took up the push for change after Henry's death in 1547. In 1549 the Book of Common Prayer, the Church of England's liturgy, was produced, followed by a revised work three years later. In Scotland, Catholicism was identified with its alliance with France and its antipathy towards England.

1530s
WAR ON THE MONASTERIES

In the 1530s, with Henry's rule over the Church of England established, the king set about on his dissolution of the monasteries. His motivation for this appears to have been a desire to win back political support in the country as well as to restore his financial position. By this time Henry VIII was bankrupt and by annexing the monasteries, he was able to redistribute wealth in England overwhelmingly in favour of the monarchy and landed gentry, and away from the Church. The dissolution of the monasteries was overseen by Thomas Cromwell. A notable thinker and writer of the age, Sir Thomas More, was executed in 1535 for his opposition to Henry's religious policies. Sir Thomas, who wrote *Utopia*, refused to deny papal supremacy.

▶ *Elizabeth I was a cautious monarch and a shrewd leader.*

1530s
THOMAS CROMWELL

Born to humble origins in 1485, Thomas Cromwell rose to become one of the pivotal figures of his age. Through Cromwell's promptings, the Privy Council, which still exists today, was established. The Council represented a streamlining of the king's decision-making process and a reform of his financial institutions, known as the King's Council. Its 19 member officers were drawn from the royal household as well as members of state. It developed its own seal in 1556. Cromwell's fate, though, was execution for treason. He fell from Henry VIII's favour after persuading the king to marry Anne of Cleves – legend has it that Henry 'found her so different from her picture ... that ... he swore they had brought him a Flanders mare'.

1553
MARY'S CHALLENGE TO PROTESTANTISM

Henry's eldest daughter, Mary, became queen of England and Ireland in 1553, following the death of her half-brother Edward VI – despite his attempts to ensure the throne passed to the Protestant Lady Jane Grey, under pressure from the Duke of Northumberland, a member of the Privy Council. Mary, the daughter of Catherine of Aragon, was a devout Catholic like her mother. Upon her succession she set about halting the anti-Catholicism practised by her father and the advisers of Edward VI. Her policies, especially her decision to marry her Spanish cousin Philip, proved unpopular. She continued with her policies and officially reconciled England to Rome. Like her father, though, she was defeated by nature. She died childless in 1558, failing to produce a Catholic heir. Her religious fervour earned her the nick-name of 'Bloody Mary'. More than 300 Protestants were executed as heretics during her reign.

1558
ELIZABETH I

Politically and economically Elizabeth I, who reigned from 1558–1603, has marked herself out as one of the most cautious rulers ever to occupy the throne. She was also a very shrewd leader. She became queen in 1558 when the country was still marked by deep religious divisions. She refused to be used as a focus point for the Protestant factions but reversed laws promoting Catholicism established by her sister Mary. Abroad, she attempted to avoid wars with the great Catholic powers, but still became entangled in a six-year long conflict with Spain. Her fame was assured through her defeat of the Spanish Armada in 1588. At home she practised economic prudence. She financed Parliament from her own money and called in coinage from previous reigns.

p. 55◀ **Distant Voices** ▶p. 59

I know I have the body of a weak and feeble woman, but I have the heart and stomach of a king, and of a king of England too; and think foul scorn that Parma or Spain, or any Prince of Europe, should dare to invade the borders of my realm.

Elizabeth I, talking of the threat posed by the Spanish Armada

The Civil Wars and the Glorious Revolution

1603–89

THE SEVENTEENTH CENTURY was one of the most turbulent centuries and also one of the most important in terms of the development of the concept of 'Britain'. It finally put the stamp on the dominance of Protestantism and also established English political dominance within the British Isles. By the beginning of the eighteenth century the Act of Union between England and Scotland had been signed. The seventeenth century witnessed the unique sight of a monarch being put on public trial and executed, another fleeing the country expecting also to be executed, civil wars, the end of the monarchy, an 11-year republic led by Oliver Cromwell, and the restoration of the monarchy. All this was accompanied by a rise in the powers and importance of Parliament.

▶ p. 62

1603
THE STUARTS

The Stuart dynasty was one of the least successful in British history despite lasting almost 400 years, first as rulers of Scotland and then of England as well. The family, which originated from the French region of Breton, ruled Scotland from 1371 to 1714 and England from 1603 to 1714. Their connection to the English throne came through the marriage of James IV to Margaret Tudor. Their granddaughter was Mary, Queen of Scots. Although Elizabeth did not recognise Mary's son, James I, as heir he still succeeded Elizabeth to the throne in 1603. In 1625 he in turn was succeeded by Charles I. The accepted spelling of Stuart is the French form of the name Stewart and eventually became the accepted form in England.

1625–49
CHARLES I

In Whitehall on 30 January 1649, Charles I became the first monarch to be tried for treason and beheaded. The road to his execution was long and complex. He came to the throne in 1625; however, his reign was permeated by disputes with Parliament over his attempts to raise revenues through taxation as well as being punctuated by protracted disputes over the long-standing issue of religion. Charles dissolved three Parliaments between 1625 and 1628. From 1629 he tried to rule without the aid of Parliament. Following a further attempt to work with Parliament which failed, civil war broke out. Captured by the Scots and handed over to the English, he escaped but was later captured and executed after his supporters were defeated.

▶ p. 62

1640s
THE SHORT AND LONG PARLIAMENTS

After an 11-year gap, Charles recalled Parliament and on 13 April 1640 he convened the Short Parliament. But after further disputes the Parliament was dissolved less than a month later. The king was trying to raise funds for the Bishops' War which had promoted further religious hostilities between Scotland and England. But many in Parliament were reluctant to grant him any revenues before their grievances for the dissolution of Parliament 11 years before were

▼ *The public execution of King Charles I, the first monarch to be tried and beheaded.*

redressed. In response Charles dissolved Parliament. The Long Parliament was politically more successful, though not for the king. Further dispute led to the outbreak of civil war in 1642. In 1648 it established the Commonwealth. In 1660 it dissolved itself in favour of the restoration of the monarchy.

1642–48
THE CIVIL WARS

There were two civil wars in England, first between 1642–46, and then again in 1648. Following the protracted dispute between Parliament and the king and the failure to find a compromise, forces representing both sides took to the battle field. Parliamentary strength lay in the south and east whereas the royalists were stronger in the north and the west. In 1643, the king's position was weakened by the decision of the Scots to support the Parliamentarian cause. In 1645, the New Model Army – a force comprising about 20,000 soldiers and commanded by Cromwell and Fairfax – led to battle being intensified. After Oxford had fallen, Charles gave himself up to the Scots. Thereafter, attempts at compromise failed again and battle ensued once more in 1648. In 1649, after decisive victories for Cromwell, the king was captured and eventually executed.

▶ p. 62

1650s
OLIVER CROMWELL

Following the civil war and the execution of Charles I, Oliver Cromwell found himself the most powerful living Englishman. A former student of Cambridge and MP for the city, Cromwell had distinguished himself during the war, although he was not without critics, especially the Royalists, the Irish and the Levellers who wanted to rid society of social distinctions but were ultimately opposed by Cromwell. His military record though was sullied by campaign in Ireland, where he controversially ordered the massacre of citizens in Drogheda and Wexford. The key player during the 11 years that England was a Republic, Cromwell assembled what was known as the Barebones Parliament in 1653. This Parliament consisted of 140 men, most of whom were chosen by Cromwell himself.

▶ *Oliver Cromwell, republican leader during the Civil Wars and later Lord Protector of England.*

▶ p. 62

1653–59
THE REPUBLIC

Between December 1653 and May 1659 England entered the period known historically as the Protectorate. This came into place after the failure of the 'Barebones' Parliament and at its head was Cromwell. He was made Lord Protector and had vast powers. But as with the monarchy there were disputes between the country's leader – Cromwell – and Parliament. Cromwell dissolved his first Parliament in 1655. The situation was reaching crisis point with the second Parliament when he died in September 1658. Despite this, the Protectorate did achieve some successes. Most notable among these was the decision to allow Jews to return to England in 1655 albeit without political equality. Education reforms were also introduced by Cromwell.

1688
THE GLORIOUS REVOLUTION

Religion remained central throughout the politics of the time. Following the restoration of the monarchy in 1660 with Charles II, James II then claimed the throne in 1685. A devout Catholic, he refused to take an anti-Catholic oath but nevertheless succeeded Charles unopposed. In 1688 a Catholic heir – Charles – was born into a period where Catholicism was reasserting itself within the English establishment. Alarmed, seven prominent statesmen invited the Protestant William of Orange to come to England. William then mustered an army which landed at Torbay, Devon, in November 1688. He marched to London virtually unopposed. James fled and was eventually defeated at the Battle of the Boyne. The succession of William and the constitutional arrangements which followed have become known as the Glorious Revolution.

▶ p. 61

1689
BILL OF RIGHTS

In October 1689 the Bill of Rights – the only one so far in British parliamentary history – was established. This legally justified the offer of the throne to William of Orange at the expense of James II. Although in retrospect it was not as radical as it could have been, especially in terms of limiting the power of the monarchy, it still established principles in law such as the supremacy of a Parliament, which would now meet more often, the freedom of speech within Parliament – still recognised today – and free elections. The bill was also important for excluding any Catholic from occupying the throne. In 1701, the Act of Settlement was signed assuring Protestant domination with the succession of the Hanoverian dynasty.

p. 57◀ **Distant Voices** ▶p. 61

They plucked communion tables down, and broke our painted glasses; they threw our altars to the ground and tumbled down the crosses. They set up Cromwell and his heir – the Lord and Lady Claypole – because they hated common prayer, the organ and the maypole.

Thomas Jordan, English poet (1652)

The Emergence of the United Kingdom

AD 789–1715

THE HISTORY OF BRITAIN has largely been written as the history of England, often ignoring the struggles which took place in Scotland and Wales. From the earliest times, the Scots – particularly during battles with the Romans – and the Welsh have both demonstrated strong, separate national identities. This spirit has often been shown in frequent battles with the English over a period of hundreds of years. Even with their entry into the Union binding the three mainland countries together – Wales first, then Scotland – these national identities have been retained and at times have flourished. They remain today shown by political moves in the late twentieth century, particularly the trend towards devolution which guarantees a Welsh and Scottish representative body.

▶ p. 69

AD 789
WELSH RESISTANCE

Originally Wales was settled by Celtic tribes. Following the Roman invasion, its inhabitants found themselves at war with the invading troops and fought with varying degrees of success. Some tribes in Wales, especially in the north, were able to resist full Roman occupation. After the Romans left Britain, the native Celtic tribes soon found themselves at war with new invaders. This time it was the Anglo-Saxons. In around AD 789, the Welsh border was marked by the construction of Offa's Dyke. This was built by the English king of Mercia, Offa; the dyke was a 113-km (70-mile) long construction of earthwork which replaced an earlier similar construction known as Wat's Dyke also built by an English king.

▶ p. 66

AD 800s
SCOTTISH RESISTANCE

Scotland was originally inhabited by the Picts, the Britons and the Angles. The race known as the Scots were found originally in Ireland, only settling in 'Scotland' from about the sixth century. By the ninth century they had completed a successful conquest of the Picts and founded the kingdom of Scotia and later Scotland. Despite several attempts, the Romans – who knew the area as Caledonia – were unable to conquer the country fully. They established the famous northern frontier at Hadrian's Wall and this was followed by the Antonine Wall further into modern Scottish territory. The Scots' successful attempts at repelling the Romans has been romanticised over the years and is cited as proof of the country's warrior-like status in ancient times.

◀ *Offa's Dyke, an earthwork that originally marked the borders of Wales.*

1300s
THE CLANS

By the ninth century, the dominant family within Scotland was the MacAlpine family, who had successfully led the Scots to victory over the Picts. The Scottish monarchy had been established and by this time Christianity had been introduced. The country occupied roughly the same space as it does now. But by the end of the fourteenth century the dominant political unit in Scotland – at least Highland Scotland – was the Clan. The culture of chieftaincy was also accepted by many of the clans, especially in the Gaelic-speaking western part of Scotland. The word 'clan' is derived from a Gaelic word meaning children or offspring. The clans took their name from the founder of the group, such as Murray, MacNab or MacDonald.

1405
THE DEFEAT OF WALES

The political unit of Wales was the kingdom. Although several strong kingdoms existed, the sheer number of these aided

p. 56◀ **Triumphs & Tragedies** ▶p. 61

1314
THE BATTLE OF BANNOCKBURN

The most important and famous battle in Scotland's long fight with the English was Bannockburn. Fought in June 1314, Robert the Bruce's forces comprehensively fought off the English armies of Edward II. The consequence of the defeat was far-reaching: Robert was able to move Scottish forces deep into English territory. The Scots though were ultimately repelled after their long march south despite their morale-boosting victories. It was the first major victory for the Scottish during the time of the 'Auld Alliance' with the French, who shared a common hatred of the English. The alliance lasted until the sixteenth century when the Scottish adopted Protestantism. Robert also tried to divert English forces by trying to raise the issue of political rule in Ireland.

English conquest, as they were able to call on vastly superior forces in terms of manpower. Between the ninth and thirteenth centuries the country's ability to repel English attackers gradually weakened. The most dominant Welsh kingdoms were those of Gruffudd ap Llywelyn who was the king of Gwynedd and Powys in the eleventh century. Other notable leaders include Hywel Dda and Llywelyn ap Iorwerth. By the thirteenth century, English supremacy had been established in Wales. In 1405, the revolt of Owain Glyndwr against Henry IV, over land issues in the north Powys region, was defeated.

1536–43
WALES BECOMES PART OF THE UNION

Wales finally succumbed to English rule in the sixteenth century. Between 1536–43, the acts of union between England and Wales were developed and became law. They were passed at the time of the Reformation by Thomas Cromwell under a sovereign – Henry VIII – whose family originated from Wales. The union gave Wales a new political make-up. The country was divided into shires and new counties were added, making 10 in total. The new shires were represented in Parliament and English law was pre-eminent following 1543. Although English dominance has no doubt diluted Welsh culture, the country still retained its own language. Christianity arrived in Wales around the time of the third century and the country adopted Protestantism in the sixteenth century.

▶ p. 63

1707
THE ACT OF UNION

In 1707 the political independence of Scotland ended. Aided by the anglophile landowners in the Scottish lowlands, the English finally secured their political and cultural dominance. The road to this arrangement began in the early seventeenth century when, in 1603, James VI of Scotland succeeded to the English throne. During the Republic, the countries were temporarily united under the Protectorate. By 1707, the Act of Union had been signed. The two Parliaments established during this time became one – with the Scottish body disappearing. Scottish MPs were now to be represented in the Parliament covering the British Isles. Despite losing political dominance, Scotland was able to retain a separate legal and religious identity, which it maintains to this day.

▲ *Leader of the eighteenth-century Jacobite rebellion, John Erskine.*

▶ *Queen Anne became the first monarch of the newly formed United Kingdom.*

p. 60◀ **Triumphs & Tragedies** ▶p. 67

1715
THE JACOBITE REBELLION

Despite the new political arrangements brought about by the Glorious Revolution and the Act of Union, some refused to recognise the new order. Those who refused were commonly known as the Jacobites, supporters of the House of Stuart who campaigned for almost 60 years for the restoration of the Stuart monarchy. The Hanoverian succession in the early eighteenth century, though, stopped any claims of the Scottish line to the throne by peaceful means. In 1715, uprisings in both Scotland and England – at Preston – were put down. Further Jacobite uprisings were attempted in 1719, 1722 and in 1745 by the 'younger pretender' Charles Edward Stuart. In Parliament, the Whigs (Scottish Presbyterians) used the long-running dispute to their advantage, claiming the Tories were Jacobite supporters.

p. 59◀ **Distant Voices** ▶p. 63

Thank God we are Saxons! Flanked by the savage Celt on the one side and the flighty Gaul on the other – the one a slave to his passions, the other a victim to the theories of the hour – we feel deeply grateful from our inmost hearts that we belong to a race, which if it cannot boast the flowing fancy of one of its neighbours, nor the brilliant esprit of the other has an ample compensation in a social, slow, reflective, phlegmatic temperament.

A nineteenth century letter to the journal *The Economist*, representing England's views of its neighbours

The Emergence of Modern Britain

1700–1837

A MAJOR ASPECT OF the nineteenth century was the Industrial Revolution, but that era and the period immediately preceding it was one which had great political relevance for Britain. The role of Parliament was evolving into one which would become more recognisable to the modern eye. The importance of political parties, however, increased over this period. As the population grew and became more urbanised fresh demands were placed on rulers. Trade unions developed, the franchise was extended and overseas, the empire was beginning to flourish despite the loss of the United States. In the middle of it all a new queen, Victoria, came to the throne; she would be the longest serving monarch in British history and would oversee the high-point of British power.

▶ p. 67

1700s
THE WHIGS

The Whigs became the dominant force in British party politics during the eighteenth century. To extend this dominance three unsuccessful Exclusion Bills were introduced, to prevent the succession of James, Duke of York. The Whigs were the first to take advantage of the new importance placed on Parliament after the Glorious Revolution. They were established in the late seventeenth century and were the forerunners of the nineteenth-century Liberals. They had been one of the driving forces behind the revolution and in the late seventeenth century and early eighteenth century assured their political dominance by forming the 'junto' – a close-knit group of Whigs who held political power under William III and Anne. Their great rivals were the Tories, over whom they enjoyed spasmodic victory throughout this time until the eighteenth century.

1700s
THE TORIES

The Tories emerged as a significant political force in the late seventeenth century. From this time, they began a period of uninterrupted power lasting almost 50 years. Many of them were closely associated with the Jacobite rebellion which led to their exclusion from power on the accession of the Hanoverian dynasty until the mid-eighteenth century. The party is a forerunner of the modern Conservative party; the term Tory derives from an Irish word – *toraidhe* – meaning outlaw. It was a term of abuse applied by Whigs against those who opposed the decision to exclude the Roman Catholic James from the throne in the late 1670s.

▶ p. 63

1714
THE HOUSE OF HANOVER

In 1714, the British monarchy passed into the hands of the Hanoverian dynasty. Their rule would last until the beginning of the twentieth century when Queen Victoria died. Their accession to the throne was assured by the act of settlement which stipulated that the Hanoverian house would rule if William III and Anne died without any heirs. The first Hanoverian king was George I. Hugely unpopular among the people, he never bothered to learn English and married a cousin whom he later imprisoned for life on the grounds of adultery. By around 1722, he left most of the political administration to Robert Walpole. He was succeeded by three more King Georges, with George III being the most famous, perhaps on account of his alleged insanity.

▶ p. 65

1721
SIR ROBERT WALPOLE

Sir Robert Walpole is generally reputed to be Britain's first ever prime minister. A Whig, his reputation was enhanced during the collapse of the South Sea Company – the crisis better known as the South Sea Bubble – in 1720. His skills saved King George I from public disgrace as the monarchy was implicated in the scheme which controlled a large part of the national debt until it collapsed owing millions of pounds. His immediate reputation assured, Walpole became First Lord of the Treasury in 1721, and thus effectively prime minister. During the 1730s he came under increasing political attack for measures such as an unsuccessful attempt to impose excise duty on wine and much else. A collector of fine art, Walpole also spent time in prison for corruption in 1712.

▲ *William Pitt, only 24 years old when he became prime minister, was a shrewd leader.*

▶ p. 69

1783
PITT THE YOUNGER

William Pitt became the youngest prime minister of the country in 1783, aged just 24. He had entered politics as an MP just three years previously. Despite his young age, his reputation as a shrewd leader became assured over the period he was in power. Son of William Pitt the Elder – also a politician – his successes came through introducing financial reforms and, at first, a commitment to Parliamentary reform. Pitt was also the leader who introduced income tax into the British political and economic system. In 1800 he steered the bill promoting the union of Great Britain and Ireland through Parliament. He died aged just 46 in February 1806.

▶ p. 65

1832
REFORM ACT

As the importance of party politics grew and a more literate nation took an ever greater interest in national matters, voting reform was desperately needed. This was first addressed in the Reform Act of 1832. Most urgently required was reform to the Rotten Boroughs. These were boroughs where the electorate had shrunk to almost nothing; borough owners could therefore nominate their own MPs, and they were sometimes used as a source of influence by the wealthy and powerful. The 1832 Act was brought in by the Whigs after much political debate. Rotten Boroughs were largely disenfranchised and the vote extended by some 50 per cent in England and Wales largely among the lower middle classes. Property owners were enfranchised and working people isolated. The effect was more limited in Scotland and Ireland.

1834
TRADE UNIONS AND POLITICAL REFORM

In 1834 six trade unionists from the Dorset village of Tolpuddle were transported to Australia amid Establishment fears at the growth of the power of organised labour. Although trade unions had been legal since 1824, the powers that be were increasingly concerned about the illegal loyalty oaths they encouraged. The trade union movement continued to develop nevertheless, and in 1868 the Trades Union Congress was formed. The early nineteenth century also saw the growth of further reforms best encapsulated in the Chartist movement. This asked for reform in six main areas: universal male suffrage, annual Parliaments, payment of MPs, equal electoral districts, voting by ballot and an end to property qualification for MPs. Despite widespread support, its importance had died out by the late 1850s.

▶ p. 68

1837
QUEEN VICTORIA

In 1837 Queen Victoria came to the throne, where she remained for 64 years. The first period of her reign was marked by political tension. As well as calls for reform to the electoral and Parliamentary system and the growth of organised labour, the queen herself sparked off a constitutional crisis. In 1839 the 'bedchamber crisis' emerged. Anticipating Parliamentary defeat, Melbourne, the Whig prime minister and favourite of the queen, resigned. Peel then attempted to put together a government and insisted on the queen dismissing those members of her bedchamber who were wives of Whigs. Victoria refused and Peel thus refused to serve. Constitutional crisis was caused by the return of Melbourne to office. The matter was only resolved when Melbourne's government eventually collapsed in 1841.

▲ *The reign of Queen Victoria saw some of the most outstanding advances in science, industry and invention in history.*

p. 61 ◀ **Distant Voices** ▶ p. 65

I will venture to say, that upon the one great class of subjects, the largest and the most weighty of them all, where the leading and determining considerations that ought to lead to a conclusion are truth, justice and humanity – upon these, gentlemen, all the world over, I will back the masses against the classes.

William Gladstone

▲ *The Tolpuddle Martyrs, who were sentenced to transportation to Australia in 1834.*

Victorian Britain

1851–1901

THE VICTORIAN ERA and the reign of Queen Victoria represents the high point of British power. During the 64 years of Victoria's rule Britain was transformed into the world's greatest industrial and military power, and its urban landscape changed forever. Parliament was strengthened, the franchise extended and the Empire reached its high-point particularly with British rule in India. Queen Victoria eventually became an especially popular monarch, strong-willed and well-loved by the population at large later in her reign. Paradoxically, despite the many achievements carried out in her name the monarchy was transformed during her reign. As the constitution evolved it limited the powers of the monarch leaving it, in the words of Walter Bagehot, to have 'the right to be consulted, the right to encourage, and the right to warn'.

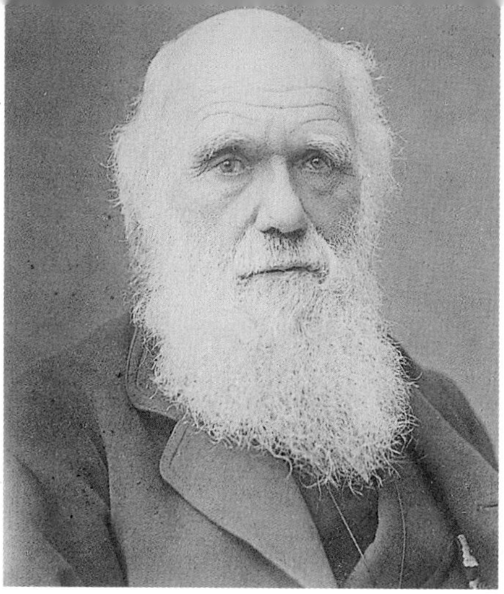

▲ *Charles Darwin, whose theories of evolution shocked the Victorian Establishment to the core.*

1851
GREAT EXHIBITION

The Great Exhibition of 1851 at Crystal Palace was more than just a day out for the more than six million people estimated to have visited it. It was a demonstration to the world of the zenith of British industrialised power. The event was loved by the public – even the act of travelling to the exhibition by train was an example of British economic strength – and it was all organised by the aristocracy. Prince Albert, Queen Victoria's husband, was the brains behind the event, which showcased over 100,000 innovative exhibits, although not all were British. The event was an unqualified success and marked a transformation in the middle Victorian period. It came to represent the onset of a calmer era in Victorian politics following the constitutional and economic crises of the 1830s and '40s.

▲ *Millions of people flocked to the Great Exhibition at Crystal Palace.*

1860s
GREAT POLITICAL THINKERS

The later Victorian era was notable for the works of great thinkers within Britain whose writings would have repercussions all around the world. As well as the concept of Darwinism, the Victorian era also gave birth to the writings of such names as John Stuart Mill, and Charles Dickens. In 1867, Karl Marx, working in London, would publish his communist theories. Walter Bagehot wrote his defining work *The English Constitution* in 1867. Darwin's great work – *On the Origin of Species* – was published in 1859 and its theories of evolution and sur-vival of the fittest proved a great worry to the Church among others. J. S. Mill's theory of utilitarianism and his defence of in-dividual freedoms promoted social reforms in the era. Dickens, brought up in poverty, used his novels to rail against the cruelties of industrialisation.

1861
DEATH OF ALBERT

The death of Prince Albert, aged 42, from typhoid in 1861, provoked an unsettled period in British political life. A distraught Queen Victoria took to mourning and seclusion for a period of 10 years. Despite her grief the amount of time Victoria spent replaced by David Lloyd George. Asquith differed from other politicians, including Lloyd George and Winston Churchill, about the need for conscription. Lloyd George, who was at first thought to have opposed the war, publicly and unequivocally supported conscription.

1917
GEORGE V

An avid stamp collector, George V was a popular monarch due to his sense of royal duty during the First World War. Also an emperor of India, the first four years of his rule witnessed two general elections, the establishment of the Union of South Africa, and a Home Rule bill for Ireland passing through Parliament. Also, in a rush of national fervour, Scott's expedition reached the South Pole. In 1917, George V was responsible for changing the Germanic name of the royal house from Saxe-Coburg into Windsor, a name which remains today. He formed the National Government in 1931 in response to the economic crisis of the time.

1918
THE RISE OF WOMEN

If there were any positive developments from the First World War, women's standing in society certainly grew. The emancipation of women, or at least the beginning of the process, has been largely linked to the Great War. It acted as a catalyst, vastly speeding up the process of female liberation than otherwise would have been the case. Their work at the front and in munitions factories led to a breaking down of the sex barriers. Previously, engineering work was seen as the preserve of men. After the war this was no longer the case. By 1918, the Representation of the People Act gave the vote to most women aged 30 and over. Women over 21 got the vote in 1928.

1918
THE DEATH OF THE LIBERAL PARTY

Prior to the war the Liberal Party enjoyed a pre-eminent position in British politics. Between 1860 and 1920, the party that emerged from the Whigs in the previous century, had spent a sustained period as the government of the United Kingdom. Lloyd George taking over in 1916 signalled the beginning of the end for the Liberal Party, as a party of government for the rest of the century. This takeover at the top prompted a split of the Liberal party. In December 1918, Lloyd George called a general election. Siding with the Conservatives in a coalition government, Lloyd George was returned as prime minister but the damage to the Liberal party, now irrevocably split was done.

1920
THE RISE OF THE CONSERVATIVES

The Liberals' split undoubtedly benefited the other political parties. The Labour Party replaced the Liberals as one of the two major political parties. The main beneficiaries, though, were the Conservatives, who became the undisputed party of government. The Conservative/Labour domination has been in place in British politics ever since. The disintegration of the Liberals allowed the Tories (Conservatives) to play to their strengths. Always regarding themselves as the patriotic party, the Con-servatives were united by the onset of war. The changing nature of the party also reflected changes in British society. No longer a party just of the landed gentry, the Conservatives were now increasingly dominated by the new class of entrepreneurs, widening their base appeal.

p. 61◀ **Triumphs & Tragedies** ▶p. 77

1918
THE END OF WAR

With the American entry into the war, the German position looked increasingly hopeless. Their only hope was to launch a major offensive to break the Allies' line. This they did in March 1918 and with some success. Paris was once again threatened by the German army. By the end of the year, however, the German effort was exhausted. The long-awaited armistice came on 11 November 1918. Despite the inevitable celebrations in London and elsewhere the losses had been on a scale never witnessed before. But it would be only 20 years before mass war would haunt Britain and the rest of Europe again.

▲ *Women replaced men in jobs they would never have been permitted to do before the War.*

p. 65◀ **Distant Voices** ▶p. 69

The road here and the ground to either side were strewn with bodies, some motionless, some not. Cries and groans, prayers, imprecations, reached me. I leave it to the sensitive imagination. I once wrote it down only to discover that horror, truthfully described, weakens to the merely clinical.

Alexander Aitken, writing of the Battle of the Somme (September 1916)

The Road Through the Second World War

1924–45

IN A LITTLE MORE THAN 20 YEARS after the end of the First World War, Britain again would be plunged into a world war. Britain's defiance of the Nazi threat through its own resistance and outside help to some represents a high point in British history through the ages. The tale of a plucky nation defying the military odds has been often told in print and on film. How much of this tale has become myth and how much is true is open to argument, but there can be little doubt that the country endured terrible deprivation during the war and the post-war years because of its stand against Hitler's regime. By the end of the Second World War Britain was an exhausted nation.

1924
THE FIRST LABOUR PARTY GOVERNMENT

The Labour Party replaced the Liberals as one of the two major political parties in Britain after the First World War. Renamed in 1906, from the Labour Representation Committee formed in 1900, the Labour Party pulled together factions from various strands of the working-class movement such as the trades unions and the Fabian Society. The party had served in the wartime coalition government and became popular after the war. The fall of the Liberals left a political vacuum. Labour, in a move which would be repeated in the 1990s, broadened its appeal to the middle classes – by taking on board more middle-class members and giving the appearance of being less radical – therefore making it more electable. In 1924, the first Labour government, headed by Ramsay MacDonald, came to power. A second government was formed in 1929 and lasted until 1931.

1926
THE GENERAL STRIKE

In May 1926, the British state faced its largest ever threat from a unified working class. Miners on strike for better pay were joined by workers from other power industries such as those in gas and electricity, as well as dockers. The strike was called by the Trades Union Congress. The strike came at a time when the power of the unions appeared to be declining, as the working classes became more vocal in their demands for better pay and conditions. The strike was also noted for its good relations between strikers and the authorities, but it ultimately proved unsuccessful, and is seen by some as the reason why the trades union movement in Britain has subsequently been largely moderate.

£ ▶ p. 71
1931
THE NATIONAL GOVERNMENT

By the 1930s, the world economy was in a state of flux. The Wall Street Crash of 1929 had proved to be a watershed for the economies of the West. In Britain the political solution to try and revive the economy was the formation of the National Government. This lasted nine years from 1931 and was headed by Ramsay MacDonald. The government included prominent Conservatives and Liberals. MacDonald was expelled from the Labour party which split and went into opposition. But the government could do little – or failed – in its attempts to turn the economy around. When the economy did pick up it appeared to be more of a result of improved trading conditions rather than governmental policies.

✠ ▶ p. 70
1936
EDWARD VIII AND THE CONSTITUTIONAL CRISIS

In January 1936, Edward VIII came to the throne. His brief reign came to an end before the year was out. Although the story of his relationship with the American divorcée Mrs Wallis Simpson has often been told as one of history's greatest-ever love stories, it also sparked a crisis among the

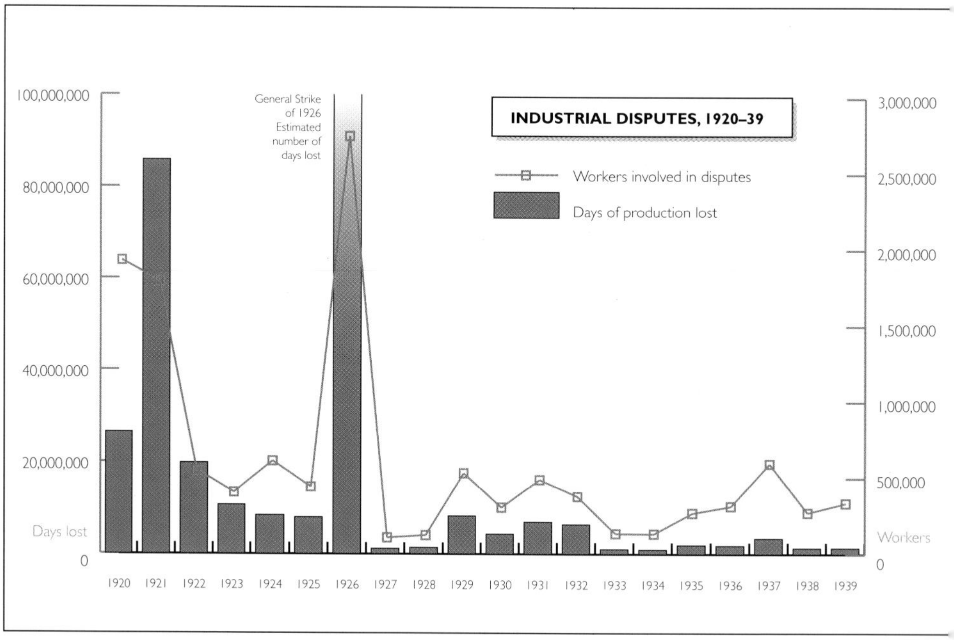

▲ *Edward VIII caused a constitutional crisis by his plan to marry divorcee Mrs Wallis Simpson.*

British establishment. The power of Parliament over the monarchy was proven when the prime minister Stanley Baldwin, backed by the Church, forbade the king from marrying Mrs Simpson if he wanted to remain king. Edward VIII chose to abdicate. With hindsight it appears the politicians were fearful of Edward's pro-Nazi leanings, though whether they used the marriage crisis as a pretext to remove him from the throne is still unclear.

▶ p. 70

1939
AT WAR ONCE MORE

On 3 September 1939 – two days after the Nazis invaded Poland – Britain was again at war with Germany. By April 1940, the German armies had successfully invaded Norway, Finland, and Denmark and also claimed their first British political casualty – prime minister Neville Chamberlain. In response to criticism of the campaign in Scandinavia, Chamberlain resigned. Chamberlain will always be associated with the discredited policy of appeasement towards Hitler (although some have recently tried to recredit this). Strongly opposed by politicians such as Churchill, appeasement was actually quite popular among the people at the time. The guarantee of peace Chamberlain secured from Hitler in 1938 at the time of the Munich crisis, though, proved to be a mirage. Chamberlain joined the Churchill government but resigned just before his death in October 1940.

▶ p. 71

1940
WINSTON CHURCHILL

A politician with a patchy record before the outbreak of war, Winston Churchill emerged at the end of war a politician whose status was assured both in Britain and abroad. Elected as a Conservative MP in 1901, Churchill crossed the floor of the House to join the Liberals in 1904. He was also elected as a constitutionalist in the 1920s. A consistent opponent of appeasement during the 1930s, Churchill was appointed First Lord of the Admiralty in 1939. When Chamberlain resigned as wartime prime minister, Churchill took over the reigns of government in May 1940. During the war he established himself as a great politician and orator. His reputation abroad was secured with his central role in the peace negotiations.

1940
THE HOME FRONT

'I'm glad we have been bombed. It makes me feel I can look the East End in the face,' so said Queen Elizabeth, now the Queen Mother to a London policeman in September 1940. This was at the height of the Blitz, often seen as a defining moment – together with the Battle of Britain – in modern British history. The Blitz of London began in September 1940 and was called off by the Germans later that month. By the time it was over, and the Battle of Britain fought during roughly the same period, the threat of Nazi invasion of Britain had receded drastically. The Blitz is often portrayed as a seminal event in British history where the general population's resistance proved central in defeating Germany.

1945
THE END OF THE WAR

By the end of 1945 the war in both Europe and in Japan was over. In Britain there would be a marked swing to the left with the landslide election of a Labour government later in the same year. Labour's massive victory – they won 394 seats, to the Tories' 210 – represented a new direction being taken in British politics. The politics of an interventionist state had been given credence during the war and Churchill's Cabinet included left-wing MPs such as Ernest Bevin. The new breed of Tories emerging also advocated a stronger role for the state after the war, both politically and economically. Seen in this context, Churchill's defeat at the polls, despite leading Britain to victory, seems less of a surprise.

◀ *Winston Churchill (seated left), the great political leader and orator during wartime Britain.*

p. 67◀ **Distant Voices** ▶p. 71

Here they were, the people who rule a fourth of the globe. They had been imperialistic and had exploited, they had subjugated. But down in the Tubes of London they were demonstrating they could take the same sort of punishment they had handed out.

A US journalist, describing the scene in the London Underground, during the Blitz (1940)

Britain After the War

1945–79

THE PERIOD AFTER the Second World War has seen various trends in British politics and a reassessment of the country's position abroad. The immediate era after war was marked by a general consensus on what was needed to aid recovery, which included a major role for the state and the public sector. By the 1980s, British politics were drastically reshaped by four successive Conservative governments who reversed many of the policies that had come before. By the late 1990s however a less conflictual politics had re-emerged. In 1945, Britain was one of the world's major powers – with an empire to boot. It ended the era with its world power diminished, and no empire any more, though it is a nuclear power and permanent member of the UN Security Council.

1948
NATIONALISATION

The Labour Party, under Clement Atlee, won the 1945 General Election and embarked upon one of its major policy initiatives – nationalisation. In basic terms this meant the purchase of private industry and business by the state so they could provide, so their supporters claimed, for the national good. The rail, gas, coal and electricity industries were among those purchased by the state. The National Health Service was established in 1948 and has been state-owned ever since, becoming the sacred cow of British politics. The policies of nationalisation were reversed by the Thatcher government in the 1980s, when many of the above industries were sold back to the private sector – a policy continued under John Major's leadership with the privatisation of the railways.

1950s
THE POLITICS OF CONSENSUS

The 1950s and early 1960s marked a conciliatory time in British politics with successive Labour and Conservative governments embarking on very similar social and economic policies, although this did not prevent intra-party feuding. This was the period of consensus politics where the tenets of social democracy and a strong welfare state were generally supported across the political spectrum. Keynesian economics were pursued by both parties in an attempt to sustain full employment. A new term – 'Butskellism' – entered the dictionary. A hybrid of a Conservative and a Labour ministers' names, Butler and Gaitskell, it was meant to demonstrate the closeness with the which the parties operated. Both parties advocated state intervention to deal with economic downturns. Internally, including in Northern Ireland, it was a time of peace.

1952
ELIZABETH II

Elizabeth II is the fourth monarch from the maunfactured House of Windsor. Her family's name was originally Saxe-Coburg but this was changed in 1917 as its German associations were seen as inappropriate during the First World War, where the main enemy was Germany. Elizabeth II came to the throne the year Britain tested its first atomic bomb and has survived 10 prime ministers, beginning with Winston Churchill. Tony Blair is the eleventh head of government during her reign. Her rule has overseen vast changes in Britain, politically, culturally and socially and many changes to the Royal Family also; although its role has not changed its tone has. Since the mid-1990s there have been increasing calls for a Republic.

► p. 72

1956
SUEZ

From the end of the Second World War, Britain retreated from its colonies, unable or unwilling to maintain an empire. India – the jewel in Britain's colonial crown since 1858 – was granted self-government in 1947. Countries around the world soon followed. But its rapidly diminishing world status was most clearly brought home to Britain during the Suez Canal crisis of 1956. When Britain, which had controlled the canal since 1875, pulled out its troops in 1956, the Egyptian government nationalised Suez. British prime minister Anthony Eden responded by sending in troops to regain control. Worldwide condemnation followed. The United States, Britain's main ally, signalled its disgust, sterling was threatened and British troops were ignominiously withdrawn.

▲ *The coronation of Queen Elizabeth II; her reign has seen some of the greatest challenges to the monarchy to date.*

▲ *The Suez Canal was the focus of an international crisis in 1956 as the Egyptian and British governments battled for control of the area.*

1957–63
HAROLD MACMILLAN

Harold Macmillan was Conservative prime minister from 1957 to 1963. His premiership oversaw the political trends which marked post-war Britain. Elected in the wake of the Suez disaster he came to power on the back of the slogan 'Most of our people have never had it so good' and a national mood reflecting a desire for domestic prosperity. Consumer-led affluence continued to create a feel-good factor following the years of war and post-war austerity. He advanced Britain's retreat from its colonies with his 'wind of change' speech in Africa and set Britain on course to gain entry to the European Economic Community, though this was vetoed by the French. Macmillan was undermined by both illness and a spy and sex scandal involving his war minister John Profumo. He retired in 1963.

1964–74
THE WILSON/HEATH YEARS

Britain entered the mid-60s seemingly prosperous and content. Just a decade later it was being labelled as the 'sick man of Europe' and was beset by political and economical problems. The Labour government under Harold Wilson between 1964 and 1970 oversaw a period of increasing social unrest underpinned by a slowly disintegrating economy. Student protests grew, as did urban disenchantment. Black communities protested about racism and the 'Troubles' in Northern Ireland erupted. Keynesian economics were unravelling, inflation was rising and industrial unrest growing. The Conservative Heath government took over in 1970 but soon found itself under pressure. It was brought down by the miners' strike of 1974 after it went to the country asking 'Who governs Britain?'.

£ ▶ p. 72

1979
A CHANGING ECONOMY

In 1976 Britain's deteriorating economic position was emphasised when the Labour government went to the International Monetary Fund for financial assistance. By 1979, the Conservatives had been returned to government after a sustained period of industrial unrest, known as the 'winter of discontent', brought down Labour. An ailing economy had refused to pick up despite the Wilson and the James Callaghan administrations watering down wage demands from the trades unions. But fears over jobs and wages refused to go away and led to a rash of strikes in the public sector in 1978–79. Even council grave-diggers went on strike. As well as ushering in a new government, the winter of discontent marked the end for the application of Keynesian economic policies in Britain.

1979
MRS THATCHER

In 1979 Britain elected its first woman prime minister, Margaret Thatcher. She became the longest-serving and one of the most controversial prime ministers of the century. Mrs Thatcher won elections in 1983 and 1987 advocating right-wing politics, a monetarist policy, sustained privatisation, and a more vigorous foreign policy, especially in Europe, which earned her the title 'Iron Lady' abroad. Her government's policies at first were deeply unpopular but she was returned to office on the back of populist opinion after the Falklands War of 1982. Although she commanded large Commons' majorities which enabled her to pursue her policies, her vote in the country was less impressive. She was driven from office by her own party in November 1990.

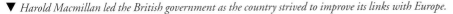

▼ *Harold Macmillan led the British government as the country strived to improve its links with Europe.*

p. 69◀ **Distant Voices** ▶p. 73

A woman of uranium, with peculiar irradiations. Compared to her, how leaden appear most of our leaders, opaque masses of flesh, austere fortresses without windows, save for the loopholes of deceit and the skylights of hidden pride. Power corrupts a man but liberates a woman and reveals her for what she is.

French newspaper *Le Quotidien* de Paris, on Mrs Thatcher (1980)

Britain and Europe

1946–99

THE ISSUE OF European political and economic union has become the most divisive issue in British politics in the late 1990s amid fears over national sovereignty. Splits over Europe were one of the contributing factors to the demise of the Conservative government in 1997. The arrival of a Euro currency in 1999, and ever-closening political ties ensured that Europe will remain a major political issue into the new century. Britain has always appeared a reluctant member, first believing closer integration was for other European countries not itself. It first applied in 1963 to join the EEC but membership was denied. A history-breaking referendum was called in 1975 to vote on Britain joining the Common Market. Britain said yes, but since then the country has sometimes appeared to be a reluctant member.

£ ▶ p. 73

1946
COLD WAR

'From Stettin in the Baltic to Trieste in the Adriatic an Iron Curtain has descended upon the Continent,' so said Winston Churchill in March 1946. Although he got one detail wrong – he should have said Lubeck, not Stettin – Churchill's premise was right. Europe after the Second World War was divided into two spheres with Britain firmly in the western, US-dominated camp. This has meant closer military ties through organisations such as the North Atlantic Treaty Organisation (NATO) as well as closer political ties through the European Union in its many forms. The basic motivation for closer integration was a sustained peace between the historically-warring European states. As peace has been secured, the Union has developed into a form of supra-national government.

▶ p. 76

1957
TREATY OF ROME

The theory of building new European political institutions began to take formal shape in 1957 with the signing of the Treaty of Rome by six countries. Britain was not one of those six countries. The government, led by Harold Macmillan, refused to join. The signatories – France, Germany, Italy, Netherlands, Belgium and Luxembourg – signed up to a treaty which established a common market and began the process of developing pan-European institutions. The concept of Europe has now grown enormously in importance and scale. Areas of policy include the Common Agricultural Policy and a Common Fisheries Policy. The Common Market became the European Community in 1967 and the European Union in 1993. Its remit now includes security and foreign policy.

1967
DE GAULLE

In 1960, Britain was a founder member of the European Free Trade Association. This comprised seven European nations and was formed after the failure of non-EEC members to extend the area of free trade throughout western Europe. Its remit focused solely on economic matters. By 1961, however, Britain had indicated it wanted to join the Common Market as a solution to economic difficulties; its application was rejected. In 1967, under Labour, Britain applied again, but was again rebuffed. Britain accused the French leader de Gaulle of blocking its attempts to join the Common Market. Some saw this as a blatant anti-British stance by the de Gaulle government but it is more likely the French premier feared Britain's relationship would threaten France's more independent foreign policy.

1975
BRITAIN JOINS THE COMMON MARKET

In 1973 after years of trying Britain, under Ted Heath, finally joined the Common Market. Denmark and Ireland joined at the same time and the EEC swelled to a membership of nine. But membership did not stop the debate in Britain about whether or not it should belong to a pan-European political organisation. In 1975, the country went to the polls in a ground-breaking referendum to vote on continued membership. A bitter campaign was fought, with the political parties largely split about which way to vote. The result was a resounding 'yes' as two-thirds voted in favour. But the splits on Europe have become no less rancorous, as Britain's continued inclusion in the European Union has developed politically.

▼ *Charles de Gaulle with US president Eisenhower at a ceremony in Washington, DC.*

▲ *Margaret Thatcher, the first female leader of the British government.*

1986
SINGLE EUROPEAN ACT

'No! No! No!' thundered Margaret Thatcher in 1990 when asked about her government's position on the prospect of more political control passing from national government to Brussels. Opposition to greater political integration in Europe was well-documented during her 11-year reign as prime minister and led to many conflicts with other European Community countries especially over budgetary contributions. On political integration she demurred; economically she promoted trade between the European partners. She vetoed Britain joining the European Exchange Rate Mechanism, until only a month before her resignation in October 1990. However, In 1986 Mrs Thatcher had signed Britain up to the Single European Act which gave fresh impetus to closer economic integration by creating a single market by 1 January 1993.

1992
BLACK WEDNESDAY

In 1979, the European Exchange Rate Mechanism was established in an attempt to stabilise the currencies of western Europe. Britain remained outside this arrangement until October 1990. When it eventually joined, it left just two years later after the events of 'Black Wednesday', when billions were wiped off the stock market as the Major government tried to rescue Britain's plunging currency. It was a deeply embarrassing episode and one from which John Major's government (in power from 1990, Major elected in 1992) never recovered. During Black Wednesday, he phoned the editor of the *Sun* newspaper to ask about his coverage for the following day. Kelvin MacKenzie said: 'I've got two buckets ... sitting on my desk and tomorrow morning I'm going to empty both of them over your head.'

1995
TORIES SPLIT

In 1990, John Major expressed his uncertainty about Britain's commitment to entering the European Exchange Rate Mechanism. The issue of Europe was one that dogged his leadership.The divisions among the Conservative Party over Europe exploded during the mid-1990s. The party, and Cabinet, was split between widely differing views of what to do about its approach to Europe. Many on the right of the party felt the leadership was not doing enough to protect British interests. In 1995 Major's leadership was challenged by Cabinet colleague John Redwood. Although Major triumphed, the number of votes in the Conservative parliamentary party gained by Redwood reflected the deep divisions among the Tories.

£

1999
THE EURO

In February 1992, the leaders of the European Union signed the Maastricht Treaty. This set out a timetable for one of

▲ *The Euro, the single European currency being phased in at the close of the millennium.*

the most ambitious projects in post-war Europe – the establishment of a European central bank and single currency by January 1999. The treaty moved the governments into greater political co-operation by agreeing foreign and security responsibilities. A reluctant Britain secured an opt-out clause freeing it from adopting the currency – the Euro. The New Labour government did not rule out joining the Euro completely, but witheld when it began on 1 January 1999. Opposition to the policy remains strong. In June 1998, the *Sun* newspaper asked about Tony Blair, 'Is this most dangerous man in Britain?' accusing Labour of warming to the Euro.

p. 71◀ **Distant Voices** ▶p. 75

This [European Monetary Union] is all a German racket designed to take over the whole of Europe.... Seventeen unelected reject politicians with no accountability to anybody, who are not responsible for raising taxes, just spending money, who are pandered to by a supine Parliament which is also not only responsible for raising taxes.

Conservative government minister Nicholas Ridley, quoted in an interview with the *Spectator* (1990)

The British Royal Family
1952–97

THE LAST YEARS of the twentieth century have been a time of drastically changing fortunes for the British monarchy. The monarchy has played a role in the life of the country – all the nations that make up Britain – for hundreds of years. Yet there can be little doubt that at the turn of the twenty-first century, it faces a crisis of confidence. The confusion over the role it should take in the new millennium has been marked, opposition has grown to the institution itself, intensified by events such as the death of Diana, Princess of Wales, in 1997. There have been criticisms that the monarchy has now lost its 'mystique' and with that much of its prestige and standing in British political life.

▲ *The role of Queen Elizabeth as monarch has changed throughout her reign.*

1952
THE REIGN OF ELIZABETH II

'I declare before you that my whole life, whether it be long or short, shall be devoted to your service and the service of our great imperial family to which we all belong,' said Princess Elizabeth in Cape Town in 1947. She was crowned in 1953 and has remained on the throne for over 45 years; during that time has witnessed great changes both at home and abroad. The role of the monarchy in British political life, aside from the ceremonial tasks, is still very central constitutionally. Paradoxically this has been demonstrated by the 'crises' that have arisen in the 1990s. Debate which has centred on the future role of the monarchy demonstrates that, as a political factor, the monarchy remains important.

▶ p. 76

1952
THE CONSTITUTION

'The British Constitution has always been confusing,' the queen remarked in the 1990s. It is also complex. Part written down, most of what has become accepted practice has emerged through convention. At its heart is the power of Parliament to make laws, laws made by the European Union, and the rule of law. The political practices which have emerged today can be traced back to the Acts of Union with Wales, Scotland and, in the nineteenth century, with Ireland. Britain has a unitary system – meaning all powers are rested with Parliament, not national or regional bodies. However, Scotland and Wales are to get their own Parliaments.

1980s
THE ROYAL FAMILY BECOMES A SOAP OPERA

'There is no doubt that those two women have done more than anyone else to bring the monarchy to this sorry state ... before they came along, the monarchy was in a healthy condition and looked to have a long and stable future. Now look how things have changed.' So thundered an article in the *Sunday Express* newspaper in 1996. Those two women were Diana, Princess of Wales and Sarah Ferguson, the Duchess of York, who married Prince Andrew in 1986. During the late 1980s the younger members of the Royal family cultivated a populist stance, appearing in television programmes and generally making the monarchy appear less formal. Traditionalists were appalled claiming they were causing great harm to the standing of the monarchy.

1990s
THE CONSTITUTIONAL ROLE OF THE MONARCHY

Walter Bagehot wrote in the 1860s, that the 'appendages of a monarchy have been converted into the essence of a republic'. Despite this, he still argued the monarchy played an essential part in the constitution. As well as the queen being the head of state, ministers are legally responsible to the monarchy, MPs have to swear an oath of allegiance to the monarchy and Parliamentary bills have to receive Royal Assent before they can become law. The ruling monarch also formally appoints the prime minister, hands out honours and reads out the legislative programme of 'my government' during the queen's speech at the beginning of Parliamentary sessions. Despite this the monarch is seen as being 'above' politics and without any personal political preferences.

1992
ANNUS HORRIBILIS

'In the words of one of my more sympathetic correspondents, it has turned out to be an *annus horribilis*.' The queen's statement in November 1992 was the first public recognition that 1992 was something of a watershed for the modern monarchy. During that year, the country witnessed the break-up of two marriages – between the heir to the throne, Prince Charles and Lady Diana Spencer, and also the marriage of the Duke and the Duchess of York. In the same year, Windsor Castle, a royal residence, was destroyed by fire. The media focus on the

▲ *Parts of Windsor Castle and many priceless collections were destroyed by fire in 1992.*

younger royals had also increased. With constant speculation about the state of their marriages, the royal family had become 'fair game' for the newspapers.

▲ *Diana, Princess of Wales, greatly improved many people's perceptions of the royal family, supporting many charities.*

1997
THE INFLUENCE OF DIANA

Married to Charles, the heir to the throne in 1981, Diana, Princess of Wales, soon proved to be a popular choice. The couple provided an heir to the throne – William – in 1982, but the marriage was to end in divorce in 1996. After the divorce, she proved more popular and controversial than ever. She criticised the Conservative government, took up the cause of the banning of landmines (Britain was one of the biggest exporters of arms) and started a relationship with a wealthy Muslim, Dodi Al-Fayed, with whom she died in a car crash in Paris in 1997. The nationwide outpouring of grief was unprecedented and could hardly have been greater if she had died the ruling monarch. Letters in the national press compared the public reaction to her death to the revolutions in eastern Europe in 1989.

1997
THE MONARCHY'S RESPONSE TO THE DEATH OF DIANA

Following the death of Diana, the British monarchy was held up to a period of scrutiny and criticism that had not previously been witnessed in Britain. It was caught floundering as public opinion and grief seem to demand a more compassionate response to Diana's death than a hiding behind tradition. A political row was simmering in London. A demand, fuelled by the tabloid newspapers, that a flag should be flown at half-mast at Buckingham Palace – usually reserved only to mark the death of the ruling monarch – as an appropriate measure of grief was the catalyst for a row over whether the Royal family was an anachronism or keeper of tradition. The queen was compelled to make a television broadcast the day before the funeral to tell the nation of her sorrow too.

1997
THE CHANCES OF A REPUBLIC?

The decline in fortunes of the monarchy allied with doubts over the usefulness of its role in the modern age have provoked calls among some sectors of the British public for the restoration of a republic. Although support for the retention of the monarchy remains in the majority, there is little doubt that opposition to the institution, at least in its present form, has grown in recent years. At the beginning of the decade support for the monarchy was between 80 and 90 per cent. According to some polls by 1997 this had slipped to around two-thirds. In an attempt to show the Royal family can adapt it has, since the death of Diana, showed signs of some modernisation, albeit largely cosmetic.

p. 73 ◀ **Distant Voices** ▶ p. 77

The Royal family has made an attempt to change but I believe that it has gone in the wrong direction.... The royals themselves have paid a terrible price for becoming stars on a stage which was not made for this purpose ... the transformation of the Royal family into a soap opera has also exacted a terrible price from the rest of us because it has reaffirmed what we were rather than what we are, and distracted us from what we might be.

Shirley Williams (1993)

Britain Today
1997–99

ON 1 MAY 1997, following a landslide election victory for Labour, Tony Blair became the youngest prime mister since Lord Liverpool in 1812. The thumping victory marked another turning point for British politics. Under Blair, Labour moved nearer to the centre of the political spectrum than at any time during the previous two decades. But despite the moderate tone of the party's winning manifesto, the government is set to unleash changes which could radically alter the status quo of British politics. Reform is on its way for the House of Lords, devolution in Scotland and Wales has begun, local government is being totally overhauled. Consensus politics is back in fashion, with high-ranking members of the Liberal Democrat Party appointed to Cabinet committees.

1997
THE END OF TORY RULE

The Conservative Party, first under Margaret Thatcher and then John Major, had ruled Britain for 18 consecutive years between 1979 and 1997. Four successive elections were won by the Tories. But on 1 May 1997, the party was all but wiped from the political map of Britain. In the fall-out from the Labour landslide victory, it was clear this was no ordinary defeat for the Tories. They returned just 165 MPs to the Commons, losing 171 seats all-in-all. No Conservative MPs were returned in either Scotland or Wales. It was the party's worst defeat for 91 years. Symbolic of their loss was the defeat of Michael Portillo, seen by many as the party's next leader, in his north London constituency, by Labour newcomer Stephen Twigg.

1997
LABOUR'S VICTORY

The general election victory in 1997 for Labour was far and away the best the party had ever recorded. Its final total number of seats, 418, was the most the party had ever won; its 13.5 million votes the highest since 1951 and its share of the vote – 43 per cent – the highest it had recorded since 1966. Under Tony Blair, party leader since 1994, Labour had become more voter-friendly, continuing a process set in place by predecessors Neil Kinnock and John Smith. Moving to the right, it courted large parts of 'middle England', usually seen as traditionally Conservative. In power it has continued to appease the middle classes, to the dismay of those on the left of the party.

▲ *Tony Blair, the Labour leader who won a landslide victory in 1997, ending 18 years of Conservative government in Britain.*

1997
REFERENDUM IN WALES

The devolution in Wales is not as radical in concept as the planned changes for Scotland. Although Wales will also elect its own MPs to the Welsh Assembly, the new body's powers will not match those being given to Scotland's Parliament. The Assembly will take control of the £7 billion budget currently controlled by the Welsh Office and decide where the money will be spent, but it will have no tax-raising powers. The plans for Welsh devolution were very narrowly accepted by the Welsh electorate in September 1997 in a referendum. Critics of the Welsh plans say proposed devolution there is 'half-baked' as it allows for only a measure of reform compared to those prescribed for Scotland.

1998
REFORM OF THE HOUSE OF LORDS

'He should leave things as they are,' said Lord Hailsham of Tony Blair's plans to reform the House of Lords. 'The system has worked since time immemorial'. But the proposals to change the House of Lords are set to go ahead regardless. Indeed, reform of the House of Lords has long been a part of Labour thinking. More radical proposals have called for its abolition but Labour is content with containing itself to the issue of hereditary peers. It wants to abolish the political rights of these peers – those who sit in the House of Lords through right of birth – and promote more life peers. This process has already begun with New Labour supporters, such as broadcaster Melvyn Bragg, being elevated to the house.

1998
NORTHERN IRELAND

The 1973 Northern Ireland Constitution Act states 'it is hereby affirmed that in no event will Northern Ireland ... cease to be part of the United Kingdom'. But a political and constitutional solution to the period of violence known as the 'Troubles' is now well under way. A ceasefire, sporadically broken, most notably in the summer of 1998 with the Omagh bombing, has now been secured

▲ *Evidence of terrorism in Northern Ireland, one characteristic of the 'Troubles'.*

and the focus now lies on the politicians rather than the military strength of all sides. The Good Friday agreement of 1998 paved the way for a referendum of the Northern Irish people who now have their own assembly with limited powers led by the Unionist first minister David Trimble. Attempts have begun to resolve the thorny issue of arms decommissioning.

p. 67◀ **Triumphs & Tragedies** ▶p. 80

1997
REFERENDUM IN SCOTLAND

One of the main tenets of Labour's election-winning manifesto was the aim, after in-party battles, of creating a Scottish Parliament and devolving more powers away from Westminster. Following a referendum of the Scottish people in September 1997, the government set about passing legislation that will see a Scottish Parliament with genuine power. The Scots will elect their own MPs to the Parliament in Edinburgh and the Parliament will have tax-raising powers and control a budget of over £17 billion. Critics have suggested the creation of a Scottish Parliament could lead to the end of the Union, with Scotland eventually choosing independence. Labour's main political competitor in Scotland is now the separatist Scottish National Party.

1998
THE MODERN ROLE OF PARLIAMENT

'Parliamentary Sovereignty is a busted flush,' said the greatest ever commentator on British constitutional affairs Walter Bagehot. Some would say his comments would still hold true today. Although reform has been proposed for the upper house, the House of Commons is coming under increasing pressure to find a new role. The strait-jacket of party politics, say the critics, means Parliament has been subjugated to the whim of the party rather than concentrating on its role as scrutiner of government policies. In 1998, with the influx of New Labour politicians and the party's strict discipline, Parliament was labelled by one critic as an 'election machine'. The rise of the European Union and its ever increasing involvement in top-level decisions has also eroded Parliament's powers.

▲ *The seat of the government in Britain, the Houses of Parliament on the River Thames.*

1999
LOCAL GOVERNMENT

Local politics is set for radical reform under the Blair government. Most well-publicised are the plans for a high-profile elected mayor of London but Labour's proposals for councils touch every corner of local government. US-style executive mayors are being encouraged for a number of metropolitan councils, backed by a cabinet-style committee. Local authorities will be placed on a more business-like footing generally. Labour says it is trying to address the lack of interest in local government and specifically increase the turnout at council elections; it has even published plans for voting in supermarkets. Many of the traditional services provided by councils are likely to be provided by the private sector instead. The last great reform of councils was in 1974.

p. 75◀ **Distant Voices** ▶p. 81

A truly terrible night for the Conservatives. I would have wished to be part of rebuilding it inside the House of Commons; I can't now do that. But I would like to do whatever I can from the wings to help rebuild a great party which has a great future.

Michael Portillo's remarks after his election defeat (1997)

Ordinary Lives

TRADITIONAL HISTORY IS about kings, queens, politicians, generals, saints, heroines and martyrs – the extraordinary people who make things happen in every age. But if you concentrate on the momentous events which they bring about, then you will only get part of the story. You will also miss the context, and the way people's diet, clothing, homes and ordinary lives contributed to the big events through the past millennia. This chapter concentrates on those ordinary lives, and the forces which shaped them. Of course, life has changed enormously from the first hunters wandering across what is now the English Channel to busy executives consulting their palmtop computer diary, but there have been similarities too – the dual carriageways which follow precisely the routes of roads laid out by the Romans within a generation of their arrival, the refugees who have arrived looking for sanctuary generation after generation, the crowded and dirty cities, the basic structures of our homes, and even our clothes – British soldiers going to war in 1914 wore helmets which would not have looked out of place on Roman or Norman invaders centuries before. The study of ordinary lives throws up unexpected parallels across the years.

KEY THEMES

- ⌘ WORK
- ✚ HEALTH
- EDUCATION
- POVERTY
- LEISURE
- CITIES
- ✂ CLOTHES
- TRANSPORT
- ↓ CRIME
- FOOD & DRINK

KEY EVENTS

1 AD 47 THE FOSSE WAY

The Fosse Way was one of a network of at least 12,000 km (7,500 miles) of Roman roads, many of them dead straight, all built to a standard of design which ensured they survived into medieval times. More than anything else, they transported Roman culture all over their new province.

2 1086 *DOMESDAY BOOK*

The *Domesday Book* was William the Conqueror's attempt to list the details of his new kingdom, setting out each community, its size, resources and tax base. It was a massive enterprise and extended the central control of the crown across the country.

3 1348 THE BLACK DEATH

The fourteenth-century series of outbreaks of bubonic plague was probably the most important event in British social history since recorded history began. Plague killed at least a third of the population, devastating all classes, but later had the effect of raising wages and contributing to the end of the feudal system.

4 1476 CAXTON STARTS PRINTING

The arrival of the first printing press in England, brought by William Caxton, combined with people's growing literacy, to produce an increasingly informed population, making the Reformation inevitable and paving the way for growing political demands.

5 1746 THE SUBJUGATION OF THE HIGHLANDS

A brutal process of pacification began in Scotland after the defeat of Bonnie Prince Charlie at Culloden. Highland dress was outlawed and so was the hereditary jurisdiction over clans by their chiefs. Scottish politics all but vanished as MPs preferred not to risk their careers by raising Scottish issues.

6 1871 THE FIRST BANK HOLIDAY

Most of the working population worked five and a half days a week with few or no holidays, until the start of bank holidays in 1871. Combined with the new railways, this marked the beginning of an new era in Britain, as city people made their way down to the seaside and into the country for the first time.

7 1916 CONSCRIPTION

The controversial introduction of conscription to feed the Western Front in the First World War had an enormous impact on society, breaking down the boundaries between classes and – because women were now doing the jobs which the men left behind – between the sexes too.

8 1969 THE DIVORCE ACT

Commentators differ about the beginning of the so-called 'permissive society'. Civil divorce had been possible since the mid-nineteenth century, but the introduction of simple fault-free divorces after the breakdown of the marriage in 1969 made it possible for anyone to end their marriages. By the 1990s, one in three marriages were breaking down, with profound implications for society.

TIMELINE

4700 BC Arrival of the first Neolithic settlers
2250 BC Stonehenge stones brought over from Prescelly Mountains, Wales
200 BC Era of the Druids
1 **AD 47** The Fosse Way completed
AD 360 Burial of the Mildenhall treasure
AD 705 Foundations laid for Wells Cathedral
AD 875 Vikings establish Jorvik (York) as trade centre on the Ouse
2 **1086** The *Domesday Book*
1209 London Bridge completed
3 **1348** First outbreaks of the bubonic plague
1381 The Peasants' Revolt
4 **1476** Caxton sets up his printing press
1547 Vagrant Act established
1563 Witchcraft made a capital offence
1565 Introduction of potatoes and tobacco by Sir Walter Raleigh
1640 End of censorship and the age of pamphlets
1652 Tea arrives in Britain, shortly after the import of Bananas
1686 Last witch hanging
1694 Bank of England established
1701 Jethro Tull invents the Seed Drill
5 **1746** The subjugation of the Highlands
1751 Gin Act introduced to control crime and alcohol consumption
1761 Bridgewater Canal built
1775 Watt and Boulton set up steam factory near Birmingham
1792 Mary Wollstonecraft publishes *A Vindication of the Rights of Women*
1795 Speenhamland System established to help the poor
1812 Gas Light and Coke Company formed
1829 Sir Robert Peel creates the civilian Metropolitan Police Force
1833 Factory Act bans employment of children under the age of nine
1837 Charles Dickens exposes London's poverty in *Oliver Twist*
1845 Railway mania hits Britain
1848 Cholera epedemic kills thousands
1857 Civil divorce becomes possible
1870 Education Act established
6 **1871** First national Bank Holiday
1895 National Trust founded by Octavia Hill
1896 First cinema shows in Leicester Square, London
7 **1916** Conscription introduced
1919 Housing Act helps to found a council housing system
1921 Marie Stopes opens the first birth control clinic
1939 All men between 19 and 41 are called up for the Second World War
1946 National Health Service provides free care for all
1958 Notting Hill Riots in response to racial tension in London
1959 The M1, Britain's first motorway, built
1967 Homosexuality and abortion legalised
8 **1969** Divorce Act becomes effective
1986 Government launches nationwide AIDS awareness campaign
1995 Rise of information technology

Beginnings
4700–100 BC

'WHO THE FIRST inhabitants of Britain were, whether natives or immigrants, remains obscure,' said the Roman historian Tacitus, but two centuries later we know they were immigrants who almost certainly wandered across the dry land which is now the English Channel in search of animals to hunt, probably in small bands of 25 people or so, settling in camps for the summer. Over the next 10,000 years or so, the inhabitants of those camps and their successors had built Stonehenge and Avebury, organised networks of hill forts across Britain, and turned themselves into a complex organisation of rival tribes – trading with people all over continental Europe, and employing increasingly sophisticated agricultural techniques. This society caught the eye of the ambitious Roman conqueror Julius Caesar.

4700 BC
ARRIVAL OF THE FIRST NEOLITHIC SETTLERS

Arriving in skin boats, clearing the forests and shrub to make pastures, Neolithic people lived in small farming communities, raising cattle, trading and fighting a continuing battle with encroaching forests. Each time the soil was exhausted from repeated plantings, the forests would creep back and would have to be fought all over again. It was a period where nature had to be kept at bay, and this could only be achieved – when it was possible at all – by communal effort, as people worked together to organise irrigation schemes or other enterprises. They probably specialised more than their hunter predecessors, spending time weaving baskets, making necklaces, bracelets and anklets, and probably drinking beer as well, with the forests always in the background.

▼ *Early communities worked together to cultivate the land and maintain healthy livestock.*

p. 77◀ Triumphs & Tragedies ▶p. 84

3100 BC
THE STONEHENGE BLUESTONES

The 123 enormous bluestones which make up the double circle at Stonehenge in Wiltshire – each of them weighing up to four tons – were brought from the Prescelly Mountains in Dyfed. This was an extraordinary feat of prehistoric engineering, with the stones either brought on seagoing ships around the coast and then dragged across country by oxen, or dragged the whole way. They were erected in a temporary structure nearby for the next two centuries before the final move to Stonehenge, where there may have been ritual activity for up to 6,000 years before the stones arrived. The final structure is related to the stars and solstices, but its exact use remains a mystery and may have changed with each generation.

⌘ ▶ p. 85

4300 BC
THE FIRST FLINT MINES

The earliest shafts for flint mining, discovered near Worthing in Sussex, were dug around 4300 BC, and this marked the beginnings of a Neolithic 'industry'. Other mines from this time have been found in Cumbria, Wales and the Highlands. There miners dug out deep pits and used deer antlers trimmed into an L-shape for digging out the flints – used for tools, fire-lighting or weapons. These flints were taken from Sussex to Cornwall, and may have been exchanged for greenstone axes brought back to Sussex and Wessex. Pottery may have been traded too, with the Neolithic entrepreneurs setting out on annual ritual trading voyages, hugging the coasts or trudging across known ways through territory which would have been minutely sub-divided.

▲ *Flint was used in the manufacture of rudimentary tools and weapons.*

▲ *The enormous bluestones at Stonehenge.*

✚ ▶ p. 97

4255 BC
THE FIRST LONG BARROWS

The first recorded long barrow was begun on open farmland around 4255 BC in Lambourn, Berkshire, beginning a trend which was to last almost 2,000 years. The barrows may have started life as wooden mortuary houses, covered over with earth later making them familiar landmarks. They were reopened, possibly for more burials over periods of centuries. They remain a mystery, given that the actual burial sites took up just one end: the rest of the mounds – anything up to 91 m (300 ft) long – contain little more than earth. Skeletons inside reveal the barrow-builders as slender, with child-like faces, and healthy – apart from suffering from osteoporosis after the age of 25. Men tended to die before the age of 35, women before 30.

2200 BC
THE END OF SKARA BRAE

When a freak storm hit the village of Skara Brae in the Orkney Islands in 1850, it blew the sand off the ruined structure of a neolithic village which had been hidden for 4,000 years. What disaster overcame its population around 2200 BC is still a mystery, but the inhabitants left behind them nine houses and a workshop, built partly below ground and linked by passageways to give protection against the elements. Whether for defensive or cultural reasons – or just because of the weather – there was only one window, so the rooms would have been lit by the light of fires. The inhabitants would probably have worn knee-length tunics, woollen caps and sandals, and decorated their faces and bodies with red ochre.

↓ ▶ p. 94

1200 BC
MAM TOR

One of the oldest and largest hill-forts, Mam Tor in Derbyshire, was occupied around 1200 BC, marking the increase in violence which seems to have characterised the Bronze Age. This may have been because of population pressures – which is why more marginal land was coming into production – or it may have been the nature of the new arrivals in Britain. For whatever reason, Bronze Age artefacts tend to be for killing and subjugation, contrasting with the Stone Age implements for handling stone and wood. Bronze Age Britain heralded an intensification of trade, particularly in weapons, developing fortifications and the spread of mixed farming. The combination of fortification and farming led to a network of defensive hills which provided home and grazing land for the people who lived there.

200 BC
THE DRUIDS

At the centre of a society which valued music, poetry, boar-hunting and horse-racing alike, Druids were a revered part of Celtic life. They fulfilled the roles of prophets, bards and priests, and had to train for up to 20 years, an apprenticeship which included learning enormous amounts of poetry. Of great significance were oak trees, mistletoe and wells – which were particularly sacred – and Druids were assisted in their duties by a class of women prophets who were not given the full privileges of Druids, but who could predict the future. When the body of a Celt, possibly a sacrificial victim, was found in a peat bog in 1984, his last meal had been wheat, barley and some kind of potion containing Druidic mistletoe.

100 BC
THE BELGIC THREAT

Danebury and other hill-forts across southern Britain were given extra defences to counter the threat from Belgic raiders from Gaul. This was a society which was orientated around the art of war. Celtic warriors had a fierce reputation, using lime to make their hair stick out before battle, wearing bright tunics and striped cloaks, and keeping the heads of dead enemies in wall niches as souvenirs. Both boys and girls were sent away to be fostered, boys to learn about fighting, girls to learn sewing and embroidery – though women like Boudicca could also lead tribes into battle. Outsiders also described the way Celtic men strained their drinks with their long moustaches as they drank.

p. 77◀ **Distant Voices** ▶p. 83

This [island] is in the far North, and it is inhabited by people called the Hyperboreans from their location beyond the Boreas, the North Wind.... There are men who serve as priests of Apollo because this god is worshipped every day with continuous singing and is held in exceptional honour. There is also in the island a precinct sacred to Apollo and suitable imposing, and a notable spherical temple decorated with many offerings. There is also a community sacred to this god, where most of the inhabitants are trained to play the lyre and do so continuously in the temple, worshipping the god with singing.

Hecateus of Abdera, describing Britain (*c.* 350 BC)

Invasion and Settlement

AD 47–1041

THE MILLENNIUM BETWEEN the Roman and Norman invasions was a period of enormous contrast for the different peoples of Britain, with times of great stability of peace, sophisticated learning, international trade and wide links to the known world – but also periods of such darkness that we only have the haziest idea of what ordinary life was like during that period. In between, there were centuries of destruction raids from invaders who themselves became settlers in turn and converted to Christianity. How different their lives were is still unclear, but by the time these islands reached the end of the first thousand years after Julius Caesar first appeared off the coast, all those new arrivals had somehow been assimilated into an uneasy social mix.

▶ p. 95

AD 47

THE FOSSE WAY

The Fosse Way, one of the main Roman roads, was mostly completed by AD 47, probably as part of a push westwards of the invasion forces. By the end of the Roman occupation, the Fosse Way stretched from Lincoln to Topsham in Devon, via Bath, Cirencester and Leicester, part of a network of roads – nearly 12,000 km (7,500 miles) of which have been identified – which linked major urban centres and helped move troops quickly around the country. The roads were planned as a hub radiating out from London, and many survived into the medieval period, forming the basis of Britain's road system right up to the advent of motorways. The roads also helped bring Roman life and trade to the countryside, from Rome to the northernmost limits of their empire.

▶ p. 89

AD 155

FIRE IN VERULAMIUM

A disastrous fire in Verulamium (St Albans) in AD 155 destroyed the town for the second time under Roman rule – the first time had been at the hands of the Iceni tribe under Boudicca in AD 61 – but both disasters enhanced its development. Like most Roman towns, it included a forum, bath, amphitheatre and temple, and the new theatre held more people than any hall in modern St Albans, offering free admission to watch bear shows and gladiatorial contests. Clustered around Verulamium and other towns were the villas, no more than half a day's travel away and including accommodation and bath houses for estate workers, which formed the backbone of the new agricultural system. As many as four mosaic schools provided the craftsmen to create lavish floors.

▼ *Armed combat between gladiators in a Roman amphitheatre.*

AD 360

BURIAL OF THE MILDENHALL TREASURE

The Mildenhall treasure was probably buried by the family of the Roman general Lupicinus, after his arrest around AD 360. But it was also sign of the growing tension as the Franks and Saxons threatened from the south and the Picts and Scots from the north. The last coins had been minted in Britain in 326, though the Emperor Magnus Maximus (d. 388) re-opened a London mint in 383. By 418, Roman rulers had gathered all the gold hoards in Britain, and either buried them or taken them to Gaul. Coins circulated until at least 430, but were then used as ornaments. Dark Age and Saxon Britain had to make do without coins, or circulate those minted on the continent, until gold *thrymsas* began to be minted in England in the first half of the seventh century.

▲ *Coins discovered amongst the ancient treasures in the burial ship at Sutton Hoo.*

AD 627

THE SHIP BURIAL AT SUTTON HOO

No bodies were ever found in the splendid ship burial at Sutton Hoo, uncovered near Woodbridge in Suffolk in the summer of 1939, but the treasures discovered there are now in the British Museum and are believed to have belonged to the powerful East Anglian king Raedwald (d. *c.* 627). What the grave showed was the wide contacts a Saxon ruler would have had at the time, stretching as far as Scandinavia and the

Mediterranean – the treasure even included a silver dish from Byzantium. It also showed how Christian symbols had become interwoven with a burial ritual which was obviously pagan. It illustrated what was probably the prevailing official technique after the arrival of St Augustine of Canterbury (d. *c.* 604) where the two traditions were integrated.

AD 705
FOUNDATION OF WELLS CATHEDRAL

Wells was one of the first great cathedrals founded by the Saxons. The people who designed and built it lived nearby in small houses with sunken floors, and wore jewellery fastened with large ornate brooches. Their social lives were orientated around great Saxon mead halls, 24 m (80 ft) or more in length, and hung inside with tapestries, ornamental drinking horns and shields. Here they would listen to minstrels with harps, and repeat popular tales like that of *Beowulf.* It was a formal society, which reserved activities like hunting and hawking for the lords, and cooking and milking for the women. But women were protected by law from marrying men they did not like, could own land and property and could easily procure a divorce.

AD 804
DEATH OF ALCUIN OF YORK

Alcuin (AD 737–804) was a sophisticated man of learning, who became Charlemagne's leading adviser on education, one of a number of English people who found roles abroad. He was also a great letter-writer, organiser and poet, and most of his life coincided with a golden age of peace, which saw the creation of some of the most beautiful illustrated gospels, the first royal charters and early codes of law, and lucrative trading settlements like the ones in Southampton and London (the remains of which are probably under what is now Trafalgar Square). Lindisfarne had been sacked and York raided before he died and the Viking raids had begun in earnest by the time of his death.

▲ *Wells Cathedral, one of the first to be built by the Saxons in England.*

AD 875
FOUNDATION OF YORK

The Vikings attacked York in AD 866 and massacred its inhabitants. They returned for good, nine years later in 875, and developed a major centre of trade on the River Ouse, building small houses where families tended to sleep and eat together in one big room, gathered around open fires in the centre, with workshops, storage and refuse at the back. Norse settlers poured into the north-east, but York remained a key Viking centre – linked to their other major centre in Dublin either by sea via lowland Scotland or by the more hazardous land journey across the Pennines, on which the last Scandinavian king of York, Eric Bloodaxe, was killed in 954. Dublin kept its Norse heritage until the city was destroyed by the Normans in 1169.

↓ ▶ p. 94

1041
THE PUNISHMENT OF WORCESTERSHIRE

Harthacnut (*c.* 1019–42) was king of England for only two years, but among his brutal reprisals was the punishment of the whole of Worcestershire after two of his tax collectors had been murdered in Worcester Cathedral. Since the reign of Aethelred the Unready (966–1016), a tax known as 'Danegeld' had been paid to the Danes to buy peace. It was later transformed into a general tax, assessed locally and based on the land unit known as a hide, which was supposed to be the amount of land needed to support a family. Church taxes, or tithes, were paid on a tenth of a family's income in either money or goods. There were other taxes as well, such as 'plough alms'.

p. 81◀ **Distant Voices** ▶p. 85

I work very hard, I go out at dawn and I drive the oxen in the field and yoke them to the plough. However stark the winter is, I dare not stay at home, for fear of my lord. I have to yoke the oxen and fasten the share and coulter to the plough, and every day I have plough a full acre or more, I have a boy who drives the oxen with a goad, and even now he is hoarse from cold and shouting. I fill the ox-bins with hay and water and I clear out the dung.

Aelfric Grammaticus, Abbot of Eynsham, describing peasant life in the tenth century

Medieval Life

1086–1290

THE MIDDLE AGES IN England saw a slow shift from the divisions between Saxons and their new Norman rulers, with a strong system of feudal allegiances holding society together, to a more complex society which included villeins who owned no land, an increasingly powerful Church and a rising class of merchants and traders. It was a period of filth and brutality, but also of learning, sophisticated herbal medicine and a growing legal system, in a world where the complicated feudal hierarchies on earth were regarded as a mirror of the great hierarchies of heaven, with every peasant owing allegiance to his lord, and via his lord to the barons, via them to the king, the Church, and directly to God.

p. 80◀ **Triumphs & Tragedies** ▶p. 86

1086
DOMESDAY BOOK

To find out the resources available in his new kingdom, William I (1027–87) ordered a complete survey of the land he had conquered, together with its people, its assets and tax base, to deterrmine what it was worth. The result, written on sheepskin, was the *Domesday Book*, which showed a population of England between one and three million, sparsely populated in the north but densely in the east. It also demonstrated, by the shift from Saxon to Norman names, how the old Saxon *thanes* and bishops were being replaced with French-speaking Normans. As king, William owned all the land. He parcelled a quarter out to bishops and nearly half to his new lords, together with licences to build castles. A complex feudal system of military service and dues was owed by people to lords, and from there to the king.

▶ p. 87

1128
THE CISTERCIAN ARRIVAL

The first Cistercians in England set up in Waverley in 1128. Their austere development of Benedictine rule was a new departure in the rapid growth of monasticism across Europe, which had begun with the spread of Benedictine communities of monks, wearing black robes. The Cistercians interpreted the rule more strictly, wearing nothing but an undyed woollen habit – which gave them the name of the white monks. They opened up more monastic opportunities by taking in lay brothers to carry out the manual labour, part of an increasingly complex hierarchy of different church roles which grew up during the Middle Ages. By 1300, there were 17,500 monks and nuns in England, providing hospitality to travellers, organising schools, hospitals and libraries. Their abbeys became immensely wealthy.

1171
MIRACLES AT CANTERBURY

Fourteen mysterious cures were recorded in the first year of the shrine of St Thomas Becket (*c.* 1120–70) at Canterbury, all within a few months of his murder by four knights loyal to Henry II (1133–89). The miracles led to a cult in Becket's name and brought pilgrims flocking from all over England along the Pilgrim's Way and all over Europe. Medieval travel was so dangerous that the church included travellers in their prayers, along with prisoners and the sick. Crosses were erected on lonely roads, lanterns kept burning in churches at night, and pilgrims would gather together – along with minstrels, bears, jugglers and herbalists – on their way to the shrines or great fairs, like Stourbridge, St Giles or Bartholomew Fairs in London.

▼ *The* Domesday Book, *a record of the population of England in the Middle Ages.*

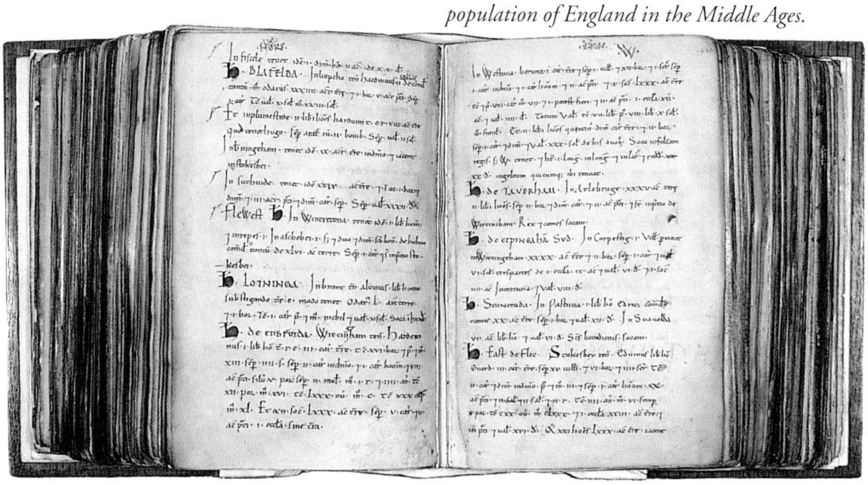

1209
OLD LONDON BRIDGE

London Bridge was the first stone bridge over the Thames, and was completed in 1209 with 19 enormous arches, which forced the water through like a millrace. Houses, shops and a chapel dedicated to St Thomas Becket were later built on it, and the bridge was one of only two ways over the river for almost 700 years. The spikes on its southern gates displayed the heads of traitors until they rotted away. The bridge was finally demolished in 1831. London was now one of only 10 towns with more than 2,000 inhabitants, which in total accounted for one in 25 of the population – and London provided a home for half of those. New towns were also being built in England, such as Hull and Devizes; and in Scotland such as Berwick and Edinburgh.

▲ *The interior of Canterbury Cathedral, with the shrine to Thomas Becket.*

▶ p. 91

1217
DEATH OF ALEXANDER NECKHAM

Alexander Neckham was a great medieval garden writer and herbalist, who described the contemporary diet in detail. Big households and monasteries had separate herb gardens, but most cottagers grew herbs too, both for flavour and medicine. Rue was used as eyewash, to clean air and add tang to cooking. Borage was added to claret or cider, but was also used to treat fevers. Angelica was used as perfume and to relieve flatulence. Rosemary became increasingly common, as a calming tea, as toothpaste or for cleaning the scalp. Meat and eggs were scarce for poorer people in these days before forks or earthenware plates, but as well as plentiful herbs and vegetables, they supplemented their diet with dairy produce, bread and ale.

▶ p. 90

1267
GUILD BATTLE

A fierce battle between the London guilds of Goldsmiths and Taylors in 1267 involved 500 people and left many of them dead. It took place against a background of the growing influence of the guilds, which were setting standards for craftsmanship, fixing prices and wages, controlling the entry of apprentices and regulating trade. The Exchequer had moved from Winchester in the twelfth century, followed by the development of permanent courts of justice in the thirteenth. By this time, London was thriving under an economic expansion, exporting wool and cloth, which was shrunk and scoured by a network of water mills around the countryside. In one 45-m (150-ft) section of London's Cheapside, as many as 15 bustling shop fronts were recorded.

1285
STATUTE OF WINCHESTER

Edward I (1239–1307) set out his solution to public order problems in the Statute of Winchester, which organised a permanent reserve army, based on muster rolls prepared ready for emergencies, by every county, hundred or township. Apart from the house-carls, the military members of the royal household, Commissioners of Array, had to select local men as paid soldiers once a year, and organise them to exercise together – creating a home guard instead of a standing army. The Statute also set out the duties of local people to act as policemen, organised by local sheriffs – formerly known as 'shire-reeves' – who had to cut the brushwood back on either side of roads to a distance of 61 m (200 ft) to reduce the risk of ambush from outlaws.

1290
THE EXPULSION OF THE JEWS

About 100 million silver pennies were in circulation in England by the thirteenth century, with labourers earning about 9d (pennies) a day, when a loaf of bread cost a farthing (a quarter of a penny). Lending money with interest – known as usury – was forbidden by religious law, but Jews were the exception. They lived under the protection of the king in the big towns, and were able to lend money and charge interest on it. But royal protection did not prevent regular out-breaks of violence against them, notably in York in 1190, where local Jews took refuge in the castle and killed themselves rather than abandon their faith. In 1290, Edward I expelled all Jews from the kingdom, along with his debts, and turned instead to the new Florentine bankers.

▼ *The expulsion of the Jews from Spain.*

p. 83◀ **Distant Voices** ▶p. 87

He shall do, sixteen working days in August and for every day he shall have one repast. He shall have ten days without the lord's food – price of a day 1/2d. He shall cart to Norwich six cartings or shall give 9d., and he shall have for every carting one loaf and one lagena of ale. Also for ditching 1d. He shall make malt for 3 ½ seams of barley and shall give 6d. Also he shall flail for twelve days or give 12d, He shall plough if he has his own plough, and for every ploughing he shall have three loaves and nine herrings....

From a survey of the village of Martham, describing the duties of the villein Thomas Knight

Age of Omens
1327–1476

IT HAS BEEN CALLED the 'calamitous fourteenth century', when war, disease and disorder spread across Europe as the feudal ties which held the continent together began to loosen. But of all those calamities, the Black Death – the most important event in recorded history for the population of Britain – was the most disastrous. But after the disaster was over, a smaller, richer, more literate population was able to extract more pay from their landowners and employers and exert themselves to break the feudal ties once and for all. A new mercantile period was beginning, when enormous sheep pastures began changing the previously arable shape of England, and cloth merchants joined the great barons as some of the wealthiest in the land.

▲ *The Plague killed thousands of people across England; poor sanitation and malnutrition aided the spread of the disease.*

p. 84◀ **Triumphs & Tragedies** ▶p. 92

1348
THE BLACK DEATH

At the time, the fatal plague known as the Black Death was a mystery, but the combined outbreaks in 1348, 1361, 1369 and 1374, left between a third and a half of the population dead – including the new Archbishop of Canterbury, just six days after his consecration. No social class escaped, and the final outbreak was particularly virulent in young people. It was known as the 'pestilence of the children'. The Black Death was probably the greatest demographic disaster in European history, and in England the population plunged from close to six million to three million, then carried on drifting downwards. In the long-term, it discouraged labour-intensive arable farming, raised wages and even led to paid holidays. Scientists did not understand that bubonic plague was spread by rat fleas for another six centuries.

▶ p. 88

1327
CIVIL UNREST

When the townspeople rose in revolt in Bury St Edmunds, Suffolk, in 1327, it marked a turning point in a disordered century. The so-called 'Little Ice Age' and floods between 1315 and 1317 had ushered in a period of serious inflation and food shortages. Prices doubled between 1305 and 1310, and by the middle of the century, the poor in Bermondsey were eating dogs, cats and even dove droppings to stay alive. This weakened people immediately before the outbreak of the Black Death. It also increased divisions in the over-crowded towns. One of the most serious outbreaks of urban violence – the St Scholastica's Day Massacre in Oxford in 1345 – saw peasants and townspeople attacking university students, shouting: 'Havak, havoc, smygt faste, gyf good knock!'

1348
KNIGHTS OF THE GARTER

Edward III (1312–77) launched his Order of the Garter with 26 knights – including himself and his 18-year-old son, the Black Prince (1330–76) – on the eve of the outbreak of the Black Death. The first meeting was held in Windsor as the first deaths began outside. Edward wanted to create a new version of the Arthurian ideal of a Round Table dedicated to chivalry and courtly love. He feasted in Windsor dressed in white and silver, wearing a tunic with the words: 'Hay, Hay, the white swan!/By Goddes soul, I am thy man'. For the population outside, romance was more

▼ *Edward III, with his Knights of the Garter, the order he founded in 1348.*

difficult than marriage: under a ruling by Pope Alexander III (d. 1181), young people could freely exchange marriage vows anywhere they liked. This remained the law in England until 1753.

✂ ▶ p. 92

1363
STATUTE OF APPAREL

Rising wages after the Black Death and a booming English cloth industry led to people of all classes adopting more striking clothing. A worried Parliament even passed a law in 1363 preventing people from dressing above their station, but it proved impossible to enforce. Instead of simple woollen tunics, people were beginning to wear stockings and the close-fitting lined tunic known as doublet and hose. Women wore their hair parted in the middle, with low-cut dresses exposing their necks, and began experimenting with the new fashion for gigantic head-dresses. Richard II (1367–1400) led the way in extravagant clothing, wearing an enormous bell-shaped gown known as a *houppelande*, with a hole in the middle for his head.

1381
THE PEASANTS' REVOLT

The Peasants' Revolt followed a third attempt to impose a poll tax on the English population, this time demanding the same sum per head. The revolt was also a response to the Statute of Labourers (1351) and other attempts to stop wage-earners benefiting from the labour shortage. The rebels came within an ace of success in London, but although the tax was dropped, their other demands – which ranged from the end of villeinage to the abolition of bishops – were ignored. The rebel arrival in London was matched by similar scenes elsewhere, including 10 days of destruction in Norwich. The university archives and library were burned in Market Square, Cambridge: 'Away with the learning of clerks!' shouted an old woman, as she threw the ancient parchments onto the flames.

▼ *The Peasants' Revolt, led by John Ball, protesting against the imposition of taxes by the government.*

1444
CITIZENS PETITION

The first commission on the filthy air of London was set up by Edward I as early as 1285, but later the burning of sea coal brought from Tyneside and the herds of animals made the experience of living in London even worse. Citizens petitioned their complaints about the 'grate stenche and so evel savour' of the swans, geese, poultry and sheep kept around the city and its outskirts. Raw sewage tended to be thrown from upstairs windows into the streets, which stank of a horrific mixture of offal, slops and kitchen refuse – in spite of the city corporation's attempts to clean the streets by setting days for putting out rubbish for collection. Homes, with their new red tiled roofs, had low boards in each doorway to stop the foul flood seeping inside.

▶ p. 90

1461
PLAYING CARDS

The first mention of playing cards in England was in a letter written by Margery Paston on Christmas Eve 1461 – she belonged to a family of Norfolk gentry whose letters to each other have survived – and she described them as if they were commonplace. Two years later, the import of playing cards was banned to encourage local producers. Most playing cards at the time were made of ivory, parchment or wood, and they were coloured by hand. Standard playing cards today carry representations of Elizabeth of York, the daughter of Edward IV (1442–83), as the queen. Board games similar to backgammon were also popular, and many games – like chess, hide-and-seek and blind man's buff, which was then known as hoodman blind – would be recognisable now.

▶ p. 98

1476
CAXTON SETS UP HIS PRESS

William Caxton (*c.* 1420–91) first came across printed books in Bruges, where print technology had spread from the work of Johann Gutenberg (*c.* 1400–68) in Mainz. Caxton went to Cologne to acquire the skill and the equipment, and produced the first printed book in English in Bruges in 1474, *The Recuyell of the Historyes of Troye*. He opened his own printing shop in Westminster two years later, and printed about 100 titles there, many of them tracts about health, law and religion. His second book, *The Game and Playe of the Chesse*, was his own translation of a book by a Dominican friar from Rheims. There were no other English printers until 1509, although English books were being imported after being printed abroad.

p. 85◀ **Distant Voices** ▶p. 89

They had a Cook with them who
stood alone
For boiling chickens with a marrow-
bone,
Sharp flavouring-powder and a spice
for savour.
He could distinguish London ale by
flavour,
And he could roast and seetre and
broil and fry,
Make good thick soup and bake a
tasty pie.
But what a pity – so it seemed to me,
That he should have an ulcer on his
knee.

Geoffrey Chaucer, *The Canterbury Tales* (1386)

Age of Shakespeare

1499–1602

WITH THE RISE OF literacy and the emergence of the Lollards a century before, the authorities were growing increasingly concerned about the rise of heresy. Scapegoats were needed at this time of enormous religious and economic upheaval, as the Reformation gripped society, and inflation – followed by deflation – beset the English economy. By 1597, English wages in real terms had reached their lowest point for seven centuries. On the other side of this, though, the new class of Scottish and English merchants were benefiting from the relative prosperity, and the Welsh relaxed with a Welsh dynasty on the English throne. In London, the first theatres were appearing, and beginning to perform plays which have survived ever since to spread English culture around the world.

1499
ERASMUS VISITS LONDON

The Dutch renaissance scholar Desiderius Erasmus (c. 1469–1536) arrived in England in 1499 for the first time, on his search for wealthy patrons and intelligent company. He particularly admired the habits of London girls: 'They kiss you when you arrive,' he wrote to a contemporary back home. 'They kiss you when they go away and they kiss you when they return. Go where you will, it is all kisses.' Erasmus was a key figure in the Renaissance. His 1516 translation of the New Testament into humanist Latin had a great impact, and by 1539 the whole Bible had been translated into English. But four years later, Henry VIII (1491–1547) had changed his mind about the translation, and forbade women, apprentices and labourers to read it.

1500s
CHANGES IN THE SOCIAL ORDER

The introduction of tobacco has been credited to Sir Walter Raleigh (1554–1618) and sweet potatoes to Sir John Hawkins (1532–95). Both spread rapidly among the growing middle classes, the previously distant gap between the rich and poor. In 1553, a law was passed that tried to regulate people's richness of clothing, reserving gold, silver, furs and crimson, scarlet and blue velvet to earls, but it was hard to enforce and the Tudors were already encouraging the new gentry. More members of the middle classes were being appointed as local justices, charged with controlling 'disorderly alehouses' and 'unlawful games'. Talented public servants from the middle ranks were being promoted, like Thomas Wolsey (*c.* 1472–1530), a butcher's son from Ipswich, and Thomas Cromwell (*c.* 1485–1540), a trader's son from Surrey.

1526
DEBASEMENT OF THE COINAGE

Henry VIII first broke the tradition of standard metal coins in 1526, reducing the quality of the silver. He did so again in 1544, just as he was having to support the biggest English army ever sent to France. The debasements worsened the serious inflation which beset the first 60 years of the sixteenth century. Food prices almost tripled in that time, which suited merchants with fixed rents but impoverished many others. A similar inflation in Scotland led to a major change in diet, from one based on meat to one based on barley and oats. Elizabeth I (1533–1603) restored the coinage, but faced a serious currency shortage as a result. She and Mary of Guise (1515–60) experimented with machine-milled coins in Scotland – to the fury of the mints.

▶ p. 92

1547
THE VAGRANT ACT

The Vagrant Act laid down that an able-bodied tramp could be defined as a slave by two magistrates, if anybody wanted him to work for them. That meant being branded with a V on the forehead and being kept in slavery for two years. The act proved impossible to enforce. Throughout the early Tudor years, people lived in fear of the beggars 'coming to town', and city gates were watched around the clock to prevent the bands of 100 or so vagrants, ploughmen thrown off their land, or former soldiers from the Wars of the Roses who wandered around the countryside from entering the cities. By the end of the century, parishes were allowed to levy local rates to pay for work for the poor, a system which became known as the Old Poor Law and stayed in force until 1834.

◀ *Coins have been made from a variety of metals throughout the ages, from pure gold and silver to alloys in times of currency shortage.*

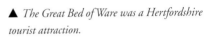

1563
WITCHCRAFT MADE A CAPITAL OFFENCE

The end of the fifteenth century marked the beginning of the 'witch craze' across Europe, as people increasingly regarded 'witches' as a scapegoat for the disorientation of the times, and by 1563 to be a witch was a capital offence in England. Before the end of the century, as many as 174 people would be indicted for 'black witchcraft' in Essex alone and half of those were executed. In the next 150 years across Europe, as many as 40,000 people – most of them women – would be put to death. The purge was particularly brutal in Scotland, where torture was legal, and by 1649 witches could be tried on the basis of unsupported anonymous allegations. As late as 1878, Essex villagers were charged with assaulting an old woman they claimed was a witch.

1571
SHAKESPEARE'S FIRST DAY AT SCHOOL

The great playwright William Shakespeare (1564–1616) was the son of a Stratford-upon-Avon glovemaker who never learned to read, but who sent his son to a free grammar school in 1571. The grammar school day, from 7 a.m to 5 p.m., included Latin, grammar, religion, geography, music and arithmetic, and pupils had to provide their own books, candles, quill pens, knives to sharpen the nib, inkhorns and boxes of sand for ink-drying. At the same time, poorer children were learning to read, sometimes in classes held in the church porches. As many as 300 new schools opened in England during the sixteenth century, and by the end of it, there had been an explosion of literacy: almost half of London's criminal classes could read.

▼ *Shakespeare (seated centre), with his contemporary playwrights.*

1590
THE GREAT BED OF WARE

Tudor times were a bawdy period of raucous innuendo, but also a period of increasing luxury and romance. The Great Bed of Ware – the 3.6-m (12-ft) square bed made around 1590 as a tourist attraction in a series of Hertfordshire inns – combined both luxury and romance, and was famous enough to be mentioned by Shakespeare in *Twelfth Night* in 1601. Homes were warmer, and beds tended to have soft feather mattresses and pillows rather than logs. Mutual love was also now an acceptable reason for marriage, though early marriages arranged by tyrannical parents remained the norm: Bishop William Chaderton (*c.* 1540–1608) disastrously married his nine-year-old daughter to a boy of 11 in 1592. The definition of husband in 1590 was one who 'hath authority over the wife'.

▲ *The Great Bed of Ware was a Hertfordshire tourist attraction.*

▶ p. 103

1602
THE GROWTH OF LONDON

The expanding population of London was a constant source of concern for the Tudors, and proclamations were issued in 1580 and 1602 forbidding multi-occupation and any new building within 7 ½ km (3 miles) of the city gates. Officials held regular inspections of houses to root out 'lodgers'. The next biggest town, Norwich, covered only two-and-a-half square kilometres (one square mile), but London's population had mushroomed from 70,000 in 1520 to 200,000 in 1600. With its close-knit muddle of warehouses, homes, markets, churches, shops and brothels, the city was described by one foreign ambassador as 'the filthiest in the world'. Katherine Wheel Alley in Thames Street had nine respectable tenements in 1584. Shortly afterwards, they had been converted to 43.

p. 87◀ **Distant Voices** ▶p. 91

One is the multitude of chimneys lately erected, whereas in their young days there were not above two or three, if so many, in most uplandish towns of the realm... The second is the great (although not general) amendment of lodging; for, said they, our fathers, yea and we ourselves also, have lain full oft upon straw pallets, on rough mats covered only with a sheet, under coverlets made of dagswain or hopharlots (I use their own terms), and a good round log under their heads instead of a bolster or pillow... The third thing they tell of is the exchange of vessel, as of treen platters into pewter, and wooden spoons into silver and tin.

William Harrison, describing three things old men remark on in his village, in *Description of England* (1587)

Age of Revolution
1613–58

THE MIDDLE YEARS of the seventeenth century in Britain were one of those rare moments in history where it really seemed for a while that the world had turned upside down. It was a period when anything seemed possible: where wild utopian theories were freely exchanged; where the growing religious tensions which had been kept in check since the Reformation exploded; and where a group of generals could execute a king. It was also a period when the first tentative explorations by English seafarers began to be consolidated by settlers like the Pilgrim Fathers and traders penetrating the coasts of America, Africa, the Caribbean and even the East Indies – bringing home new kinds of food and a new international sense of being English.

▶ p. 95

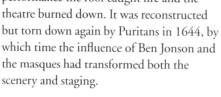

1613
BURNING OF THE GLOBE

The area of London known as Bankside, which had been, until 1546, a neighbourhood of prostitutes licensed by the Bishop of Winchester, became in the late seventeenth century the site of London's new theatres. The Globe was the home of the King's Men, including Shakespeare and Richard Burbage (*c.* 1569–1619), the son of the builder of the first English playhouse. It was built out of timber in 1599 near Southwark Cathedral and saw the first performances of many of Shakespeare's great plays. During one performance the roof caught fire and the theatre burned down. It was reconstructed but torn down again by Puritans in 1644, by which time the influence of Ben Jonson and the masques had transformed both the scenery and staging.

▲ *The reconstructed Globe Theatre on London's South Bank.*

▶ p. 96

1615
MERCHANT ADVENTURERS

The Merchant Adventurers of London had gradually consolidated themselves as England's main overseas trading body. They were granted royal charters in 1486 and 1505, and concentrated on the export of cloth to Germany and the Netherlands. They regained their monopoly in 1615 after the Cockayne scheme had failed to rival their power, when the government tried to break their dominance by banning unfinished cloth exports – an attempt to kick-start the English finishing industry. The cloth industry had by then concentrated in towns and areas of high rural population, causing economic disruption in other regions. In 1614 English traders recorded their highest ever cloth export figures, but they halved again with the bad harvests in the following eight years.

1637
THE 'SHIP MONEY' CASE

'Ship money' had originally been a levy on certain ports in time of war. It was extended inland in the 1590s to help finance the war against Spain and revived by Charles I (1600–49) as part of his struggle for revenue during his 11 years of direct rule – an example of his unParliamentary 'tyranny', according to his enemies. The puritan politician John Hampden (1594–1643) came close to winning a test case against the tax in 1637, having refused to pay it, and ship money was finally declared illegal in 1642. At the same time, the abolition of the Court of Wards freed landowners from all remaining feudal duties owed to the crown, and from the money substitutes which had grown up instead. Future state finance lay in the taxing of income or property.

1637
THE COVENANT

Covenants against Catholicism had been emerging in Scotland since the Reformation, but Charles I's attempt to impose a new prayer book in 1637 led to the covenanting movement – a commitment to restore the purity of the national Kirk. It attracted signatures all over Scotland and served as a manifesto for the 1640s. The Scots contribution to the Civil War, on both sides, was intended to protect

▼ *A seventeenth-century merchant and his clerk working on their books*

this national revolution, but the war ruined the new Jacobean prosperity in Scotland with recession, plague and famine, culminating in 48 hours of murder and pillage by English forces in Dundee in 1651. The Restoration brought no success either: as many as 300 covenanting ministers were thrown out of their parishes during the re-introduction of bishops to Scotland in 1661–63.

1640
END OF CENSORSHIP

Mary I (1516–58) had first imposed a registration system on the Stationers' Company in 1556–57, and from 1586 new publications had to get licences from the Archbishop of Canterbury or the Bishop of London. When the system collapsed in 1640 in the run-up to the Civil War, it led to an upsurge in publishing and – in a period of great political idealism – the great age of the pamphlet. In 1640 there were just 22 pamphlets published; by1642 there were nearly 2,000. The free-for-all was followed by more controls under Oliver Cromwell (1599–1658) and a statutory licensing of the press after the Restoration. The pamphlets added to the hothouse atmosphere of radicalism during and after the Civil War, where people felt able to talk of 'the world turned upside down'.

1647
PUTNEY DEBATES

With the Civil War temporarily abated, the victorious New Model Army gathered at Putney Church and Whitehall in London to discuss the shape of the country after the war. The Putney Debates included ordinary soldiers as well as senior officers and discussed a range of radical ideas, ranging from those of the Levellers – votes for all men except servants and the abolition of tithes – to the Diggers' outright opposition to property. The language alarmed more conservative elements: 'If the unruly rout have once cast the rider, it will run like wildfire through all the counties of England,' said Cromwell. The Levellers were suppressed in 1649 after army mutinies, and the Putney Debates ultimately achieved little.

▲ *Tobacco, first introduced to Britain in the seventeenth century, is now an important cash crop.*

▶ p. 93

1652
THE ARRIVAL OF TEA

With the discoveries in the New World and other places, and the journeys of the two John Tradescants, father and son, a range of exotic new foods began arriving in England, notably bananas in 1633 and tea in 1652. The tea arrived in the form of a small amount captured in a Dutch ship, but by 1660 it was already so popular as a fashionable medicinal drink that it was subject to tax. Loose tobacco was also now widely available, with the first coin-in-the-slot vending machines introduced into taverns in 1615. John Tradescant Junior built up a large collection of historical and natural curiosities, open to paying visitors in Lambeth in the 1650s, and which formed the basis of Oxford's pioneering Ashmolean Museum in 1683.

1653–59
THE PROTECTORATE

From 1653 until 1659, Cromwell ruled the country as Lord Protector; in this role he found himself increasingly at odds with his Parliaments, and decided eventually on direct rule. To oversee local government in all its various forms, he briefly appointed major-generals to run each of the 11 districts of England, with powers to interfere in a range of country pleasures: such as horse-racing, bear-baiting and cock-fighting, to force the 'idle' to work, to make people responsible for their servants' behaviour and to make sure laws against blasphemy, drunkenness and sabbath-breaking were enforced. News items could no longer be published without permission, and secretary to the Council of State, John Thurloe (1616–68), oversaw the only two surviving newspapers. This scheme, however, was quickly superseded.

p. 89◀ **Distant Voices** ▶p. 93

To preserve your body from the infection of the plague, you shall take a quart of old ale, and after it hath risen upon the fire and hath been scummed, you shall put thereinto of aristolochia longa, of angelica and of celandine of each half a handful, and boil them well therein; then strain the drink through a clean cloth, and dissolve therein a drachm of the best mithridate, as much ivory finely powdered and searced, and six spoonful of dragon-water, then put it in a close glass; and every morning fasting take five spoonful thereof, and after bite and chew in your mouth the dried root of angelica, or smell, as on a nosegay, to the tasselled end of a ship rope, and they will surely preserve you from infection.

Gervase Markham on plague prevention, *The English Hus-wife* (1615)

Restoration
1665–1701

CHARLES II WAS warmly welcomed when he was restored to the throne in 1660, by people who were exhausted by the old divisions, and he set about trying to restore the nation to 'its good old manners, its good old humour and its good old nature'. The gigantic maypole erected in the Strand in London the following year was intended to symbolise a break from the puritanism of the past, and the country set about finding a way through the murderous issues which had torn it apart. For the ordinary people, the effects of the Restoration included a deliberate attempt to allow morris dances and Christmas carols once more, but also encouraged a new interest – led by the new king – in the scientific breakthroughs of Newton and Boyle and the new architectural styles of Wren and Hawksmoor.

◀ *The Great Fire of London in 1666 destroyed over 13,000 homes and many public buildings, including St Paul's Cathedral.*

p. 86◀ **Triumphs & Tragedies** ▶p. 94

1665–66
THE GREAT PLAGUE AND GREAT FIRE OF LONDON

The plague and fire were together the cause of London's biggest ever exodus. The plague itself killed 15 per cent of London's 450,000 population, but other badly-affected cities included Newcastle, Norwich, Portsmouth, Southampton and Sunderland. Infected houses were isolated and sealed, and mass graves established on the outskirts of the cities. London's Great Fire in September 1666 finally destroyed the infection there, together with 13,200 houses. A coal duty was imposed to pay for repairs, and strict building regulations drafted to cut the risk of fire. Many of the grandiose rebuilding schemes of Sir Christopher Wren (1632–1723) never came to fruition, but his churches remain a testament to the new brick city that emerged. His St Paul's cathedral makes Westminster Abbey 'look like crinkle-crankle', said the diarist John Evelyn (1620–1706).

✣ ▶ p. 97

1671
THE GAME LAWS

By the end of the seventeenth century, the country gentry were on the rise at the expense of the yeoman farmers. Nothing divided them further than the laws passed in 1671 by the Cavalier Parliament which ruled that freeholders worth less than £100 – the vast majority – could no longer kill game, even on their own land. Farming families had long since made a good meal out of a pheasant which had strayed onto their farms, but an artificial definition now divided them from their richer neighbours. Shooting was taking over from hawking as the respectable way for the gentry to kill game birds, which meant that even more birds were killed – and the pickings for the rest, now defined as 'poachers', were all the more meagre.

✂ ▶ p. 102

1685
INTRODUCTION OF SILK-MAKING

The French king Louis XIV revoked the Edict of Nantes, which had guaranteed the position of the French Protestants, in 1685, prompting half a million refugees to flood into Britain to add to the existing Huguenot communities. Among them were craftsmen skilled in clock-making, ironwork and the beginnings of silk manufacture. This contributed to what was a fashionable period of bright clothes and wigs, which had been in vogue since Charles II (1630–85) adopted the idea to cover up his greyness in 1666. The writer Anthony Wood (1632–95) described it as 'a strange effeminate age when men strive to imitate women in their apparel, viz. long periwigs, patches in their faces, painting, short wide breeches like petticoats, muffs, and their clothes highly scented, bedecked with ribbons of all colours'.

1686
LAST WITCH-HANGING

Alice Molland from Exeter became, in 1686, the last witch to be hanged in England, although the witch trials in Salem, Massachusetts, would not begin for another four years. It was a sign that the old paranoid superstitions were beginning to fade, but the witch hunts had caused enormous suffering

▲ *The Game Laws, introduced in 1671, proved very unpopular amongst farming families.*

– mainly to country women. The last witch trials took place in England in 1711 and in Scotland in 1722. In 1736, the laws against witchcraft were repealed in both countries. Life was changing in the countryside at the same time: by 1683, the wild boar – which had once roved the medieval forests – was finally extinct in Britain. In 1663 the first turnpike tolls had been levied, sending new roads deep into the countryside.

1692
THE FOUNDATION OF LLOYD'S

London café-owner Edward Lloyd (d. 1713) opened a coffee shop in Tower Street in 1692, and it became the meeting place for the new profession of marine insurers. He published a bulletin of maritime news, which developed into *Lloyd's List*. By 1774, the institution had moved to the Royal Exchange buildings where it formed a crucial part of Britain's growing shipping strength and advised the Admiralty. The Great Fire of London had also given rise to the idea of fire insurance. The first companies insuring property emerged in 1696, with householders paying an annual fee which was proportionate to the value of their house. The London Insurance Corporation and the Royal Exchange Insurance Corporation were established in 1711.

◀ *The last witch-hanging occurred in 1686, but the fear of witchcraft continued for many years afterwards.*

▶ p. 101

1693
OPENING OF WHITE'S

The famous White's chocolate house opened in St James's Street, London in 1693, and by 1697 proprietors were already having to move it to larger premises on the other side of the street. It was soon notorious as a gaming house, influential in the development of the Tory party and White's Club, and attracting such clamorous interest that the fashionable clientele moved upstairs to avoid the crowds. Coffee houses became increasingly widespread after the first one opened in Oxford in 1650, and there were 2,000 in London by the end of the century. Wine consumption was down because of taxation, but consumption of spirits and beer was shooting up. One tavern in London's Ludgate Hill, Belle Sauvage, offered a drink and a look at a rhinoceros for a shilling.

1694
THE BANK OF ENGLAND

The government passed a bill in 1694 for a lottery funnelling £1 million into government coffers, but it was clear that William III (1650-1702) still needed another £1.2 million to fund his French wars. The idea of a reserve bank was launched a month later and the money was raised within 10 days, with the king and queen subscribing first. The bank invested heavily in government stock and used this as security to issue bank notes – though as £10 was the smallest denomination, notes were pretty rare. Even so, the paper money began to fuel inflation, and the price of bread doubled between 1693 and 1699. A Window Tax followed in 1696, as an innovative way of taxing property according to size, and stayed in force until 1851. The Bank of Scotland was founded in 1695.

1701
AGRICULTURAL ADVANCES

The great agricultural improver Jethro Tull (1674–1741) invented his famous seed drill around 1701. In 1714 he used his observations of agriculture on the Continent to develop a horse-drawn hoe to pulverise the soil, and described them in his book *Horse Hoeing Husbandry*. Tull may not have had quite the impact which contemporaries attributed to him, but he was still a key figure in the agricultural revolution which – between 1660 and 1850 – allowed farmers to feed a population that had quadrupled in size, at the same time as improving the quality of the food produced. By 1700, about half of England's agricultural land had been enclosed as a way of using more modern growing methods, but from then on, the process was going to be accelerated.

p. 91 ◀ **Distant Voices** ▶ p. 95

Up, and angry with my maids for letting in watermen, and I known not who, anybody that they are acquainted with, into the kitchen to talk and prate with them, which I will not endure. To dinner, where Creed came, who I vexed devilishly with telling him a wise man, and a good friend of his and mine, did say that he lately went into the country to Hinchingbrooke; and, at his coming to town again, had shifted his lodging, only to avoid paying the Poll Bill, which is so true that he blushed, and could not in words deny it. My wife do begin to give me real pleasure with her singing.

Samuel Pepys' diary (6 May 1667)

Age of Reason

1720–59

THE EIGHTEENTH CENTURY was a time of growing prosperity around Britain, but elements of the old brutality were still prominent: where amputations – popular after the invention of the tourniquet in 1672 – were regularly carried out, without anaesthetic, where fashionable people rushed to replace all their rotting teeth with ivory imitations, where up to 14,000 black slaves lived in English country houses, and where men wandering alone in ports might find themselves press-ganged into the brutal world of naval discipline. It was a period where growing learning and ignorance battled for control in the dark corners of England and Scotland. Between 3–14 September 1752, the country shifted to using the Gregorian calendar, leading to widespread rioting.

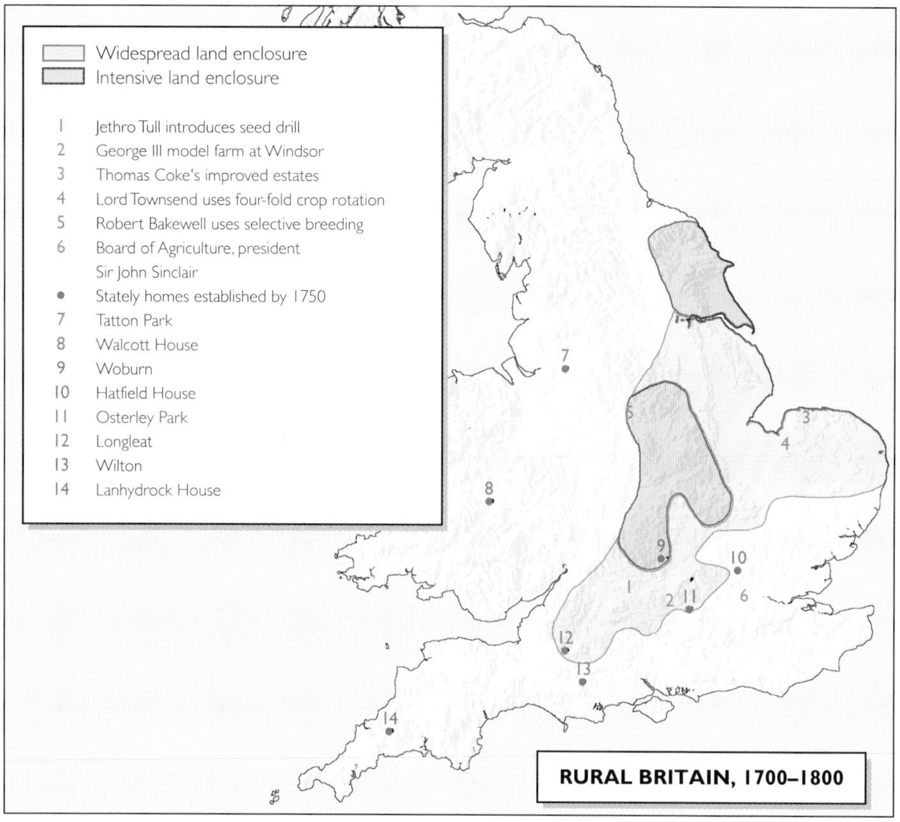

RURAL BRITAIN, 1700–1800

1720
THE SOUTH SEA BUBBLE

The South Sea Company was set up in 1711 to trade with South America, but also as an alternative source of government funds to the Whig-dominated Bank of England and East India Company. Eight years later, its scheme to take over part of the government debt – achieved partly by bribery – led to wild speculation in the company's stock, until the bubble burst in September 1720. Many prominent people, including George I (1660–1727) lost heavily. This was a period when the financial term 'bubble' passed into the language, following financial crashes in Amsterdam and – encouraged by the Scottish financier-turned-gambler John Law (who had been forced to flee to France) – in Paris. The South Sea debacle led to wide restrictions on forming companies, except by the difficult and expensive route of royal charters.

↓ ▶ p. 98

1739
EXECUTION OF DICK TURPIN

John Gay's *Beggar's Opera* in 1723 revealed the existence of a nether world of tramps, cheats, thieves, prostitutes and highwaymen – a world of which travellers were only too aware. There was no official police force to protect travellers, except for a small patrol of 50 mounted men who guarded the approaches to London. 'One is forced to travel, even at noon, as if one is going into battle,' said prime minister Sir Robert Walpole (1676–1745). The most celebrated highwayman, Dick Turpin (1705–39), was finally hanged in York. He bowed to the ladies in the watching crowd, and flung himself off the scaffold. The crowd was so delighted that they stole his body and buried it in quicklime to stop it being sold to the infamous anatomists.

p. 92◀ **Triumphs & Tragedies** ▶p. 104

1746
THE SUBJUGATION OF THE HIGHLANDS

A brutal process of pacification began in Scotland after the defeat of Bonnie Prince Charlie (1720–88) at Culloden in 1746. Highland dress was outlawed, and so was the hereditary jurisdiction over clans by their chiefs. Scottish politics all but vanished, as MPs preferred not to risk their careers by raising Scottish issues at Westminster. The collapse of kelp prices after 1815 destroyed the remaining economic power in the highlands, and the Clearances that followed replaced much of the population with sheep. Paradoxically, the intellectual and business ferment, known as the Scottish Enlightenment, was under way in Edinburgh at the same time, led by thinkers like David Hume (1711–76) and Adam Smith (1723–90). By the end of the eighteenth century, Scotland was generating 50 times more money than it had at the beginning.

▲ *The tales recounted about highwayman Dick Turpin have given him legendary status.*

▶ p. 102

1742
RANELAGH GARDENS

Ranelagh Gardens, which became a major centre of fashionable life, was first opened to the public in 1742 as a profit-making entertainment centre near London's Chelsea Hospital, offering fashionable concerts, balls, fireworks and masquerades. It rivalled the slightly rowdier Vauxhall Gardens, which cost a shilling to enter and had been London's premier pleasure gardens since the 1730s. Ranelagh's main attraction was promenading round the Rotunda, a big building lined with dining boxes and boasting its own orchestra. Outside London, the equivalent of the gardens were the spa towns. The population of Bath multiplied 11-fold during the eighteenth century, and was attracting 12,000 visitors to its elegant squares every June to October. Ranelagh was demolished in 1805.

1751
GIN ACT

Gin was introduced into Britain from the Netherlands in the 1690s and became extremely popular as a cheap route to oblivion. The 'gin era' was immortalised by the Gin Lane engraving by William Hogarth (1697–1764) and, at its peak, there were 8,659 'dram shops' in London alone – not to mention another 6,000 alehouses. It was widely believed that gin-drinking encouraged vice and idleness, and the government tried to control it by increasing the duties in 1729, and introducing stiff penalties for anyone infringing the regulations in 1736. Both actions proved unpopular and ineffective, so that the duties were reduced again seven years later. The era was finally ended when a moral panic about crime resulted in the Gin Act in 1751. It massively raised the tax on gin once more.

▼ *The* Gin Lane *engravings by William Hogarth depicted scenes of squalor and lewd behaviour.*

▶ p. 96

1753
INLAND TRANSPORT IMPROVES

The first Turnpike Act had been passed in 1663 and allowed the operators to charge tolls to pay for and repair roads. As much as 18,500 km (11,500 miles) of turnpike road were built between 1750 and 1770, speeding up journey times, but sometimes attracting the rage of the locals – notably in the rioting that occurred near Leeds and Bradford in 1753. By then, there were six different companies operating wagons between London and Manchester. 'However incredible it may appear,' said one advertisement, 'this coach will actually arrive in London four days after leaving Manchester'. In 1700 it took 10 days to get from London to Edinburgh by coach; by 1750 it was six days and by 1800 only three. By 1763 there were as many as 30 coaches a day between London and Birmingham.

1753
ARRIVAL OF THE UMBRELLA

The eccentric traveller Jonas Hanway (1712–1786) was the first British man with the nerve to carry a parasol in case of bad weather, and he was ridiculed for it after his return to London in 1753. But by the end of his life, the umbrella had been widely adopted, not so much as a means of keeping dry as to stop the dirty city rain staining people's clothes. This was a period of increasing wealth among the middle classes – especially among the growing bands of lawyers, apothecaries and surgeons – which translated itself into a new interest in fashion. Handbags were introduced in the 1760s, and by the end of the century were being listed as 'indispensibles'. By 1800, there were 153 fashion shops in London's Oxford Street alone.

1759
FOUNDATION OF WEDGWOOD POTTERIES

Josiah Wedgwood (1730–95) founded his celebrated pottery business in Staffordshire in 1759, and developed an innovative approach to marketing and assembly line manufacturing, determined to 'make such machines of the men as cannot err' and thereby to transform himself into the 'Vasemaker General to the Universe'. His mass-produced dishes could be stacked, his teapots poured accurately, and broken pieces could be replaced. His pottery was soon to find its way into the homes of all classes, replacing their old pewter dishes. By his death, Wedgwood was a fellow of the Royal Society, leaving a fortune of £500,000. His medallion depicting a slave with the slogan 'Am I not a Man and a Brother?' helped popularise the anti-slavery movement at the end of the century.

p. 93◀ **Distant Voices** ▶p. 97

Sweet smiling village, loveliest of the lawn,
Thy sports are fled, and all thy charms withdrawn;
Amidst thy bowers the tyrant's hand is seen
And desolation saddens all thy green:
One only master grasps the whole domain,
And half a tillage stints thy smiling plain; ...
Sunk are thy bowers, in shapeless ruin all,
And the long grass o'ertops the mouldering wall;
And trembling, shrinking from the spoiler's hand,
Far, far away thy children leave the land....

Oliver Goldsmith, *The Deserted Village* (1770)

Industrial Revolution

1775–1812

WHILE THE FRENCH across the Channel were experiencing a violent political revolution, which marked the end of the *ancien regime*, the British were embarking on a more peaceful – but sometimes just as painful – revolution of their own. By the end of this period, the centre of economic power had shifted to the new factories in the north and the Midlands, and the new machines and agricultural changes had provided the basis for economic dominance in the next century. But this was also the era of the dark brutality of the new factories, and poverty was more widespread and more desperate than it had been before. Political pressures to regulate the system, or to set it in a powerful moral framework, were also getting stronger.

▶ p. 103

1775
WORK CONDITIONS DURING THE REVOLUTION

Steam pioneer James Watt (1736–1819) and his partner Matthew Boulton (1728–1809) set up their factory in Soho outside Birmingham in 1775, and the following year they produced the first commercial steam engine. Birmingham had already become an important centre in the Industrial Revolution, and visitors reported that the locals stank of oil, and had red eyes and hair stained green by the brass foundries. Some industrialists were responsible employers; some were not, literally chaining men, women and children – sometimes straight from the workhouses – to the tireless new machines. The 1802 Health and Morals of Apprentices Act tried to outlaw children working before 6 a.m. or after 9 p.m., but it was hard to enforce. The nature of industry was becoming a central social issue.

▼ *The Bridgewater Canal, which enabled the transport of heavy goods to previously inaccessible areas.*

▶ p. 100

1792
CANAL MANIA

The English enthusiasm for canals dated back to the 1761 opening of a canal linking the coal mines in Worsley, Lancashire, with the outskirts of Manchester; it was built by the Duke of Bridgwater (1756–1803) and the self-educated engineer James Brindley (1716–72). The canal was described as 'perhaps the greatest artificial curiosity in the world'. By 1792, the year of 'canal mania', 42 new canals were projected, and canal shares were being bought enthusiastically by local merchants, landowners and manufacturers. At its height, there were 6,500 km (4,000 miles) of inland waterway in Britain, built mainly on local initiative, and dramatically cutting the cost of transporting goods. When the first boatload of coal arrived in Oxford from Coventry in 1790, the church bells were rung in celebration.

1792
A VINDICATION OF THE RIGHTS OF WOMEN

Inspired by the French Revolution and Tom Paine's *The Rights of Man*, the 1790s were a time of radical turmoil, centred around political societies like the Sheffield Society for Constitutional Information (1791) which advocated pensions, free education and votes for all men. The societies were banned after social disorder which began with the bread riots in 1795, when a mob broke the windows of 10 Downing Street, shouting 'No war, no famine, no Pitt, no king!'. Formal proscription evetually occurred in 1799. Paine's ideas were applied to the position of women by the pioneer feminist Mary Wollstonecraft (1759–97) in *A Vindication of the Rights of Women*, published in 1792, and other tracts, which demonstrated the double standards of the day. 'In marriage, husband and wife are one person,' said the great lawyer Sir William Blackstone (1723–80), 'and that person is the husband'.

▶ p. 99

1795
SPEENHAMLAND SYSTEM

A meeting of Berkshire magistrates at Speen in 1795 responded to the poor harvest and

▲ *Pioneer feminist Mary Wollstonecraft, author of* A Vindication of the Rights of Women.

high prices, by drawing up a system of poor relief which could apply to agricultural labourers both out of work and in. The system took account of the size of families and the price of bread, and made up earnings to a basic minimum. The system – known as the Speenhamland System – was widely adopted across southern England. Parliament criticised the idea, and so did the Royal Commission on the Poor Laws in 1832–24, because they believed it depressed wages and was a disincentive to work and save money and an incentive to delay marriage. Most labouring families were then reduced to meals of bread and cheese six days a week, and Speenhamland showed how far real wages had fallen. Money wages increased very rapidly in the 1790s.

✚ ▶ p. 100

1796
MANCHESTER FEVER HOSPITAL

Manchester Fever Hospital opened in 1796 after a series of local typhus epidemics. It was able to take in about 440 patients a year, one in nine of which died. Hospitals were still rare, though Thomas Coram (1667/8–1751) had started the Foundling Hospital in London in 1739 to look after the abandoned babies often found on the streets of the city – helped by fund-raising concerts given by Handel (1685–1759). People who really needed hospitals rarely reached them, because the parishes would not pay to send people from workhouses there. Most people stayed at home when ill. 'It was a common sight,' wrote one doctor, 'to see two or three children laying in the same bed, with such a load of pustules that their skins stick together.'

1801
GENERAL ENCLOSURE ACT

By the end of the eighteenth century, up to three million open fields had been enclosed in the Midlands alone, and the 1801 Act meant that the process became even simpler. Woods and wasteland disappeared, making way for a new pattern of hedges, walls and fences. Some of those who had depended on using common land were thrown off unceremoniously to become labourers or paupers. 'When farmers became gentlemen, their labourers became slaves,' complained the radical William Cobbett (1763–1835). Under the influence of agricultural reformers like Arthur Young (1741–1820), land was becoming more productive and monstrous new breeds of cattle were appearing. Even George III (1738–1820) was writing a regular agricultural column, under the pseudonym 'Mr Robinson'.

1811
THE LUDDITES

The new factories and machines were also taking the livelihood away from handloom weavers, framework knitters and others, especially in the north and Midlands, a situation that was made even worse by the impact of Napoleon's ban on trade with Britain from occupied Europe. Organised machine-breaking took place in Nottingham in 1811, associated with a legendary youth called Ned Ludd or 'King Ludd' who gave his name to the Luddite movement. Others attacked warehouses and carried off food. After an 1812 raid on Cartwright's Mill near Huddersfield, 17 were executed in York. An army of 12,000 men – bigger than Wellington's army in Spain – was sent north to suppress the Luddites. There were outbreaks of Luddism again, but the York executions had already broken the movement.

1812
GAS LIGHT AND COKE COMPANY

There had been experiments with street-lighting, starting with animal fat and moving onto oil, during the eighteenth century, but it was now technically possible to light city streets using coal gas, in a system developed by Boulton and Watt. The Gas Light and Coke Company was formed in London in 1812 to do so, lighting Westminster Bridge in 1813 and replacing the oil-lamps in the parish of St Margaret's, Westminster, the following year. Gaslight was also being introduced into Manchester cotton mills, and by the middle of the nineteenth century, the gas industry was using a million tons of gas a year. Lighting streets made them safer, lighting factories meant workers could work longer and better, and lighting concert halls meant more social activity for the upper and middle classes.

p. 95◀ **Distant Voices** ▶p. 99

Dinner was announced soon after our arrival, which consisted of the following things, Salmon boiled & Shrimp Sauce, some White Soup, Saddle of Mutton rosted & Cucumber &c., Lambs Fry, Tongue, Breast of Veal ragoued, rice Pudding the best part of a Rump of Beef stewed immediately after the Salmon was removed. 2nd course. A Couple of Spring Chicken, rosted Sweetbreads, Jellies, Maccaroni, frill'd Oysters, 2 small Crabs, & made Dish of Eggs... We got home about half past nine, as we went very slowly on Account of Briton's walking, who ... was very imprudent indeed, but I believe he had been making too free with Mr Mellishs Beer &c.

The Rev James Woodforde's diary (20 April 1796)

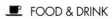

Age of Reform
1816–40

THE HORRORS OF THE slave trade, together with stories of mothers and daughters clutching lighted candles in their teeth down the mines, or children working 12-hour days in appalling factory conditions – all formed part of the debate after the Napoleonic wars. Although the reforms were controversial at the time – critics feared they would take the edge off business profitability – the reformers were winning the arguments about slavery, prisons, factories, democracy and schools. This was a period of utilitarianism, and the 'scientific analysis' of social issues, as followers of the philosopher Jeremy Bentham intervened in the various debates, organising systems, setting up commissions and institutions, and setting the moral tone for much of the century.

▲ *The prison reformer Elizabeth Fry, visiting female prisoners.*

1816
DEMOBILISATION

The Battle of Waterloo and the end of the war was an unexpected economic disaster for Britain, as the demoralised markets on the continent were unable to absorb stockpiles of British goods, and up to 400,000 members of the armed forces were suddenly thrown onto the labour market. The result was serious unemployment. The 10 per cent income tax was abolished, but replaced with taxes on other products. The poor existed on a diet of potatoes, condensed milk, tea from used tea leaves, white bread mixed with chalk, and water from the sewers. The result was serious political upheaval, fuelled by the urban discontent which led to events such as the Peterloo massacre in 1819, mass demonstrations after the transportation of the Tolpuddle Martyrs in 1834 and the Chartist disturbances later.

▶ p. 100
1828
THE APPOINTMENT OF DR ARNOLD

The basic education of working class children was carried out by the Sunday schools and of street children by the ragged schools. Under the 1833 Factory Act, which banned the employment of children under nine, employers became responsible for educating their child workers. The education of the upper classes was the responsibility of unreformed and sadistic 'public schools'. The appointment of Thomas Arnold (1795–1842) as headmaster of Rugby in 1828, marked the beginning of a new 'moral' approach, however, with a broader curriculum, and a disciplinary code which reduced the bullying – and helped regenerate the public school system. His style of 'muscular Christianity' was popularised in *Tom Brown's Schooldays* (1857), written by the Christian socialist Thomas Hughes (1822–96).

◀ *The early years of the nineteenth century were a turbulent time for the Church*

▶ p. 103
1829
THE METROPOLITAN POLICE

The prison reformer Elizabeth Fry (1780–1845) made her first horrifying visit to Newgate in 1813, and her campaign to improve conditions coincided with an increase in the number of prisoners. Home secretary Sir Robert Peel (1788–1850) ended the brutal death sentences for theft and began replacing transportation to Australia with penal servitude in Britain, knowing that juries were refusing to convict. The resulting influx of convicts were housed in prison hulks on the rivers. Peel's new police force in London was deliberately created to be more civilian than military – armed only with a truncheon and top hat – because of political distaste for the system of spies and soldiers on the Continent. It took another 10 years before counties were allowed to have their own police force.

1829
CATHOLIC EMANCIPATION

Changing the law to stop discrimination against Catholics was a dangerous business, as the Gordon Riots showed in 1780. Small reforms had been made, though, and Irish Catholics were allowed to buy freehold land from 1782. Yet the Test Act still barred Catholics from Parliament and other civil offices. The failure of the Irish harvests in 1817, 1823 and 1826 made the issue more urgent, but the 1828 election to Parliament of the Irish Catholic leader Daniel O'Connell (1775–1847), the leader of the Catholic Association (probably the first political mass movement) brought it to a head. George IV (1762–1830) was finally persuaded to sign the Catholic Emancipation (Relief) Act in 1829, which removed all the remaining disqualifications.

▶ p. 107

1834
POOR LAW AMENDMENT ACT

The poor had been the responsibility of parishes since Elizabethan times, though in Scotland they were helped by a loose system of charity organised by the kirk. But the influence of utilitarian reformers like Jeremy Bentham (1748–1832) led to a new system. The Poor Law Amendment Act attempted to make applying for poor relief a demeaning and degrading exercise and the spectre of the workhouse, with its harsh regime and segregation of the sexes sent a chill down the spine of many working people – as it was intended to do. Parishes were organised into Poor Law Unions, run by elected 'guardians', responsible to a London-based Poor Law Commission. Workhouses, said the scheme's architect Edwin Chadwick (1800–90), should be 'uninviting places of wholesome restraint'. The new law caused riots in the northern textile towns.

1837
OLIVER TWIST

The novelist and reformer Charles Dickens (1812–70) was enjoying his first success with *The Pickwick Papers* when he published *Oliver Twist*, an expose of the urban underclass through the eyes of an orphan who is caught up in a gang of child pickpockets. It came two years after the Municipal Corporations Act, which helped the development of a system of elected local government in the new urban areas. At the same time, the socialist Friedrich Engels (1820–95) was about to embark on his study of social conditions in Manchester, describing tiny houses with an average of 20 people in each, and one lavatory for every 120 people. 'Heaps of refuse, offal and sickening filth are everywhere interspersed with pools of stagnant liquid,' he wrote.

1837
FIRST TELEGRAPHIC MESSAGE

During the Napoleonic wars, urgent messages were sent from the Admiralty to the dockyards by a system of semaphore stations relayed from high spots like church towers. Messages from London took just 12 minutes to reach Portsmouth. But that all changed in 1837 when the first telegraphic message was sent, by means of electro-magnetic signals which made a needle point to letters of the alphabet from Camden Town Station to Euston. Morse Code was invented the following year, and the first railway telegraph system was working between Paddington and Slough by 1842. Racing news from Newmarket was sent telegraphically in 1854, the news agency Reuters was founded five years later. Once the Atlantic cable had been laid in 1866 telegraphic messages could be sent to the United States as well.

1840
THE PENNY POST

The penny post owed its existence to the persistence of the educational reformer Sir Rowland Hill (1795–1879), who struggled to develop the idea over five difficult years. Before that, the upper classes had used the privileges of MPs and high officials to use franked post, but most other letters were charged on an elaborate scale depending on how far they had travelled, and the postman had to wait at each house to be paid. Hill's proposal introduced a uniform charge for any package weighing less than 15 g (half an ounce), and within 25 years, 642 million letters and packages were being sent every year. 'The aristocracy are very furious about it,' said the Earl of Ilchester, 'and think it beneath their dignity to understand anything about a penny.'

▲ *An early telegraphic machine, used to send messages by way of electro-magnetic signals.*

p. 97◀ **Distant Voices** ▶p. 101

At what age are children employed? *Never under five, but some are employed between five and six in woollen mills: they go to work between five and six a.m.; in the summer they work until ten in the evening – as long as they can see.* How do they eat? *They get breakfast as they can; they eat and work – generally water porridge, with a little treacle that they take when they get a minute.* Suppose our Bill forced owners to close down their mills? *This would mean domestic work, the greatest blessing for England; the factory system is slavery.'*

Evidence to the Committee on the Factory Bill (1831)

Society on the Move
1845–63

THE TROUBLE WITH railways, said the Duke of Wellington, is that they 'encourage the working classes to travel about'. He was right: the upheaval caused by cutting railway tracks through already over-populated cities was nothing to the social upheaval they caused. Poorer people could travel for the first time, sometimes on the new day excursions, sometimes every day to get to work. They were able to see things they had never seen before, like the 1851 Great Exhibition, and assert themselves in new directions. The first Trades Union Congress (1868) was a portent of things to come, just as the Married Women's Property Act (1870) was a sign that women were also beginning to assert themselves, particularly in education and health.

▶ p. 104 **1845**
RAILWAY MANIA

'Railway mania' arrived in full force between 1845–47 when 576 companies were set up and over 14,000 km (8,700 miles) of new track were agreed. Armies of navvies were cutting tracks or building the new railway towns like Swindon or Crewe – Crewe did not even appear as a place-name in the 1841 census. Former draper George Hudson (1800–71), known as the 'Railway King', was making a fortune speculating in railway shares, although he was also on his way to prison and ruin. Under an 1844 Act, companies had to run at least one train every weekday at no more than a penny a mile. The advent of trains had already forced towns to synchronise their times: Bristol, for example, used to run its clocks according to latitude, 10 minutes behind those in London.

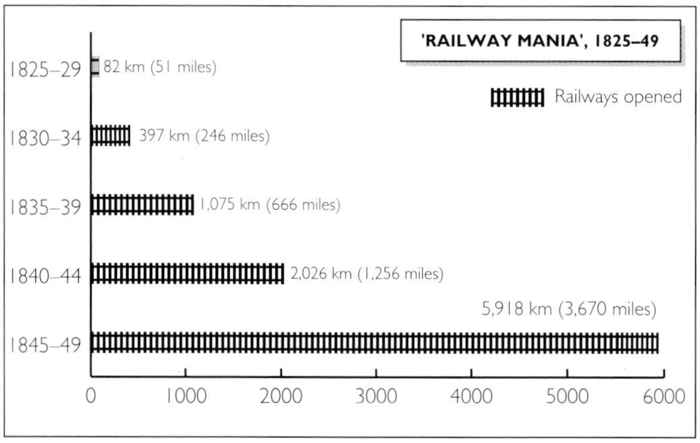

✚ ▶ p. 110 **1848**
CHOLERA EPIDEMIC

City conditions were such that the mortality rate in cities such as Liverpool was extremely high. The cholera epidemic in 1848, which claimed 53,000 lives, swung public opinion behind reformers like Edwin Chadwick (1800–90), head of the Board of Health, and his campaign for a modern sewage system. As the famine raged in Ireland, the poor of London were scraping together the guinea it cost to have their relatives' names carved near unmarked graves. Public health acts followed in 1848 and 1869, and by the end of the century, soap was the most advertised product. 'There have been at work among us three great social agencies,' said one non-conformist preacher, 'the London City Mission, the novels of Mr Dickens, the cholera.'

1851
EXCURSIONS

Prince Albert's brainchild, the Great Exhibition, demonstrated the domination of British technology and industry, as symbolised by the 24-ton block of coal by the entrance to the exhibition. It also attracted as many as 6.2 million visitors, some of whom walked all the way from Penzance. Most came on the new excursion trains, which were such an important departure in social history. Rail had first arrived in Blackpool in 1846, but the day excursions were started by travel agent Thomas Cook (1808–92), who first persuaded Midlands Counties Railway to provide cheap tickets for 500 temperance delegates from Loughborough in 1841. 'We must have railways for the millions,' he said. By 1869, Cook had gone on to many other things, and was present at the opening of the Suez Canal.

▶ p. 102 **1853**
START OF FORMAL EDUCATION FOR GIRLS

The Christian socialist F. D. Maurice (1805–72) opened Queen's College in London's Harley Street in 1848, and among those women who attended lectures there were some of the pioneers in teaching and medicine: Dorothea Beale, Frances Mary Buss and the medical pioneer Sophia Jex-Blake. Miss Buss (1827–94) founded the North London Collegiate School for Girls in 1853 as an instrument for asserting the independence and professional advancement of women. Miss Beale

▼ *Early tunnel construction was dangerous work for the railway 'navvies'.*

(1831–1906) took over Cheltenham Ladies College in 1858, and founded St Hilda's College, Oxford in 1890. In 1863, girls were allowed to take the same 'middle class examinations' at 15 or 16 and 18 as boys. The experiment continued, and Bedford College, London, awarded the first degrees to women in 1878.

▶ p. 108

1855
SUNDAY OPENING RIOTS

Beer had long been the staple drink of the masses – it was safer than drinking water – but temperance campaigners and preachers increasingly included it along with spirits as the cause of drunkenness. No games were held on Sundays, and morning prayers were read by the head of middle class households, but the pubs were open nevertheless. In 1854, they forced them to close at midnight on Saturday and – except for brief periods for Sunday lunch and evening – not re-open until 4 a.m. on Monday. Complete Sunday closing was enforced in Scotland from 1853 and Wales from 1881. Furious pub-goers rioted throughout the summer of 1855 in Hyde Park, breaking the windows of carriages in protest. But in 1864, pubs were forced to close every night from 1 a.m. to 4 a.m.

1857
THE START OF DIVORCE

Civil divorce became possible in 1857, though it was still difficult and expensive to achieve – especially for women, who also had to prove cruelty or desertion. It was considered a disgrace. Queen Victoria (1819–1901) refused to let even the innocent parties of a divorce attend her court until 1887. The public divorces of two major politicians – Sir Charles Dilke (1886) and Charles Stewart Parnell (1890) – ruined their careers, and by the end of the century only 0.2 per cent of marriages finished in divorce. This was the high point of Victorian respectability and confusion about women: 'God! She is like a milk-white lamb that bleats for Man's protection,' wrote John Keats. At the same time, nevertheless women were beginning to force their way into the world of men.

1863
THE FIRST DEPARTMENT STORES

Describing himself as the 'Universal Provider', William Whiteley (1831–1907) opened London's pioneering department store (which still bears his name) in 1863. Inspired by the Great Exhibition, his store in Bayswater employed staff working from 7 a.m. to 11 p.m., and claimed to be able to supply anything 'from a pin to an elephant at short notice'. He broke every agreement about trading demarcations, and in this way so enraged other shopkeepers that he was burnt in effigy by local butchers in 1876. Chain stores were also beginning to open in high streets. Jesse Boot, the Nottingham chemist, would have 181 shops by the end of the century. Thomas Lipton opened his first shop with £100 in 1871. By 1914 he had 500 shops and his name was known all over the world.

1863
THE NEW COMMUTERS

The word 'commuter' was first used in the 1850s, by which time there were 800 horse-drawn buses in London, and traffic jams were so common that new streets like Corporation Street in Manchester or Shaftesbury Avenue in London were being built to relieve the congestion. The first tram appeared in Liverpool in 1863, and the underground Metropolitan Railway opened between Paddington and Farringdon Street in London in 1862, backed by the City of London and Great Western Railway, to speed people into work. By then, London's new Victoria Station had provided access to new suburbs in south London for the new middle classes, where they could live in relative health and still commute to work every morning.

▼ *An early horse-drawn omnibus, forerunner of the modern public transport system.*

p. 99◀ **Distant Voices** ▶p. 103

The first shock of a great earthquake had, just at that period, rent the whole neighbourhood to its centre... Houses were knocked down; streets broken through and stopped; deep pits and trenches dug in the ground; enormous heaps of earth and clay thrown up; buildings that were undermined and shaking, propped up by great beams of wood.... A brand-new Tavern, redolent of fresh mortar and size, and fronting nothing at all, had taken for its sign The Railway Arms.... The Excavator's House of Call had sprung up from a beer shop; and the old-established Ham and Beef Shop had become The Railway Eating House, with a roast leg of pork daily.

Charles Dickens, describing the coming of the railway navvies, *Dombey and Son* (1848)

The New Voters
1870–90

THE EXTENSION OF THE voting franchise was a slow business, making little leaps forward in 1867 and 1884, extending voting to artisans in towns – though still not to women. The voting changes coincided with a more democratic age in other fields as well. People were enjoying days out on bank holidays, travelling along approximately 1,500 km (9,000 miles) of railway track – described by the art critic John Ruskin (1819–1900) as 'the iron veins that traverse our country'. Fashions were becoming more democratic too, as women exerted their rights to play games or travel independently. An increasingly articulate system of local government was also beginning to tackle the health and efficiency of the burgeoning towns and cities.

▶ p. 113

1870
EDUCATION ACT
Religious disagreements and the rising ethic of laissez-faire resulted in the state taking a role in providing education, with the 1870 Education Act. The new law set out a secular system of primary schooling (made compulsory 10 years later) run by about 2,000 elected school boards. It was a belated recognition of the importance of education in an industrial democracy, and a response to the concern felt since the 1850s for the lack of basic technical understanding among new recruits to the factories. 'Upon the speedy provision of elementary schools depends our industrial prosperity,' said the Liberal minister W. E. Forster (1819–86), who introduced the act to Parliament. Girls and boys, normally segregated by sex, were taught reading, writing and arithmetic together. Responsibility was handed over to local authorities in 1902.

▶ p. 110

1870
THE AGE OF THE BUSTLE
Artisan clothes were disappearing, and with the arrival of cheap ready-made suits, clothing was becoming increasingly classless, with most people dressing like office clerks. Bowler hats were making an appearance, but the biggest changes were to richer women's clothes. The crinoline was disappearing by 1870 and was being replaced by the bustle, which used tight corsets of steel and whalebone to produce an unnaturally narrow waist, with dresses trailing up to a yard behind. By 1890, the bustle was going out of fashion, and women were liberating themselves by wearing knickers instead of thick petticoats. These knickers were long and frilled at the bottom, encouraged shorter skirts and were much lighter. As such, they made a real contribution to the liberation of women.

▶ p. 105

1871
BANK HOLIDAYS
The banker and scientist Sir John Lubbock (1834–1913) designed his Bank Holiday Act as a deliberate method of giving the general populace – then usually working five and a half days a week – four days off a year. The bill went through Parliament easily, defining the days for England, Wales and Ireland – with slight variations for Scotland – when the banks would close; the first bank holiday took place in August 1871. The response was enormous and immediate; special trains laid on failed to cope with the rush for the seaside. Paid holidays for most workers were rare at this time, and the event marked the beginning of leisure time for the people of Britain, who were carried by day excursion trains to the seaside, rivers and pleasure gardens.

1885
THE WHITE SLAVERY CASE
The underside of Victorian respectability was the dark world of prostitution. According to the campaigning journalist W. T. Stead (1849–1912), the editor of the *Pall Mall Gazette*, there were as many as 50,000–60,000 prostitutes working in London alone. He made this claim during his trial for buying a girl of 13 for £5 in Marylebone, something he did with the help of members of the new Salvation Army, as a way of revealing the existence of white slave traffic in children from London to Paris and Brussels. Stead's story had two results: he was sent to prison, but the 1885 Criminal Law Amendment Act made trafficking criminal, raised the age of consent from 13 to 16 and extended the legal protection of women.

1886
SCOTTISH HOME RULE ASSOCIATION
By the mid-1880s, prime minister W. E. Gladstone (1809–98) was convinced of the need for Irish home rule, but a growing Celtic revival was also having an influence on culture and politics in Wales, Scotland and Ireland. The Scottish Home Rule Association was launched in 1886, followed a year later – the year of Queen Victoria's Golden Jubilee – by the launch of Yo Cymru Fydd (Young Wales). The Cross Commission in 1888 proposed bi-lingual teaching in Welsh, and in spite of generations of official discouragement, about half the population of Wales spoke Welsh by 1900. A similar scheme was already running in Scotland, and in both Ireland and Scotland, Gaelic football and hurling clubs were emerging to preserve national past-times.

▶ p. 105

1888
NEW COUNTY COUNCILS
'Be more expensive,' the Liberal thinker John Bright (1811–89) urged his party as they began to take responsibility for the decaying cities. Birmingham was showing the way forward: under former screw

▲ *Slums in the East End of London; poverty was rife in the early nineteenth century.*

manufacturer Joseph Chamberlain (1836–1914), the city had taken over its gas and water supplies and embarked on a programme of urban regeneration. Manchester had opened its public baths back in 1846 and the first free library in 1852. The introduction of elected county councils in 1888, followed by district and parish councils in 1894, directed more of this energy towards local improvements. Women were allowed to vote for the new councils, as they had been for school boards since 1870 and for poor law guardians since 1834, but were still excluded from voting for Westminster governments.

◀ *Victorian prime minister William E. Gladstone, who believed in a Home Rule policy in Ireland.*

↓ ▶ p. 115

1888
JEWS IN LONDON

The series of horrific 'Jack the Ripper' murders of prostitutes in Whitechapel in 1888 has never been solved. At the time, the mystery gripped the public and brought widespread condemnation of the police, but it also heightened tensions over the latest influx of immigration to east London, and at least one attempt was made to implicate local Jews. From 1870– 1914, as many as 120,000 Jewish refugees from the pogroms in Russia and eastern Europe made their homes in London's East End, Manchester and Leeds. As many as 29 per cent of the new wave became tailors, leading to a revival of the rag trade in east London. Others played a prominent role in the tobacco trade: both Player's factory (1882) and Imperial Tobacco in Glasgow (1888) were Jewish enterprises.

✂ ▶ p. 106

1890
UNIONS AND STRIKES

The last three decades of the nineteenth century saw a massive growth in trade unions, and by 1890, there were 1.5 million members. The 1871 Trade Union Act gave unions limited legal immunity, and the government of Benjamin Disraeli (1804–81) went even further, making peaceful picketing legal as well. But it was the 1888 Match Girl's Strike, led by the feminist orator Annie Besant (1847–1933), and the Great Dock Strike – led by Ben Tillett (1860–1943) and John Burns (1858–1943) – which gave the movement a major boost. The London dockers fought successfully for an extra penny an hour and for better working conditions, and had a dramatic effect on middle class opinion, drawing in even Cardinal Manning (1808–92), the Catholic Archbishop of Westminster, as a mediator.

p. 101◀ **Distant Voices** ▶p. 105

The passengers were packed on decks and paddleboxes like herrings in a barrel, and so great was the hunger of the crowd on board one of the vessels that the steward declared himself to be 'eaten out' in ten minutes after the vessel left Thames Haven. Margate Jetty was simply blocked so far as to be impassable, whilst thousands of excursionists who came down by rail wandered along the cliffs. How many may have gone down is impossible to say. The people arrived at Cannon Street and Charing Cross for Ramsgate at 8am and it was 10 o'clock before the surprised but active officials of the South Eastern could accommodate all their customers.

The *News of the World*, reporting on the first bank holiday (August 1871)

Fin de Siècle
1894–1913

'NO LANGUAGE CAN EXPRESS the sense of personal loss,' said a newspaper editorial on the death of Queen Victoria in January 1901, just as the new century began. Most of the population could not remember a time before she was on the throne, presiding over an unprecedented increase in the power and wealth of the country. But at the height of British imperial power, conflict between the classes and between the sexes was growing rapidly. Fierce strikes in 1910–12 culminated in troops being used against strikers in Tonypandy and the militant campaign for votes for women was having an increasing impact on public life. There were still two million servants in British homes, but all the old certainties seemed to be crumbling.

▶ p. 112

1894
THE FIRST MOTOR CAR

The first motor car seen in Britain was a Benz, imported in 1894, and stopped by police as it crossed London for the first time. Two years later, the law which laid down a speed limit of 4 mph and insisted on a man in front carrying a red flag – designed for older heavier steam-powered vehicles – was repealed, and the Earl of Winchelsea burned the flag ceremonially at the first London-Brighton rally that same year. A new speed limit of 20 mph was imposed in 1904 and by 1914 there were 140,000 cars in the country – and motor accident deaths were running at almost 1,500 a year. 'What pair of horses could carry a load, as my Daimler has done, of 250 pounds of baggage, myself and my man?' said one advertisement.

1895
THE NATIONAL TRUST

The conservation organisation, the National Trust, was founded by the housing reformer Octavia Hill (1838–1912) and others, to protect areas of natural beauty. The Lake District had been saved from the railways only eight years before, and the Ancient Monuments Bill – protecting Avebury and other sites – had finally been passed in 1882. All that was needed was the success of the bicycle – and specifically the invention in Belfast of the pneumatic tyre in 1888 – to complete the 1890s cult of the open air. Bicycles cost about £4.50 in the 1890s, and they had an enormous influence on women's fashion, women's emancipation and in engendering a sense of fellowship – via the 1878 Bicycle Touring Club – and freedom of the road.

◀ *The first cars, similar to this early Benz, appeared on the streets of Britain in 1894.*

p. 94◀ **Triumphs & Tragedies** ▶p. 109

1912
THE SINKING OF THE *TITANIC*

The sinking of the British liner *Titanic*, after striking an iceberg in 1912, happened to coincide with the deaths of the ill-fated British Antarctic expedition, led by Captain Robert Falcon Scott (1868–1912). Both tragedies became mythic events, wrapped in tales of heroic self-sacrifice, which set the tone for the enormous casualties of the First World War. This was a period of chivalric ideals, brought to a head in the apotheosis of British imperialism celebrated during Queen Victoria's Diamond Jubilee in 1897, with 50,000 troops marching through London and a gigantic celebration outside St Paul's Cathedral. Responsibility and sacrifice were also the ideals of the Boy Scouts (1908) and Girl Guides (1909), organisations created by the hero of the siege of Mafeking, Sir Robert Baden-Powell (1857–1941).

▲ *Charlie Chaplin, the British-born star who became known as the 'King of Comedy' in early cinema.*

1896
THE DAILY MAIL

Alfred Harmsworth, later Lord Northcliffe, (1865–1922) was the son of an impoverished barrister. He launched his first newspaper in 1888, along with his first publication for boys, *Comic Cuts.* But it was his *Daily Mail*, launched in 1896 and costing a halfpenny a copy, which made his fortune and invented popular journalism. Within three years, the *Mail* had a circulation of half a million; within 10, Harmsworth controlled *The Times.* He launched the *Daily Mirror* for women in 1903, converted it into the first morning picture paper, and it was the first newspaper to reach a million readers. Prime minister Lord Salisbury (1830–1903) dismissed the *Mail* as 'a journal produced for office boys by office boys'.

▶ p. 108

1896
THE FIRST CINEMAS

The enormous late Victorian music halls provided the main popular entertainment, but a revolution was beginning with the first cinema shows in London's Leicester Square in 1896. The first purpose-built cinema appeared in Colne, Lancashire, and was known as the Central Hall – the word 'cinema' was not coined until 1910. Most of the silent movies shown were American, but the pre-eminent silent star was British. Charlie Chaplin's first film appeared in 1913, the same year that censorship started, after which films were classified as U (universal) or A (adult). There were fears about indecent behaviour in the dark but, according to one London cinema owner, this was usually no more than 'the privileged manifestation of affection between the sexes'.

1898
GARDEN CITIES

When the Parliamentary shorthand writer Ebenezer Howard (1850–1928) published his book, later called *Garden Cities of Tomorrow*, he launched an influential movement which led to the development of town planning and ultimately to the post-war new towns. His idea was to move the overcrowded populations of the inner cities to self-supporting green towns, owned by the residents, and surrounded by a green belt of farmland. The first garden city began in Letchworth in 1903, where the pioneering designs for public housing with gardens were widely adopted, but mainly – in spite of Howard's urging – developments began on the edges of towns, like Hampstead Garden Suburb (1907). The Town Planning Institute was founded in 1914 to emancipate the nation from 'the beast of ugliness'.

1909
THE PEOPLE'S BUDGET

The People's Budget, formulated by the Chancellor of the Exchequer David Lloyd George (1863–1945), was the culmination of a series of measures to tackle poverty by the Liberal government. Parliament backed old age pensions for the over-70s, which reduced the threat of the workhouse for the old. Labour exchanges followed in 1909, and a limited national insurance scheme was introduced in 1911. These measures followed a string of detailed reports revealing inner city poverty by leading sociologists like former shipping magnate Charles Booth (1840–1916) and Seebohm Rowntree (1871–1954), the son of a chocolate magnate. 'A West End and an East End', wrote the American journalist Jack London (1876–1916) in 1902, '...one end is riotous and rotten, the other end sickly and underfed'.

1913
DEATH OF EMILY DAVISON

The leading suffragette Emily Davison (1872–1913) received eight prison sentences in her militant battle for women's votes, and was force-fed 49 times. The Women's Social and Political Union (WSPU) had been founded in 1903 by Emmeline Pankhurst (1858–1928) and her daughter Christabel (1880–1958) as a breakaway movement from the suffragists, who had been dedicated to achieving the same end through peaceful political argument. Wrapped in a WSPU banner, Emily Davison tried to grab the reigns of the king's horse as it rounded Tattenham Corner at the Epsom Derby in 1913, shouting 'Votes for Women!'. She died later of her injuries, and 10 bands and 2,000 women supporters followed her coffin at her funeral.

p. 103◀ **Distant Voices** ▶p. 107

What is our task? To make Britain a fit country for heroes to live in.

David Lloyd George (1945)

▲ *As men left their jobs to fight the War, their places were taken by women, in the first step towards female emancipation.*

War and Depression
1915–37

IN FOUR SHORT YEARS, the First World War put life in Britain through one of its most traumatic social transformations, leaving it poorer by a whole generation of men, plunging the economy into depression, undermining conventions and re-defining the relationship between the sexes. After playing their part in the war effort, organising voluntary schemes, tending to the wounded at the front, working in almost every profession, it no longer seemed tenable to exclude women from voting. By 1919, Britain's first woman MP – Nancy Astor – had taken her seat in Parliament. It was a time of new informalities, and suburban living, with many families owning homes and cars for the first time. For others grinding unemployment was their lot.

1915
THE SINKING OF THE *LUSITANIA*

The sinking by a German U-boat of the transatlantic liner *Lusitania* in 1915 helped bring the US into the war, but it also brought to a head the intolerance among the public who were cut off from the realities of war on the Western Front. After the sinking, an angry mob stormed through the East End of London, smashing shops with German-sounding names. Busy-bodies handed out white feathers – indicating cowardice – to men not wearing uniform; one particularly notorious government propaganda film, *Once a Hun, Always a Hun*, urged people not to trade with Germans after the war. 'Refuse to be served by an Austrian or German waiter,' said one advertisement in the *Daily Mail*. 'If your waiter says he is Swiss, ask to see his passport.'

1916
CONSCRIPTION

Compulsory military service divided the ruling Liberals, but before the Military Service Act of 1916, the New Army of Lord Kitchener (1850–1916) relied on volunteers, 2.25 million of which came forward. At the outbreak of war, so many men came forward at Great Scotland Yard that the duty officer took 20 minutes just to reach his desk. It was not enough: British men in the armed forces reached a peak of 5.3 million. The 16,000 conscientious objectors were screened by local tribunals, and 41 were condemned to death by the military – but imprisoned instead after a political outcry, joining the 6,000 others who spent some time in prison for the same reason. The public was extremely hostile to them, but influential figures like the philosopher Bertrand Russell (1872–1970) supported their cause.

◀ *Lord Kitchener, whose 'New Army' at the start of the War, relied on volunteers.*

⌘ 1916
WOMEN BUS CONDUCTORS

The shortage of men on the home front meant that women were beginning to fill roles which would have been unthinkable for them a few years before. Women became bus conductors from 1916, housemaids fled their jobs to go into factories – with as many as 900,000 women in the munitions factories by the end of the war – and the number of women working in banks multiplied by seven in the same period. Others played prominent roles in wartime voluntary organisations, distributing 12 million bandages, 16 million books and 232 million cigarettes to the troops. These new roles changed women's fashions for ever, leading to shorter skirts – 15 cm (6 in) above the ground – and by 1916 the brassiere was beginning to replace the old-fashioned camisole.

1918
MARRIED LOVE

A war babies scare in 1915 emphasised the changing relations between the sexes because of the war. Women were working, smoking and eating out alone, middle class chaperones were becoming obsolete, and the *Daily Mail* was attacking a new hedonism among young people. Illegitimacy rates were up 30 per cent by 1918, but contraception was also increasingly common. By the end of the war, every village chemist was selling condoms, one in 10 men were using them and in 1919 the first successful diaphragms were sold. At the forefront of the revolution was Marie Stopes (1880–1958), whose 1918 books *Married Love* and *Wise Parenthood* had openly discussed contraception and sold 700,000 copies. She opened the first birth control clinic in the country in 1921.

1919
THE HOUSING ACT

The ideal of a 'land fit for heroes to live in' was given added impetus by the obvious health of American and Australian troops compared to their under-nourished comrades from the British cities – then the 1919 influenza epidemic killed another 150,000. The post-war coalition government concentrated on education and housing, raising the school leaving age to 14, and passing the Housing and Town Planning Act steered through Parliament by Christopher Addison (1869–1951). Local authorities were told to survey local housing needs – in Glasgow, one in five families were still living in one room – and put forward building plans for subsidy. Although both education and housing suffered under the Geddes Axe (1922), the principle of council housing was set.

1920
THE UNKNOWN SOLDIER

In an out-pouring of national grief in 1920, the Unknown Soldier was buried in Westminster Abbey, and the Cenotaph – designed by Sir Edwin Lutyens (1869–1944) – was unveiled in Whitehall. With nearly a million British Empire deaths and over two million wounded, barely a family remained untouched by the war. By 1922, 900,000 war pensions were being paid out; six years later, 65,000 shell-shock victims were still in mental hospitals. A revulsion against jingoism spread through the country as the true horrors became apparent, described in the bleak war paintings of Paul Nash (1899-1946) and the writing of Robert Graves (1895–1985) and a determination that peace-time should be better. 'We cannot return to the old ways, the old abuses, the old stupidities,' said Lloyd George.

▲ *Westminster Abbey, the site of the tomb of the Unknown Soldier.*

1931
THE MEANS TEST

Unlike competitor countries, Britain faced mass unemployment right through the 1920s and into the Great Depression, reaching a peak of 22.5 million in 1932. It was a period of deep poverty in the industrial cities, and disastrous labour relations leading to the General Strike in 1926 and the Jarrow March of 1936. The Means Test was an emergency measure introduced by the National government in the Autumn of 1931, applying to anyone receiving unemployment benefit beyond the statutory six months. Claimants had to be checked by the Public Assistance Committees, which had taken over from the Poor Law Guardians, who took all income, savings, gifts or furniture into account, thereby causing great bitterness. By January 1931, 180,000 had been denied unemployment insurance.

1937
THE FIRST MOTOR SHOW

While the old economy based on coal and steel was in depression, a new economy – cars, aeroplanes, chemicals, plastics, wireless sets and artificial fibres – was moving into metroland. Hire purchase agreements multiplied 20-fold from 1919 to 1939, and so did the number of cars on the road. Driving tests began in 1934 and the first Motor Show was held in Olympia in 1937. This was the period of speculative building of semi-detached homes, available for £500, and built along the new bypasses known as 'ribbon development'. With its new commuter suburbs like Hendon, Morden and Wembley, London grew to a peak population of eight million, and the millionth Morris car rolled off the assembly line at their Cowley works in Oxford just before the outbreak of war in 1939.

p. 105◀ **Distant Voices** ▶p. 109

The third England, I concluded, was the new post-war England, belonging far more to the age itself than to this particular island. America, I supposed, was its real birthplace. This is the England of arterial and by-pass roads, of filling stations and factories that look like exhibition buildings, of giant cinemas and dance-halls and cafes, bungalows with tiny garages, cocktail bars, Woolworths, motor-coaches, wireless, hiking, factory girls looking like actresses, greyhound racing and dirt tracks, swimming pools and everything given away for cigarette coupons.

J. B. Priestley, describing the new generation, *English Journey* (1934)

The Home Front

1939–42

IF THE FIRST WORLD WAR began to undermine distinctions between the classes, the Second World War took the process very much further, as rich and poor alike found themselves on the front line – each with their own identity cards and ration books. One volunteer bomb disposal squad, killed defusing their 35th bomb in May 1941, consisted of the Earl of Suffolk, his chauffeur and his secretary. Bombing did not result in the expected breakdown of morale, any more than it did in Germany under Allied bombing, but it had a devastating effect on property, health and sanity. As the war progressed, there was increasing interest in the kind of society after victory, driven on by the Beveridge Report and culminating in the Labour general election victory in 1945.

1939
CONSCRIPTION AGAIN

Conscription began again in May 1939 after Germany's annexation of Czechoslovakia. Four months after war began, all men aged between 19 and 41 were called up, but by 1943 conscription had been extended as far as unmarried women between the ages of 18 and 50 – who were required to work on the land or in the factories. By 1944, there were 500,000 women in the forces, 200,000 in the Women's Land Army and over 300,000 working in the civil service. Up to 60,000 people applied to be conscientious objectors; 5,000 of them were prosecuted and most of those sent to prison. But there was little bitterness against them this time because it was obvious that civilians were also in the front line: before September 1941, it was more dangerous to be a British civilian than a soldier.

1939
THE START OF ITMA

The BBC had been broadcasting since 1922, and under the dour control of Sir John Reith (1889–1971) until 1938, it became a rigorously respectable organisation where announcers were expected to wear evening dress before addressing the microphones. At the outbreak of war, the BBC's experimental television broadcasts were shut down, but wireless really came of age. Listeners tuned into the Home Service, the news on the BBC's European Service – broadcasting in 36 languages to occupied Europe – and one in six even listened regularly to the Nazi propagandist Lord Haw-Haw (William Joyce, 1906–46), broadcasting from Bremen. But it was the BBC's comedy show ITMA (*It's That Man Again*) that really caught the public's imagination, and held it from 1939 to the death of its main star Tommy Handley in 1949.

1939
EVACUATION

To avoid air attack, the government planned to evacuate urban children – and sometimes their mothers and teachers – to safety in the countryside. In the event, 1.5 million went – more than had been planned for. Another two million left of their own accord, but by early 1940, a million had returned home to the cities. A second wave followed when the Blitz began later that year. There were problems from the start, such as providing evacuees with country shoes and warm clothing. The arrival of slum children was a revelation for the better-off homes they stayed in, and helped to increase support for a post-war welfare state. Some government departments also left London, including part of the Admiralty which moved to Bath.

1940
THE START OF RATIONING

German U-boats were already threatening food supplies, and food rationing began in 1940. It was based on a formula related to people's nutritional requirements, and covered butter, bacon and sugar. Its first effect

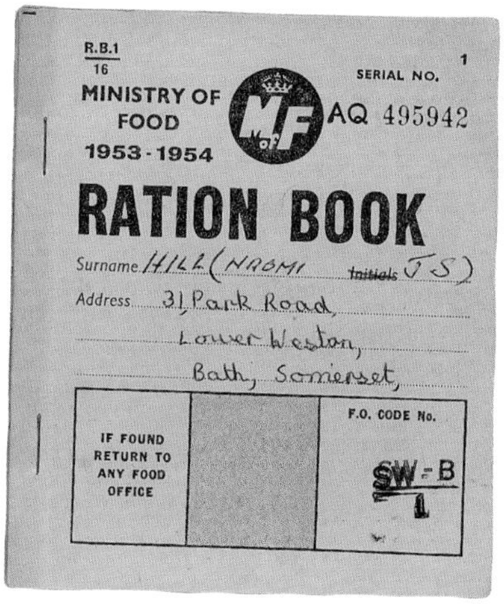
R.B.1
16
MINISTRY OF FOOD
1953-1954
SERIAL NO. 1
AQ 495942
RATION BOOK
Surname HILL (NAOMI   Initials J S)
Address 31, Park Road,
Lower Weston,
Bath, Somerset,
IF FOUND RETURN TO ANY FOOD OFFICE
F.O. CODE No.
SW-B
1

▼ *As city children were evacuated, the country people who took them in were forced to realise the appalling conditions endured by many in the cities.*

was to raise food consumption, because people liked to buy their whole ration. Meat was also rationed soon after, followed by most other foods except for bread and potatoes, under direction of the food minister Lord Woolton (1883–1964), the former chairman of John Lewis. Clothes rationing began in 1941, leading to the government campaign, urging people to 'Make do and Mend' and to the simple 'utility' look, designed by Norman Hartnell (1901–78). School meals doubled early in the war and became a social service, canteen eating was encouraged, and so was the campaign to 'Dig for Victory'.

1940
THE HOME GUARD

The Home Guard was launched by Winston Churchill (1874–1965) within days of his taking office in May 1940. Starting as the Local Defence Volunteers, it changed its name to the Home Guard in July. Members were exempt from military service, because of their age or occupation, and came to symbolise Britain's determination to resist invasion. Although the Home Guard reached a peak of 1.6 million in 1942, it was almost unarmed in its early months. Nazi propagandists reported gleefully about old soldiers doing drill with broom handles and the desperate radio appeals for shotguns. The force was never called into action, though they did man anti-aircraft guns during the Blitz, and were eventually disbanded at the end of 1944.

1940
OPERATION SEALION

The Nazi invasion of Britain was continually postponed through the autumn of 1940, as the German Luftwaffe battled for control of the skies. But elaborate precautions were put in place in case the invaders arrived, an event which was to be heralded by the ringing of church bells; indeed they did ring before the expected invasion on September 8. Iron railings had already been removed for the war effort, and from May 1940, all signposts, station nameboards, memorial placenames and milestones were also removed. Concrete blocks and pill-boxes appeared at crossings, anti-glider arches on main roads, and open spaces were filled with bits of old machinery to deter parachutists. The leaflet *If the Invader Comes* was distributed to every household in June, urging them to 'stay put'.

p. 104◀ **Triumphs & Tragedies** ▶p. 113

1940
DESTRUCTION FROM THE SKIES

The expected aerial deluge from the Germans over Britain did not happen for almost a year after the outbreak of war. A black-out was enforced immediately and car headlights banned – deaths on the road doubled during the first month of the war. When it came in 1940, the Blitz was a military failure for the Germans but caused enormous damage to cities – especially London, Liverpool, Manchester, Sheffield and Coventry. More raids followed in 1942, and the V-rocket raids in 1944. 60,000 civilians were killed during the war and 200,000 houses destroyed. People broke into underground stations for shelter at first, and this became institutionalised, though even at the height of the Blitz, six out of 10 people slept at home.

1942
THE BEVERIDGE REPORT

A month after the Battle of El Alamein, the influential report was published by the Liberal economist Sir William Beveridge (1879–1963). It was to become a blueprint for the post-war 'welfare state' – a term coined by the radical Archbishop of Canterbury, William Temple (1881–1944). Beveridge set out a national insurance scheme designed to banish what he called the 'five giants': want, disease, ignorance, squalor and idleness. It caught the imagination of the public, was widely discussed by ordinary servicemen, and sold 635,000 copies. A sceptical government proceeded with the battle against ignorance in the form of free secondary education for all, as outlined in the 1944 Education Act, steered through Parliament by R. A. Butler (1902–82).

▲ *Cities across Europe suffered extensive damage through aerial raids during the Second World War.*

p. 107◀ **Distant Voices** ▶p. 111

Just before darkness fell we took the chairs down to the dugout, and as we came back our two guests arrived, very thankful to come out again for a night's sleep. We left them to chat to Kate while we had supper, and when Kate came in with a khaki rice pudding (made from condensed milk and queer!) and damsons she said sirens had sounded a quarter of an hour before. We had not heard them, but we listened and heard the first plane – or perhaps second or third – over and decided to finish our meal and wait a while before descending. Soon we heard the big guns pounding 'pom-pom', so got into our warm things and came down, while Kate decided to stay with our guests and get under the stairs if necessary.

Clara Milburn's diary, living outside Coventry (26 October 1940)

Never Had It So Good

1946–59

'LET'S BE FRANK ABOUT IT,' said prime minister Harold Macmillan in a speech in Bedford in July 1957, 'most of our people have never had it so good.' The phrase was borrowed from the 1952 election slogan by the Democrats in the USA, and passed into the language, because it struck a chord. Three years after the end of food rationing people were increasingly better off, and the new welfare state seemed to be taking the edge off poverty. It was a period of great optimism and increasing consumerism, as more households saved up the money needed for a car, washing machine and other labour-saving devices. The Diners Club launched the first credit card in 1950, and – apart from the shadow of the Cold War – everything seemed possible.

✚ ▶ p. 114

1946
THE NATIONAL HEALTH SERVICE

Free medical service was passed by the Labour government in 1946, after difficult negotiations with the medical profession conducted by health minister Aneurin Bevan (1897–1960), fulfilling some of the objectives of the Beveridge Report. It was believed that demands on the NHS would reduce as people became healthier, but the opposite was the case – and by the 1970s it was the biggest employer in Europe. Bevan resigned in protest at the introduction of charges for dentures and spectacles, due to financial pressure during the Korean War in 1951. The NHS was part of the new welfare state, which included comprehensive national insurance and a National Assistance Act which meant that neighbours were no longer responsible for the poor.

▼ *As free medical treatment became available for all on the NHS, so waiting lists grew.*

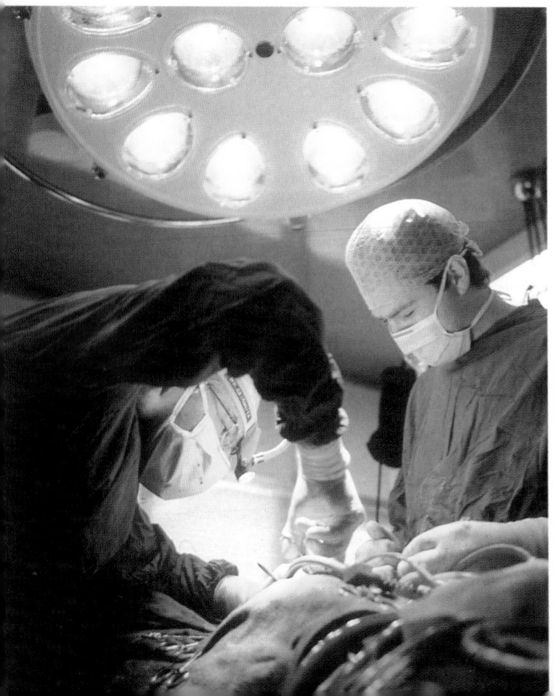

1947
AUSTERITY

The conditions for renewing the US war loans proved impossible to meet, and with reserves dangerously low, Labour's Chancellor of the Exchequer Sir Stafford Cripps (1889–1952) was forced to tax and ration above wartime levels, and shift domestic production towards exports to earn hard currency, leading to the drastic devaluation of the pound in 1949. Bread was rationed from 1946–48, potatoes in 1947 and sweets and other food stayed rationed until 1954. The policy was successful economically but disastrous politically, contributing to Labour's election defeat in 1951. Petrol rationing ended in 1950, but the Austerity period led to a widespread black market: that same year, the liner *Franconia* was found to be carrying smuggled nylon stockings worth £80,000.

✂ ▶ p. 112

1947
THE NEW LOOK

The New Look dresses emerged after the coldest winter in Europe for 40 years, launched in Paris by the French designer Christian Dior (1905–57). Designers turned their backs on the utility looks of the war, designing garments with padded shoulders, low waists and sumptuous billowing skirts. Their luxury and expensive designs flew in the face of British government Austerity recommendations about conserving cloth, and were condemned by Sir Stafford Cripps and other government officials, afraid that such extravagence would undermine policies of exporting clothes to earn badly needed foreign currency. However, it thrilled women in the year that enormous queues were regularly forming just to buy nylon stockings. So successful was it, that the New Look dominated fashion until 1954.

1948
STEVENAGE

The Uthwatt and Barlow Commissions before and during the war were adamant that the cities were over-crowded and polluted, and so was the influential report on the future of London by Sir Patrick Abercrombie (1879–1957). The 1945 Labour government responded with the New Towns Act 1946. By 1948 they had set up green belts around the major cities to stop them spreading further, and designated the sites for eight new towns around London to house 'overspill' population in homes with gardens, separated from polluting industries where classes would be mixed. The first such town was Stevenage in Hertfordshire, and more followed in Scotland and northern England. The 29th and final new town – Milton Keynes in Buckinghamshire – was designated in 1967.

1951
THE HOUSING PROMISE

With homelessness and widespread squatting by angry families at epidemic proportions after the war, the government of Clement Attlee (1883–1967) offered local authorities a subsidy of £16 10s per house built. The result was 900,000 new homes by 1951, less than their promised 240,000 a year. The new Conservative housing minister Harold Macmillan (1894–1986) promised 300,000 – later 400,000 – and made his political reputation by achieving it. He did so by removing some building controls, raising subsidies, and ending the need for private licences to build homes. By 1957, 1.5 million homes had been built, opening a disastrous period of subsidised homes through the 1960s. These were sometimes system built, often high-rise, and were so unpopular with tenants that by the 1980s many were being demolished.

1953
THE CORONATION OF ELIZABETH II

The coronation of Elizabeth II (b. 1926) in 1953 was a sumptuous affair, marking the end of the Austerity years and the beginning of the television age, building on the popular success of the Festival of Britain two years before. Although it rained throughout, TV pictures of the 25-year-old queen excited a sense that the country was on the verge of a second Elizabethan age – enhanced when the news was released the same day that a British team had become the first to conquer Mount Everest. It also marked the beginning of a period when the monarchy would have to respond increasingly to media coverage, often intrusive, with a greater openness about the workings of the royal household.

▼ *As Britain crowned its new queen, Edmund Hillary and his team reached the top of Everest.*

◀ *The coronation of Queen Elizabeth II drew huge television audiences for the first time, as well as widespread celebrations around the country.*

1958
THE NOTTING HILL RIOTS

Given the right to settle in Britain under the 1948 British Nationality Act, the first immigrants from the new Commonwealth arrived in Britain that same year on the liner *Empire Windrush*. They included 492 new arrivals from Jamaica. It was the latest in a series of waves of immigration to British cities which stretches back centuries. London Transport had a deliberate policy of recruiting West Indians, while Asians often found themselves in the clothing industry, particularly in east London and Bradford. Integration was occasionally difficult, and tensions led to serious rioting in 1958 in Nottingham and London's Notting Hill; but in spite of the occasional pessimistic predictions, race never became the central issue it had become in the USA.

1959
THE MINI

Car designer Sir Alec Issigonis (1906–88) launched his Mini in 1959, shaving the length of the car by mounting the engine crossways. It was an immediate success, the summit of the 1950s consumer boom, and its design has remained essentially unchanged ever since. By 1961, a million Morris Minor saloons – Issigonis' previous creation – had been bought and 800 supermarkets had opened. As many as 32 per cent of households owned a car and 16 per cent had fridges. The writer J. B. Priestley (1894–1984) coined the phrase 'admass' in 1955 – the year TV advertising began in the UK – to describe the increasing proliferation of consumer advertising and high-pressure selling. But there was something essentially British about the Mini: 'We think Lancias are the kind of cars hairdressers drive,' said actor Michael Caine in its defence.

p. 109◀ **Distant Voices** ▶p. 113

It used to be fun, Dad and old Mum,
Paddling down Southend
But now it ain't done, never mind
chum,
Paris is where we spend out outings.
Grandma's trying to shock us all
Doing knees-up rock an' roll
Fings ain't what they used to be.

Lionel Bart, *Fings Ain't What They Used to Be* (1959)

The Swinging Age
1959–78

WHEN THE 1960 PROSECUTION of Penguin Books for publishing D. H. Lawrence's novel *Lady Chatterley's Lover* collapsed, it seemed to mark the start of a more permissive age. But 1960s Britain, with its youth culture, protests and its relative economic comfort, ran up against the disappointments of the 1970s, where inflation and the energy crisis sapped the confidence of the country, and people flirted with private armies and the breakdown of civilisation. Post-war hope came up against the intractability of Britain's social and economic problems. Even so, the country had never been richer, better educated, more mobile and healthier, and – after the success of the Clean Air Acts – cleaner, though the inexorable rise of motor traffic threatened to spoil it.

1959
THE FIRST MOTORWAY

Prior to the opening of the M1 in 1959, Britain had been the only country in western Europe, apart from Switzerland, not to have a comprehensive motorway system. It was soon making up for lost time, and the transformation was very fast: most 1950s homes were built without garages, but the number of cars on the roads doubled between 1958 and 1965 to about nine million – and continued to grow rapidly, undermining the progress on smoke control achieved in the 1950s and '60s. By the 1970s, the first experiments in town centre pedestrianisation were taking place, but the growth of the car seemed unstoppable. The 1963 report by British Rail chairman Richard Beeching (1913–90), led to one third of Britain's railway stations being cut, and by the 1990s, 90 per cent of freight goods had been shifted onto the roads.

1964
BBC2

The BBC's director-general throughout the 1960s, Sir Hugh Greene (1910–87), promised to aim the corporation 'right into the centre of the swirling forces that were changing life in Britain'. It was in the 1960s that TV began to play its central role in British life, witnessed by the televised coverage of the World Cup final (1966) and the first man on the moon (1969). Apart from the introduction of colour television in 1967, it was the 1964 launch of the BBC's second channel – the 'highbrow' BBC2 – which set the pace for the TV decade, launching three weeks after the pirate radio station Radio Caroline. Cinema-going halved from 1971–84, and average Britons were soon approaching their current daily average of more than three hours of TV every day.

1965
THE MINI-SKIRT

The fashion designer Mary Quant (b. 1934) had been running her Bazaar shop in London's King's Road since 1955, but it was a decade later that she developed the item of clothing, the mini-skirt, which came to symbolise the decade – reaching its shortest in 1967–68. The mini-skirt stood for a new generation of women, modelled by a new generation of achingly thin models, and helped make the King's Road the centre for fashion in the Beatles and hippy eras (although it was briefly overtaken by London's Carnaby Street). With the emergence of people like Quant and the Beatles, fashion, music and youth culture rapidly became among Britain's main export earnings – a trend which has continued into the 1990s.

▶ *The mini-skirt was the fashion item of the 1960s, designed by Mary Quant.*

1969
THE DIVORCE ACT

Commentators differ about the beginning of the so-called 'permissive society'. Did it begin with legalising suicide in 1959, ending conscription in 1960, or legalising abortion and homosexuality in 1967 under the regime of Labour home secretary Roy Jenkins (b. 1920)? The Sexual Offences Act only legalised homosexuality between consenting adults over 21 in private, and only for England and Wales, but it was part of a string of legal changes that changed the moral atmosphere of Britain. Others included the introduction of the contraceptive pill, the abolition of the death penalty and the reduction of the voting age to 18. The most influential, however, was probably the 1969 Divorce Act, which allowed fault-free divorce after the 'irretrievable breakdown' of the marriage. The divorce rate has risen steadily ever since.

1969
THE SALE OF THE *NEWS OF THE WORLD*

The left-leaning *Daily Mirror* was the top-selling newspaper in Britain in 1960,

▲ *The Australian media-magnate Rupert Murdoch.*

developing a whole new language of journalism to popularise issues. But it was the arrival of the Australian press-magnate Rupert Murdoch (b. 1931) which developed tabloid journalism in its present form – part comic, part magazine, part picture paper, with minimal news content. He bought the *News of the World* in 1969, followed quickly by the ailing trade union paper the *Sun,* which he turned into a tabloid. Most of the other national newspapers followed this style; all of them except the *Mirror* and later *Today* leaning to the right, which was widely regarded as having contributed to the election victory of Margaret Thatcher (b. 1925) in 1979. By 1981, Murdoch also owned *The Times.*

1971
OPEN UNIVERSITY

A modern economy needed more higher education, said the Robbins Report of 1963, recommending a target of 60 universities in Britain by 1980. They never reached it, but universities like East Anglia, Essex, Lancaster, Sussex, Warwick and York all received charters in the 1960s, and by 1972 there were 45 – plus a growing sector of polytechnics, which themselves became universities in 1993. The number of students had doubled in a decade, and many were ready to play a leading role in the ferment of 1960s youth politics. The Open University was a scheme of prime minister Harold Wilson's (1916-95), and used radio, television and correspondence courses to take university education to adults at home. Its innovative techniques have been copied all over the world.

1978
THE WINTER OF DISCONTENT

The attempt by Labour minister Barbara Castle (b. 1910) to control growing trade union power, outlined in the white paper *In Place of Strife,* was defeated by the cabinet and TUC in 1969. By 1975, a Gallup poll voted the general-secretary of the Transport and General Workers Union Jack Jones (b. 1913) as the most powerful person in the country. By 1978, relations between the government and unions had broken down completely over a five per cent pay limit announced by the government of James Callaghan (b. 1912), and a number of key trade unions went on strike. The impact of the strikes was made worse by the severe winter, and the experience paved the way for the anti-trade union legislation of the Thatcher government, which took office in 1979.

▲ *Sussex University, one of the few establishments to receive a charter in the 1960s.*

p. 109◀ **Triumphs & Tragedies** ▶p. 122

1968
THE COLLAPSE OF RONAN POINT

A small explosion in the 22-storey Ronan Point flats in east London brought part of the block collapsing like a pack of cards. The public inquiry that followed found that a 97 kph (60 mph) wind could have done the same. So, although 1968 was the peak year for flat-building – 400,000 were finished – Ronan Point spelled the effective end of high-rise flats. People were leaving the cities instead: London lost half a million people during the 1970s, while both Liverpool and Glasgow lost a third of their population from 1951–81. Having already lost half its woodlands since the war, southern England was the main destination for ex-Londoners. 'The maps of population change in the 1980s are almost the precise inverse of those of the 1880s,' wrote the geographer Peter Hall.

p. 111◀ **Distant Voices** ▶p. 115

Sexual intercourse began
In nineteen sixty-three
(Which was rather late for me) –
Between the end of the Chatterley ban
And the Beatles' first LP.
Up till then there's only been
A sort of bargaining,
A wrangle for a ring,
A shame that started at sixteen
And spread to everything.

Philip Larkin, *Annus Mirabilis*
(16 June 1967)

The Computer Age
1981–96

DISCOVERY OF NORTH SEA OIL changed the nature of the British economy completely by forcing up the value of the pound to make British manufacturing expensive abroad. The epic Miners' Strike of 1984–85 confirmed the change. Britain was becoming a service economy instead of a manufacturing one. But the real changes in post-war society are apparent from the changes in the government's basket of essential goods used to work out the rate of inflation. In 1947, these included radios, bicycles and custard powder. In the 1950s, rabbits and candles were dropped for brown bread and washing machines. The 1970s added yoghurt and duvets, the 1980s oven-ready meals and video tapes, and the 1990s microwave ovens and camcorders.

1981
BRIXTON RIOTS

A misunderstanding in Brixton in April 1981 was all that was needed to unleash the most destructive riot in Britain since the war. Later in the summer, riots in Southall, Toxteth and a series of copycat disturbances around the country followed. There was only one death – a disabled man run down by a police van in Toxteth on the day of the royal wedding – but a combination of tension between police and the black community, plus youth unemployment, exploded to shift government attention on to the inner cities. A report by the Church of England in 1986, after a second Brixton riot in 1985, urged action to tackle social disintegration. Even the Prince of Wales (b. 1948) spoke publicly about his fears of 'inheriting a divided kingdom'.

1982
THE START OF THE HERITAGE INDUSTRY

Wigan Pier was the centre of a searing 1930s indictment of social conditions by George Orwell (1903–50), but in 1982 Wigan Council resurrected the memory by developing eight acres of derelict industrial land as the Wigan Heritage Centre, including the Orwell Pub and Pier Shop, selling Victorian perfume and model miners' lamps. The centre marked the beginning of the heritage industry which became one of the buzz-words of the 1980s, attracting 30,000 visitors in its first year – to a town with more derelict land than any other in England. By the mid-1980s, more people in Wales were working in the new heritage industry than in the old mainstays of coal and steel – often dressed as working people representing the very industries which had laid them off.

1985
STANSTED AIRPORT

Most manual workers were getting three weeks paid holiday a year by 1971, and increasingly people were swapping their traditional holidays in Britain with package tours abroad – organised by the rapidly multiplying tour operators in the Mediterranean or beyond. Heathrow Airport opened in 1946, the result of a late government requisition in 1944, and was soon supplemented by Gatwick. The long process of choosing a site for the third London airport ended in 1985 with the decision to develop Stansted in Essex. By 1993, British people were taking 23 million foreign holidays a year, and over 130 million passengers were travelling through British airports – a third of them through over-crowded Heathrow, now the busiest airport in the world.

✚ 1986
THE AIDS PUBLICITY CAMPAIGN

Margaret Thatcher came to power in 1979 promising that the NHS was 'safe with us', but the strains were beginning to show. Although smoking was on the decline and inoculation was defeating the old diseases,

▲ *Awareness of AIDS and HIV was heightened by a government campaign and public demonstrations.*

the stresses of modern life and the progress of medical science were taking their toll on NHS funding at a time when successive governments were trying to squeeze public spending. The arrival of Aids in 1981 highlighted the problem: fearing an epidemic, the government launched an unprecedented public information campaign in 1986. The epidemic never happened, and the impact of Aids was blunted by an expensive cocktail of drugs.

1988
THE GREEN CONSUMER GUIDE

By the mid-1990s, 10 times as many people were members of environmental organisations than political parties, and by far the most influential recruit to the movement was Prince Charles. It was he who persuaded Margaret Thatcher to declare herself a 'friend of the earth' in 1988, the year before the Green Party's success in the European elections. The movement continued to be influential on government and business policy, but it was the publication of *The Green Consumer Guide*, demonstrating that up to a third of shoppers were prepared to pay more for environment-friendly products, which propelled the movement into the mainstream. Violent protests over the M3 extension (1996) and the Newbury bypass (1997) were also influential in the development of transport policies.

1990
THE STRANGEWAYS RIOT

The prison riot at Strangeways in Manchester in 1990, when inmates took control of the building for 25 days, was a symbolic moment in the growth of crime – a continuing story since the 1960s. Recorded crimes mushroomed from 2.7 million a year in 1980 to a peak of 5.6 million in 1992 in England and Wales; the peak of 590,000 a year came earlier in Scotland in 1991. Most crimes are traditionally committed by young men – 80 per cent by men under 35 – so the shrinking population of teenagers was beginning to feed through into better figures. But because of an enthusiasm for prison as a solution among successive home secretaries, the prison over-crowding crisis continued.

1995
THE LAUNCH OF MONDEX

The launch in Swindon of Mondex – the computerised money system developed by NatWest, Midland and BT – was a sign of the growth of information technology in every area of British life. The first cashpoint in Britain was opened by Barclays in Enfield in 1967, but the wide distribution of credit cards in the 1980s also changed the way people used money, as well as contributing to a total of over £500 billion in personal debt. Computer technology filtered into UK homes and offices, taking off in the mid-1990s with the arrival of the internet. By 1998, as much as seven per cent of the UK population had access to it – and this figure is rising at a rate of 75 per cent every year, with 250,000 online shopping transactions taking place every month.

1996
THE ROYAL DIVORCE

The divorce of the Prince and Princess of Wales in 1996 was one of the most public estrangements of all time, after their wedding had been seen by record numbers around the world in 1981. It fuelled the growing debate about the future of the British monarchy, but it also provided a mirror to the British people – who were divorcing faster than any other European country apart from Denmark. The increase in the divorce rate had widespread implications for planning and welfare. As many as 10 per cent of households were headed by a single parent, and a quarter contained just one person – twice as many as 1961. The result was growing isolation and a prediction of 4.4 million new homes needed for southern England.

◀ *A prisoner on the roof of Strangeways Prison during the riots of 1990.*

▼ *Cashpoints have become a familiar sight in high streets all over Britain since the launch of Mondex.*

p. 113 ◀ **Distant Voices** ▶ p. 119

Imagine all the American architects with their psychological training taking the little English planners out to lunch. Imagine Evening Standard *readers commuting 250 miles every day. Imagine faxes tripping down wires; currency dealers being measured for suits at their workstations. Imagine rows of unregistered BMWs and Porches, prowling VAT men, armed policemen, thousands of tourists each making a feature video, freelance wheel clampers, sponsored litter bins; one-room flats at £1,000 a week. Imagine all this in London and then wake up in a cold sweat. Get me a lawyer!*

Architecture critic Martin Pawley, on the 1980s boom, *Blueprint* magazine (June 1988)

Britain in the World

AT SOME POINT IN prehistoric times, the British Isles parted company from the mainland of Europe. Not only did this make invasions of Britain far more difficult, but it also, in the long run, turned the British away from Europe to look elsewhere in the world. In AD 43, Britain became very much a part of Europe, as a province of the Roman Empire. In 1066 Britain became part of a European empire once again, but from 1453, British interests were increasingly diverted elsewhere. For more than 500 years Britain avoided permanent contact with Europe, although there were many occasions when Britain formed alliances with continental powers and many other occasions when Britain intervened decisively in European affairs. Instead, Britain created a vast empire, with possessions scattered throughout then-known world. In 1961 the wheel began to turn full circle. Britain applied for the membership of the EEC. Although she was not admitted until 1973, ties with Europe have grown stronger ever since. In an age when Imperialism has been rejected, Britain has once again become part of the European community in a more complete sense than at any time since the Roman Empire.

KEY THEMES

- CONQUEST
- VICTORIES
- HEROES
- MONARCHS
- EMPIRES
- EXPLORATION
- WAR
- TRADE
- POLITICS
- AGREEMENTS

KEY EVENTS

1 AD 43
THE CLAUDIAN INVASION

In AD 43 the Romans invaded Britain. After being held up at the Medway in Kent, the army crossed the Thames and closed in on Colchester. Once victory was in sight, Claudius hurried from Rome with a band of elephants to lead his army in triumph.

2 AD 410
THE WITHDRAWAL OF THE LEGIONS

In the fourth and early fifth centuries a number of emperors were proclaimed by the British legions and attempted to march on Rome. None was successful. In the meantime the province of Britain continued to be prosperous and remained so long after the last legionaries were recalled to Rome in AD 410 by the Emperor Honorius.

3 1066
THE BATTLE OF HASTINGS

King Harold advanced to meet William of Normandy at Hastings in 1066. On 14 October the English army was defeated at Hastings and Harold was killed. On 25 December William was crowned king of England in Westminster Abbey.

4 1485
THE END OF THE HUNDRED YEARS' WAR

Defeat in the Hundred Years' War turned English attention inwards. For the next 30 years the barons of England fought over the succession to the crown. A struggle that was only decided when Richard III was defeated and killed by Henry VII at the battle of Bosworth Field in August 1485.

5 1588
THE DEFEAT OF THE SPANISH ARMADA

On the night of 27 July 1588, Drake attacked the Spanish fleet with fireships; many cut their anchor cables in order to escape. On 29 July the only full-scale battle was fought between the demoralised Spanish and the triumphant English. The remnants of the Armada then fled north and returned to Spain around the north coast of Scotland.

6 1763
THE TREATY OF PARIS

At the Treaty of Paris in 1763 France agreed to withdraw from Canada and to reduce her interests in India to a purely commercial basis. Cuba was returned to Spain in exchange for Florida. In the West Indies Grenada, St Vincent, Dominica and Tobago were retained by Britain, but Martinique and Guadeloupe were returned.

7 1815
THE BATTLE OF WATERLOO

The Prussian army arrived at Waterloo and fell on the flank of the French. Wellington ordered a general advance and the French army disintegrated. It marked the end of the Napoleonic Wars. Napoleon fled and surrendered to a British warship. He was exiled to St Helena and never returned.

8 1940
DUNKIRK

As the BEF crowded onto the beaches of two ports at Dunkirk, the Royal Navy attempted to rescue the force. 310,000 British troops were rescued from the beaches, although almost all their equipment was lost.

TIMELINE

50 BC Julius Caesar carries out the conquest of Gaul
1 **AD 43** Emperor Claudius invades and conquers Britain
2 **AD 410** Last Roman legionaries leave British Isles
3 **1066** Harold killed at Battle of Hastings
1189 Richard the Lionheart becomes king and leaves for Third Crusade
1214 King John loses empire in France to Philip II of France
1272 Henry III succeeded by Edward I
1333 Edward III invades France to claim the French throne
1346 Edward III defeats the French army at the Battle of Crécy
1415 Battle of Agincourt
4 **1485** End of the Hundred Years' War
1553 Mary Tudor becomes queen
1558 Elizabeth I becomes Queen
1577 Drake circumnavigates the globe
5 **1588** Defeat of the Spanish Armada
1600 British East India Company established
1689 Start of second Hundred Years' War
1756 Start of the Seven Years' War
6 **1763** Treaty of Paris signed
1768 Captain Cook embarks on his first voyage of discovery
1788 Penal colony established at Botony Bay
1789 Storming of the Bastille; French Revolution begins
1801 Nelson destroys Danish fleet in Copenhagen
1805 Battle of Trafalgar
1808 Peninsular War
7 **1815** Battle of Waterloo; end of Napoleonic Wars
1830 Lord Palmerston becomes British foreign secretary
1831 James Ross reaches magnetic north
1836 Great Trek made by the Boers in South Africa
1840 First British colonists arrive in New Zealand
1849 David Livingstone begins exploration of Africa
1854 Crimean War begins
1857 Indian mutiny within the East India Company leads to its demise
1867 Canada established as the first Dominion
1879 War between British and Zulus in South Africa
1889 Cecil Rhodes etablishes British South Africa Company
1900 Commonwealth of Australia Act passed
1902 Captain Robert Scott begins exploration of Antarctic
1907 Signing of the Triple Entente
1914 British Expeditionary Force (BEF) sent to defend Belgium
1916 Battle of the Somme
1919 Treaty of Versailles
8 **1940** BEF rescued from the beaches of Dunkirk and Calais; Battle of Britain
1944 D-Day
1945 United Nations set up
1947 India and Pakistan gain independence
1956 Britain and France seize control of Suez Canal
1957 European Economic Community formed
1982 Falklands War
1990 Nelson Mandela released

A Province of Rome

55 BC–AD 410

FOR ALMOST 400 YEARS Britain was a province of the Roman Empire. It formed part of the frontier between the Roman world and the Barbarians (as the Romans called outsiders). It was a wealthy province and supplied raw materials to the empire in the form of wheat and metals. British dogs were also highly prized for hunting. But Britain's exposed position on the edge of the known world meant that there was always the risk of attack, especially when the Romans gave up their attempts to conquer the whole island. In the early third century and on a number of occasions in the fourth Britain was invaded from the north. Eventually the garrison of three Roman Legions was withdrawn by the Emperor Honorius and the Britons were left to fend for themselves.

✦ ▶ p. 120

55 BC
JULIUS CAESAR'S INVASION

In the 50s BC Julius Caesar carried out the conquest of Gaul, modern France. From the north coast the Roman legionaries could see the white cliffs of present-day Dover about 20 Roman miles away. The Romans already knew a good deal about Britain, but after the conquest of Gaul there was an extra incentive to take a closer look. Fugitives had fled to Gaul and were soon raiding the new Roman province. In 55 BC Julius Caesar decided to teach the British a lesson. He landed briefly in Kent, but returned the following year with a much larger force of four legions. He led his army in a wide sweep around London smashing the resistance of the British tribes. But having forced them to submit, he left Britain and returned to Gaul.

◀ *Julius Caesar, emperor of Rome and leader of the first raids into Britain.*

AD 43
CLAUDIUS' INVASION

In AD 43 the Romans invaded Britain again and this time they came for good. A British chieftain appealed to Rome for help in a war against Caractacus of the Catuvallauni and the emperor, Claudius, sent an army of 40,000 men. Claudius had just become emperor after the murder of his nephew Caligula in 41 and he was anxious to win a great victory. After being held up at the Medway in Kent, the army crossed the Thames and closed in on Colchester. Once victory was in sight, Claudius travelled to the British Isles to oversee the final triumph. He was only in Britain for 15 days before he returned to Rome leaving his generals to carry out the rest of the conquest.

AD 60
RESISTANCE TO ROME

The Romans soon overran all of Britain to the south-east of a line from the Severn to the Humber, but further progress proved much more difficult. The area to the north and west was more rugged and difficult. In AD 60, Suetonius Paulinus was trying to conquer Anglesey, when he heard of a serious revolt by the Iceni tribe under their queen, Boudicca. According to legend her daughters had been raped by the Romans. In response, the tribe turned on the garrison of Colchester and then rampaged through the south-east butchering thousands. Paulinus marched southeast and met Boudicca's army somewhere in the Midlands. The Roman legions held firm against the massed charges of the British and Boudicca's revolt collapsed. The queen herself committed suicide.

AD 84
AGRICOLA

In the AD 70s and 80s the Romans gradually extended their control of Britain. The most important conquests were the work of Agricola. He advanced into Scotland and built a legionary fortress at Inchtuithil. He planned to cross to Ireland and bring that under Roman control, but after he was recalled to Rome the attempts to occupy Scotland ended and Inchtuithil was abandoned. From then onwards Roman Britain was garrisoned by three legions based at York, Chester and Caerleon in south

▲ *The emperor Claudius, who finished the job begun by Caesar nearly 100 years previously, by conquering England.*

▼ *An ancient Scottish warrior with kilt, winged helmet, weapons and shield.*

Wales. For the next 200 years the Romano-British enjoyed an almost unbroken period of peace and increasing wealth. This can still be seen in the remains of a huge number of villas, which were built right across southern England from the second to the fourth centuries.

AD 122
HADRIAN'S WALL

Emperor Hadrian decided to try to stabilise the borders of the empire. Several eastern provinces were abandoned and borders were strengthened in central Europe. He also decided to build a permanent border between Britain and Scotland to the north. From AD 122 to 129, Roman soldiers constructed what came to be known as Hadrian's Wall. It was 117 km (80 Roman miles or 73 imperial miles) long, with a series of 13 forts and milecastles. Most of the structure was of stone, but the western third was turf-built. Twenty years later the Emperor Antoninus Pius pushed the frontier further north and built the Antonine Wall. Between the two walls was the huge area of southern Scotland. In 211, the Antonine Wall was abandoned once and for all and Hadrian's Wall became the permanent frontier again.

AD 193
SEPTIMIUS SEVERUS

Septimius Severus was the first African to become emperor of Rome when he succeeded in AD 193. This was at a time of considerable unrest and Septimius spent much of his time restoring order. In 205 the Scots had overrun Hadrian's Wall and invaded Britain. Septimius travelled to Britain himself, becoming the first emperor to visit the province since Claudius. He re-established imperial power in Britain and authorised the permanent withdrawal from the Antonine Wall. He died at York in 211, and was the only Roman emperor to be buried in Britain. The reign of Septimius led to a long period of peace for Britain. For the next 60 years there were constant civil wars throughout the empire, but Britain escaped the worst effects of all of them.

AD 367
DECLINE OF THE SAXON SHORE

At the beginning of the fourth century the Roman Empire began to be attacked by tribes from northern Europe. Britain was attacked by the Saxons from northern Germany, who raided towns on the east and south coasts. The Roman response was to build a series of forts along these coasts and a commander was appointed to take charge of them. He was called the Count of the Saxon Shore. Many of these forts still stand today; Pevensey and Portchester are very good examples. The Count also had naval forces, which he could use to attack the raiders. The new measures worked for about 70 years, but from AD 367, when there was a mass attack on Britain, they began to break down completely

✳ ▶ p. 121

AD 410
BRITAIN CHANGING HANDS

Throughout the third century the Empire saw an increasing number of civil wars as ambitious generals tried to seize power. Britain was an obvious place to start a rebellion. Not only was it a remote province, but it also had a garrison of three legions, much more than most provinces. In AD 286 Pausanias seized control of Britain and held it for nearly 10 years. In the fourth and early fifth centuries a number of emperors were proclaimed by the British legions and attempted to march on Rome. None was successful. In the meantime the province of Britain continued to be prosperous and remained so long after the last legionaries were recalled to Rome in 410 by Emperor Honorius.

p. 115◀ **Distant Voices** ▶p. 121

I ran my ships aground on an evenly sloping beach, with no rocks. The Britons seeing my plan had sent forward their horsemen and a number of the chariots they use for fighting. The rest of the troops followed close behind – they were ready to stop us landing. We were really up against it. The size of our ships meant that they ran aground in fairly deep water. Our men held back, chiefly because of the deep water, the man who carried the Eagle of the 10th legion cried in a loud voice, 'jump down my comrades, unless you want to surrender the Eagle to the enemy'. At this, our soldiers jumped together from the boats.

Extract from Caesar's *Gallic Wars*, describing Britain (54 BC)

1066 And All That

1066–1272

FROM 1066 UNTIL the sixteenth century England was closely involved in the affairs of Europe. At first, French rulers invaded and took possession of England, but later, as kings of England, they attempted to seize the crown of France. The series of events began with the Norman invasion in 1066, and continued until the last English possession in France, Calais, was recaptured by the French in 1558. This period of history is commemorated to this day on the royal standard, which includes the Fleur de Lys, the emblem of the French royal family, along with the emblems of England and Scotland.

▶ p. 121

1066
HAROLD GODWINSON

On 5 January 1066, Edward the Confessor died. He was childless. Edward had been a weak king and it was perhaps no surprise when Harold Godwinson, Earl of Wessex, was proclaimed king almost immediately. He had been at Edward's side when he died and stated that Edward had named him king at the point of death. Although no one had actually heard Edward say this, no one challenged him. There is little doubt that Harold was a popular king. He was the most powerful man in England and a very successful general. Although there appears to have been no immediate opposition to Harold's succession, he soon found that he had two rivals – the king of Norway and William of Normandy.

1066
HARALD HARDRADA

Harald Hardrada was king of Norway and a descendant of the Danish king of England, who had reigned from 1016 to 1042. When he heard news of Edward's death, he decided to try to seize the throne of England. Harald was a famous warrior and he was supported by Sweyn, the king of Denmark and by Tostig, the brother of Harold Godwinson, who had been exiled in 1064. He was obviously a very dangerous opponent and in September he landed in Yorkshire and defeated an English army at the battle of Fulford Gate, near York. But while Harald was celebrating, King Harold marched north and made a surprise attack on the Norwegian army. Harald, Sweyn and Tostig were all killed and the army was destroyed at the Battle of Stamford Bridge on 25 September. It appeared that, for the moment, England was safe.

◀ *Carved and painted panels, showing Edward the Confessor and Henry VI.*

▶ p. 122

1066
WILLIAM OF NORMANDY

William of Normandy was an old friend of Edward the Confessor. He claimed that Edward had promised him the throne of England when he died. More important still, he stated that in 1064 Harold Godwinson had been shipwrecked on the coast of France and had sworn to support William's claim to the throne when Edward died. When William heard of Edward's death, he began to collect an army and prepared to invade England. In early August 1066 he had about 7,000 men in the small port of St Valery at the mouth of the River Somme. But William's plans went wrong. For six weeks he was unable to sail because the wind was in the wrong direction. It was not until 28 September that William was able to land in England.

▲ *The death of King Harold, depicted in the Bayeux Tapestry.*

▶ p. 129

1066
STAMFORD BRIDGE AND HASTINGS

William of Normandy landed in England only three days after the battle of Stamford Bridge. When Harold heard the news he marched south immediately and advanced to meet William at Hastings. For some reason he did not wait to collect reinforcements and so arrived at Senlac, the site of the battle, with less men then it would seem the situation demanded. Harold may have been over-confident, he was after all the king of a large country and William was only a duke, or Harold may have been trying to prevent damage to his estates in Sussex. Whatever the reason, Harold's decision to bring fewer men proved a fatal one. On 14 October the English army was defeated at Hastings and Harold was killed. On 25 December 1066 William was finally crowned king of England in Westminster Abbey.

✳ ▶ p. 124

1100s
A PROVINCE OF NORMANDY

The Norman conquest changed England dramatically. William took possession of all land and only eight per cent was left in English hands. French became the language of government. England also changed from being a powerful independent kingdom, to become a province of an increasingly influential empire based in north-west France. William obviously preferred Normandy and spent most of his time there; his eldest son took the title of duke of Normandy when William died in 1087, and Henry II, who became king in 1154, spent only about one-third of his reign in England. As far as Henry was concerned, it was his French possessions that were the most important.

1189
RICHARD THE LIONHEART AND THE THIRD CRUSADE

Henry II died in 1189 and he was succeeded by his son Richard. Richard had taken a vow to go on a crusade only a few months before his father's death and left England almost immediately. He was away for almost five years. The crusade lasted for two years, but on his way home Richard was taken prisoner by Leopold, duke of Austria, and was held to ransom for 150,000 gold marks, a sum equal to two years' taxes. It was the effort to collect this vast sum which rendered so many impoverished and gave rise to the legend of Robin Hood. When Richard finally returned, he left again to fight a series of campaigns in France. He was shot by an archer in 1199.

1214
THE BATTLE OF BOUVINES

After Richard's death his brother John became king. He was not a successful general and the French empire was gradually lost to the advances of Philip II of France. By 1204 all English lands north of the River Loire had been lost. The lands south of Loire, in Gascony, remained loyal to John. In 1214, John summoned an army and invaded northern France. His intention was to recapture the lost lands, but instead he was heavily defeated at the Battle of Bouvines and forced to evacuate France. It was partly as a result of this defeat that John was forced to meet the Barons at Runnymede in 1215.

▶ *Edward I, who attempted to restore English control in France and regain many of the territories that had been lost under his predecessors.*

✠ ▶ p. 122

1272
EDWARD I

When King John died in 1216 he was succeeded by his nine-year-old son Henry III. He made several attempts to invade France and these were partly responsible for his increasing unpopularity with the Barons. In 1264–65 there was a civil war between the Barons – led by Simon de Montfort – and Henry's forces, led by his son Edward. When Henry died in 1272, his son succeeded as Edward I. He attempted to restore English prestige and sent expeditions to Gascony to re-establish English authority. Edward was able to retain control over Gascony, but was unable to regain any of the lands in northern France.

p. 119◀ **Distant Voices** ▶p. 123

At last the English began to weary. Evening was now falling, they knew that their king with two of his brothers and many other great men had been killed. Those that remained were almost exhausted, and they realised they could expect no more help. They began to flee as swiftly as they could, some on foot, some along the roads, but some over the trackless country.

From *The Deeds of William*, by William of Poitiers (1071)

The Hundred Years' War

1327–1485

THE HUNDRED YEARS' War began in 1338 and lasted until 1453. It was a series of attempts by the English kings to establish their claim to the throne of France. At first the English were very successful, but towards the end of the fourteenth century many areas were recaptured by the French. Henry V then regained control of much of France and his son, Henry VI, was the only English king to be crowned king of France. After Henry V's death, however, the English possessions were gradually lost during the reign of Henry VI, who suffered from mental illness. When the wars came to an end in 1453, only Calais remained in English hands.

✠ ▶ p. 126

1327
EDWARD III

Edward III became king at the age of 15 in 1327. After defeating the Scots at Halidon Hill in 1333, Edward turned his attention to France. The French king, Philip VI, was supporting the Scots and Edward wanted to stop their interference in English affairs. In 1338 he invaded France, in response to attacks on Gascony by Philip VI of France. Edward also claimed the throne of France through his mother Isabelle, who was a French princess. In 1340 the English navy won its first great victory at Sluys and gained control of the Channel. Edward then made a truce with the French until 1345.

p. 113◀ **Triumphs & Tragedies** ▶p. 127

1415
HARFLEUR AND AGINCOURT

Henry V invaded France in 1415. He advanced through Normandy, seizing the port of Harfleur, then facing the French army at Agincourt on 25 October 1415. The English were vastly outnumbered, but Henry chose a muddy field for the battle, where the French knights would be forced to attack between two woods which would restrict their movement. It was very similar to the battlefield of Waterloo, which Wellington would choose in 1815 for the final struggle with Napoleon. Henry used the same tactics as those that had been used at Crécy and Poitiers. As the French knights charged they were showered with arrows from the English longbows, and Henry's army triumphed.

✌ ▶ p. 136

1346
CRÉCY

In 1346, Edward III invaded France and met the French army at Crécy. The result was a catastrophic defeat for the French. For the first time on the continent, Edward used the longbow, which the English had encountered in Wales. Almost 2 m (6 ft) in length and requiring tremendous strength, it had the power to penetrate chain mail and even plate armour on occasions. When the French knights charged, they galloped into a hail of arrows. This sequence of events was to be repeated in several battles during the next 80 years. Edward followed up his victory at Crécy by capturing Calais in 1347, using artillery. The surrender of the burghers of Calais is commemorated in a statue in the town to this day.

▲ *The longbow was perhaps the most successful advance in weaponry in the Middle Ages.*

1356
POITIERS

After Crécy, Edward III agreed a truce with the French for eight years. But in 1355 his son Edward, the Black Prince, led an army to Bordeaux in Gascony. The English marched north and met the French Army at Poitiers. Using the same tactics as at Crécy, the Black Prince inflicted an even more crushing defeat on the French, capturing John, the king of France and many French knights. In 1359 Edward invaded France again and reached Paris. The French agreed to surrender Gascony and the area around Calais and to pay a ransom for King John. Edward agreed to give up his claim to the throne of France. The two countries signed the Treaty of Bretigny, which brought to an end the first period of the war.

🏃 ▶ p. 128

1360
THE BLACK PRINCE

After the Treaty of Bretigny in 1360, Edward, the Black Prince, governed Aquitaine, the area in south-west France that included Gascony. He became involved in a series of campaigns against the French, led by Bertrand du Guesclin. The French avoided battle and concentrated on wearing the English out by a war of attrition. The people of Aquitaine became more and more opposed to the English as Edward imposed extra taxes to pay for the cost of the war. Eventually, in 1371, he left France and returned to England. Edward, the Black Prince, died in 1376 from plague, just a year before his father, Edward III. He is buried in Canterbury Cathedral and there is a chapel dedicated to him in the crypt.

▲ *Effigy to Edward, the Black Prince, who died in 1376, a victim of the Plague.*

1370
JOHN OF GAUNT

The Black Prince was replaced in France by his brother, John of Gaunt. John proved to be an incompetent soldier and within three years most English possessions in France had been lost. By 1375 only five towns remained in English hands: Calais, Cherbourg, Brest, Bayonne and Bordeaux. John of Gaunt returned to England in 1374 and tried to take power, but when Edward III died in 1377, he was succeeded by Richard II, the son of the Black Prince. Richard reigned for 22 years, before being deposed by John of Gaunt's son, Henry in 1399. Richard was probably murdered in 1400 and Henry IV established the House of Lancaster. During the reigns of Richard II and Henry IV there was little fighting in France, but when Henry IV died in 1413, his son Henry V invaded once again.

1422
HENRY VI

The success at Agincourt led to the reconquest of Normandy and the Treaty of Troyes in 1420.

▲ *The ineffective king of France, Henry VI, with his bishop.*

Henry V was appointed Regent of France, and when he died in 1422, his son Henry VI was acclaimed king of France. At the time, however, Henry VI was only six months old and, although he was crowned king of France in Paris in 1431, during his reign English control of France gradually slid away. Paris was lost in 1436 and Gascony in 1442. Normandy was recaptured by the French in 1448 and all English attempts at reconquest failed. By 1453 only the town of Calais remained in English hands. The Hundred Years' War was over. The English kings had failed in their attempt to conquer France, although their claim lives on in the Royal Standard.

1485
THE BATTLE OF BOSWORTH FIELD

Defeat in the Hundred Years' War turned English attention inwards. For the next 30 years the barons of England fought over the succession to the crown. The struggle was decided when Richard III was defeated and killed by Henry VII at the battle of Bosworth Field in August 1485. Henry VII (1485–1509) avoided all foreign wars, except for an invasion of France in 1492, which he called off when the French offered him £50,000. From being a major power in Europe during the reign of Henry V, England was now of almost no importance. Henry VII concentrated on security and financial strength at home and was prepared to leave foreign adventures to others.

p. 121◀ **Distant Voices** ▶p. 125

The French army was crowded together between two small woods. The knights hardly had room to raise their lances. It had rained all night, and the ground was too soft for the horses. The heavy armour worn by the French knights made things worse. The English knights were on foot and advanced in good order. The archers were at the sides of the field. When they fired the arrows fell so fast that the French knights did not dare look up.

A French account of the battle of Agincourt, written by a knight who took part (1415)

Westward Ho

1497–1783

IN THE SECOND HALF of the fifteenth century the nations of Europe began to explore the world. The Portuguese were the first: Prince Henry the Navigator sent sea captains south along the coast of Africa, until Vasco da Gama reached India in 1497. Portuguese and Spanish sailors began to explore the Americas and, in 1497, the first English expedition set sail under John Cabot. For the next 400 years the English explored all corners of the known and unknown world. By the end of the nineteenth century they had created an enormous 'empire on which the sun never set'. In the eighteenth century the most important part of that empire was the American Colonies.

▶ p. 126

1497
JOHN CABOT

John Cabot was a Genoese merchant who settled in England in 1495. He had travelled extensively in the eastern Mediterranean and, when he heard about Christopher Columbus' discoveries, decided to sail west to try to find a short cut to Asia. He set sail on 2 May 1497 and reached land on 24 June. Almost certainly this was the coast of Newfoundland. He returned to England and then led a second expedition the following year with five ships. One turned back, but the other four were all lost. Cabot's second expedition had come to nothing, but he had begun a tradition in English seafaring and had started the English occupation and conquest of North America.

▲ *John Cabot, whose exploratory expeditions were some of the first of many such voyages that were to set sail from England at that time.*

1584
SIR WALTER RALEIGH

English interest in the Americas was revived in the 1560s, when John Hawkins began transporting slaves from Africa to Spanish America. His nephew, Francis Drake, sailed around the world from 1577 to 1581, attacking Spanish colonies on the way. But the real breakthrough in the colonisation of America came in 1584, when Walter Raleigh sent out an expedition to found a colony in what he called 'Virginia', in honour of Queen Elizabeth I, the 'virgin queen'. Raleigh also believed the legend of 'El Dorado', the Golden Man, which stated that American Indians threw a golden figure into a lake as sacrifice. In 1616 he led an expedition up the Orinoco River in South America in attempt to discover it, but failed and returned in disgrace.

▶ p. 138

1604
VIRGINIA

The colony of Virginia was set up in 1584, but in both 1586 and in 1591 supply ships found it deserted. Not until 1604 was a permanent settlement created and even then it was only the beginning of the cultivation of tobacco in 1612 that really established the colony. In 1607 the colony was saved by Captain John Smith, who held the colonists together in a period of great difficulty and famously married the Indian princess Pocahontas. Virginia led to further colonies being established in America. Massachusetts was settled in 1606 and the colony was given a royal charter in 1629. Connecticut, Rhode Island and Maryland were all settled in the 1630s and were given their royal charters in the 1660s.

▼ *Sir Walter Raleigh, who began the colonisation of America in the area he called 'Virginia'.*

▶ p. 130

1664
NEW YORK

The English were not the only people to establish colonies in America. In 1612 the Dutch set up a trading station on Manhattan Island, and in 1626 they bought the island from the Indians for 24 dollars. The colony became known as New Amsterdam. In 1664 the colony was handed over to the English and was renamed New York after the brother of Charles II, James, duke of York. The new colony led to the establishment of two more. To the west, the Quaker William Penn set up Pennsylvania and New Jersey was created to the south. Charles II's reign also saw the settlement of the Carolinas and finally in 1733 the state of Georgia was set up.

1733
THE 13 COLONIES

When Georgia was set up as a penal colony in 1733, there were 13 colonies in America. Each one was different and there were frequent disputes between them over territory. To the north were the more industrial, heavily populated states. Here the most important political factors were merchants and trade. To the south were the more agricultural and rural states, where landowners were predominant. North and South were divided by the line finally drawn by two surveyors, Mason and Dixon, in 1767. It ran due west between Pennsylvania and Maryland. What held the colonies together was the constant fear of Indian attacks, and, from the 1660s, attacks by French forces from their colonies along the St Lawrence River.

▶ p. 129

1755–59
THE FRENCH AND INDIAN WAR

In 1755, war broke out between the American Colonies and the French and their Indian allies. At first the war went badly for the colonists and the French captured Forts Oswego, George and Ticerondoga. But in 1758 the tide began to turn. Louisburg, Fort Frontenac and Fort Duquesne were captured by the British and in 1759 General Wolfe attacked Quebec, the centre of French Canada. At the Battle of the Heights of Abraham in September 1759, the British forces destroyed the army of General Montcalm and then captured Quebec five days later. French power in North America was ended. At the Treaty of Paris in 1763 the French gave up Canada and all land east of the Mississippi River.

1773
THE BOSTON TEA PARTY

The Treaty of Paris in 1763 greatly reduced the threat from the French to the American Colonies. It also meant that the colonists had much less need of British protection; so when the British government tried to tax the Americans to pay for the costs of the war, it met increasing opposition. At the forefront of the opposition was the city of Boston. In 1770, the Boston Massacre took place and when the British government tried to sell tea from India in America in 1773, Bostonians threw it into the harbour. In retaliation the British government closed the port of Boston in 1774, but this only increased tension. The other colonies rallied to the support of Massachusetts at the First Continental Congress in September 1774 and when British troops tried to stop colonists seizing military stores at Concord in April 1775, the American rebellion started.

◀ *The Boston Tea Party: a rebellion against British trade restrictions in America.*

1783
THE AMERICAN REBELLION

War broke out in America in 1775 and lasted until 1781. It resulted in the total defeat of the British. Until 1778 the colonists fought against the British on their own, but from 1778 the colonists were supported by the French, who were looking for an opportunity to avenge Britain after the French and Indian War. The French navy prevented supplies being sent to the British forces in America and the French army besieged General Cornwallis in Yorktown in Virginia. In 1781 Cornwallis was forced to surrender. In 1783 the British and the Americans signed the Treaty of Versailles, which guaranteed American independence.

p. 123◀ **Distant Voices** ▶p. 127

Just before the dissolution of the meeting, a number of brave and resolute men, dressed in Indian manner went on board Captain Hall's ship, where they hoisted out the chests of tea. There was the greatest care taken to prevent the tea from being purloined by the populace. One of the Monday papers says that the masters and owners are well pleased that their ships are thus cleared.

An extract from the *Massachusetts Gazette*, describing the Boston Tea Party (1773)

The Struggle with Spain
1553–1604

UNDER THE TUDOR monarchs the power of the feudal barons was destroyed and a strong centralised state began to be formed. The turmoil of the Wars of the Roses was ended by Henry VII and a new majestic style of monarchy was created by Henry VIII and Elizabeth I. But just as one form of discord disappeared, another, religion, took its place. Henry VIII's decision to divorce Catherine of Aragon led to a long period of discord between different religious groups in England, as each tried to establish that their version of Christianity was the most appropriate for salvation. The rejection of Catholicism also brought England into conflict with Spain, the most powerful country in Europe, in the second half of the sixteenth century.

1553
BLOODY MARY TUDOR

Mary Tudor became queen in 1553; she was the daughter of Catherine of Aragon and had been brought up as a Catholic. During her reign Catholicism was revived in England and it is estimated that 300 Protestants – including the Archbishop of Canterbury – were burnt at the stake. More unpopular, however, was Mary's marriage to Philip of Spain. The marriage treaty stated that, while Philip would have the title king of England, he could not interfere in the government and also could not succeed Mary if she died. The marriage drew England into a war with France in 1557, which at first showed signs of success. In January 1558, however, the French captured Calais, the last English possession across the Channel. Mary died soon afterwards; she said that Calais was engraved on her heart.

✠ ▶ p. 128

1558
ELIZABETH I'S FOREIGN POLICY

Elizabeth succeeded her elder half-sister in 1558. She signed the treaty of Cateau-Cambresis with France in 1559, which promised the return of Calais to England in eight years' time. However, in 1564 Elizabeth gave up all claims to Calais in exchange for 220,000 crowns. Elizabeth wanted to restore the depleted English treasury and avoid any foreign entanglements. She followed the same policy with Spain, carrying on extended negotiations with Philip II and trying to prevent English sea captains attacking Spanish ships and colonies. But as the scale and wealth of Spain's American empire grew, Elizabeth found the task increasingly difficult. Philip II was also a devoted Catholic and wanted to return England to what he believed was the true faith. In the 1570s and early 1580s there were many sources of friction.

▲ *Queen Elizabeth I, whose reign saw the victory of the English naval fleet over the Spanish Armada.*

✝ ▶ p. 132

1577–81
DRAKE'S CIRCUMNAVIGATION

Francis Drake was a nephew of John Hawkins, the main founder of the slave trade. Like other sea captains, Drake began to attack Spanish ships in the 1570s and in 1577 sailed west in an attempt to

▲ *Sir Francis Drake practised piracy on Spanish ships during his circumnavigation of the globe.*

circumnavigate the world. This was the first great voyage of exploration by English ships. Drake crossed the Atlantic to the Spanish Main, then sailed down the coast of South America, through the Straits of Magellan and up the west coast of South America. He sailed as far north as Drake's bay in California, naming the region New Albion and claiming it for England. He then crossed the Pacific, sailed through the East Indies and across the Indian Ocean, round the Cape of Good Hope and north to England in 1581. Overall the voyage showed a profit of 4,700 per cent.

1587
ENGLISH PIRACY

Philip II was not prepared to tolerate English attacks on Spain's empire and put into operation a plan to reintroduce Catholicism in England. In 1587, a huge battle fleet was assembled in Lisbon ready to attack England. The plan was to sail up the Channel, collect a Spanish army in the Netherlands and land it in

England. As the Spanish infantry were the most feared fighting force in Europe at the time, Philip expected an easy victory. Before the Armada could sail, however, it was attacked by Drake. In April 1587, Drake raided Cadiz and destroyed thousands of tons of shipping and supplies, occupied Cape St Vincent and then blockaded Lisbon. Before returning to England he seized a Spanish treasure ship with £114,000 on board. Drake became known to the Spanish as *El Draque* – 'the Dragon'.

p. 122◀ **Triumphs & Tragedies** ▶p. 131

1588
THE SPANISH ARMADA

The 132 ships of the Spanish Armada sailed in May 1588 and reached Cornwall on 19 July. The English fleet avoided a major battle and instead shadowed the Spanish ships up the Channel. The smaller, lighter English ships sniped at the large, slow-moving galleons, but did little real damage to them. When the Armada anchored off Calais on 27 July, it was still more or less intact. The following night Drake attacked the Spanish fleet with fireships; many Spanish ships cut their anchor cables in order to escape. On 29 July the only full scale battle was fought between the demoralised Spanish and the triumphant English. The remnants of the Armada then fled north and returned to Spain around the north coast of Scotland.

1590
THE FLOTA

The defeat of the Armada in July 1588 ended any prospect of an invasion of England, but it did not end the war with Spain. English ships continued to raid Spanish ships and in 1589, 91 were brought into English ports. The greatest prize of all, however, was the Flota, the Spanish treasure fleet that sailed each year from the Spanish Main. In 1590, Philip II took the extraordinary step of ordering it not to sail, and in 1591 it was only allowed to sail with a heavy escort. Even so, it was attacked off the Azores by Sir Richard Grenville. Although the attack failed, the Spanish ships were so badly damaged that most sank in the severe storms that followed the battle.

1595
THE DEATH OF FRANCIS DRAKE

After his heroics against the Armada, Drake planned an even bigger adventure for 1589. He intended to destroy the remnants of the Armada at anchor in Spanish ports and then land in Portugal and support Don Antonio of Portugal in an attempt to overthrow Philip II. He persuaded the queen to back him to the extent of about £60,000; it was a disaster. Although Drake seized Corunna, little more was achieved. The force marched on Lisbon, but failed to take it. When Drake returned home in disgrace he had lost 8,000 of his 15,000 men. He went into retirement, but planned one more expedition in 1595 along with his uncle, John Hawkins. It was to be an attack on New Spain in the Caribbean. It, too, failed and Drake and Hawkins were both killed at Nombre de Dios.

1604
PEACE

The war with Spain dragged on until 1604, but after the death of Philip II in 1598, it lost much of its focus. Philip III, who succeeded his father, had no interest in attacking England. He lived as a virtual recluse and devoted himself to religion. James I, who had succeeded Elizabeth I in 1603, brought the war to an end in 1604. English rivalry with Spain soon disappeared. Spain became involved in a series of wars with France and was also dragged into the Thirty Years' War. From 1640 onwards there was also a serious revolt in Catalonia. Following peace with Spain, the English kings became heavily involved in internal politics, which led to the civil war in 1642 and the execution of Charles I in 1649.

▲ *The defeat of the Spanish Armada off the coast of Cornwall in 1588.*

p. 125◀ **Distant Voices** ▶p. 129

The king of Spain's plans are to invade England and Ireland. His preparations include 350 ships from Spain, 80 from Venice and Genoa and one from Florence. 12,000 men maintained by Italy and the Pope, 6,000 by the Spanish clergy, 12,000 by the nobles of Spain. It is reported that 10,000 of these are horsemen. I think it is not all true, but some of it is.

Part of a speech made by the lord chancellor to Parliament (1587)

The Second Hundred Years' War
1688–1783

IN 1689, WAR BROKE OUT once more between France and England. Fighting was to continue, on and off, for almost 100 years. At first the struggle was restricted to Europe, but increasingly the main areas of conflict were India, America and the Caribbean as the two countries competed for colonies and dominance in trade. Trading posts in India, islands in the West Indies and forts in North America were captured, recaptured and then handed back at the end of the war. By 1763 Britain had won the struggle for empire, but France exacted revenge by interfering in the American Rebellion from 1778 onwards. The rivalry finally came to an end in 1783 with the independence of Britain's American colonies and the bankruptcy of the French monarchy. Six years later Revolution broke out in France as a result.

▲ *John Churchill, 1st Duke of Marlborough, who led a triumphant army in the Battle of Blenheim.*

1688
WILLIAM III

In 1688, William of Orange, the Stadtholder of the Netherlands, became king of England, when James II fled. French support for James and William's desire to protect the Netherlands, led to England being drawn into war with France in 1689. William joined the League of Augsburg and landed in the Netherlands with an army. He was defeated in a series of battles from 1692 to 1694, but managed to avoid total disaster. At sea, the English navy won an important battle over the French at Cap la Hogue in 1692. This marked the beginning of English dominance at sea, which was to continue until the twentieth century.

1702–13
THE WAR OF THE SPANISH SUCCESSION

In 1700 Charles II of Spain died without an heir. There were two claimants, one French and one Austrian. In his will Charles named Louis XIV's grandson, Philip of Anjou as his successor. England and Austria formed an alliance to prevent this happening. The English feared that it would lead to a union between France and Spain. The ensuing war led to important changes to Britain's position in Europe. In 1704 Gibraltar was captured from Spain and it was ceded at the Treaty of Utrecht in 1713. At the same time the French gave up all claims to Hudson's Bay and Newfoundland in Canada. England also signed the Methuen Treaty with Portugal, which became England's oldest ally. When the war ended in 1713 Britain was a major European power for the first time for almost 100 years.

◀ *William of Orange with his wife, Mary; their ascension became known as the 'Glorious Revolution'.*

▶ p. 130

1704
THE DUKE OF MARLBOROUGH

The greatest successes during the War of the Spanish Succession came, unusually, on the Continent. English and British armies had a poor record in Europe for much of the eighteenth century. They usually landed in the Low Countries, as William II had done in 1692 and achieved little; but in 1704 the opposite happened. The Duke of Marlborough led his army 480 km (300 miles) across Europe and destroyed the French at the Battle of Blenheim. In the next five years the duke won three more victories at Ramilies, Oudenarde and Malplaquet. The secret of his success was the discipline of the British infantry, steady under fire and also under attack from the French cavalry. Exactly the same discipline was to win the battle of Waterloo in 1815.

1739
JENKINS' EAR

In 1738, Robert Jenkins – a sea captain – arrived in London with one of his ears preserved in a bottle. He claimed that it had been cut off by the Spanish. Anti-Spanish feelings had been growing in Britain during the 1730s and there were also many tales of British sailors being thrown into Spanish prisons and being badly treated. These stories revived memories of the days of Drake and

Hawkins and some began to imagine raiding parties descending on the Spanish colonies in the Caribbean. Jenkins' Ear was one of the catalysts that led to war being declared on Spain in 1739. There followed a series of attacks on the Spanish colonies in central America, and Porto Bello was taken in November 1739, but little else was achieved.

▶ p. 139

1740
THE WAR OF THE AUSTRIAN SUCCESSION

In 1740 Holy Roman Emperor Charles VI died, leaving only a daughter, Maria Theresa. Three claimants tried to take the throne and a major European war ensued. As in the Spanish War of Succession, Britain was involved on the side of Austria, but the British position was more complicated than before: since the Hanoverian succession in 1714 the British kings were also Electors of Hanover in northern Germany. George II was anxious to defend his electorate and even led the British army to victory at the battle of Dettingen in 1743. The British then suffered a series of defeats and by 1747 the French were about to occupy the Low Countries. Two naval victories in 1747 turned the tide for Britain. At the Treaty of Aix-la-Chapelle (1748), all conquests were returned and the status quo was accepted.

1756
THE SEVEN YEARS' WAR

In 1756 war broke out again between France and Britain, caused by clashes between the forces in America and Canada. The war resulted in total victory for Britain over France; after some initial military defeats in Europe and the disastrous loss of Minorca, British forces won a series of victories around the world. Most spectacular of all was 1759 – the *Annus Mirabilis.* In this year, the British army defeated the French at Minden and the Royal Navy won victories at Lagos and Quiberon Bay. In America the Battle of the Heights of Abraham ended French power in Canada. In the West Indies, almost all the French islands were occupied, as well as the Spanish colony of Cuba. Senegal and Goree were captured from France in Africa and Manila was captured from Spain.

▲ *The tomb of William Pitt in Westminster Abbey; Pitt was great leader during the Seven Years' War.*

▶ p. 135

1763
THE TREATY OF PARIS

At the Treaty of Paris in 1763 France agreed to withdraw from Canada and to reduce her interests in India to a purely commercial basis. Cuba was returned to Spain in exchange for Florida. In the West Indies, Grenada, St Vincent, Dominica and Tobago were retained by Britain, but Martinique and Guadeloupe were returned. Britain regained Minorca in exchange for the return of Belle-Ile. On balance it was a great triumph for Britain, although the government was criticised for not driving a hard enough bargain. In fact France was humiliated and looked for the earliest opportunity for revenge during the American Rebellion. Spain also resented its losses and backed the American colonists from 1779.

▶ p. 136

1783
THE TREATY OF VERSAILLES

By 1780 Britain found herself at war not only with the American colonies, but also with France, Spain and Holland. In addition, a League of Armed Neutrality was formed between Russia, Denmark and Sweden to protect shipping at sea from attacks by the British navy. Many of the territories gained during the Seven Years' War were lost, including Florida and Senegal and many of the West Indian Islands. However, Gibraltar survived a siege lasting almost three years from 1779 to 1782 and in the final year of the war the balance was once again shifted by the navy. In 1782 Admiral Rodney won the Battle of the Saints in the West Indies. The Treaty of Versailles in 1783 confirmed American independence as well as most of the conquests of the war.

p. 127◀ **Distant Voices** ▶p. 131

I have not time to say more, but to beg you will give my duty to the Queen, and let her know her army has had a glorious victory. Tallard and two other generals are in my coach and I am following the rest. The bearer my aide de camp Colonel Parker will give her an account of what has passed.

A note written by Marlborough to his wife after the battle of Blenheim (1704)

India
1600–1947

THE ENGLISH ARRIVED in India, for the first time, in 1603 (the name India here refers to the whole sub-continent including the modern countries of India, Pakistan and Bangladesh). The British did not leave until 1947. India became in due course, the finest 'jewel in the crown', a place of fascination and mystery, and some British people came to think of themselves as its rightful rulers. Yet the history of the English and British in India went through many stages, and real political control by Britain was only achieved in the nineteenth century. Until then, the British were often more interested in the wealth of India than they were in helping the people.

▶ p. 133

1600
THE EAST INDIA COMPANY

The East India Company was set up in 1600. It was one of a number of trading companies established at the time. It sent its first mission, headed by John Mildenhall, to India in 1603 and gained the right to trade from the Mughal Emperor in 1608. Over the next 50 years, the Company set up trading stations around India: Surat in the north-west; Madras in the south-east; and Bombay on the west coast. Later Calcutta in the north-east was also occupied. In 1664, a similar French company was set up and established its first trading station at Pondicherry in 1674. For almost 100 years the two companies competed for control of the trade of India.

1750s
ROBERT CLIVE

Robert Clive was an officer in the East India Company army. In the 1750s he led a series of campaigns against the French forces and their Indian allies, which smashed French power and established British authority in India. In 1751 he seized the town of Arcot and in 1757 recaptured Calcutta. In the same year he captured the French trading station of Chandernagore and then annihilated the army of the Nawab of Bengal at the battle of Plassey in June 1757. Pondicherry, the main French trading station was captured in 1759 and the French East India Company was dissolved in 1769. This left the British in control of a number of small areas on the coast and the state of Bengal, which Clive governed until 1767, when he returned to Britain accused of corruption.

▼ *Western-style buildings such as these still stand in cities throughout India as testimonies to the era of British rule.*

1772
WARREN HASTINGS

Warren Hastings was the governor of Bengal from 1772 to 1785. He began a programme of reforms, introducing a new coinage and tax system and beginning the study of Muslim and Hindu law. In 1773, a Supreme Court was set up and the actions of the East India Company's officers were controlled. They were prevented from trading privately and taking gifts. When war broke out with France in 1778, Hastings seized the remaining French trading stations and also attacked the Maratha confederacy. Hastings sometimes acted highhandedly and, after his retirement in 1785, he was accused of corruption by one of his colleagues, Philip Francis. His trial dragged on from 1788 to 1795, when he was acquitted.

1775
THE MARATHA WARS

The Marathas were Hindu princes from southern India, who attacked the Mogul Empire at the end of the seventeenth century. The Marathas were organised into a loose confederacy and for a century they fought both amongst themselves and against the Mughal Empire for control of India. By the late eighteenth century, most of central India was under the control of Maratha princes and this led them into conflict with the British in 1775, when the first Anglo-Maratha War broke out. The Second Maratha War broke out in 1802 and led to the defeat of the Marathas at the battles of Laswaree and Assaye. Most Indian states were then brought under British control.

▶ p. 137

1915
GANDHI

Mohandas Gandhi returned to India in 1915, having already led campaigns against racist laws in South Africa. He had supported Britain during the First World War and, like many Indians, expected that the British would introduce substantial changes to India by way of a reward. When they did not, he became the leader of the Congress and began a series of campaigns of civil disobedience. He preached *satyagraha* (non-violent protest). Gandhi wanted a united India, in which people of all faiths could live together, he opposed the efforts by Hindus, Muslims and Sikhs to create their own states, but in the end he failed. The violence that erupted in India after the Second World War convinced him that unity was impossible. He was murdered in January 1948 by a Hindu extremist, who believed that he had favoured Muslims.

▲ *Mahatma Gandhi, with Lord Mountbatten, viceroy of India, and his wife.*

▶ p. 134

1919
THE INDIAN NATIONAL CONGRESS

The Indian National Congress was set up in 1885 to campaign for Indian independence. Until the First World War most demands were moderate, but from 1919 onwards they became more extreme. 1,200,000 Indians served in the British armed forces during the First World War and something was expected in return. Reforms were introduced in 1919, but they only gave provincial authority to Indians. Even worse, in April 1919, 376 Indians were killed by the British army in the Amritsar massacre. This, it seemed to many nationalists, was what the British intended for India in the future. Further changes in the government of India were introduced in 1935, giving Indians control over some areas of national policy, but by then it was too late. Congress wanted complete independence.

▲ *The Indian Mutiny marked the beginning of nationalist campaigns in India.*

1947
INDEPENDENCE

India and Pakistan became independent on 15 August 1947. The Labour government in Britain wanted to end British rule as quickly as possible and sent Lord Mountbatten to India as the last viceroy in February 1947. Since August 1946 there had been many outbreaks of violence between Hindus and Muslims, and Mountbatten realised that Partition was the only way of preventing widespread violence and set up a commission to decide on a boundary between the two states of India and Pakistan. Even so, thousands of Hindus and Muslims were killed when they discovered they were on the 'wrong' side of the border. Sikhs, who had nowhere to go, were even worse off.

p. 127◀ **Triumphs & Tragedies** ▶p. 132

1857
THE INDIAN MUTINY

By 1857, the East India Company, a private corporation, governed virtually the whole of the sub-continent. The only limit on its authority was the reduction of its monopoly of trade. Since 1800 the East India Company had made enormous improvements in its territories. In 1857 some of the soldiers of the East India Companies army mutinied. The most serious trouble occurred in northern India around Delhi – caused by the introduction of a new cartridge; rumours spread that it was smeared with either pig fat – which was unclean to Muslims – or cow fat, which was a sacred animal to Hindus. Some Indians see this as the first real show of Indian nationalism, but at the time, the revolt was ruthlessly suppressed. It led to the end of the East India Company, however. In 1858 the British government took over the government of India.

p. 129◀ **Distant Voices** ▶p. 133

How can you even dream of Hindu-Muslim unity? We have no intermarriages. We have not the same calendar. The Muslims believe in a single God, and the Hindus are idolatrous. Now again, the Hindus worship animals. They consider cows sacred. We want to kill cows. We want to eat them. There are only two links between the Muslims and the Hindus: British rule – and the common desire to get rid of it.

From a speech made by M. A. Jinnah, leader of the Muslim League (1940)

The Wider World
1740–1914

UNTIL THE MID-EIGHTEENTH century, British attention was mostly focused on the empire in North America and India. From the 1740s, however, British explorers began to venture into the South Pacific and this became even more significant after the loss of the American colonies in 1783. In the nineteenth century there was a revival of interests in polar exploration and in the efforts to find the 'North-west Passage', the route from the Atlantic to the Pacific around the north coast of Canada, which had fascinated Tudor explorers. Increasingly, however, there was a desire to explore the continent of Antarctica and find the routes to both the North and South Poles.

▲ *Cook and his crew engraving the name of their ship* Endeavour *on to the bark of a tree on their arrival in Australia.*

▶ p. 133

1740
ANSON

When war broke out between Britain and Spain in 1739, the three most senior admirals in the Royal Navy had an average age of 70, so heroics were perhaps unlikely. Neverthless, Commodore Anson was sent off to South Anerica, in 1740, with a raiding party. In fact, Anson made few attacks on Spanish shipping and the voyage became one of exploration. He rounded Cape Horn, sailed across the Pacific and circumnavigated the world, just as Drake had done 150 years earlier. When Anson returned in 1744, he had made no significant discoveries, but he had helped to revive interest in Britain in the exploration of the Pacific and Antractica.

1768–79
CAPTAIN COOK

Captain James Cook followed in the footsteps of Anson and made three voyages to the Pacific. In 1768 to 1771 he sailed around New Zealand, proving that it was an island, and then returned to Britain around the Cape of Good Hope. From 1772 to 1775 he became the first man to cross the Antarctic Circle and sailed around Antarctica and claimed South Georgia for Britain. His final voyage was from 1776 to 1779. He sailed north through the Bering Strait looking for passages to the north-west and the north-east to the Atlantic. He discovered Christmas Island and Hawaii, but was killed before he could return home. Cook's great achievement was that he mapped huge areas of the Pacific and began to disprove the long held theory of the existence of a great southern continent, the *Terra Australis.*

◀ *Captain James Cook, the first man to cross the Antarctic Circle.*

p. 131◀ **Triumphs & Tragedies** ▶p. 147

1912
SCOTT OF THE ANTARCTIC

Captain Robert Scott led an expedition to Antarctica in 1902. In 1903 he landed on the continent and marched south to 82 degrees, a new record. Scott returned in 1910. Although he was mainly interested in scientific research, he became involved in a race to the true South Pole and set out, with four others, in November 1911. He reached the pole on 16 January 1912, only to find that the Norwegian Roald Amundsen had beaten him by exactly one month. Scott's refusal to use dog sledges was one reason for his failure. On the return journey, Scott and his party all died from exhaustion in a blizzard on about 29 March 1912.

1788
BOTANY BAY

The first Europeans to reach Australia were Dutch explorers in the early seventeenth century. Captain James Cook explored the east coast during his first voyage, naming it New South Wales. It was his reports that led the British government to set up a penal colony at Botany Bay in 1788. Convicts had been sent to Georgia in the American colonies, but that was impossible after 1783. On 26 January 1788, 11 ships with 717 convicts landed at Port Jackson, later to be known as Sydney. After serving their sentences, the convicts were emancipated and given between 30 and 50 acres of land each. Soldiers were given about 100 acres. These were the first European inhabitants of Australia.

▶ p. 137
1800s
NEW ZEALAND

Traders from Australia began to exploit New Zealand at the end of the eighteenth century. Whalers set up settlements on South Island and Sydney merchants bought timber and flax from Maori chieftains on New Zealand's North Island. The New Zealand Company was set up in 1839 and it sent the first British colonists in 1840. The Treaty of Waitangi was signed with about 500 Maori chiefs. They handed over sovereignty to Britain, but in return were guaranteed their lands and other possessions. The capital was established at Auckland. French settlers also arrived at the same time, but did not remain for long. The New Zealand Company was dissolved in 1851 and the British government took full control of the colony.

1819–47
JOHN FRANKLIN

In 1819, Lieutenant John Franklin was part of an expedition sent to map the north coast of Canada. In 1825 he returned to explore the Mackenzie River and in 1845 led a third expedition to try to find the Northwest Passage in his two ships, the *Erebus* and the *Terror*. Although Franklin was well prepared, his ships became trapped in ice during the winter of 1846–47. He himself died in June 1847 and the rest of the party died the following winter. The bodies of some of the men have been discovered recently and they were found to have died from lead poisoning. Franklin had carried supplies of food in lead cans, unaware of the risk that this entailed.

▶ p. 140
1848
JAMES ROSS

James Ross took part in an expedition to the North-west Passage in 1829-33, reaching the magnetic north pole on 1 June 1831. In 1841 he was sent by the Admiralty to Antarctica and reached 78 degrees south, a record which stood for 60 years. He mapped many areas of Antarctica and claimed possession of them for Britain. In 1848 Ross set out on the first of a series of expeditions to try to find Sir John Franklin's ships. He followed Franklin's route, but turned back before he reached the point where they had been trapped in ice. More expeditions followed and the records of the party were discovered in 1854.

▶ *The great British explorer, Ernest Shackleton, who died on his fourth expedition to the Antarctic.*

1914
SHACKLETON

Ernest Shackleton was a member of Scott's expedition in 1902. He returned on his own in 1907 and reached 88 degrees south, only 156 km (97 miles) from the true pole. Food shortages forced the party to turn back, however. Members of his party crossed Antarctica and reached the magnetic South Pole. In 1914 Shackleton set out on a third expedition planning to cross Antarctica. His ship the *Endurance* became trapped in ice and was crushed in November 1915. The crew escaped in boats and landed on Elephant Island. Shackleton and five others sailed the 1,287 km (800 miles) to South Georgia and then returned to rescue the remainder of the crew. Further explorations of Antarctica were carried out by Sir Douglas Mawson in 1929-33 and John Rymill from 1934–37.

p. 131◀ **Distant Voices** ▶p. 135

I, who had ambition not only to go farther than any one had gone before, but as far as it was possible for man to go, was not sorry at meeting with this interruption as it in some measure relieved us, at least shortened the dangers and hardships inseparable with the navigation of the Southern Polar Regions. Since therefore, we could not proceed one inch farther to the south, no other reason need be assigned for my tacking and standing back to the north.

An extract from the journal of Captain James Cook, describing meeting ice on his journey to Antarctica (1774)

Revolution

1793–1801

FROM 1793 TO 1815 Britain and France were at war for all but 13 months. This was a war of a quite different nature to those of the previous hundred years. The wars in Europe from 1688 to 1783 had been fought between rival royal families, each trying to gain territory and prestige from the others, or between rival empires competing for dominance in trade. But the events of 1789 to 1792 released a new form of energy in France and the French Revolutionary War became a struggle between nations; it was a struggle in which the French had an enormous advantage: nationalism. When war restarted in 1803, its nature had changed once again. To the nationalist ideals of the Revolution were added the magnetism and ambition of Napoleon Bonaparte.

▶ p. 139

1793
THE FRENCH REVOLUTION

On 14 July 1789 a Paris mob stormed the Bastille – a royal fortress and prison in France – and killed the governor. During the next three-and-a-half years the French Revolution became more and more violent, culminating in the execution of Louis XVI in January 1793. Austria and Prussia had both attacked France in 1792, but Britain had not become involved. Many people in Britain had at first welcomed the French Revolution. They saw it as suitable penance for France's interference in America in 1788. It was regarded as the French equivalent of the Glorious Revolution of 1688. But as events grew more violent, there were increasing appeals for action, all of which were turned down by William Pitt the Younger, the prime minister. The balance was finally tipped on 1 February 1793, when the French invaded the Low Countries.

▲ *The storming of the Bastille in Paris, the first step towards revolution in France – an ominous move for the aristocracy.*

1793
WALCHEREN

The British government responded to war, as it had done so often in the past, by sending an expedition to the Low Countries to protect the River Scheldt. It was led by King George III's brother, the duke of York and it landed at Walcheren, a boggy unhealthy island near the mouth of the Scheldt. For nine months the army traipsed around inconclusively, while a mocking nursery rhyme was made up to describe its inactivity. Then having achieved nothing it returned home. It was a sign that the traditional British strategy of trying to safeguard the Low Countries was no longer relevant. This war was going to be fought on a far wider scale and for far bigger prizes.

1793
TOULON

In April 1793, a British force under Admiral Hood seized the French port of Toulon, hoping that royalists would rally to its support. This did not happen. Although there were revolts against the Revolutionary government in some areas of France, such as the Vendee in the west, the big cities and the south in particular were strongly Republican. Hood held Toulon until December 1793, but was then forced to evacuate it. An important factor in his decision was the use of artillery by a young officer, Napoleon Bonaparte, who dragged his cannon onto high ground from where he was able to bombard the city. This was the first time that Napoleon achieved any degree of fame. The British forces learnt another lesson. This war was not going to be fought in the rather gentlemanly manner of some past European wars.

▶ *Napoleon Bonaparte, the French general who established a dictatorial regime at the turn of the nineteenth century.*

1793
BLUE WATER

William Pitt the Younger had been prime minister for almost nine years when he declared war on France in 1793. After the failure of the Walcheren and Toulon expeditions, he adopted the same policies as his father had used during the Seven Years' War. He began to mop up French possessions around the world and particularly in the West Indies, where the sugar islands had always been regarded as great prizes. In previous wars these had been used as bargaining counters in the final peace treaty. But the French Revolutionary

▲ *William Pitt, who declared war on France in his capacity as prime minister.*

government simply paid no attention. It was not interested in West Indian islands when it was fighting for its life in Europe. Pitt's strategy had almost no impact on the war in Europe.

1794
PITT'S GOLD

By 1794 it was obvious that Britain would not be able to interfere in any significant way in the war on the Continent. Nevertheless, the British government wanted to see France defeated. Pitt adopted a policy that had been used during the War of the Austrian Succession; he began to pay subsidies to the continental powers to persuade them to carry on the fight against France. 'Pitt's Gold' as it became known was little more than a bribe to Austria and Prussia to keep them at war with France. Over the next 10 years or so more than £3,000,000 was sent abroad to provide support for the Austrian and Prussian armies. But it made little difference. In 1797 and 1801 the Austrians and Prussians were forced to accept French terms for peace after crushing defeats.

1797
BLOCKADE

Pitt's most successful strategy in the French Revolutionary War was the use of the naval blockade. From 1793 the main ports of France were bottled up by British fleets. At first the blockade was not completely successful. In June 1794 the Channel Fleet failed to capture a large convoy carrying wheat to France and in 1797, the French fleet escaped and nearly landed an army in Ireland. In addition the Channel Fleet mutinied for a month in April 1797 and the North Sea Fleet mutinied for seven months. Despite these setbacks, there were two important naval victories in 1797. In February Admiral St Vincent destroyed a Franco-Spanish Fleet at Cape St Vincent near Cadiz and in October Admiral Duncan defeated the Dutch fleet at Camperdown. Both Spain and the Netherlands had declared war on Britain.

▶ p. 148

1798
BATTLE OF THE NILE

The decisive action at the battle of Cape St Vincent in February 1797 was taken by Captain Horatio Nelson, who disobeyed orders and put his ship between the two sections of the enemy fleet. This led to a rapid rise to the rank of admiral and command of the Mediterranean Fleet in 1798. His task was to blockade Toulon. In May 1798 Napoleon sailed with an army of 35,000 men from Toulon bound for Egypt. His fleet slipped past Nelson in a storm and Napoleon landed in Egypt and captured Cairo. Nelson arrived 10 days later, having searched the Mediterranean for Napoleon. He found the French fleet at anchor in Aboukir Bay at the mouth of the Nile and ordered an immediate attack. The French fleet was almost totally destroyed.

1801
COPENHAGEN

In 1801, Austria and Prussia made peace once again with France, and Russia formed the League of Armed Neutrality with Sweden and Denmark. A fleet under Admiral Hyde Parker was sent to Copenhagen to investigate; Nelson was his second-in-command. When the fleet reached Copenhagen, Hyde Parker ordered Nelson to reconnoitre the approaches to the harbour, where he found the Danish fleet at anchor. Nelson attacked immediately. When Hyde Parker realised what had happened, he ordered Nelson to break off the action by hoisting a flag signal. Nelson put his telescope to his right eye, in which he was blind, and said to Captain Hardy, 'You know Hardy, I have only one eye, I have a right to be blind sometimes. Do you know, I really do not see that signal'. The Danish fleet was destroyed and the League of Armed Neutrality collapsed.

p. 133◀ **Distant Voices** ▶p. 137

The first man who jumped into the enemy's mizzen-chains was Captain Berry, late my first lieutenant. He was supported by a soldier of the 69th regiment. I followed as soon as possible. I found the cabin doors fastened, and the Spanish officers fired their pistols at us through the windows, but having broke open the doors, the soldiers fired, and the Spanish brigadier fled as retreating to the quarter-deck. It was not long before I was on the quarter-deck when the Spanish captain on bended knee presented me with his sword.

From Nelson's report on the battle of Cape St Vincent (1797)

The Corsican Tyrant
1802–15

IN 1795, NAPOLEON BONAPARTE emerged from almost total obscurity to defeat Austria within a year and then seize power in France in 1799. Five years later he created himself emperor and then set about establishing himself as the legitimate ruler of France. Napoleon had the ability to create almost complete devotion amongst his soldiers. When he reviewed his army he would stop and address men by name and refer to the battles they had fought. In fact, this familiarity was usually set up. He learnt the names of men in advance and used the trick as a way of encouraging loyalty. As an instinctive commander on the battlefield, however, Napoleon had no equal and for more than 10 years there was no one who could match him.

▲ *Admiral Nelson, on the deck of his flagship, the HMS* Victory*, during the Battle of Trafalgar, in which he was fatally wounded.*

▶ p. 138

1802
THE TREATY OF AMIENS

By early 1802, Britain was once more fighting France on her own. In March 1802 Britain and France signed the Treaty of Amiens, which led to the cessation of hostilities for more than a year. Britain returned all of her conquests to France and her allies, except Trinidad and Ceylon, which were ceded to Britain. France agreed to hand back Malta to the Knights of St. John. But nothing else was settled and Napoleon was left free to continue to redraw the map of Europe. War broke out again in May 1804, partly because Malta had not been handed back, but also because Napoleon was angry at attacks made upon him in the British press.

1805
THE CAMP AT BOULOGNE

From 1803 to late 1805 Napoleon had one principal aim, to invade and subdue Britain. He collected an army of 150,000 men at Boulogne and prepared to ferry them across the Channel in flat-bottomed barges and land in Kent. There was only one thing in his way, the British navy, which controlled the Channel. Napoleon considered a number of alternatives, digging a tunnel and using balloons, but he eventually decided upon a complicated plan, which would involve the Toulon Fleet escaping, sailing to the West Indies and then returning to the Channel to shepherd his troops across. In May 1805, the French commander at Toulon, Admiral Villeneuve, escaped from Toulon and set sail across the Atlantic to set the plan in motion.

▲ *Napoleon Bonaparte looking across the Channel, planning his invasion of England.*

▶ p. 137

1805
TRAFALGAR

When the French fleet escaped from Toulon in May 1805, Napoleon's plan to invade Britain seemed to be working even better than he had expected. Nelson, who had been blockading Toulon for two years, at first thought that the French might be heading for Egypt. Only when Nelson had sailed as far as the Straits of Messina did he head west and follow Villeneuve across the Atlantic. The French plan was to make Nelson think they were going to attack the West Indian islands, but instead return to Europe. Nelson guessed what was going on and sent word to the Admiralty by a fast ship. When Villeneuve reached France, he was unable to force his way up the Channel and sailed south to Cadiz. On 21 October Nelson tracked him down and destroyed his fleet at the Battle of Trafalgar, where he was killed.

▶ p. 139

1806
THE CONTINENTAL SYSTEM

By 1805, the Grande Armee was already heading east from Boulogne. In December Napoleon defeated the Austrian and Russian armies at Austerlitz and in 1806 he defeated Prussia. In November 1806, he issued the Berlin Decree, which declared that Britain was in a state of blockade and banned all trade with her. This was repeated by the Milan decree in December 1807. The whole European coastline from Sweden to Spain was closed to British trade. Napoleon knew that he could not invade Britain, so he tried to bring her to her knees by starving her out. His attempt was more successful than the British government would have liked. Wheat prices doubled and there was severe unrest in the north of England, but the System crumbled when Russia broke away in 1811.

1808
THE PENINSULAR WAR

In 1808 a British army landed in Portugal to try to inspire a revolt against the French, who had occupied Spain and Portugal earlier that year. At first the British were very successful, but in October Napoleon arrived in person and drove the British back to Corunna. The army was forced to embark and return to Britain. A second army landed later in 1809 commanded by Lord Wellington. He established a base at Lisbon and protected it with massive lines of fortifications, the lines of Torres Vedras. For the next four years the army of the Peninsular spent each winter in Lisbon and then ventured out each spring to harry the French. They were supported by Spanish irregulars, who attacked French supply lines. These became known as 'guerrillas'.

1810
COLONIAL CONQUESTS

With French attention increasingly occupied by events in Europe, British forces took the opportunity to occupy colonies around the world. Many of these were returned at the end of the war, but some key additions were made to the empire. Ceylon and the Cape of Good Hope, which became the basis of South Africa, were taken from the Netherlands, Malta was occupied and retained, the islands of Tobago, St Lucia and Mauritius were taken from France and Heligoland was also occupied. On the map these additions to the empire looked unimpressive, but they were to prove very significant. The age of sail was about to give way to the age of steam, and many of these were to prove important coaling stations throughout the nineteenth century.

▶ p. 141

1814
WELLINGTON

Wellington's scorched earth strategy in the Peninsular played an important part in the defeat of Napoleon. For four years, 250,000 French troops tramped around Spain becoming increasingly disillusioned and demoralised. The same tactics were used by the Tsar in Russia in 1812, and the attempt to march to either end of Europe proved too much for the French army. In 1813 the Allies began a general advance on France and in 1814 they closed in on Paris. Wellington captured Bordeaux in March and then defeated Soult at Toulouse. The following month Napoleon surrendered and was exiled to Elba. However, after only 11 months he escaped and returned to France. The Allies quickly put an army together and Wellington was appointed the commander of the allied forces.

▶ p. 151

1815
WATERLOO

When Napoleon returned from Elba in March 1815, he knew that he had to defeat the Allied forces quickly as 200,000 Austrian and Russian troops were advancing from the east. He struck north immediately and met Wellington at Waterloo on 18 June. The French army attacked the British line all day, but the British infantry held out against the French cavalry, just as Marlborough's forces had at Blenheim. At about 5.30 p.m. the Prussian army arrived and fell on the flank of the French. Wellington ordered a general advance and the French army disintegrated. Napoleon fled and surrendered to a British warship. This time he was exiled to St Helena where he died in 1821.

▼ *Napoleon fighting against Wellington's forces at the Battle of Waterloo.*

p. 135◀ **Distant Voices** ▶p. 139

I return you many thanks for the honour you have done me; but Europe is not saved by any single man. England has saved herself by her exertions, and will, I trust, save Europe by her example.

A speech made by William Pitt the Younger in reply to a toast at a banquet in London (1805)

British Foreign Policy
1815–54

IN SEPTEMBER 1814 the representatives of the Allies met at Vienna to decide the future of Europe. Although the Congress of Vienna was interrupted by Napoleon's return from Elba, the meetings continued, but the terms imposed on France after Waterloo were much stricter. The Congress of Vienna was the first of a series of Congresses, which met in the years after the end of the war. They were the first sign of the great powers working together to ensure the peace of Europe. However, cohesion soon broke down. It became clear that the chief aim of Russia, Austria and Prussia was to prevent reform and the creation of constitutional government, and Britain and France took less and less part as a consequence.

▶ p. 141

1815
THE TREATY OF VIENNA

The Treaty of Vienna brought the Napoleonic war to a close and attempted to re-establish the status quo in Europe. All the Allies supported the principle of legitimacy, which restored the rulers of Europe to the thrones they had occupied before the outbreak of war. Only Germany was changed substantially, with the number of independent states being reduced from nearly 400 to less than 40. Britain's main interests were the retention of colonies conquered during the wars and the security of Europe. She joined the Quadruple Alliance, guaranteeing to provide 60,000 men if there was any further violation of treaties by France, but Britain did not sign the Holy Alliance, which was later used to suppress liberalism in western Europe. Castlereagh, the British foreign secretary called it a piece of 'sublime mysticism and nonsense'.

1818
VISCOUNT CASTLEREAGH

Viscount Castlereagh was the British representative at the Congress of Vienna and remained foreign secretary until he committed suicide in 1822. In Britain he was regarded as a conservative reactionary, but abroad he was seen as a dangerous liberal. He refused to agree to the demands of Russia, Austria and Prussia to be allowed to interfere in the internal affairs of countries in Europe. He could do little about the Austrian domination of Italy, but he used his influence to protect France, Spain and Portugal. His position led to a split between the Allies at the congresses after 1815. Castlereagh's policies were published in his state paper of May 1820, in which he set out his belief that the internal affairs of different countries were their own concern.

✳ ▶ p. 144

1820s
THE EASTERN QUESTION

From the 1820s the Eastern Question loomed ever larger in the minds of British foreign secretaries. It concerned the fate of the provinces of the Turkish Empire in the Balkans. As Turkish authority grew weaker, public opinion in Britain usually sided with their Christian subjects, as in the case of Greece in the 1820s, but British governments became increasingly concerned that the decline in Turkish power would lead to an advance by Russia towards the Mediterranean. British policy was normally to support the Sultan against attacks by Russia and attempts by his governors to break away from the authority of Istanbul. So when the governor of Egypt, Mehmet Ali tried to become independent in the 1830s and 1840s, Britain backed the Sultan.

▲ *The Turkish Sultan Abdul Aziz.*

1822
GEORGE CANNING

After Castlereagh's suicide in 1822, George Canning became foreign secretary. Although he had fought a duel with Castlereagh in 1809 and the two men had been enemies

▲ *English statesman George Canning, who became foreign secretary after the death of Castlereagh.*

ever since, their approaches to foreign policy were very similar. Canning believed even more strongly than Castlereagh that the great powers should not interfere in events outside their own countries. He supported the Greek rebellion in the 1820s, which led to the creation of the Greek state and he threatened to use the British navy to prevent intervention in the revolts, which broke out against Spanish rule in South America. He said, 'I have brought in the New World to redress the balance of the Old'.

▶ p. 142

1830
LORD PALMERSTON

In 1830, Lord Palmerston became British foreign secretary. Until his death in 1865 his policies dominated British foreign policy. Palmerston was a strange mixture. On the one hand he was a skilled diplomat, who settled the difficult question of Belgian independence in 1839, on the other hand, he was a keen exponent of gunboat diplomacy and did not hesitate to use force to support British interests around the world. In 1850 he compelled the Greek government to pay compensation to an extremely dubious character, Don Pacifico, who claimed that he had lost documents worth more than £20,000 in a fire in Athens. At the same time Palmerston supported liberal revolutions throughout Europe. In 1860 he allowed British warships to protect Giuseppe Garibaldi as he crossed from Sicily to Naples during his campaigns in southern Italy.

1836
THE GREAT TREK

In 1833, slavery was abolished in the British Empire. Only two areas were affected by this decision: the West Indies and South Africa. In the West Indies compensation was paid to slave owners, but in South Africa the slave-owning Boers left the colony and travelled north to set up two new states, the Orange Free State and the Transvaal. Their journey became known as the Great Trek and acquired huge significance in the history of South Africa. The two new states retained their independence until the 1870s, when they were threatened by the Zulus. The refusal of the Boers to accept the abolition of slavery was the basis of the Apartheid system, which developed formally in South Africa after the Second World War.

▲ *The South African slave-owners moved to the Transvaal on the official abolition of slavery.*

1839
CHINA

In 1839 fighting broke out between Britain and China over the opium trade, which was illegal in China. Lord Palmerston, the British foreign secretary, wanted to force the Chinese to accept opium and occupied Canton in 1840. Far more serious, however, was the Second Opium War, which began in 1857 after the Chinese authorities seized the *Arrow*, a ship carrying opium. Britain and France forced the Chinese to accept European diplomats in China and opened 11 ports to European traders. When the Chinese refused to allow western diplomats into Peking, the British occupied the city and burnt the Emperor's Summer Palace.

▶ p. 140

1854
THE CRIMEAN WAR

Russia had occupied the provinces of Moldavia and Wallachia in 1853, in an effort to put pressure on Turkey to allow Orthodox priests the right to control the holy places in Jerusalem, and the following year this dispute grew into a major war, which involved an invasion of the Crimea by a Franco-British force of 125,000 men, because the British government was afraid that Russia was planning to expand into the Balkans and try to take control of the Straits. The army spent two years besieging Sevastopol in the most appalling conditions, and suffered very heavy losses from disease. This suffering was relieved by the arrival of Florence Nightingale, who took over the hospital at Scutari. The British army displayed incredible heroism at the battles of the Alma, Balaclava and Inkermann.

p. 137◀ **Distant Voices** ▶p. 141

In our cavalry fight today we had 13 officers killed or missing, 156 men killed or missing; total, 169; 21 officers wounded, 197 men wounded; total, 218. Total killed, wounded or missing, 387. Horses, killed or missing, 394; horses wounded, 126; total, 520.

From a report that appeared in *The Times*, describing the Charge of the Light Brigade at the battle of Balaclava (1854)

The Scramble for Africa

1849–1902

IN THE SECOND HALF of the nineteenth century the European powers raced each other to occupy the continent of Africa. By 1914 there were only two independent African countries: the ancient kingdom of Ethiopia and Liberia, which had been set up in 1823 as a home for liberated American slaves. In northern Africa France was the dominant power, in the south Britain occupied vast areas, and people like Cecil Rhodes dreamt of a railway running from the Cape to Cairo, never leaving British soil. Elsewhere, Belgium occupied the Congo, tens of times its size, Portugal occupied Angola and modern Mozambique and Germany held modern Namibia.

1849–71
DAVID LIVINGSTONE

One reason for the Scramble for Africa was the wealth that Africa was believed to hold, but some Europeans were in Africa for a very different reason. David Livingstone was a Scottish missionary and explorer who made extensive journeys across Africa in the mid-nineteenth century. In 1849 he crossed the Kalahari Desert and in 1853–56 crossed the entire continent, discovering the Victoria Falls on the way. In 1858 he set off from the Zambezi and discovered Lake Nyasa and in 1866 discovered Lake Tanganyika. By this time his travels had caught the attention of the world and when he failed to emerge from Tanganyika, H. M. Stanley, an American journalist, set out to find him. The two men met in the famous encounter on the shores of Lake Tanganyika in 1871.

▼ *The Scottish missionary and explorer, David Livingstone.*

1877
THE BOERS

The Boers were the descendants of the original Dutch settlers of the Cape of Good Hope. When slavery was abolished in the British Empire in 1833, the Boers marched north and set up the Orange Free State. They had to fight bloody battles against the Zulus, led by Dingaan, but in 1838 defeated them at the battle of Blood River. In 1843 Natal was made a British colony and more Boers left, crossing the Vaal River to form the Transvaal, which became the South African Republic in 1856. In 1852 at the Sand River Convention, the British recognised the independence of the Boers. In 1877 diamonds were discovered in Griqualand on the Orange River and the British annexed the area, despite Boer protests. Later, they went even further and annexed the South African Republic.

▶ p. 146

1879
THE ZULU WAR

In 1879 war broke out between the British in South Africa and the Zulus, led by King Ceshwayo. At the battle of Insandhlwana, in January, a British column was massacred, but the Zulus lost so many men in the attack that Ceshwayo tried to restrain any further attacks. His decision was backed up by the experience of a Zulu army, which attacked a small British force at Rorke's Drift, a mission station. However, the British were not prepared to leave the Zulus alone. Reinforcements arrived from Britain and the Zulus were crushed at the battle of Ulundi in July. Ceshwayo surrendered the following month. During the Zulu War, the Boers had accepted the annexation of the South African Republic, but once the threat was removed they wanted independence.

1880
THE FIRST BOER WAR

In 1880 the Boers in the Transvaal revolted against British rule. At Laing's Nek and Majuba Hill they defeated British forces and the government signed the Treaty of Pretoria in 1881, which gave the South African Republic its independence. Foreign Policy was to be handled by the British government, however. In 1886 the whole situation was transformed, when gold was discovered in the Transvaal. Miners rushed from all over the world and the city of

▲ *Zulu warriors performing a war dance before meeting the British in the Zulu Wars.*

▲ *The discovery of gold in the Transvaal in South Africa led to the famous Gold Rushes.*

Johannesburg appeared almost over night. By 1890 it had a population of 100,000 and there were 450 mining companies operating in the area. The Boers treated the miners as foreigners, *Uitlanders*: they had no rights, could not vote and paid extra taxes. The miners began to look to Britain to protect them.

1890
CECIL RHODES

Cecil Rhodes founded the De Beers Mining Corporation in 1880, to dig for diamonds. In 1888 it was amalgamated with his main rival, Barnato's, and his company, Consolidated Gold Fields, soon controlled a large share of the gold industry. In 1889 he set up the British South Africa Company, which was allowed to explore the area north of the Transvaal. He occupied Mashonaland in 1890 and built the city of Salisbury. In the same year he became prime minister of Cape Colony. One of Rhodes's aims was to set up a customs union between Cape Colony, Natal, the Orange Free State and the South African Republic, but Kruger, the President, refused on behalf of the government in Johannesburg. In December 1895, Rhodes decided to try to force Kruger's hand.

1895
THE JAMESON RAID

The Jameson Raid was a futile attempt to create trouble in the South African Republic. Cecil Rhodes believed that there was an impending revolution in Johannesburg and organised an armed raid by his friend Starr Jameson, along with 600 men, into the Republic. Rhodes heard too late that the revolt was not going to take place and tried to stop the raid. He was unsuccessful and it was a disaster. Jameson and his men were either killed or rounded up and he was handed over for trial in Britain. In disgrace, Rhodes was forced to resign as prime minister of Cape Colony; it was virtually the end of his career. He died soon afterwards.

1900
THE SECOND BOER WAR

In 1897, Sir Alfred Milner became British High Commissioner in South Africa. He demanded that the *Uitlanders* be given the vote and refused to compromise. Kruger declared war on 12 October 1899, realising the weakness of British forces in South Africa. Until the end of the year, the British suffered defeat after defeat, but the arrival of General Roberts with reinforcements in January 1900 turned the tide. By September both Boer republics had been occupied and their capitals captured. The war dragged on for another 18 months as the Boers resorted to guerrilla tactics. General Kitchener, who took over command in November 1900, built blockhouses to defend railway lines and herd Boer civilians into concentration camps before he forced their leaders to surrender.

▶ p. 142

1902
THE TREATY OF VEREENIGING

The Treaty of Vereeniging brought the Second Boer War to an end in May 1902. The Boers accepted British control, but were granted £3,000,000 to rebuild their farms. In 1910 the Union of South Africa was set up, with four provinces, Cape Colony, Natal, Orange Free State and Transvaal. Capetown became the seat of the Parliament, Pretoria became the capital and Bloemfontein became the seat of the Court of Appeal. Dutch and English both became official languages. This was, therefore, a real attempt at compromise. In 1910, two Boer leaders, Botha and Hertzog, set up the South African Party, but in 1914, Hertzog broke away to form the Nationalist Party, which became exclusively Boer and drew most of its support from rural areas.

p. 139◀ **Distant Voices** ▶p. 143

The battle began soon after daybreak with a heavy rifle fire, opened up by the Boers from the river bed upon the mounted infantry while still at their breakfast. After some fairly severe fighting, the mounted infantry succeeded in driving back the Boers and cleared the river bed for about a quarter of a mile. The Shropshires and Canadians advanced by a series of short rushes in the most gallant style, the Canadians especially showing a magnificent and almost reckless courage.

A newspaper report of the battle of Paardeberg, during the Second Boer War (1900)

Splendid Isolation

1856–1907

AFTER THE CRIMEAN WAR, Britain increasingly avoided any permanent involvement in European affairs. This was partly because attention was focused more and more upon the empire, but also because British governments preferred not to take part in the alliance system, which became ever more complex from 1870. After the accession of Kaiser Wilhelm II in 1887 and the resignation of Bismarck in 1890, Britain became increasingly concerned at the more aggressive attitude adopted by Germany and ended her 'Splendid Isolation' in 1902. By 1914, Britain had developed a joint naval strategy with France, although the British army was to resist real co-operation with France until almost the end of the First World War.

▲ *The German kaiser, Wilhelm II.*

▶ p. 148

1856
THE TREATY OF PARIS

The Treaty of Paris brought the Crimean War to an end in 1856. It guaranteed the integrity of Turkey and forced Russia to evacuate the provinces of Moldavia and Wallachia. The Dardanelles were to remain closed to warships during peacetime, which meant that Russian warships would not be allowed into the Mediterranean. This was ignored by Russia only 15 years later, when France went to war with Prussia. But the Treaty could not rebuild the Turkish Empire, or reform the rule of the Sultans and the empire continued to disintegrate; Britain found itself increasingly supporting a regime which was transparently corrupt and often violent.

1861
BRITAIN AND THE AMERICAN CIVIL WAR

In 1861, civil war broke out between the states of the US. Thirteen slave-owning states in the South attempted to secede from the union and the president of the USA, Abraham Lincoln, sent the Federal army into action against them. The British government sympathised with the South, from where Britain obtained most of its cotton. When representatives of the Southern states were taken off a British ship, the *Trent*, by Federal officers there appeared to be a risk that Britain might enter the war on the Confederate side, but the crisis blew over. It soon became clear that public opinion in Britain backed the North. Cotton workers in Lancashire accepted long lay-offs when the blockade of southern ports by the Federal navy prevented supplies reaching Britain.

▶ p. 145

1878
THE CONGRESS OF BERLIN

In 1877, Russia went to war with Turkey to protect Slavs in the Turkish Empire. The treaty of San Stefano, which brought the war to an end in March 1878, set up a new large state of Bulgaria as well as granting independence to Montenegro and Serbia. This worried both the British and Austrian governments. They believed that the new state might easily fall under the control of Russia and both Montenegro and Serbia were likely to be pro-Russian. A conference was arranged at Berlin to settle the crisis. Bulgaria was divided into three parts and both Serbia and Montenegro were reduced in size. Austria was given the right to occupy Bosnia-Herzegovina. At the time this seemed a satisfactory compromise, but later events were to prove otherwise.

1900
THE NAVAL ARMS RACE

In 1898, the First German Navy Law was passed and was swiftly followed by the Second in 1900. The two laws laid out plans for the construction of a large navy designed to rival Britain's by 1917. This was an example of the Kaiser's determination to make Germany a world power. In Britain the Laws were viewed with alarm since there was no apparent reason why Germany needed a navy, except to attack Britain. The British government responded by beginning a programme of warship construction intended to maintain the 'two-power standard', which had been the basis of naval policy in the late nineteenth century. It simply stated that the British navy should be as big as the next two largest navies combined.

1902
JAPAN

Fear of the expansion of the German navy was one of the reasons why Britain began to look for allies at the beginning of the twentieth century. A natural choice was Japan, with whom Britain already had close ties. Since 1870 many Japanese naval cadets had been trained in Britain and the Japanese navy had been reorganised on British lines. The Treaty signed in 1902 meant that, in the event of war, the Japanese navy would look after British interests in the Far East, allowing the British navy to concentrate on European waters. This was the first break in Britain's policy of Splendid Isolation.

▲ *Japanese cadets trained in Britain combined the skills of the Japanese and British armies.*

1904
ENTENTE CORDIALE

A much more important step in British foreign policy was the Entente Cordiale signed between Britain and France in 1904. It was not a treaty as such, but a settling of long-standing sources of friction. Britain recognised French influence in Morocco and the French recognised British influence in Egypt. Territorial disputes in Canada, Africa and Indo-China were also settled. More significant, however, was the fact that the Entente led subsequently to discussions on naval issues. The two navies agreed to divide responsibility for European waters. In 1912 the British navy withdrew its forces from the Mediterranean and the French navy withdrew its forces from the Channel.

1906
DREADNOUGHT

In 1906, the British navy launched HMS *Dreadnought*, a battleship which made all existing battleships out-of-date. It carried ten 12-inch guns and had a top speed of 21 knots. The German navy responded by building dreadnoughts of its own and the Naval Arms Race speeded up. Between 1906 and 1914 the British built 29 dreadnoughts and the Germans built 17. By 1914 the ships carried 15-inch guns and their oil-fired turbine engines could reach a top speed of 25 knots. The British public became very much involved in the race. In 1909 the popular cry was, 'We want eight, we won't wait', and a Navy League was formed to campaign for more and more ships. This added to anti-German feelings, which had become increasingly prevalent since 1890.

1907
THE TRIPLE ENTENTE

In 1907, Britain signed an Entente with Russia. As in the case of the Entente Cordiale, its most immediate effects were the settlement of outstanding disputes between the two countries in Persia, Afghanistan and Tibet. But the agreement also drew Britain into the system of alliances, which had dominated European politics since 1870. Britain was now clearly aligned with France and Russia against the powers of the Triple Alliance: Germany, Austria-Hungary and Italy. The Triple Entente, as it came to be known, did not commit Britain to defend or support the other two powers, but it did make British support for them much more likely in the event of war.

▼ *The steam battleship that was to change the face of naval warfare after 1906 – the* Dreadnought.

p. 141◀ **Distant Voices** ▶p. 145

While great naval power in the hands of Britain cannot constitute a menace, in the hands of Germany it will be a great peril to the world, the more so as the recent history of German policy is one of daring aggression and as the want of space at home compels Germany to conquer the colonies of others or perish.

From an article in the *Daily Mail*, describing the growth of the German navy (1903)

From Empire to Commonwealth

1867–1994

AT THE END OF THE nineteenth century, the British Empire covered about one quarter of the inhabited world. Children in British schools coloured in maps to show the extent of the empire on which the 'sun never set'; but almost as soon as it reached its peak, the empire began to break up and in 1931, the Statute of Westminster declared that the dominions were independent members of a free 'Commonwealth of Nations'. Although the British monarch is the head of the Commonwealth, individual countries can be republics or retain the monarch as their head of state and in the Commonwealth all member countries are equal. It is the second largest international organisation in the world; only the United Nations is bigger.

THE DEVELOPMENT OF THE BRITISH EMPIRE, 1815–1914

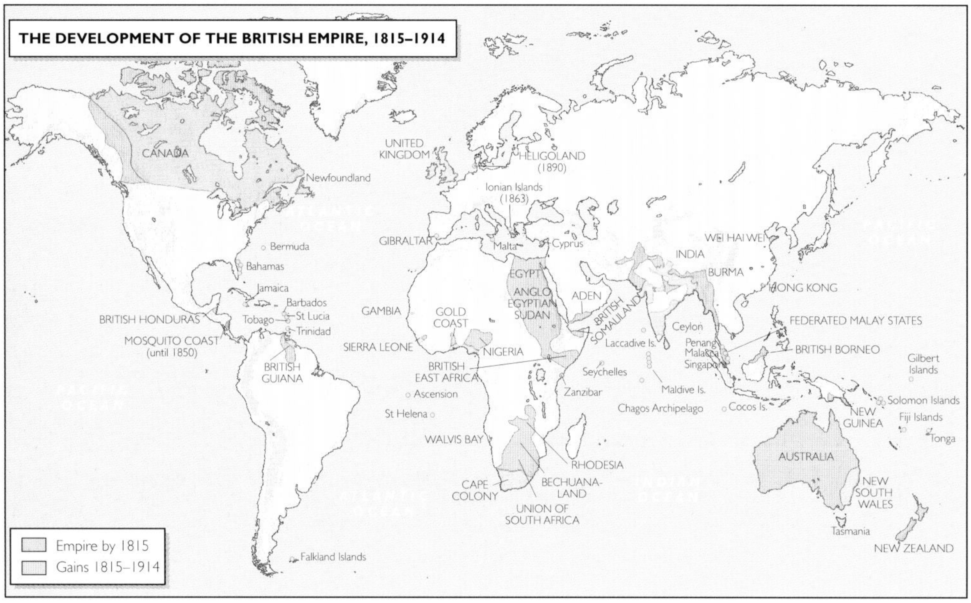

✳ 1867–1910
DOMINIONS

Dominion status meant the creation of an integrated self-governing country within the British Empire. The idea was first put forward in the Durham Report of 1839, which investigated the causes of riots in Canada in 1837. The first dominion to be founded was Canada in 1867, then Australia in 1900, New Zealand in 1907 and South Africa in 1910. Until these dates each of these countries had been made up of individual colonies, which often competed between themselves, particularly in the cases of Canada and South Africa, which had different racial groups. Each dominion was given a central government, but also state or provincial governments. They were free to develop their own policies, but supported Britain in both the First and Second World Wars.

1867
CANADA

The Dominion of Canada, comprising Quebec, Ontario, New Brunswick and Nova Scotia was set up by the British North America Act in 1867. It had a central government in Ontario. Manitoba joined the dominion in 1870 and British Columbia in 1871. This led to the building of the Canadian Pacific Railway, which linked the provinces together even more firmly. Alberta and Saskatchewan both joined in 1905. Although dominion status helped to ease the differences which existed between the British and French settlers, they did not go away and are now stronger than ever. Quebec is one of the few areas of the Commonwealth from where people have made a determined effort to leave.

1900
AUSTRALIA

Australia was originally colonised by the British as a collection of small settlements, which were vast distances apart. In 1855, Victoria, New South Wales, South Australia and Tasmania were all given their own Parliaments; Queensland followed later that year and Western Australia in 1890. In 1900, with Germany having occupied Papua and the French in Tahiti, the Commonwealth of Australia Act was passed, which united the states into a dominion. It was believed that this would make the defence of Australia against foreign attack more effective. Many Australians served at Gallipoli in the First World War and in the Far East in the Second World War.

1907
NEW ZEALAND

New Zealand became a British dominion in 1907, despite fierce resistance to British settlement there in the early years of the nineteenth century. As the century progressed, Britain became increasingly determined to annexe the country. The Treaty of Waitangi ceded North Island to the British Crown in 1840, and Britain later staked its claim to South Island by right of discovery. Although the status of dominion was granted in 1907, it was not until after the Second World War that New Zealand acknowledged its independence. The country had fought on the Allied side during the First World War, mainly with its Australian cousins at Gallipoli.

▲ *Mixed bathing on a beach in Durban, South Africa, after the decline of the apartheid regime.*

1949
APARTHEID

The beginnings of apartheid can be traced back to the Great Trek of 1836, when the Boers chose to leave Cape Colony rather than free their slaves. Many whites in South Africa regarded the native Africans as inferior, and apartheid really began in 1949 with the founding of the National Party. In theory apartheid meant 'separate development', the idea that blacks, whites and coloureds should live their lives apart. What made the system so objectionable was that apart came to mean completely different standards, which were controlled by the whites. A black African had to carry a pass at all times, was not allowed in certain areas and could not use the same facilities or schools as a white. In the 1960s and 1970s these laws were rigorously enforced – violently if necessary.

1950s
DECOLONISATION

Decolonisation is the withdrawal of Britain from its colonies in the period after the Second World War. The first example was the independence of India and Pakistan in August 1947; this was followed by independence for most of Britain's colonies in Africa in the 1950s and 1960s. Ghana was the first in 1957 and then Nigeria in 1960. In most cases British withdrawal was achieved without violence, but in Kenya the Mau Mau, a terrorist organisation, began to attack white settlers. It took four years of fighting (1952 to 1956) to defeat them.

▶ p. 153

1965
UDI

Rhodesia, which had been founded by Cecil Rhodes in the 1890s, was dominated by about 200,000 white settlers. When the neighbouring colonies gained independence in 1964, the white Rhodesians decided to prevent a similar occurrence by declaring UDI, a Unilateral Declaration of Independence. This was announced by the prime minister, Ian Smith on 11 November 1965. For 10 years Rhodesia survived, but in the late 1970s there were increasing attacks from guerrillas led by Robert Mugabe. Eventually sanctions forced Ian Smith to allow free elections in 1980 and Mugabe's party won 57 seats out of 80. He became the first prime minister of the new country of Zimbabwe.

1994
SOUTH AFRICA

On 11 February 1990, Nelson Mandela, the vice-president of the African National Congress, was released from prison in South Africa, where he had been since 1963. He had been in prison since 1963. From this time, there was increasing pressure on South Africa by Britain, the Commonwealth and the United Nations to end its policy of apartheid. By releasing Mandela the South African government hoped that it would be possible to reach a compromise with the ANC. This did not happen. Talks dragged on for four years before a general election was held in April 1994. The ANC won with 62.5 per cent of the votes and Nelson Mandela became the president of South Africa. One of his first actions was to apply for readmission to the Commonwealth, which the old regime had left in 1961.

▼ *Nelson Mandela, leader of the ANC, was a key figure in the fight against the oppression of the black African population.*

p. 143◀ **Distant Voices** ▶p. 147

I told de Klerk that the ANC had not struggled against apartheid for 75 years only to yield to a disguised form of it; if it was his true intention to preserve apartheid through the Trojan horse of group rights, then he did not truly believe in ending apartheid.

From *The Long Walk to Freedom* by Nelson Mandela (1994)

The First World War
1914–18

IN AUGUST 1914 Britain declared war upon Germany to honour the promise made in the Treaty of Westminster in 1839 – and entered the First World War. Most people in Britain supported the war and the news was greeted with great enthusiasm, Recruiting stations were besieged and within a month one million men had volunteered to join the army. It was to be the greatest war in history, on so big a scale that from 1919 it was known simply as the Great War, no other name seemed appropriate. There was hardly a person in Britain who did not feel intense relief when the war finally ended on 11 November 1918. There were also few who did not share the view that this must be the 'war to end all wars'.

1914
DECLARATION OF WAR

On 4 August 1914 Germany declared war on Belgium and put into practice the Schlieffen Plan. This involved German forces marching through Belgium to attack the French army from the rear. The Belgian government appealed to Britain for support. When Belgium had become independent in 1839, Britain had guaranteed to defend it, and in 1914 this promise was kept. 160,000 British troops were hastily assembled and sent across the Channel as quickly as possible. Even London buses were sent to speed their arrival in Belgium. By 21 August the British troops were taking up positions near the town of Mons ready to meet the German army.

1914
THE BEF

The troops sent to Belgium in August 1914 were part of the British Expeditionary Force, the BEF, commanded by Sir John French. On 23 August they were attacked by the Germans and fought a five-day battle, slowly retreating before the German attacks. Outnumbered many times, the BEF had no chance of defeating the Germans, but it did play an important part in preventing the Schlieffen plan from succeeding. The German advance was slowed sufficiently to allow the French army to recover and face the Germans at the Marne on 5 September. The Germans were stopped and then forced back. By the end of October the frontline was stabilised and the armies dug themselves into trenches. They were to be there for four years.

▶ p. 150

1915
YPRES

By the end of October 1914 the remnants of the BEF found itself in Ypres. The town was very low-lying and surrounded by shallow hills, which were occupied by the Germans. It contained an enormous cloth hall and a cathedral, both with tall spires. They made excellent targets for the German gunners. The British held Ypres (they called it 'Wipers') for four years and by 1918 there were virtually no buildings

▲ *Destruction being wreaked around the Ypres salient during the First World War.*

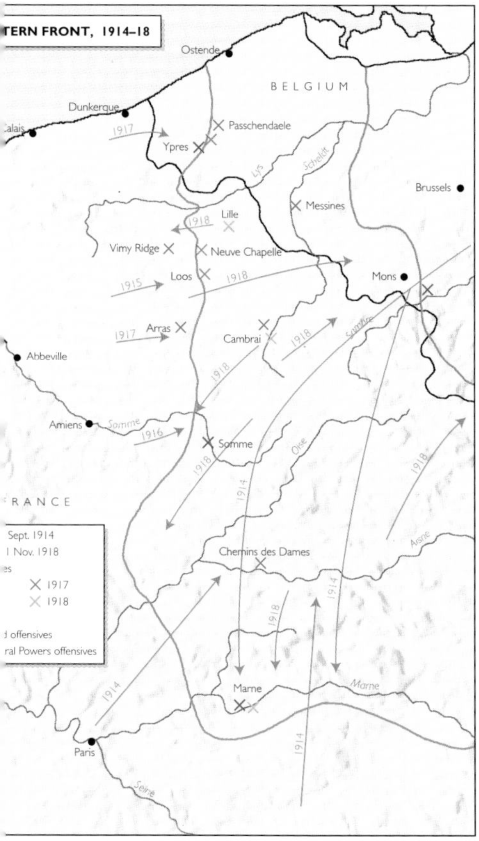

left standing. In 1915 the Germans attacked from the north at Langemarck and used poison gas for the first time. 8,000 soldiers were killed. In 1917 the British tried to break out and dug 18 enormous mines under the German lines and exploded them. The intensity of the blast wreaked death and havoc amongst the German troops.

1915
GALLIPOLI

The impossibility of breaking through the front lines on the Western Front in France led to an attempt to strike at the enemy from the south. In April 1915, Allied forces landed at Gallipoli in Turkey. The aim was to force Turkey, Germany's ally, out of the war and then link up with the Russian army. The landings succeeded, but little further progress was made. The Allied troops had to attack uphill against well-trained and well dug-in Turkish troops. A second landing was made at Suvla Bay in August, but this failed to break the deadlock. In December 1915, the Allied forces were evacuated by night. This was the most successful part of the disastrous operation.

1916
THE WAR AT SEA

For most of the war the Royal Navy commanded the high seas. The German fleet, which had been built since 1900 made little attempt to leave port and fight. Only on one occasion was there a major naval battle, in May 1916 off Jutland. The result was inconclusive. Britain lost more ships, but the German ships returned to port and did not emerge again. Instead the Germans launched unrestricted U-boat warfare, in an attempt to starve Britain out. In the first half of 1917 this was very successful and many ships were sunk, but the introduction of the convoy system reduced losses and Britain survived. At the same time the Royal Navy imposed a strict blockade on Germany, which produced severe shortages by early 1918.

1917
PASSCHENDAELE

Haig's second major battle was at Passchendaele, north of Ypres, which began in August 1917. Once again it was preceded by a massive artillery bombardment, which this time destroyed not the German positions, but the drainage systems. When the British troops tried to advance they had to lay duckboards to prevent themselves drowning in mud. Once again the battle was called off in November, after an advance of six miles. Even today the bodies of soldiers from the First World War are dug up in the fields around Ypres and the names of 54,000 soldiers who have no known grave are recorded upon the Menin Gate at the eastern end of the town.

1918
THE ARMISTICE

In March 1918 the German army launched a massive attack on the Allied lines. They had recently been able to move a million soldiers from the Eastern Front after the surrender of Russia and they knew that American troops would soon be arriving in Europe. The attack was very successful at first and the Allies were driven back more than 50 miles, but there the line held. When the Allies counterattacked the Germans had no prepared defences and they in turn were forced back. By the end of October the German army was on the brink of collapse and the Allies were about to invade Germany. The Socialist government, which had seized power on 9 November, agreed to an armistice, which took effect at 11.00 a.m. on 11 November 1918.

p. 132◀ **Triumphs & Tragedies** ▶p. 149

1916
THE SOMME

In December 1915, Douglas Haig became the commander-in-chief of the British forces on the Western Front: He believed that the deadlock could be broken by weight of numbers and prepared for a major battle in 1916. Originally he intended to attack near Ypres, but the German attacks on Verdun, which began in February, made him change his plans. Instead the attack would take place near the River Somme and would, it was hoped, take pressure off the French forces further east. Haig believed that a heavy bombardment would destroy the German defences. The infantry would then walk across and clear the way for a massive cavalry advance. On the first day of the battle the British army suffered 70,000 casualties and when the attacks were called off in November, less than five miles of land had been gained.

p. 145◀ **Distant Voices** ▶p. 149

We stay in the front line eight days and nights; then go out for the same period. The men are practically without rest. The are wet through much of the time. They are shelled. They work all night, and a good part of each day, digging filling sandbags, and repairing the trench. The temperature is icy. They have not even a blanket.

From a diary of an officer who served during the First World War (1916)

Collective Security

1919–39

THE IMPACT OF THE First World War was so enormous that the leaders of the Allies decided to set up an international organisation to prevent such an event ever recurring; it was known as the League of Nations. The most important characteristic of the years from 1919 to 1939 was the failure to maintain and support the aims and ideals expressed in the Covenant of the League of Nations. One country after another either ignored the Covenant or failed to enforce its terms on others when it was broken. Yet, despite these failings, many people in Britain continued to believe in the League long after it had been proved to be an ineffective force.

1919
THE TREATY OF VERSAILLES

The leaders of the Allies met at Versailles, France, in March to discuss the peace terms to be imposed on Germany. David Lloyd George, the British prime minister, had fought a general election in December 1918 with the slogan 'Make Germany Pay', but when he arrived at Versailles he wanted to avoid really harsh conditions, for fear that these might provoke a backlash in Germany. Lloyd George did manage to tone down the demands of the French to some extent, but overall the Germans came to see the Treaty as humiliation. Britain gained most of the German colonies, under League of Nations mandates, and was handed the German fleet. When the German crews heard the terms of the treaty they scuttled all of the ships in Scapa Flow.

1920
THE LEAGUE OF NATIONS

The League of Nations came into being on 1 January 1920. It was intended to have a Council of nine members, five of them permanent, an Assembly, which met once a year and a secretariat headed by a secretary-general. Despite President Wilson's leadership, the US did not join, as Congress refused to ratify Wilson's actions. Although the League could apply military sanctions against members, it did not have any military forces and had to persuade members to declare war on countries that broke the Covenant. But in the long run its most fundamental weakness was that three of the permanent members of the Council, Japan, Italy and Germany, left in the 1930s, and after this the remaining two, Britain and France, bore the whole burden of enforcing the League's decisions.

◀ *The controversial prime minister during and after the war years, David Lloyd George.*

1931
MANCHURIA

In 1931, Japan invaded Manchuria, which was a province of China, claiming that they were acting in self-defence. The Japanese set up the puppet state of Manchukuo, with the last emperor of China, Pu Yi, as its head. The League of Nations set up a Commission of Inquiry under the Earl of Lytton to investigate. In October the Lytton Commission reported that there was no evidence that the Japanese had acted in self-defence and recommended that Manchuria should be an autonomous region under Chinese control. The Japanese ignored the report and the condemnation from the League and resigned in 1933.

1935
ABYSSINIA

In October 1935, Italy attacked the African kingdom of Abyssinia (Ethiopia). Consequently, in November, the League of Nations imposed economic sanctions upon Italy, but did not include oil, which the Italian dictator Mussolini later said would have forced him to withdraw. Britain attempted to

▼ *The Italian dictator Benito Mussolini, who set up a fascist regime during the Second World War.*

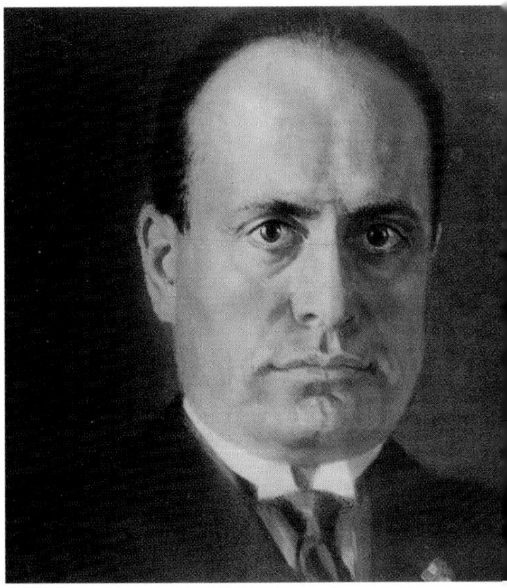

▲ *Hitler attempted to 'cleanse' Germany of those he deemed undesirable, most notably the Jews.*

reach a compromise with Mussolini and put forward the Hoare-Laval Pact, in conjunction with France. This would have allowed Italy to retain a large part of Abyssinia, but the Pact failed. Britain's actions in proposing the Pact and in opposing sanctions involving oil were prompted by her desire to keep Mussolini as an ally against Hitler, who had left the League of Nations in 1933 and who had begun to rearm in 1935. Italy left the League in 1937 and signed the Pact of Steel with Germany.

1938
APPEASEMENT

Increasingly the British and French governments began to adopt the policy of Appeasement towards the dictators in the 1930s. This was the belief that if the demands of the dictators were met they would be satisfied. In Britain, Appeasement had widespread support, partly because memories of the horrors of the First World War were still in many people's minds, but also because Hitler was seen as a successful leader who was curing unemployment and who might be a useful ally against Communism in the future. So when Hitler reoccupied the Rhineland in March 1936 and occupied Austria in March 1938, the protests from Britain and France were only half-hearted.

1939
CZECHOSLOVAKIA

In March 1939, Hitler occupied the rest of western Czechoslovakia. Chamberlain realised that Appeasement had failed and immediately signed defensive agreements with Poland and Romania. These guaranteed that Britain would defend these countries if they were attacked. Chamberlain intended that this should be a warning to Hitler and he backed it up by ordering the beginning of conscription in Britain in June 1939, the first time that this had ever happened in peacetime. Hitler ignored the warning and in August signed the Nazi-Soviet Pact with Stalin. This was to ensure that Stalin did not attack Germany when Hitler invaded Poland, his next target.

1939
POLAND

Hitler invaded Poland on 1 September 1939. On 2 September the British government sent a note to Berlin demanding that the German forces withdraw, or agree to withdraw, by 11.00 a.m. on 3 September. Hitler ignored the note and the invasion continued. He believed that Chamberlain was bluffing as he had not taken any action in the past. Chamberlain now had no option as the British government had promised to defend Poland; on the other hand, in the past Britain had had no such treaty obligations to Czechoslovakia or Austria. At 11.00 a.m. on 3 September, Britain went to war with Germany. Chamberlain announced the declaration on the BBC Home Service in a special broadcast at 11.45 am. Everything he had worked for had collapsed.

p. 147◀ **Triumphs & Tragedies** ▶p. 150

1938
MUNICH

In September 1938, Hitler demanded self-government for the Sudeten Germans who lived in Czechoslovakia. Neville Chamberlain, the British prime minister, flew to Germany to meet Hitler and agreed to his demands. Chamberlain persuaded the French government and the Czechs to accept the situation; he then returned to Germany to give Hitler the news. He found that Hitler had new demands. The Sudetenland must be handed over to Germany immediately. Chamberlain returned to Britain and prepared for war, but at the last moment Mussolini suggested a four-power conference to discuss the matter. Germany, Italy, France and Britain met at Munich on 29 September and agreed to hand over the Sudetenland. Chamberlain returned in triumph to London with an agreement signed by Hitler, who had promised never to go to war with Britain again.

p. 147◀ **Distant Voices** ▶p. 151

I had established a certain confidence which was my aim in spite of the hardness and ruthlessness I thought I saw in his face, I got the impression that here was a man who would be relied upon when he had given his word.

From a letter written by Neville Chamberlain to his sister, after meeting Hitler (September 1938)

Never in the Field of Human Conflict
1940–44

WHEN PEOPLE IN Britain heard Neville Chamberlain's speech on the wireless on the morning of 3 September 1939, they had many ideas of what war might entail. In 1937, newsreel of the bombing of Guernica had shown what damage could be done to undefended cities and the worst was expected. In fact, for over seven months, very little happened, and it was not until the late summer of 1940 that the full effects of total war were felt in Britain. Then for 12 months Britain faced Hitler alone. Even then, it took three more years before British forces landed in Normandy and a further 11 months before Germany surrendered in the spring of 1945.

p. 149◀ **Triumphs & Tragedies** ▶p. 151

1940
DUNKIRK

In September 1939 a British Expeditionary Force had sailed to Belgium, just as in 1914. In May 1940, the German advance cut it off from the French forces and it was pushed back towards Calais and Dunkirk. As the BEF crowded onto the beaches of the two ports the Royal Navy attempted to rescue it. Fortunately, at this point, Hitler made one of his periodic interventions in military strategy. He ordered the German tanks to halt on the outskirts of Dunkirk. Possibly he believed that this would give the British government a chance to ask for terms, but instead 310,000 British troops were rescued from the beaches. Almost all their equipment was lost, however.

1940
THE PHONEY WAR

Only minutes after Chamberlain's announcement of the declaration of war, air-raid sirens sounded in London. This was a familiar sound as there had been many practices both in September 1938 and during the recent weeks. But it was a false alarm. There was no bombing of London or of any other city in Britain in 1939, or in the early months of 1940. The evacuees began to return home, air-raid precautions began to be relaxed, and people began to wonder if there was going to be a war after all. In fact almost nothing happened until Easter 1940, when Hitler suddenly invaded Holland and Norway, then struck through Belgium and into France.

1940
THE BATTLE OF BRITAIN

In August 1940, the Luftwaffe began to attack the Royal Air Force. It was assumed in Britain that this was a prelude to an invasion. At first radar stations on the coast were attacked and then airfields were bombed. Finally the Luftwaffe attempted to destroy Fighter Command. The British fighters – the Hurricane and the Spitfire – were more than a match for the opposition, but Britain had only a limited number of trained pilots, and it was this that began to tip the balance at the beginning of September. Hitler intervened and ordered the Luftwaffe to stop attacking Fighter Command on 7 September and attack London instead, by night. This gave the RAF a chance to recover. When the next daytime attack took place on 15 September, the RAF defeated the Luftwaffe. The Battle of Britain was over.

1940
THE BLITZ

When the Luftwaffe lost the Battle of Britain, it began to bomb London and the other cities of Britain, night after night: this was the Blitz. The aim of Hitler was to break the morale of the British people and force the government to surrender. He nearly succeeded. Although the newspapers were full of stories describing people's resilience, the winter of 1940–41 was very difficult, as bombing destroyed homes, lives and families. London was bombed continuously for 53 nights and the raid on Coventry in November killed 500 people. Every major

▼ *A Hawker Hurricane plane, used by the British during the Second World War.*

town and city in the British Isles was attacked. In 1941 the bombing slackened off as Hitler prepared to attack the USSR.

1941
THE BATTLE OF THE ATLANTIC

From 1941, Hitler attempted to starve Britain by attacking convoys in the Atlantic. U-boats were sent out in packs to attack supply convoys from the USA. Winston Churchill later confessed that this was the only time during the war that he was really frightened. In the Spring of 1941, more than 300 ships were sunk, and even when the US joined the war in December 1941, little could be done to stop German U-boats. The battle was not finally won until 1943. By then convoys could be escorted all the way by warships and also be given air cover by long-range flying boats.

1942
NORTH AFRICA

At the beginning of the Second World War, Egypt and Palestine were held by Britain. Italy was occupying Libya and invaded Egypt in September 1940. The invasion failed completely and the British were able to force the Italians back and take more than 100,000 prisoners. In April 1941, German General Rommel was sent to support the Italians and he advanced into Egypt once again. He captured Tobruk and then reached El Alamein about 113 km (70 miles) from Alexandria. In October 1942 the British Eighth Army, under General Montgomery, attacked Rommel at El Alamein and drove the Germans out of Egypt. In December, US forces landed in Morocco and by May 1943 all of North Africa was in the hands of the Allies.

p. 150◀ **Triumphs & Tragedies** ▶p. 156

1944
D-DAY

On 6 June 1944, Allied forces landed on five beaches in Normandy to begin the liberation of Europe. British and Commonwealth forces landed on three beaches and US forces on the other two. Breaking out of the beachhead took more than a month, but after that Paris was liberated in early August and the Rhine was reached in September. The British army tried to seize the bridges across the Rhine at Arnhem, but failed. Germany was not invaded until the following spring. On 30 April 1945, Hitler committed suicide in Berlin, and eight days later Germany surrendered to the Allies.

▼ *The bombing of the US naval base Pearl Harbor by the Japanese.*

▲ *Allied forces land on the beaches of Normandy on D-Day, one of the greatest amphibious manoeuvres in the history of warfare.*

1942
THE FAR EAST

After the attack on Pearl Harbor by the Japanese in December 1941, most British territories in the Far East were overrun. Hong Kong surrendered in December 1941 and Malaya and Singapore in February 1942. A force of British warships on its way to Singapore was overwhelmed by Japanese aircraft and destroyed. The Japanese then overran Burma and tried to invade India. British and Commonwealth prisoners of war were forced to build the notorious Burma-Siam railway and 60,000 died in the process. But from that point the Allies began to strike back. In 1944, British forces drove three Japanese armies out of Burma, with 350,000 Japanese casualties.

p. 149◀ **Distant Voices** ▶p. 153

The whole of the warring nations are involved, not only soldiers, but the entire population. The fronts are everywhere. Every village is fortified. Every road is barred. The front lines run through the factories. The workmen are soldiers with different weapons, but with the same courage.

From a speech made by Winston Churchill (1940)

No More a Superpower

1945–82

THROUGHOUT THE SECOND WORLD WAR, Winston Churchill attended all the conferences as one of the Allied leaders. Great Britain was, in fact, the only one of the Allies to be at war constantly from September 1939 to August 1945. By the end of the War, however, it was already becoming clear that the leader of the western Allies was Franklin Roosevelt, the US president. He, and his successor, Harry Truman, took all the key decisions in the final months of the War. Churchill and his successor, Clement Attlee, attended the conferences at Yalta and Potsdam and took responsibility for one zone of Germany. It soon became clear, however, that Britain was not able to match the economic and military might of the two Superpowers, as the USA and the USSR were to be known in the future.

1945
YALTA AND POTSDAM

The British prime ministers attended the conferences at Yalta and Potsdam as of right. Britain had led the struggle against Germany for the first two years of the war and there was no question of her being excluded from the decisions to be taken on the future of Europe. However, it was already clear that the USA was taking the lead in western policy. Roosevelt had turned down Churchill's suggestion of an Allied drive to Berlin in 1945 and seemed prepared to trust Stalin's promises about free elections in eastern Europe. Although Britain was granted equal status in the occupation of Germany, the main western voice at both conferences was the USA's.

1945
THE UNITED NATIONS

The United Nations was set up in April 1945. The name had been chosen by Franklin Roosevelt to describe the countries which were fighting against the Axis powers during the Second World War and all three Allies had agreed to take part in the UNO at the conferences of Yalta and Potsdam. Britain, along with the USA, the USSR, France and China, became a Permanent Member of the Security Council. This gave her special importance, prestige and power. It meant that Britain was right at the heart of the UNO and could also veto any Security Council Resolution. Britain has retained her place on the Security Council ever since.

1947
THE GREEK CIVIL WAR

Several areas of Europe remained unsettled after 1945, one was Greece, where a civil war broke out between the government and Communist rebels. Britain supported the government with financial and military aid, but in 1947, in the face of severe austerity at home, the government decided that it could no longer afford to back the Greek government. Truman, the US president, offered to step in and took the opportunity to announce the Truman Doctrine. This offered US support to any country where the legitimate government was being attacked by a minority either from inside the country or from outside. This was the first time that the US undertook the defence of the free world. When Marshall Aid was offered soon after, Britain was one of the first countries to accept it.

1948
THE BERLIN AIRLIFT

In 1947, Britain and the US united their zones of Germany in what was called 'Bizonia' and set about helping the country to recover from the effects of the War. In 1948, the French were also included. When the Allies attempted to introduce a new currency in the western zones, Stalin closed the borders with the west, preventing contact by land, canal or rail with the Allied sectors in Berlin. For 10 1/2 months the Allies supplied West Berlin by air, approximately one third of the flights were undertaken by Britain. When the blockade was lifted in May 1949, Britain, the USA and France established the Federal Republic of Germany, with its capital in Bonn.

1949
NATO

The North Atlantic Treaty Organisation was set up in 1949 in response to the Berlin Blockade. Thirteen countries signed the treaty including Britain and the US. The most important aspect of the treaty was the clause that stated that an attack on one member would be taken to be an attack on all of the members. This was intended to deter any attacks from eastern Europe. By signing the treaty Britain was linking her security to that of western Europe. US bases were set up in Britain and eventually nuclear weapons were located there. This was the first time that Britain had undertaken a long-term treaty commitment to continental Europe. To this day, none of the members of NATO has been attacked.

▼ *The original North Atlantic Treaty, signed by 13 member countries.*

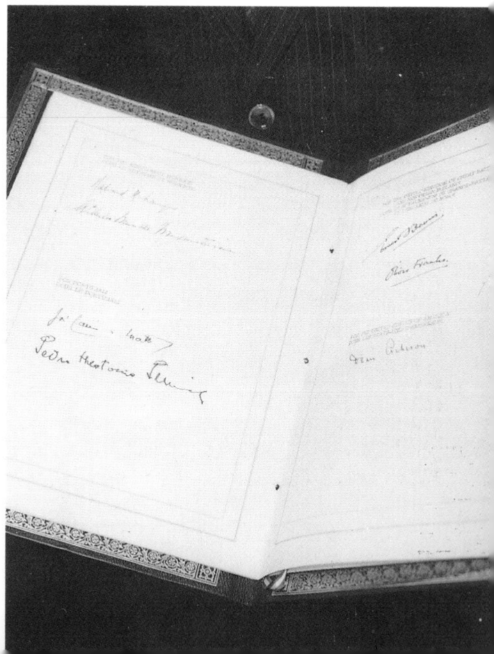

▲ *The takeover by Egypt of the Franco-British run Suez Canal Company, led to the Suez Crisis in 1956.*

1956
THE SUEZ CRISIS

Britain held responsibility for Egypt from the 1880s until 1922, and continued to station troops in the Suez Canal Zone. In 1952 there was a revolution in Egypt, which forced the king to abdicate and then set up a republic. In 1954 the British troops were forced to leave, British and French banks were nationalised and in 1956 the Suez Canal Company, which was owned by Britain and France, was taken over. In October 1956, Britain and France landed troops and seized control of the Canal. The Israeli army invaded Egypt at the same time. The action was condemned by the United Nations and by the US government. The British forces were withdrawn and Britain had to accept the actions of the Egyptian government, led by President Nasser.

1973
THE EEC

In the late 1940s, there was a series of discussions about plans to unify Europe. These led to the setting up of the European Coal and Steel Community in 1951, which was the basis of the European Economic Community when it was formed in 1957. Britain took little part in these proceedings, believing that her links with the Commonwealth and the USA made them irrelevant. But it soon became clear that the Common Market, as it came to be known, was a success. In 1961 and 1967 Britain applied to join, but was prevented by the French president Charles de Gaulle. He believed that Britain's links with the US were too strong and that she was not committed to Europe. After de Gaulle's death in 1970, Britain applied for a third time and became a member in 1973.

1982
THE FALKLANDS WAR

Britain took possession of the Falkland Islands in 1771. In 1838, Argentina tried to force Britain to hand them back and Britain blockaded the Argentine coast in reply. Further demands were made in the twentieth century but all were refused. In March 1982, 10,000 Argentine troops landed on the Falkland Islands and South Georgia was occupied at the same time. The handful of British troops on the islands surrendered. A task force of 3,500 men was assembled in Britain to retake the islands. The first landings were made at San Carlos and then forces moved south to Goose Green and East to Tumbledown. The Argentine forces surrendered in June. Altogether more than 330 British servicemen were killed retaking the islands.

◀ *Marines training aboard ship during the Falklands conflict between Britain and Argentina.*

p. 151◀ **Distant Voices** ▶p. 157

I urge you to avoid the use of force, at least until it has been proved to the world that the United Nations is incapable of handling the problem. To invade Egypt merely because that country has chosen to nationalise a company, will be seen by the world as power politics and raise a storm of resentment.

From a letter by President Eisenhower to Anthony Eden, the British prime minister, during the Suez Crisis (1956)

Industry and Invention

MAN, IN CONTRAST WITH other species, does not possess highly developed instinctive reactions but he does have the incredible ability to think systematically and creatively about techniques. It is because of this he can innovate and consciously modify his environment in a way no other species has ever managed. A monkey may occasionally use a stick to knock bananas out of a tree but a man can fashion the stick into a cutting tool and gain a whole bunch of bananas. Over the history of man he has grown through these techniques to build up civilised cultures, complex industries and incredible inventions. This chapter shows the growth and development of British invention and industry over the centuries. It shows how British manufacture grew from its basic origins in metal goods, pottery and textiles through to industry, assuming a greater economic significance with the coming of the Industrial Revolution in the eighteenth and nineteenth centuries. In addition it will show how, through the study of warfare and the input of many great British thinkers and inventors, our small country has often led the world in inventions and innovations of great significance, and not just in war.

KEY THEMES

- TRANSPORT & TRAVEL
- AGRICULTURE
- EXTRACTION & PROCESSING
- POWER & ENERGY
- INVENTIONS
- MATERIALS
- CONSTRUCTION
- MEDIA & COMMUNICATIONS
- MANUFACTURING
- TOOLS & WEAPONS

KEY EVENTS

1 3100 BC
A MONUMENT IN THE MAKING

Stonehenge, the monumental circular setting of large standing stones surrounded by a circular earthwork, was built around 3100 BC and is located about 13 km (8 miles) north of Salisbury, England. The Stonehenge that survives today is considerably ruined, many of its stones having been pilfered by medieval and early modern builders.

2 AD 896
A GREAT HISTORY OF LEARNING

Alfred the Great aimed at supplying men with 'the books most necessary for all men to know' in their own language. He had acquired an education despite great difficulties, and he translated some books himself with the help of scholars from the Continent. Compilation of the *Anglo-Saxon Chronicle* began in his reign.

3 1300s
SHOOTING AHEAD OF THE COMPETITION

The English longbow was introduced to European battlefields in the fourteenth century and made the arrow a formidable battlefield missile. The longbow was as tall as a man and the arrow about half that length. An English archer could shoot six aimed shots a minute, and his effective range was about 183 m (200 yd).

4 1570
A WAY TO MAP THE WORLD

Precise mapping began with the development of the theodolite by English mathematician Leonard Digges in 1570. The theodolite measures horizontal and vertical angles. It consists of a telescope mounted between two side supports in a trunnion. The angles through which the telescope moves are measured from circular, graduated scales.

5 1698
FULL STEAM AHEAD

In 1698, Thomas Savery patented a pump with hand-operated valves to raise water from mines by suction produced by condensing steam. In 1712 another Englishman, Thomas Newcomen, developed a more efficient steam engine with a piston separating the condensing steam from the water. This was then improved on in 1765 by James Watt.

6 1804
THE GREAT TRAINS

Railed trucks had been used for mining as early as 1550, but the first self-propelled locomotive ever to run on rails was one built by Richard Trevithick (1771–1833). It was demonstrated over 14 km (9 miles) with a 10.2-tonne load and 70 passengers in Penydaren, Glamorgan, on 21 February 1804.

7 1830s
BRITAIN DEVISES THE COMPUTER

In the 1830s, inventor Charles Babbage developed plans for the analytical engine. In this device he envisioned the capability of performing any arithmetical operation on the basis of instructions from punched cards, a memory unit in which to store numbers, sequential control, and most of the basic elements of the computer.

8 1926
THE FIRST TELEVISION PICTURES

In 1926, John Logie Baird demonstrated a mechanical scanner able to convert an image into a series of electronic impulses that could then be reassembled on a viewing screen as a pattern of light and shade. In 1929 the British Broadcasting Company began broadcasting experimental TV.

TIMELINE

PREHISTORY Choppers and axes invented
PREHISTORY Generation, control and understanding of fire
PREHISTORY Structures built, including tombs, homes and monuments
PREHISTORY Oxen and donkeys used for transport
8000 BC Flint mined and tools made
7500 BC Grain cultivated in an organised way
4000 BC Metal and beaten copper tools appear, including spears
3500 BC Basic plough invented
1 **3100 BC** Stonehenge
1000 BC First use of coal
55 BC Romans start mass road construction
AD 600 Ironworks spread throughout country
AD 800 Invention of the scythe
2 **AD 896** Alfred the Great begins compilation of *Anglo-Saxon Chronicle*
AD 900 Horse and plough used together after invention of the rigid collar
1000 Architecture develops
1100 Cannons and windmills invented
1200 Gunpowder invented; fortifications strengthened on Norman castles
3 **1300s** Longbow invented
1386 Mechanical clock developed
1400 Bellows and furnaces invented to help the smelting of iron
4 **1570** Leonard Digges invents the theodolite
5 **1698** Thomas Savery patents his mine pump
1712 Thomas Newcomen develops piston engine
1733 Faster shuttle looms patented by John Kay
1748 Artificial refrigeration demonstrated by William Cullen
1754 English porcelain developed
1764 Spinning Jenny invented
1775 Rotary action engine adopted by Sir Richard Arkwright
1797 Screw-cutting lathe invented
1799 Perfecting of industrial bleaching and dyeing industries
6 **1804** Richard Trevithick invents self-propelled engine
7 **1830s** Analytical engine invented by Charles Babbage
1831 Relationship between electricity and magnetism discovered
1837 Electric telegraph invented
1856 First production of synthetic dye
1892 Vacuum flask invented
1900 Electric lighting and the filament bulb invented
1901 First transatlantic radio communication
1903 Gas turbine engine invented
1922 Development of the radar
8 **1926** Scanner demonstrated by John Logie Baird
1939 Jet-powered aeroplane invented
1943 Laboratory opened to build the atom bomb
1947 Jet propulsion developed
1956 Nuclear power station, Calder Hall, opens
1966 Optical fibres used to transmit infra-red signals
1995 Nuclear power fed into the National Grid for the first time

Beginnings

Prehistory–3500 BC

APART FROM A FEW short references in classical literature, knowledge of Britain before the Roman conquest (begun around AD 43) is derived entirely from archeological research. It is thus lacking in detail, for archeology can rarely identify personalities, motives, or exact dates. All that is available is a picture of successive cultures. This period was one of discovery, of power, of learning to use the land and what man found around him. Most significant was the beginning of the use of tools. A degree of specialisation in toolmaking was achieved by the time of Neanderthal man (70,000 BC); more advanced tools, requiring assemblage of head and haft, were produced by Cro-magnon *Homo sapiens* (35,000 BC), while the application of mechanical principles was achieved by pottery-making Neolithic man (6000 BC).

▲ *Early man used simple stone tools to protect themselves from wild animals.*

▶ p. 158 **PREHISTORY**

CHOPPERS AND AXES

Dating back to around 2.6 million years ago, the beginning of the Paleolithic Age, the earliest known tools consisted of variously sized examples of the pebble tool, or chopper. The chopper is thought to be the first tool made and used by human beings. It typically consisted of a water-worn, fist-sized rock, chipped away at one end to create a roughly serrated edge. It was used to cut through the skin and sinews of hunted animals. This was the only tool used by man for almost two million years, until the hand axe, a superior version of the chopper was invented. In this tool both the faces of the rock were chipped making the edge of the hand axe considerably sharper than that of the earlier chopper.

p. 151◀ **Triumphs & Tragedies** ▶p. 161

PREHISTORY

MAKING FIRE

The use of fire was a technique mastered at some unknown time in the Old Stone Age. The discovery that fire could be tamed and controlled and the further discovery that a fire could be generated by friction between two dry wooden surfaces were momentous. Fire was the most important contribution of prehistory to power technology, although little power was obtained directly from fire except as defence against wild animals. For the most part, prehistoric communities remained completely dependent upon manpower but, in making the transition to a more settled pattern of life in the Neolithic, or New Stone Age, man began to derive some power from animals that had been domesticated. The bones of a dog, possibly used for hunting about 8500 BC, have been discovered in the western USA.

▶ p. 159 **PREHISTORY**

THE FIRST BUILDINGS

Prehistoric building techniques underwent significant developments in the Neolithic Revolution. Nothing is known of the building ability of Paleolithic peoples beyond what can be inferred from a few fragments of stone shelters, but in the Neolithic Age some impressive structures were erected, primarily tombs and burial mounds and other religious edifices, but also, toward the end of the period, domestic housing in which sun-dried brick was used for the first time. In northern Europe, the Neolithic transformation

▲ *The markings on fragments of stone such as this enable us to understand how such tools were made.*

began later than it did around the eastern Mediterranean and lasted longer. There, huge stone monuments, of which Stonehenge in England is the outstanding example, still bear testimony to the technical skill and the imagination and mathematical competence, of the later Stone Age societies.

PREHISTORY
THE FIRST CRAFTS

Manufacturing industry had its origin in the Neolithic Age, with the application of techniques for grinding corn, baking clay, spinning and weaving textiles, along with those of dyeing, fermenting, and distilling. Some evidence for all these processes can be derived from archeological findings, and some of them at least were developing into specialised crafts by the time the first urban civilisations appeared. In addition, the early metalworkers were beginning to learn the techniques of extracting and working the softer metals: gold, silver, copper, and tin. All these early fields of specialisation implied developing trade between different communities and regions, and again the archeological evidence of the transfer of manufactured products in the later Stone Age is impressive.

▶ p. 167

PREHISTORY
BECOMING MOBILE

Paleolithic man presumably depended entirely on his own feet for transport, and this remained the common mode of transport throughout the Stone Age. Domestication of the ox and the donkey undoubtedly brought some help, although not being able to harness the horse long delayed its effective use. The dugout canoe and the birch-bark canoe had showed man that water transport was a possibility and there is some evidence that by the end of the Neolithic Age the sail had already emerged as a means of harnessing the wind for small boats, beginning a long sequence of developments in marine transport and showing the extent to which humans were already applying their minds to problems.

8000 BC
EARLY MINING

Archeological discoveries indicate that mining was conducted in prehistoric times. Apparently, the first mineral used was flint which, owing to its concoidal fracturing pattern, could be broken into sharp-edged pieces that were useful as scrapers, knives, and arrowheads. During the Neolithic Period (about 8000–2000 BC), shafts up to 100 m (330 ft) deep were sunk in soft chalk deposits in France and Britain in order to extract the flint pebbles found there. Other minerals, such as red ochre and the copper mineral malachite, were used as pigments. Gold was one of the first metals utilised, being mined from streambeds of sand and gravel where it occurred as a pure metal because of its chemical stability.

7500 BC
EARLY ANIMALS AND CROPS

It is generally assumed that Europe, prior to the introduction of agriculture from the East, was inhabited by hunter-gatherers, apart from the earliest known incidence in the Old World of the domesticated dog at Star Carr in Yorkshire, England (about 7500 BC), cattle in Greece (about 6000 BC), and a possibility of domesticated pigs in the Crimea at an earlier date. It has been suggested that the grain called Fat Hen (*Chenopodium album*) was cultivated at Iron Age settlements in Denmark, as well as Gold of Pleasure (*Camelina sativa*). Since cultivation of these grains is regarded as typifying a late form of agricultural development, it follows that agriculture must have taken about 3,000 years to spread from Greece to Denmark and the British Isles.

▶ p. 158

3500 BC
TILLING THE LAND

The very early farmers used pointed wooden sticks, sometimes weighted with a stone, to till the soil, but they could only scratch the top soil and this did not produce good crops. These sticks soon developed into a variety of implements including hoes, spades and forks. As early as 3500 BC the greatest basic invention in agriculture had been made, that of the plough. Typically, ploughs were made of wood in the shape of a letter A, curved at the pointed end so that it made a furrow in the ground when it was dragged along, steered by the ploughman walking behind. It was dragged initially by men then later oxen. By 500 BC an iron blade had been added and by AD 1000, wheels.

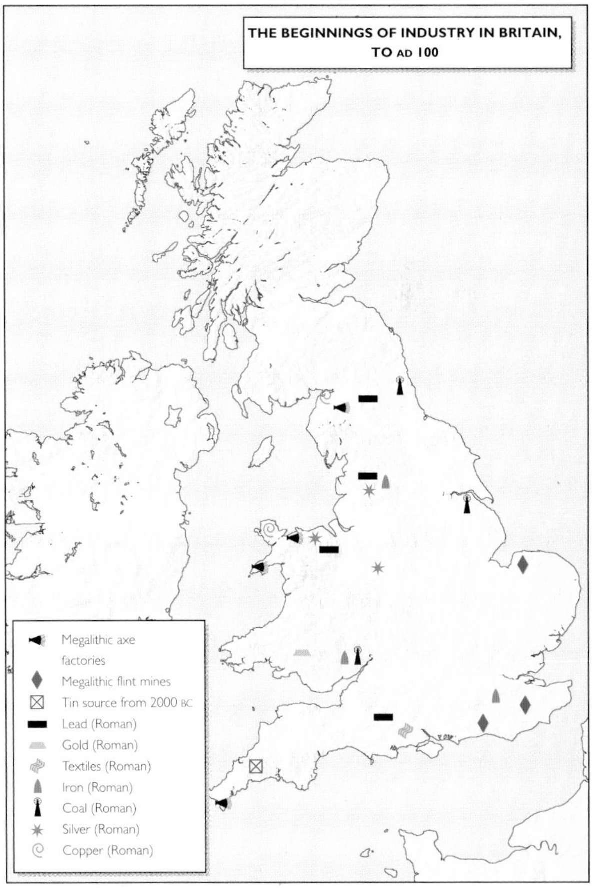

p. 153◀ Distant Voices ▶p. 159

Ads are the cave art of the twentieth century.

Marshall McLuhan (1911–80), Canadian theorist

Ancient Britain

4000–1000 BC

A MAJOR CHANGE OCCURRED in Britain around 4000 BC with the introduction of agriculture by Neolithic immigrants from the coasts of western and possibly north-western Europe. They were pastoralists as well as tillers of the soil. Tools were commonly made of flint from mining, but axes of volcanic rock were also traded by prospectors exploiting distant outcrops. The dead were buried in communal graves and other evidence of religion comes from enclosures (e.g., Windmill Hill, Wiltshire), which are now believed to have been centres of ritual and of seasonal tribal feasting. British Neolithic culture thus developed its own individuality. The technological change took place very slowly over a long period of time, in response to only the most basic social needs, the search for food and shelter.

▶ p. 163

4000 BC
SPEARS FOR BATTLE

Around 4000 BC the stone axes of the Neolithic Period began to give way to the first tools made from metal, usually from beaten copper. Centuries later, people learned how to smelt copper and, much later, iron, and the use of metal tools spread throughout the world. For the first time it was possible for individuals to have specialised tools for particular tasks. In addition, axes and spears began to gain military use, bronze spearheads closely followed the development of alloys hard enough to keep a cutting edge and represented, with the piercing axe, the earliest significant military application of bronze. Spearheads were also among the earliest militarily significant applications of iron, because existing patterns could be directly extrapolated from bronze to iron.

4000 BC
THE BEGINNING OF METALLURGY

The agricultural skills of the Neolithic Period had made possible a growth in population which created a need for the products of specialised craftsmen in a wide range of commodities. These craftsmen included metalworkers, first those treating metals easily obtained in metallic form then those extracting certain metals from ores in which they occur. Probably the first used was the carbonate of copper known as malachite, then already in use as a cosmetic and easily reduced to copper in a strong fire. This slowly led to the development of metallurgy and the encouragement of trade in order to secure specific metals. Metallurgy contributed substantially to the emergence of urban societies, as it relied heavily upon trade and manufacturing industries, and so helped the rise of the first civilisations.

◀ *As primitive technological advances were made, stone axes and spears such as these gave way to stronger, sharper, metal tools.*

4000 BC
SEA TRAVEL

During this early period the sailing ship assumed a definitive shape, progressing from a vessel with a small sail rigged in its bows and suitable only for sailing before the prevailing wind up the River Nile, into the substantial ocean-going ship of the later Egyptian dynasties, with a large rectangular sail rigged amidships. Egyptian and Phoenician ships of this type could sail before the wind and across the wind, but for making headway into the wind they had to resort to manpower. Nevertheless, they accomplished remarkable feats of navigation, sailing the length of the Mediterranean. Although in Europe none of this technology was available, it was due to these developments that the Romans would later invade the British Isles.

▶ p. 165

4000 BC
THE START OF IRRIGATION

Techniques of food production began to show many improvements over Neolithic methods, including one outstanding innovation in the shape of systematic

▼ *Cutting tools such as scythes began to be developed, improving farming methods.*

irrigation. This was first developed in the civilisations of Egypt and Mesopotamia, which depended heavily upon the two great river systems, the Nile and the Tigris-Euphrates, both of which watered the ground with their annual floods and rejuvenated it with the rich alluvium they deposited. The Nile flooded with regularity each summer, and the civilisations building in its valley early learned the technique of basin irrigation, ponding back the floodwater for as long as possible after the river had receded, so that enriched soil could bring forth a harvest before the floods of the following season.

4000 BC
FOOD AND DRINK

Local crafts and manufacturing in the early civilisations concentrated on such products as pottery, wines, oils and cosmetics, which had begun to circulate along trade routes before the introduction of metals. These became the commodities traded for the metals. In pottery, the potter's wheel became widely used for spinning the clay into the desired shape, but the older technique of building pots by hand from rolls of clay remained in use for many purposes. In the production of wines and oils, various forms of presses were developed, while the development of cooking, brewing and preserving demonstrate that the science of chemistry began in the kitchen. Cosmetics, too, evolved as an offshoot of culinary art.

⊞ ▶ p. 166
3100 BC
STONEHENGE

Stonehenge, a monumental circular setting of large standing stones surrounded by a circular earthwork, was built in prehistoric times beginning about 3100 BC. It is located about 13 km (8 miles) north of Salisbury, England. The Stonehenge of today is considerably ruined as many of its stones were stolen by medieval and early modern builders (there is no natural building stone within 21 km (13 miles) of Stonehenge); its general architecture has also been subjected to centuries of weathering. It is thought to have been built in three phases: in Stonehenge phase 1 (3100 BC), a circular ditch was excavated using deer antler picks; in 2100 BC, phase 2 saw the erection of 80 bluestone pillars, transported from Wales; phase 3 (2000 BC) erected the large sarsen stones, transported 30 km (19 miles).

▶ p. 164
3000 BC
BRONZE AND IRON

During the second millennium, the use of true bronze, an alloy of copper and tin,

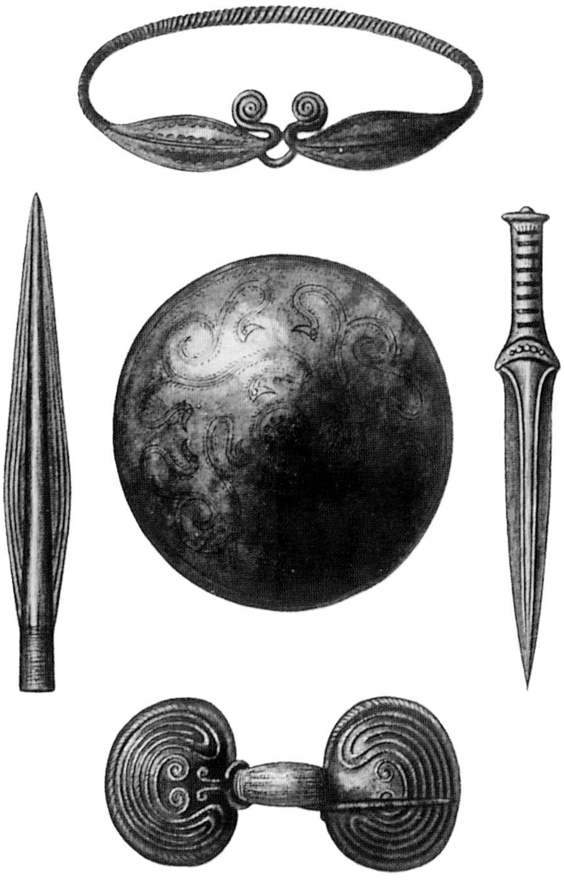

▲ *Bronze and iron artefacts, including jewellery, vessels, weapons and simple armour have been discovered across the British Isles.*

greatly increased. The tin deposits in Cornwall, England, were much used. Bronze was made before 3000 BC, although its use in artefacts did not become common until much later. Bronze is harder than copper as a result of alloying that metal with tin or other metals. Bronze is also more readily melted and is therefore easier to cast. It is harder than pure iron and more resistant to corrosion. The substitution of iron for bronze in tools and weapons from about 1000 BC was the result of iron's abundance compared to copper and tin rather than any inherent advantages of iron.

1000 BC
THE FIRST USE OF COAL

The discovery of the use of fire helped to distinguish humans from other animals. Early fuels were wood (and charcoal derived from it), straw and dried dung. References to the early uses of coal are meagre. Aristotle referred to 'bodies which have more of earth than of smoke' and called them 'coal-like substances'. Coal was used commercially by the Chinese long before it was in Europe. Although no authentic record is available, coal from the Fu-shun mine in north-eastern China may have been employed to smelt copper as early as 1000 BC. Cast-iron Chinese coins dating to about the first century BC are thought to have been made using coal. Coal cinders found among Roman ruins in England suggest that the Romans were familiar with its use before AD 400.

p. 157◀**Distant Voices**▶p. 161

Even God cannot change the past.

Agathon (466 BC)

Roman Britain

100 BC–AD 122

EVEN IN ROMAN TIMES, Britain lay on the periphery of the civilised world, and Roman historians, for the most part, provide for this period only a framework into which the results of archeological research can be fitted. Britain truly emerged into history only after the Saxon settlements in the fifth century AD. The Romans did provide advancements for Europe, the contributions of Greece and Rome in philosophy and religion, political and legal institutions, poetry and drama, and in the realm of scientific speculation are well known. Their mechanical innovation was not distinguished, however, and even in the realms of military and construction engineering, in which they showed great ingenuity and aesthetic sensibility, their work represented more a consummation of earlier lines of development than a dramatic innovation.

▲ *The Romans laid out an extensive network of roads that enabled their soldiers to march directly and quickly to the site of any crisis.*

100 BC
THE DISCOVERY OF IRON

One of the outstanding technological feats of the Greco-Roman world was the smelting of iron. This technique, derived by unknown metallurgists, probably in Asia Minor about 1000 BC, spread far beyond the provincial frontiers of the Roman Empire. Iron ore, long a familiar material, could not be reduced into metallic form because of the extreme heat required to perform the chemical transformation, about 1,535°C (2,795°F), compared with the 1,083°C (1,981°F) necessary for the reduction of copper ores. To reach this temperature, furnace construction had to be improved and ways devised to maintain the heat. These conditions were achieved only on a small scale, in furnaces burning charcoal and using foot bellows to intensify the heat.

▶ p. 162

100 BC
NEW POWER TECHNIQUES

The Romans were responsible, through the application and development of machines that were already available to them, for an important technological transformation in the world. This included the widespread introduction of rotary motion. This was exemplified in the use of the treadmill for powering cranes and other heavy lifting operations, the introduction of rotary water-raising devices for irrigation works (a scoop wheel powered by a treadmill), and the development of the waterwheel as a prime mover. The first-century BC Roman engineer Vitruvius gave an account of watermills, and by the end of the Roman era many were in operation. Water and man power remained the mainstay of energy in this period.

100 BC
POTTERY TRADE

The Romans made good quality pottery available throughout their empire from the first century BC to the third century AD through the manufacture and trade of the bright-red, polished red ware called *terra sigillata*. The term means literally 'ware made of clay impressed with designs'. *Terra sigillata* was made in Gaul from the first century AD at La Graufesenque (now Millau, France) and later at other Gallic centres, whence it was exported in large quantities to outlying parts of the Roman Empire, including Britain. The body of the ware was generally cast in a mould. Relief designs, taken from a wide repertory of patterns and figurative scenes, were also cast in moulds (which had been impressed with stamps in the desired pattern) and then applied to the vessels.

55 BC
TRANSPORT IN THE ROMAN EMPIRE

By the time of the first invasions of Britain in 55 BC sailing ships were equipped with a square or rectangular sail to receive a following wind and one or more banks of oarsmen to propel the ship when the wind was contrary.

▼ *Romans built kilns to fire their pottery, which was then distributed around Britain and abroad.*

p. 156◀ **Triumphs & Tragedies** ▶p. 169

AD 122
A WALL TO STOP BARBARIANS

Hadrian came to Britain in AD 122 and arranged for the building of the famous Hadrian's Wall from AD 122–126. This was a continuous Roman defensive barrier that guarded the north-western frontier of Britain from barbarian invaders. The wall extended from coast to coast across the width of Britain, running for 118 km (73 miles) from Wallsend (Segedunum) on the River Tyne in the east to Bowness on the Solway Firth in the west. At every ⅓ Roman mile there was a tower, and at every mile a fortlet (milecastle) containing a gate through the wall, presumably surmounted by a tower, and one or two barrack-blocks. The fortlets, towers, and forts continued for at least 42 km (26 miles) beyond Bowness down the Cumbrian coast.

▲ *The remains of a Roman fort situated on Hadrian's Wall.*

The carvel-built hull (with planks meeting edge-to-edge rather than overlapping) was developed. The Romans gave much more attention to inland transport than to the sea, and constructed a network of carefully aligned and well-laid roads, often paved over long stretches, throughout the provinces of the empire. Along these highways the legions marched rapidly to the site of any crisis at which their presence was required. The roads also served for the development of trade, but their main function was military, as a vital means of keeping a vast empire in subjection.

▶ p. 169

AD 0
CEMENT

The origin of hydraulic cements goes back to ancient Greece and Rome. The first materials used were lime and a volcanic ash that slowly reacted with it in the presence of water to form a hard mass. This formed the cementing material of the Roman mortars and concretes of 2,000 years ago and of subsequent classic construction work in western Europe. Volcanic ash mined near the city of Pozzuoli was particularly rich in essential aluminosilicate minerals, giving rise to the pozzolana cement of the Roman era, used by the Romans in many of the fine buildings of their Empire. The term cement, meanwhile, derives from the Latin word *caementum*, which meant stone chippings such as were used in Roman mortar, not the binding material itself.

AD 43
DEEPER PLOUGHING

Iron Age technology was applied to agriculture in the form of the iron, or iron-tipped, plough, which opened up the possibility of deeper ploughing and of cultivating heavier soils than those normally worked in the Greco-Roman period. The construction of ploughs improved slowly after the Roman conquest in AD 43, but the moldboard for turning over the earth did not appear until the eleventh century, so that the capacity to turn the sod depended more on the wrists of the ploughman than on the strength of his draft team, and as a result heavy ground was not often tilled. The potential of the heavy plough was thus not fully exploited in the temperate areas of Europe until after the Roman period.

AD 43
THE ARCHIMEDES SCREW

There were some slight but significant mechanical achievements in the Greco-Roman civilisations of this period which gradually filtered through to the rest of Europe. The world had one of its great mechanical geniuses in Archimedes, who devised remarkable weapons to protect his native Syracuse from Roman invasion and applied his powerful mind to such basic mechanical contrivances as the screw, the pulley, and the lever. The Archimedes screw was a machine for raising water and consisted of a circular pipe enclosing a helix and inclined at an angle of about 45° to the horizontal with its lower end dipped in the water. Rotating the device caused the water to rise in the pipe.

p. 159◀ **Distant Voices** ▶p. 163

People coming from the country see lots of houses but they do not see the city.

Gnaeus Agricola (AD 37–93), Roman general and politician

The Early Medieval Period

AD 400–800

THE MILLENNIUM BETWEEN the collapse of the Western Roman Empire in the fifth century AD and the beginning of the colonial expansion of western Europe in the late fifteenth century has been known traditionally as the Middle Ages, and the first part of this period consists of the five centuries of the Dark Ages. We now know that the period was not as socially stagnant as this title suggests. In the first place, many of the institutions of the later empire survived the collapse and profoundly influenced the formation of the new civilisation that developed in western Europe. Although this age was marked by frequent warfare there was much development in the making of superior weapons, and a resurgence in the interest of learning.

▶ p. 162

AD 400s

THE RISE OF THE HORSE

With no large slave labour force to draw on at the beginning of the Middle Ages, Europe needed alternative sources of power and the introduction of labour-saving machinery. The first instrument of this power revolution was the horse. With the invention of the horseshoe, the padded, rigid horse collar, and the stirrup, all of which first appeared in the West in the Dark Ages, the horse was transformed from a beast of burden useful only for light duties into a highly versatile source of energy in peace and war. Once the horse could be harnessed to the heavy plough by means of the horse collar, it became a more efficient draught animal than the ox, and the stirrup made the mounted warrior supreme in medieval warfare.

AD 400s

A STEP BACKWARDS

The disappearance of Roman power in western Europe during the fifth century led to a decline in building technology. Brickmaking became rare and was not revived until the fourteenth century. The use of domes and vaults in stone construction was also lost. Building techniques fell to Iron Age levels, using log construction, packed clay walls, mud brick, and wattle and daub. Meanwhile advanced building technologies were developing in China in this same period during the Sui (AD 581–618) and T'ang (AD 618–907) dynasties. In the third century BC, the completion of the Great Wall, about 6,400 km (4,000 miles) in length and following a sinuous path along the contours of rugged terrain, showed remarkable achievements in masonry technology and surveying methods, which it would take Europe many centuries to develop.

AD 500s

IRON EVERYWHERE

Beginning about the sixth century AD, and for the next thousand years, the most meaningful developments in metallurgy centred on iron-making. Great Britain, where iron ore was plentiful, was an important iron-making region. Iron weapons, agricultural implements, domestic articles, and even personal adornments were made. Fine-quality cutlery was made near Sheffield. Monasteries were often centres of learning of the arts of metalworking. Monks became well known for their iron making and bell founding, the products made either being utilised in the monasteries, disposed of locally, or sold to merchants for shipment to more distant markets. In 1408, the bishop of Durham established the first water-powered bloomery, where the ore was melted down to large solid lumps or blooms, with the power apparently operating the bellows.

▶ p. 166

AD 500s

THE POWER OF WATER

Medieval technology soon applied itself to harnessing water and wind power. The Romans had pioneered the use of water-power in the later empire, and some of their techniques probably survived. The type of water mill that flourished first in northern Europe, however, appears to have been the Norse mill, which used a horizontally mounted waterwheel to drive a pair of grindstones directly, without the intervention of gearing. Examples of this simple type of mill survive in Scandinavia and in the Shetlands. It is possible that a proportion of the 5,624 mills recorded in the *Domesday Book* in 1086 were still of this type. Most of the *Domesday* water mills were used for grinding grain, but later they were also used for sawing wood, and crushing vegetable seeds for oil.

▼ *With the disappearance of the Romans, building technologies reverted to earlier techniques, with the use of wattle-and-daub, wood, straw and clay.*

▲ *The power of water began to be more effectively harnessed with the development of the rudimentary water wheel.*

AD 500s
FURNITURE

With the collapse of the Roman Empire during the fourth to fifth centuries, Europe sank into a period in which little furniture, except the most basic, was used: chairs, stools, benches and primitive chests were the common items. Several centuries passed before the invading Teutonic peoples evolved forms of furniture approaching the Roman standard of domestic equipment. Certain ancient traditions of furniture making, particularly turnery, influenced early medieval craftsmen. Turnery was used in making chairs, stools and couches in Byzantium, and it seems that this technique was known across Europe as far north as Scandinavia. The Anglo-Saxon epic poem *Beowulf*, which gives some glimpses of the domestic economy of western Europe in about the seventh century, mentions no furniture other than benches and some kind of seat or throne for the overlord.

▶ p. 164

AD 600s
A NEW AGE OF LEARNING

The early medieval period actually saw a resurgence of interest in learning. The finest centre of scholarship was Northumbria. There, Celtic and classical influences met, missionaries brought books from Ireland, and many Englishmen went to Ireland to study. Other Northumbrians went abroad, especially to Rome, and among them was Benedict Biscop. Benedict returned from Rome with Theodore (AD 668–669), spent some time in Canterbury, and then brought the learning acquired there to Northumbria. He founded the monasteries at Wearmouth (AD 674) and Jarrow (AD 682). *Beowulf*, considered the greatest Old English poem, is sometimes assigned to this age, but the dating is uncertain. The Hiberno-Saxon (or Anglo-Irish) style of manuscript illumination also evolved at this time, its greatest example being the *Lindisfarne Gospels*.

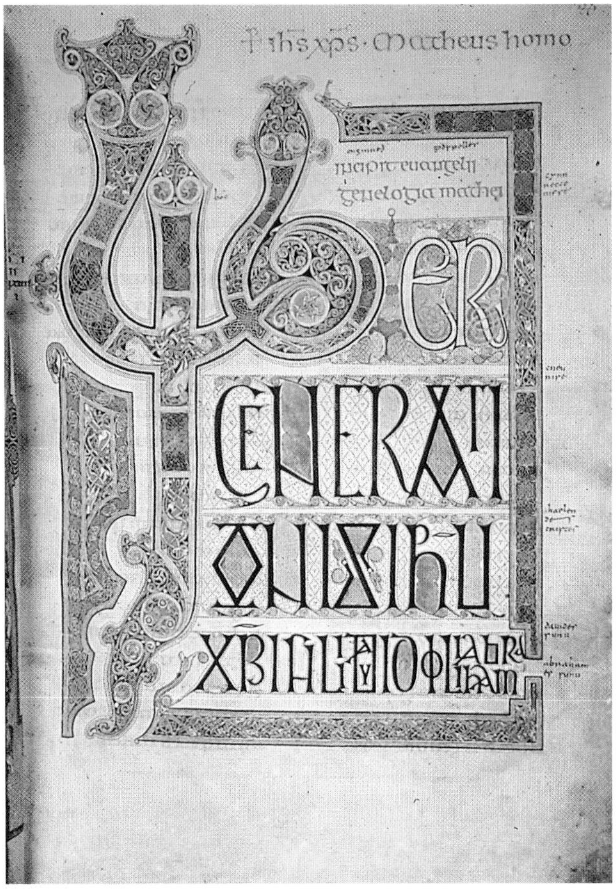

▲ *The* Lindisfarne Gospels *are some of the best examples of early manuscript illumination.*

▶ p. 164

AD 700s
THE SCYTHE

The scythe is probably one of the most important of all agricultural hand tools, consisting of a curved blade fitted at an angle to a long, curved handle and used for cutting grain. In modern scythes the handle has a projecting peg that is grasped by one hand, facilitating control of the swinging motion by which grass and grain are cut. The exact origin of the scythe is unknown, but it seems it was little used in the ancient world. Its widespread use only came with the agricultural developments of the Carolingian era (eighth century AD) in Europe, when the harvesting and storing of hay became extremely important in order to support livestock through cold winters.

AD 800
THE OPEN FIELD

The precise origin of the open-field arrangement, which had long scattered strips of arable land separated from each other by a furrow, balk (ridge of land left after ploughing) or mere (boundary), is obscure. The earliest examples of this system date from about AD 800, the year Charlemagne was crowned emperor of the West. Usually these strips of land, normally about one acre in size, were laid out in two or three large fields. Each farmer in the village worked a number of these acres: the units forming his holding were scattered among those of other men. The open-field system continued as more land was reclaimed and lasted for many centuries, longer, of course, in some places than in others.

p. 161◀ **Distant Voices** ▶p. 165

Justice is the constant and perpetual wish to render everyone his due.

Emperor Justinian (482–565)

Vikings and Anglo-Saxons

AD 800–1050

THE TEUTONIC TRIBES who moved into a large part of western Europe did not come empty-handed, and in some respects their technology was superior to that of the Romans. They were people of the Iron Age, and although much about the origins of the heavy plough remains obscure, these tribes appear to have been the first people with sufficiently strong iron ploughshares to undertake the systematic settlement of the forested lowlands of northern and western Europe, the heavy soils of which had frustrated the agricultural techniques of their predecessors. The invaders came almost as colonisers and, although regarded as 'barbarians' by the Romanised inhabitants of western Europe who resented their intrusion, the newcomers provided an element of innovation and vitality.

AD 800s
WAGONS AND HORSES

During the early Middle Ages heavy wagons of the sort known for centuries were still in use, though with improved harnessing that allowed for the replacement of two horses by a single animal. Shafts were more often used, and the distances covered could be increased to 24–32 km (15–20 miles) a day. The higher state of Celtic carriage building and driving meant that significant advances in transportation technology became possible. Thus, at the onset of the high Middle Ages Europe was poised for considerable transport advances. At the beginning of that era Europe was not notably advanced in transportation, being at about the same stage of development as China.

▶ p. 167

AD 800s
SOAP FOR TEXTILES ONLY

The technique of making soap appears to have been a Teutonic innovation of the Dark Ages, being unknown in the ancient civilisations. The process consisted of decomposing animal or vegetable fats by boiling them with a strong alkali. Early soapmakers dispersed wood or plant ashes in water, added fat to the solution, then boiled it, adding ashes as the water evaporated. During the process the neutral fat underwent a chemical reaction with the ash, a process called saponification. Long before it became popular for personal cleansing, soap was a valuable industrial commodity for scouring textile fabrics. Its manufacture was one of the first industrial processes to make extensive use of coal as a fuel, and led to the development of the coal industry in northern Europe.

AD 800
THE LONG BOAT

The most formidable mode of travel at this time was the Viking ship. Vikings used double-ended, clinker-built (with overlapping planks) fighting galleys put together with iron nails and caulked with tarred rope. By AD 800 the Viking craft had a mast and a single, large, reinforced square sail, which was lowered in battle; high bow and stern, with removable dragon heads; and a single side rudder on the starboard (steer-board) quarter. At first the Vikings made no distinction between war and cargo ships, but later they built larger ships specifically designed for war. By 1000 they sailed three categories: those with fewer than 20 thwarts (40 rowers); those with up to 30; and the 'great ships' with more than 30, the battleship of the time.

▶ *Viking long-boats were incredibly strong and fast, using as many as 60 rowers.*

▶ p. 169

AD 896
THE LEARNED ALFRED

Alfred the Great saw the Viking invasions of AD 892–896 as a punishment from God, especially because of a neglect of learning, without which men could not know and follow the will of God. He deplored the decay of Latin and enjoined its study by those destined for the church, but he also wished all young freemen of adequate means to learn to read English, and he aimed at supplying men with 'the books most necessary for all men to know' in their own language. Alfred had acquired an education despite great difficulties, and he translated some books himself with the help of scholars from Mercia, the Continent, and Wales. Compilation of the *Anglo-Saxon Chronicle* began in his reign.

▶ p. 173

AD 900s
MINING TECHNIQUES

The mining techniques around the tenth century remained unsophisticated for as long as coal was obtainable near the surface, but as the search for the mineral led further underground the industry copied methods

that had already evolved in the metal-mining industries of north and central Europe. The extent of this evolution was summarised by Georgius Agricola in his *De re metallica*, published in 1556. This large, abundantly illustrated book shows techniques of shafting, pumping (by treadmill, animal power and waterpower) and of conveying the ore won from the mines in trucks, which anticipated the development of the railways. It is impossible to date precisely the emergence of these important techniques, but the fact that they were well established when Agricola observed them suggests that they had a long ancestry.

AD 900s
HORSE AND PLOUGH

A wheeled asymmetrical plough is known to have been in use in some parts of western Europe by the late tenth century. Illuminations of manuscripts and calendars a little later in date show a plough with two wheels fitted with a rudimentary mouldboard and a coulter. This plough could invert the soil and turn a true furrow, thus making a better seedbed. The horse collar, which replaced the old harness band that pressed upon the animal's windpipe, was one of the most important inventions in the history of agriculture and appeared at this time in Europe. The rigid, padded horse collar enabled the animal to do heavier work, ploughing as well as haulage. Many peasants continued to use oxen because horses were more expensive to buy and to keep.

▼ *The invention of the plough enabled people to utilise animal power to make proper seed-beds.*

▶ p. 170

AD 900s
EXPANSION OF FARMLAND

Widespread expansion of farmed land occurred throughout western Europe between the tenth century and the later years of the thirteenth. In France, new villages were built and new farms carved out of the forest and the waste while, in England, a great deal of land on the boundaries of the open fields was taken in and cultivated. All this new cultivation was carried out with the same old implements and tools; the same crops were cultivated and animals bred as before. In remote and desolate places, monastic organisations created great estates. These estates were formed to feed growing populations rather than to improve technical skills. A new literature of farming arose, although this was directed to the attention of great lords and ecclesiastical magnates rather than to the illiterate majority of husbandmen.

1050
THE ROMAN INFLUENCE

Relatively few structures survive from the Dark Ages, but the later centuries of this period were an age of improvement in building. Romanesque and Gothic architecture embodied significant technological innovations. The architect-engineers studied classical building techniques and solved the problems of constructing very tall masonry buildings while preserving as much natural light as possible. They used the cross-rib vault, the flying buttress, and great window panels which provided scope for the new craft of the glazier. The Romanesque style, with stone arches, vaults and domes spanning interior spaces, did not really begin until the later part of the eleventh century. Stone was very important and from 1050 to 1350 more stone was quarried in France alone than in the whole history of ancient Egypt.

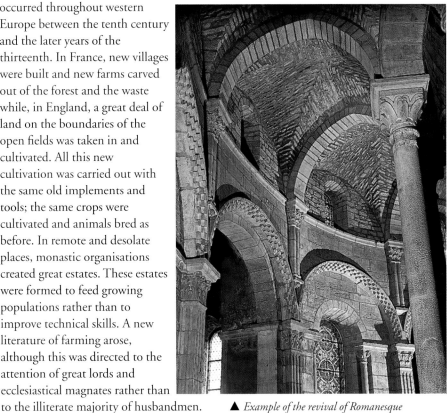

▲ *Example of the revival of Romanesque architecture.*

p. 163◀ **Distant Voices** ▶p. 167

Then began I ... to turn into English the book that is named in Latin Patoralis ... one-while word for word, another-while meaning for meaning.

King Alfred (AD 849–901), Preface to the Anglo-Saxon version of *Gregory's Pastoral Care*

The Normans and Beyond

1086–1300s

AROUND 1000, the conditions of comparative political stability necessary for the re-establishment of a vigorous commercial and urban life had been secured by the success of the kingdoms of the region in either absorbing or keeping out the last of the invaders from the East, and thereafter for 500 years, the new civilisation grew in strength and began to experiment in all aspects of human endeavour. Much of this process involved recovering the knowledge and achievements of the ancient world. In Britain this was a time of great urban development, with larger towns and better construction and building techniques, as well as a period of understanding how to harness wind and water power.

▶ p. 171

1086

THE POWER OF THE TIDE

The oldest reference to a water mill dates from about 85 BC, but ocean tides were also used to drive waterwheels. Tidal water was allowed to flow into millponds, controlled initially through lock-type gates and later through flap valves. Once the tide ebbed, water was let out through sluice gates and directed onto the wheel. Sometimes the tidal flow was assisted by building a dam across the estuary of a small river. Tidal mills were widely used by the twelfth century. The earliest recorded reference to them is found in the *Domesday Book* (1086), which also records more than 5,000 water mills in England south of the Severn and Trent rivers. A tidal mill for pumping water was built in the River Thames in 1582.

▶ p. 172

1100s

A CHANGE OF CASTLE

The twelfth century saw the evolution of the fortified stronghold from the Anglo-Saxon motte and bailey (a timber tower encircled by a timber and earth wall) to the fully developed masonry castle, which became outdated by the end of the Middle Ages because of the development of artillery. Intrinsic to this change was the invention of gunpowder and the development of techniques for casting metals, especially iron. Gunpowder appeared in Europe in the mid-thirteenth century, although it was known in the Far East long before then. It was a mixture of carbon, sulphur and saltpetre. The first two were available from charcoal and deposits of volcanic sulphur in Europe, but saltpetre had to be crystallised by a noxious process of boiling stable sweepings and other decaying refuse.

1100s

THE CANNON

The first effective cannon appeared at this time made of wrought-iron bars strapped together, but although barrels continued to be made in this way for some purposes, the practice of casting cannons in bronze became widespread. The technique of casting in bronze had been known for several millennia, but the casting of cannons presented problems of size and reliability. Bronzesmiths drew on the experience of bell founders experienced in medieval church building, as the casting of a large bell posed the similar problems of heating a substantial amount of metal and of pouring it into a suitable mould. Bronze, however, was an expensive metal to manufacture in bulk, so that the widespread use of cannon in war had to wait for improvements in iron-casting techniques.

1100s

THE POWER OF WIND

The sail had been used to harness wind power from early civilisations, but the

▲ *Many masonry castles, such as Battle Abbey in Sussex, still stand throughout Britain today.*

windmill was unknown in the West until the end of the twelfth century. Present evidence suggests that the windmill developed spontaneously in the West; though there are precedents in Persia and China. The windmill certainly became widely used in Europe in the Middle Ages. The first type of windmill to be widely adopted was the post-mill, in which the whole body of the mill pivots on a post and can be turned to face the sails into the wind. By the fifteenth century, however, many were adopting the tower-mill type of construction, in which the body of the mill remains stationary with only the cap moving to turn the sails into the wind.

1100s
HEATING

Although Roman hypocaust heating disappeared with the empire, a new development in interior heating appeared in western Europe at the beginning of the twelfth century: the masonry fireplace and chimney began to replace the central open fire. Previously large roof openings over central fires let in wind and rain, so each house had only one and larger buildings had as few as possible. The chimney did not let in much air or water and could remove most of the smoke. Although much of the heat went up the flue, it was still a great improvement, and it could be used to heat both small and large rooms. Houses, particularly large ones, were now broken up into smaller, more private spaces each heated by its own fireplace.

▼ *The Miller, one of the pilgrims to feature in Chaucer's* Canterbury Tales*; the horse was the fastest mode of transport for the early traveller.*

1180
THE PILGRIM

Medieval technology made very little contribution to inland transport, although this period did see some experimentation in bridge building and in the construction of canals. Lock gates were first developed on canals as early as 1180, when they were employed on the canal between Brugge (Bruges, now in Belgium) and the sea. Roads remained indifferent where they existed at all and were not looked after or maintained in any way, and vehicles were clumsy throughout the period. Most wayfarers, like the pilgrims described by Chaucer in his *Canterbury Tales*, travelled on horseback (or on foot), and this was to remain the best mode of inland transport for several centuries to come.

▶ p. 174

1270
THE LURE OF THE SEA

The Middle Ages produced a decisive technological achievement in the creation of a reliable ocean-going ship depending entirely on wind power instead of a combination of wind and muscle. Firstly, the traditional square sail was combined with the triangular lateen sail developed in the Arab dhow; this allowed ships to sail close to the wind. Secondly, the adoption of the sternpost rudder gave greatly increased manoeuvrability, allowing ships to take full advantage of their improved sail power in tacking into a contrary wind. Finally the introduction of the magnetic compass provided a means of checking navigation on the open seas in any weather. Soon navigational charts were used, with the first recorded use on board ship in 1270. The world began to open up to Europe.

▶ p. 174

1300s
THE ENGLISH LONGBOW

The origins of the bow and arrow are prehistoric. In Europe, it was the development of the crossbow, which had been known in ancient times but was perfected in the Middle Ages, and the English longbow, introduced to European battlefields in the fourteenth century, that made the arrow a formidable battlefield missile. The longbow, which probably originated in Wales, was as tall as a man and the arrow about half that length. The bow was held with outstretched arm and the arrow drawn back to the bowman's ear. An English archer could shoot six aimed shots a minute, and his effective range was about 183 m (200 yd), although an arrow could go twice as far in the right hands.

▲ *The arrow became a formidable missile weapon on the battlefields of Europe.*

p. 165◀ **Distant Voices** ▶p. 169

Had I been present at the Creation, I would have given some useful hints for the better ordering of the universe.

Alfonso the Wise, king of Castille (1221–84), said after studying the Ptolemaic system

The Quickening Pace of Change
1300–1455

THE TECHNOLOGICAL HISTORY of the Middle Ages was one of slow but substantial development. In the succeeding period the tempo of change increased markedly and was associated with profound social, political, religious and intellectual upheavals in western Europe. This period was one of expansion. This expansion became possible after advances in naval technology opened up the ocean routes to Western navigators. The development of voyages of discovery into imperialism and colonisation was made possible by the new firepower including the iron cannon. Back at home, there was much significant development of the printing industry and the Peasant's Revolt saw the beginnings of an improvement in conditions for workers in industry.

1300s
THE RISE OF CRAFT GUILDS

Craft guilds, also called mystery (from Latin *ministerium*, 'occupation'), were European medieval occupational associations, usually comprising all the artisans, and often the suppliers, retailers and wholesale merchants, concerned with a specific branch of industry or commerce. A weavers' guild is recorded at Mainz as early as 1099 and in London and other cities of England during the reign of Henry I (1100–35); but the greatest period of guild expansion occurred during the fourteenth century. The primary economic objective of most craft guilds was the establishment of a complete monopoly over all who were associated together inthe pursuit of a common profession, but the ability of the craft guilds actually to exercise their authority was subject to serious practical limitations.

1300
ALCHEMY AS SCIENCE

In the twelfth century, Christian scholars began to make translations from both Arabic and Greek works including the literature of alchemy. By 1250 alchemy was familiar enough to enable such encyclopedists as Vincent of Beauvais to discuss it fairly intelligibly, and by 1300 the subject was under discussion by the English philosopher and scientist Roger Bacon and the German philosopher, scientist and theologian Albertus Magnus. To learn about alchemy was to learn about chemistry, for Europe had no independent word to describe the science of matter. In the works of Bacon and Magnus, change was discussed in a truly chemical sense, with Bacon treating the newly translated alchemy as a general science of matter for which he had great hopes.

1362
REACHING TO GOD

As new building designs stretched skywards, the spire at Salisbury Cathedral was built over the crossing of the nave and transept, which had not been designed to accommodate it, and the tall crossing piers began to buckle under the added weight. Strainer arches had to be added between the piers to brace them against buckling. This was the first time that stone columns were slender and heavily loaded enough to be observed to bend or buckle. Salisbury's spire was therefore built as a composite structure of stone cladding laid over a timber frame and tied together at the base with iron bands to resist spreading, and it rose to a total height of 123 m (404 ft) when it was finished in 1362.

▶ *An early pendulum clock, housed in a magnificent gold casing.*

1364
FIREARMS

As cannon became larger and more powerful, gunsmiths were reducing the size of other guns to supply the requirement for firearms. The earliest known firearms are dated 1364. Such weapons were hand-held cannons or arquebuses, which needed two people to operate them, with the heavy barrel supported by a tripod or a pole. Soon, such long arms had been refined to make the weapons more practicable since they could be operated by a single marksman, and light enough to carry in the hand. The musket was favoured for accuracy in the field, while short arms, such as carbines and pistols, were the weapons for close quarters. Firing mechanisms developed from the matchlock to the wheel-lock and flint-lock.

▶ p. 171

1386
A SENSE OF TIME

Medieval interest in mechanical instruments flourished, as shown by the development of the mechanical clock. The oldest example, driven by weights and controlled by a verge, an oscillating arm engaging with a gear wheel, and dated 1386, survives in Salisbury Cathedral, England. Clocks driven by springs had appeared by the mid-fifteenth

century, making it possible to construct more compact mechanisms, thus preparing the way for the portable clock. The problem of overcoming the diminishing power of the spring as it unwound was solved by the invention of a simple compensating mechanism, the fusee: a conical drum on the shaft that permitted the spring to exert an increasing momentum, or tendency to increase motion, as its power declined.

▶ p. 173

1400s
MELTING IRON

Iron has long been considered one of the most important metals. It was originally made by heating an ore such as haematite, which contains iron oxide, in a charcoal fire. When the fire died down, a spongy mass of iron remained which could be hammered into shape. Bellows were invented in the European Middle Ages and were commonly used to speed combustion, as in a blacksmith's or ironworker's forge, or to operate reed or pipe organs. In the fifteenth century, cylindrical furnaces were built and cold air was pumped in at the base. These were the forerunners of the modern blast furnaces. The temperature was high enough to melt the iron so that it could be run off at the bottom as pig or cast iron.

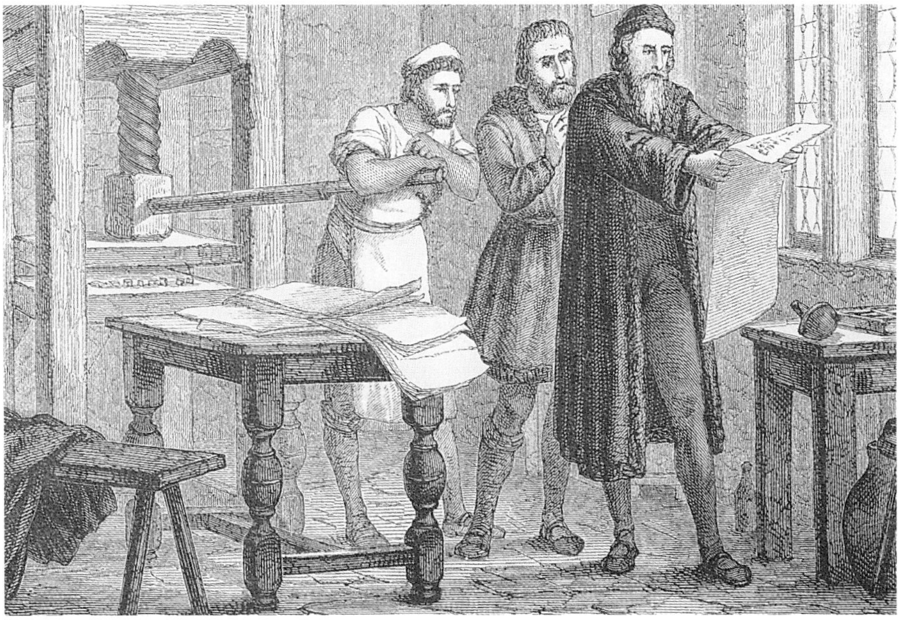

▲ *Johannes Gutenberg studying a page of his Bible, produced from the revolutionary new printing press in the workshop in Mainz.*

▶ p. 176

1455
A NEW WAY OF PRINTING

It was in the fifteenth century that printing with movable metal type was made possible. The first large-scale printing workshop was the one established at Mainz by Johannes Gutenberg, which was producing a sufficient quantity of accurate type to print a Vulgate Bible in about 1455. The printing press itself, vital for securing a firm and even print over the whole page, was an adaptation of the screw press already familiar in other applications, including the winepress. The printers found an enormous demand for their product, so that the technique spread rapidly and by 1500 almost 40,000 recorded editions of books had been printed in 14 European countries, with Germany and Italy accounting for two-thirds of this number.

p. 161◀ **Triumphs & Tragedies** ▶p. 172

1400s
LITTLE BOMBS

Grenades are small explosive, chemical or gas bombs that are used at short range. The word 'grenade' probably derived from the French word for pomegranate, because the bulbous shapes of early grenades resembled that fruit. Grenades came into use around the fifteenth century and were found to be particularly effective when exploded among enemy troops in the ditch of a fortress during an assault. They eventually became so important that specially selected soldiers in seventeenth century European armies were trained as grenade throwers, or grenadiers. After about 1750, grenades were virtually abandoned because the range and accuracy of firearms had increased, lessening the opportunities for close combat. Grenades did not come back into use on an important scale until the Russo-Japanese War (1904–05).

▲ *A French grenadier igniting a grenade.*

p. 167◀ **Distant Voices** ▶p. 171

I will make covered chariots, safe and impregnable, which may enter among the enemy and his artillery and defeat any body of men....

Leonardo Da Vinci (1452–1519), Italian painter and engineer

Renaissance

1500–1659

AN ASPECT OF THE Renaissance often overlooked is the scientific revolution that accompanied it. For centuries the authority of Aristotle in dynamics, of Ptolemy in astronomy, and of Galen in medicine had been taken for granted. Beginning in the sixteenth century their authority was challenged and overthrown, and scientists set out by observation and experiment to establish new explanatory models of the natural world. There was a fundamental shift of emphasis to a progressive, forward-looking attitude and to increasingly seek practical applications for scientific research. Meanwhile, the traditional crafts flourished within the expanding towns, where there was a growing market for the products of the rope makers, barrel makers (coopers), leatherworkers (curriers) and metalworkers (goldsmiths and silversmiths), to mention only a few of the more important crafts.

▲ *Advances in medical science occurred in tandem with the study of alchemy, chemistry and the development of laboratory equipment.*

1500s
ALCHEMY AND MEDICINE

Medical chemistry was defined in Europe by its great publicist, Paracelsus (1493–1541), who was the sworn enemy of the malpractices of sixteenth-century medicine and a vigorous advocate of 'folk' and 'chemical' remedies. By the end of the sixteenth century, medicine was divided into warring camps of Paracelsians and anti-Paracelsians, and the alchemists began to move *en masse* into pharmacy. Paracelsian pharmacy was to lead, by a devious path, to modern chemistry, but the alchemist's pursuit of gold-making still persisted, though methods sometimes differed. The impression given is that many believed they had the secret of gold making but that most of them had acquired it from someone else and not from personal experimentation.

1550
THE HUMBLE POTATO

The potato was used by Andean Indians for 200 years but was not introduced to Europe until the mid-sixteenth century, reputably to England by the explorer, Sir Walter Raleigh. Potatoes began being imported properly in 1550 and they became the staple diet for many people. The crop was, for many years, stored by piling the potatoes up into clamps which were tightly covered with straw and earth. The crop failed in successive years caused by late blight fungus which destroyed the tubers, of the potato plant. Potato crisps were invented in France but manufactured from 1920 in England by Frank Smith.

▶ p. 177

1565
GROWTH OF WORLDWIDE HABIT

When Christopher Columbus discovered the Americas, he found the natives using tobacco in much the same manner as it is used today. The American Indians believed it to possess medicinal properties, which was the main reason for its introduction into Europe. Tobacco was important in Indian ceremonies, such as the smoking of the pipe of peace. Evidently the natives of North and South America had developed crude methods of tobacco culture. The extension of tobacco growing to practically all parts of the world began with its introduction into Europe: France, 1556; Portugal, 1558; Spain, 1559; and England, 1565. Portuguese and Spanish sailors then took tobacco from Europe to all parts of the world.

▼ *Tobacco can now be found growing on plantations throughout the Tropics.*

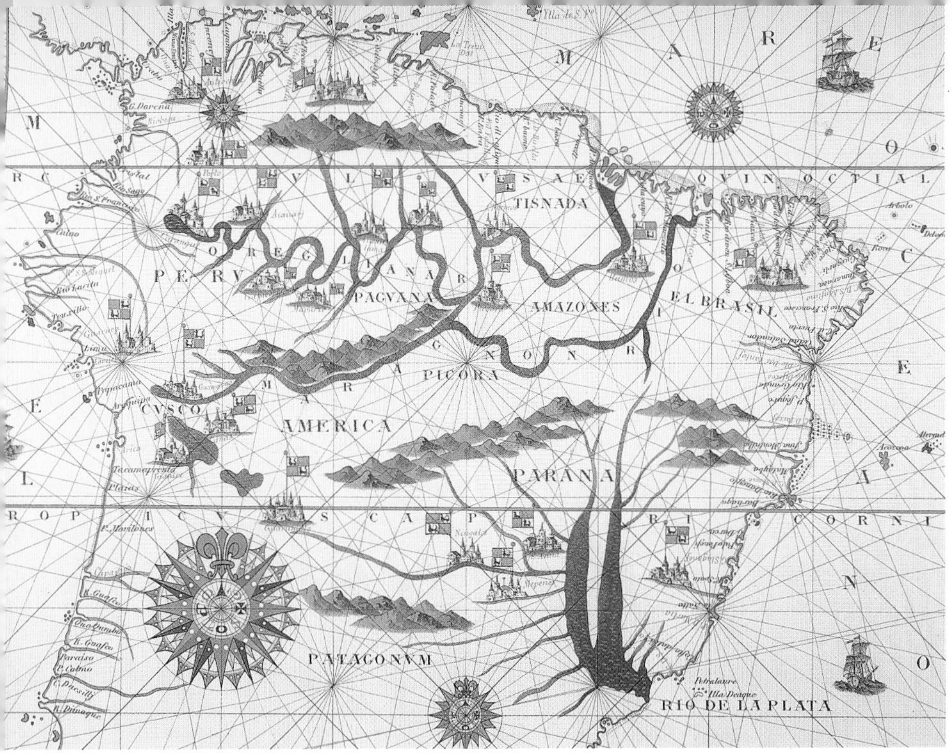

▲ *The earliest maps were often seen as works of art rather than accurate geographical representations of newly charted territory.*

1570
BETTER MAPS

The earliest maps were drawn from observations made by travellers and could be very inaccurate over large areas. Considerable evidence was gathered using the information brought back by explorers in the fifteenth and sixteenth centuries but more precise mapping began with the development of the theodolite by a self-educated English mathematician, Leonard Digges, in 1570, and triangulation in 1617. The theodolite was based on an instrument designed by Hero around AD 100 and measures horizontal and vertical angles. It consists of a telescope mounted between two side supports in a trunnion so that it can be moved up and down in a vertical plane, whilst the trunnion can also be rotated horizontally. The angles through which the telescope moves are measured from circular, graduated scales.

1600s
NEW HEATING

The efficiency of interior heating was improved throughout the seventeenth century by the introduction of cast-iron and clay-tile stoves, which were placed in a free-standing position in a room. The radiant heat they produced was then distributed uniformly throughout the space. In addition, these stoves lent themselves to the burning of coal, a new fuel which was rapidly replacing wood in western Europe. When European builders had rediscovered the technology of the classical world in brick, stone and timber, a stable plateau was reached in the development of the building arts with little further advancement. These available materials and techniques were well-suited to the churches, palaces and fortifications that their patrons required.

1608
LOOKING FOR STARS

The first optical telescope was invented in the Netherlands by spectacle-maker Hans Lippershey in 1608. A year later the Italian Galileo Galilei improved the design. These telescopes consisted of two lenses mounted in a tube whose length was the difference between the focal lengths of the two lenses. Galileo was the first to observe mountains on the moon and the four satellites of Jupiter. His astronomical work led him to believe that Copernicus' world view, that the Earth circled the Sun, was correct, which brought him into conflict with the Catholic Church in 1632. The telescope had a great effect on navigation and travel as well as on the whole science of astronomy.

▶ p. 175 **1620**
THE FIRST CALCULATOR

In 1620, Edmund Gunter, professor of astronomy at Oxford University, replaced printed logarithmic tables by etching a line of logarithms along a 60-cm (2-ft) wooden ruler. This could be used for adding or subtracting lengths measured from the line by dividers. The idea was improved upon by the Rev. William Oughtred in 1621, when he did away with the dividers by sliding one scale over the other. In 1630 this was developed still further into an early type of slide rule by Robert Bissaker. This ruler had fixed and sliding log scales and later a sliding cursor was added. Many more scales were added to slide rules allowing them to be used for many different computations.

▶ p. 177 **1659**
NATURAL GAS IN EUROPE

The first discoveries of natural gas seeps were made in Iran between 6000 and 2000 BC. Many early writers described the natural petroleum seeps in the Middle East, especially in the Baku region of what is now Azerbaijan. The gas seeps, probably first ignited by lightning, provided the fuel for the 'eternal fires' of the fire-worshipping religion of the ancient Persians. The use of natural gas was mentioned in China in about 900 BC. Natural gas was unknown in Europe, however, until its discovery in England in 1659, and even then it did not come into wide use for some time. Instead, gas obtained from carbonised coal (known as town gas) became the primary fuel for illuminating streets and houses throughout much of Europe from 1790.

p. 169◀ **Distant Voices** ▶p. 173

There is no greater hatred in the whole world than that of ignorance for knowledge.

Galileo Galilei (1564–1642), Italian mathematician and astronomer

Experiment and Expansion
1698–1750

PROBABLY THE MOST important innovations of this period were in power. The researches of a number of scientists, especially those of Robert Boyle of England with atmospheric pressure, of Otto von Guericke of Germany with a vacuum, and of the French Huguenot Denis Papin with pressure vessels, helped to equip technologists with the theoretical basis for the generation of steam power. Thomas Savery took out a patent for a 'new Invention for Raiseing of Water and occasioning Motion to all Sorts of Mill Work by the Impellent Force of Fire' in 1698. Although waterpower and wind power remained the basic sources of power for industry, a new prime mover had appeared with the steam engine, with tremendous potential for further development as and when new applications could be found for it.

▲ *The combination of brick and timber remained popular into the seventeenth century.*

p. 169◀ **Triumphs & Tragedies** ▶p. 173

1698
THE ARRIVAL OF STEAM

The earliest steam engines were the scientific novelties of Hero of Alexandria in the first century AD, but not until the seventeenth century were attempts made to harness steam for practical purposes. In 1698, Thomas Savery patented a pump with hand-operated valves to raise water from mines by suction produced by condensing steam. In about 1712 another Englishman, Thomas Newcomen, developed a more efficient steam engine with a piston separating the condensing steam from the water. In 1765 James Watt greatly improved the engine by adding a separate condenser to avoid heating and cooling the cylinder with each stroke. Watt then developed a new engine that rotated a shaft instead of providing the simple up-and-down motion of the pump and, along with other improvements, produced a practical power plant.

▶ p. 177

1700s
A CHANGE OF FACE

The practice of building in stone and brick became common, although timber remained an important building material for roofs and floors, and, in areas in which stone was in short supply, the half-timber type of construction retained its popularity into the seventeenth century. After that brick and tile manufacturing spread and provided a cheap substitute, although its use declined in the eighteenth century, when classical styles enjoyed a vogue and brick came to be regarded as inappropriate for facing such buildings. Cast iron was coming into use in buildings for decorative purposes. Glass was also beginning to be

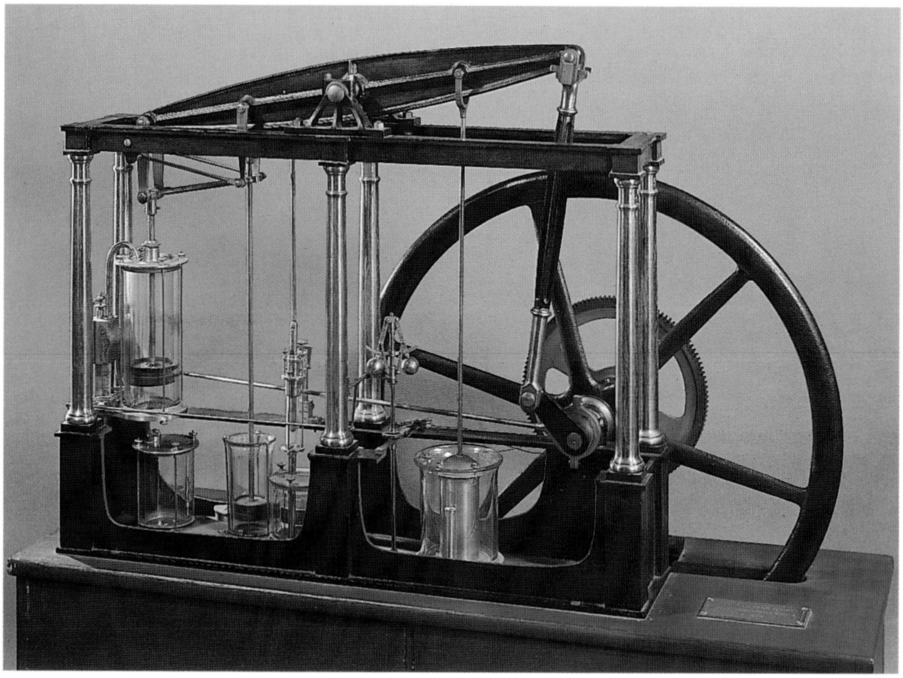

▶ *Watt's steam engine, built using the principles displayed in Thomas Newcomen's earlier model, but much improved on.*

used on many buildings, developing the industry that still relied on the ancient skill of fusing sand to make glass.

1718
THE FIRST MACHINE GUN

From the very first introduction of firearms in the late European Middle Ages, attempts were made to design a weapon that would fire more than one shot without needing to be reloaded. In 1718 in London, James Puckle patented a machine gun that was actually produced; a model of it is in the Tower of London. Its chief feature, a revolving cylinder that fed rounds into the gun's chamber, was the first basic step toward the automatic weapon; what prevented its success was the clumsy and undependable flintlock ignition. The introduction of the percussion cap in the nineteenth century led to the invention of numerous machine guns in the United States, several of which were employed in the American Civil War (1861–65).

▶ p. 174
1733
FASTER LOOMS

The son of a wool manufacturer, John Kay, made many improvements in dressing, batting and carding machinery. On 26 May 1733, he received a patent for a 'New Engine or Machine for Opening and Dressing Wool' that incorporated his flying shuttle. In previous looms, the shuttle was thrown, or passed, through the warp threads by hand, and wide fabrics required two weavers to pass the shuttle. Kay mounted his shuttle on wheels in a track and used paddles to shoot the shuttle from side to side when the weaver jerked a cord. This meant one weaver could weave fabrics of any width more quickly than two could before. Woollen manufacturers in Yorkshire were quick to adopt the new invention, but they organised a protective club to avoid paying Kay a royalty.

▶ p. 175
1742
MAKING STEEL

Making steel involves lowering the carbon content of pig-iron to below 1.5 per cent and controlling the presence of other impurities. This was first successfully achieved in 1742 by Benjamin Huntsman, an English clockmaker. He melted wrought iron in a clay crucible and added the required amount of carbon. This method, however, proved very expensive and could only be carried out on a small scale. It was replaced by a process invented independently in the 1850s by American William Kelly and Englishman Sir Henry Bessemer. It came to be known as the Bessemer Process. In 1864, Frenchman Pierre Martin and naturalised Briton Sir William Siemens invented the open hearth process. Both processes lasted for 100 years but were replaced by oxygen and electrical processes.

p. 172◀ **Triumphs & Tragedies** ▶p. 178

1701
TULL'S SEED DRILL

Attempts to mechanise the process of sowing seeds had been made around 1000 BC in Mesopotamia, when ploughs were fitted with a separate piece of wood containing a hole through which seeds were dropped from a tube into the soil. However, the first efficient seed drill was invented by the Englishman Jethro Tull who, after reading law at Oxford, devoted his life to studying soil fertility. He invented the seed drill, which was based on the arrangement of the groove, tongue and spring in the sound board of an organ, in 1701. The drill was pulled along by a horse and the seeds dropped from hoppers down tubes and were sown in rows. This enabled him to use a special hoe, which he also invented, between the rows.

1748
A WAY TO STAY COOL

The first known artificial refrigeration was demonstrated by William Cullen at the University of Glasgow in 1748. Cullen let ethyl ether boil into a partial vacuum; he did not, however, use the result to any practical purpose. In 1805, an American inventor, Oliver Evans, designed the first refrigeration machine that used vapour instead of liquid. Evans never constructed his machine, but

▲ *Jethro Tull's hoe-plough, with two horses harnessed to it.*

one similar to it was built by an American physician, John Gorrie, in 1844. Commercial refrigeration is believed to have been initiated by an American businessman, Alexander C. Twinning, in 1856. Shortly afterward, an Australian, James Harrison, examined the refrigerators used by Gorrie and Twinning and introduced vapour-compression refrigeration to the brewing and meat-packing industries.

1750
NEW MINES

The period from 1500 to 1750 witnessed a steady expansion in the mining of minerals other than coal and iron. Queen Elizabeth I introduced German miners to England in order to develop the mineral resources of the country, and one result of this was the establishment of brass manufacture. This metal, an alloy of copper and zinc, had been known in the ancient world and in Eastern civilisations but was not developed commercially in western Europe until the seventeenth century. Metallic zinc had still not been isolated, but brass was made by heating copper with charcoal and calamine, an oxide of zinc mined in England in the Mendip Hills. Other non-ferrous metals such as tin and lead were sought out and exploited with increasing enterprise in this period.

p. 171◀ **Distant Voices** ▶p. 175

If you have great talents, industry will improve them; if you have but moderate abilities, industry will supply their deficiency.

Sir Joshua Reynolds (1723–92), to the students of the Royal Academy

The Early Industrial Period

1754–97

THE FIRST UNMISTAKABLE EXAMPLES of manufacturing operations, carefully designed to reduce production costs by specialised labour and the use of machines, appeared in the eighteenth century in England. They were signalled by important inventions in the textile industry including John Kay's flying shuttle (1733); James Hargreaves' Spinning Jenny (1764); Richard Arkwright's water frame (1769); and Edmund Cartwright's power loom (1785). The steam engine was perfected by James Watt and this was the key to further rapid development. Once human, animal and water power could be replaced with a reliable, low-cost source of motive energy, the Industrial Revolution was clearly established, and the next 200 years would witness invention and innovation the likes of which could never have been imagined.

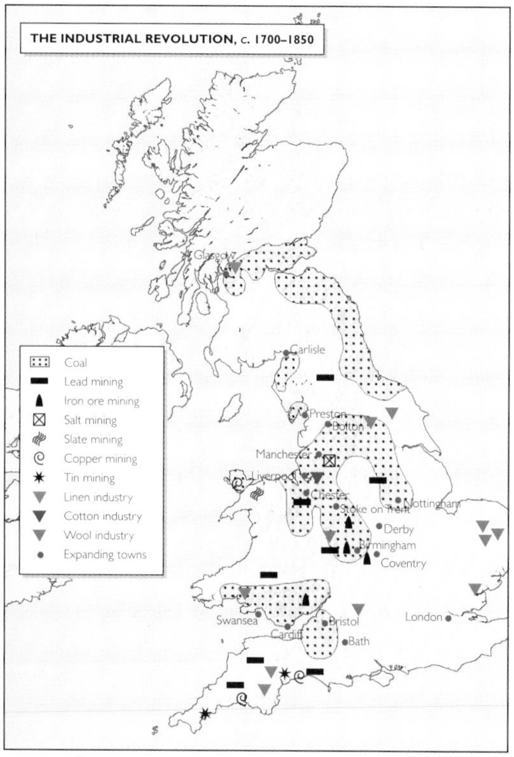

▶ p. 175 **1754**

ENGLISH PORCELAIN

During the eighteenth century, European porcelain had reached a stage where it rivalled that from China. It remained a luxury, however, until it was brought into general use by two Englishmen – Josiah Wedgwood and Josiah Spode. Wedgwood came from a family of Staffordshire potters and, in 1754, he established his own pottery, trying to make cheap earthenware that could compete with porcelain. In 1763 he patented cream-coloured queen's-ware, and followed it with blue jasper-ware. In 1769 he built a new factory near Hanley, where he practised mass-production methods to make crockery for everyday use. His work was supplemented by Spode's invention of bone china in 1800; this looked like porcelain, but was cheaper and stronger. It became widely used and popularised by Spode's willow pattern.

◀ *Josiah Wedgwood, the English potter who enabled mass-produced, high-quality china to become a household item.*

▶ p. 179 **1756**

THE RETURN OF CEMENT

The use of cement declined after the fall of the Roman Empire and it was not until the eighteenth century that it was resurrected by an English civil engineer, John Smeaton, for building the fourth Eddystone Lighthouse off the south-west coast of England between 1756 and 1759. He made his cement by heating clay containing limestone rock, which occurs quite widely. The successor to this cement was Portland cement invented by Joseph Aspdin of Leeds, who in 1824 took out a patent for a material that was produced from a synthetic mixture of limestone and clay. He called the product Portland cement because the material, when set, resembled Portland stone, the limestone used for building in England.

▶ p. 177 **1757**

PLOTTING A COURSE: THE SEXTANT

Early mariners used the sun by day and the North pole star by night in order to estimate their position. As time went on, better methods of navigation were found with the astrolabe, popularised by Portuguese explorers around 1500, then in 1731 the octant was demonstrated independently by John Hadley of England and Thomas Godfrey of Philadelphia. The more accurate sextant was first made to resemble its present form by a Scot, Captain John Cambell, in 1757. In use, the horizon is viewed through a telescope and a fixed half-silvered mirror, while a second mirror is rotated to bring the sun or a particular star into view alongside the horizon. The angle of rotation gives the altitude of the sun from which the latitude position can be calculated.

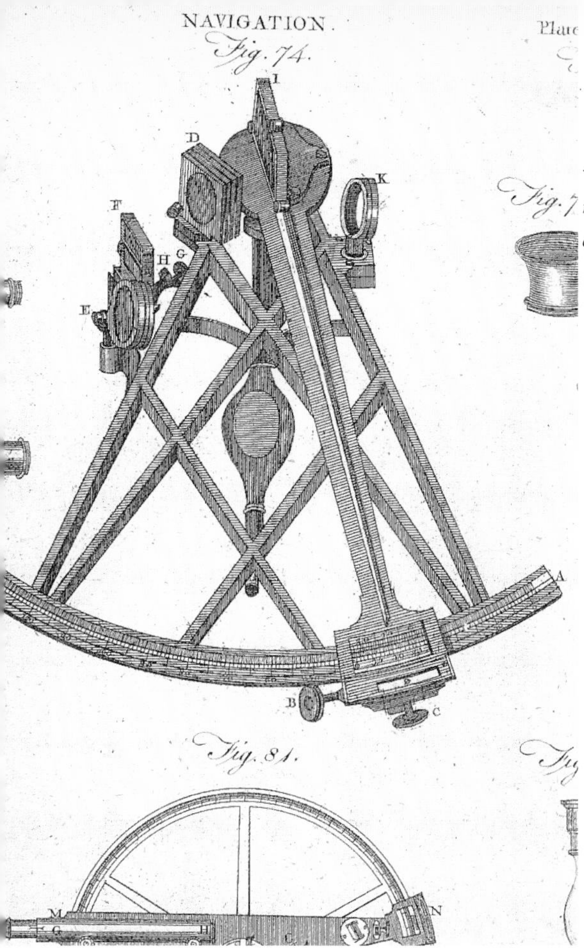

◀ *The sextant, one of the earliest nautical instruments available to sailors, enabling them to navigate the oceans.*

1764
A NEW WAY TO SPIN

James Hargreaves was the English inventor of the spinning jenny, the first practical application of multiple spinning by a machine. In about 1764, Hargreaves conceived the idea for his hand-powered multiple spinning machine when he observed a spinning wheel that had been accidentally overturned by his young daughter Jenny. As the spindle continued to revolve in an upright rather than a horizontal position, Hargreaves reasoned that many spindles could be so turned. He constructed a machine with which one individual could spin several threads at one time. When he began to sell the machines to help support his large family, local hand spinners, fearing unemployment, broke into his house and destroyed a number of jennies, causing Hargreaves to move to Nottingham in 1768.

▶ p. 176

1775
DRIVING THE WHEELS OF INDUSTRY

Between 1775 and 1800, the period over which Watt's patents for his engines were extended, the Boulton and Watt partnership produced some 500 engines, which, despite their high cost in relation to a Newcomen engine, were eagerly acquired by the tin-mining industrialists of Cornwall and other power users who badly needed a more economic and reliable source of energy. Basically, they converted the engine from a single-acting (applying power only on the downward stroke of the piston), atmospheric pumping machine into a versatile double-acting engine which could be applied to rotary motion, thus literally driving the wheels of industry. The rotary action engine was quickly adopted by British textile manufacturer Sir Richard Arkwright for use in a cotton mill which demonstrated the feasibility of applying steam power to large-scale grain milling.

▶ p. 187

1783
EASIER IRON

Brittle pig-iron, used for cookers, manhole covers, railway lines etc., was originally converted to wrought iron by removing most of the carbon and other impurities by repeated hammering, hence the term 'wrought'. Wrought iron is malleable and more ductile. This laborious procedure was finally replaced from 1783 by a puddling process invented by Englishman Henry Cort. This process involved heating the pig-iron with haematite whilst stirring (puddling) the mixture with long iron rods. As the impurities were removed the melting point of the mixture rose until it became pasty. At that stage, it was removed, hammered and rolled into shape. Cort's invention greatly increased the use of iron. Unfortunately Cort got into debt and his patents were confiscated by the government.

1784
SHRAPNEL

The Shrapnel shell was invented in 1784 by the British Lieutenant (later General) Henry Shrapnel. Shrapnel projectiles contained small shot or spherical bullets, along with an explosive charge to scatter the shot as well as fragments of the shell casing. A time fuse set off the explosive charge in the latter part of the shell's flight, when it was near opposing troops. The resulting hail of high-velocity debris was often lethal; shrapnel caused the majority of artillery-inflicted wounds in the First World War. During the Second World War it was found that a high-explosive bursting charge fragmented the shell's iron casing so effectively that the use of shrapnel balls was unnecessary, and it was thus discontinued. The term shrapnel continued to be used to designate the shell-casing fragments.

▶ p. 179

1797
A NEW LATHE

The lathe is one of the oldest and most important machine tools. Wood lathes were in use in France as early as 1569. During the Industrial Revolution the machine was adapted for metal cutting. The rotating horizontal spindle to which the work-holding device is attached is usually power-driven at speeds that can be varied. On a speed lathe, the cutting tool is supported on a tool rest and manipulated by hand. In 1775 John Wilkinson of England built a precision machine for boring engine cylinders. In 1797, Henry Maudslay designed and built a screw-cutting engine lathe. Maudslay had equipped his lathe with 28 change gears that cut threads of various pitches by controlling the ratio of the lead-screw speed to the spindle speed by 1800.

p. 173◀ **Distant Voices** ▶p. 177

Avarice, the spur of industry, is so obstinate a passion, and works its way through so many real dangers and difficulties.

David Hume (1711–76)

Power and Machines

1799–1833

THE INDUSTRIAL REVOLUTION was really a worldwide phenomenon, but beyond any doubt it occurred first in Britain, and its effects spread only gradually to continental Europe and North America. By 1800 Britain was by far the most industrialised state in the world and its rate of economic growth rapidly accelerated in the last third of the eighteenth century. The increase in mechanisation ruined the livelihoods of some skilled craftsmen, most notably the handloom weaver, although it is probable that without industrialisation the social costs of rapid population growth in Britain would have been far greater. It undoubtedly helped that Britain was richly endowed with coal and iron ore, and these minerals were often located close together in counties such as Staffordshire, Northumberland, Lancashire and Yorkshire.

▶ p. 181

1799
THE BIRTH OF THE CHEMICAL INDUSTRY

The growth of the textile industry at this time brought a sudden increase of interest in the chemical industry, because of the problem of how long natural bleaching techniques took, relying as they did on sunlight, rain, sour milk and urine. The modern chemical industry was virtually called into being in order to develop more rapid bleaching techniques for the British cotton industry. Its first success came in the middle of the eighteenth century, when John Roebuck invented the method of mass-producing sulphuric acid in lead chambers. The acid was used directly in bleaching, but it was also used in the production of more effective chlorine bleaches, and in the manufacture of bleaching powder, a process perfected by Charles Tennant at his St Rollox factory in Glasgow in 1799.

▶ p. 178

1802
FIRST IMAGES

In 1802, Thomas Wedgwood, son of the famous potter Josiah Wedgwood, reported his experiments in recording images on paper or leather sensitised with silver nitrate. Although he could record silhouettes of objects placed on the paper, he was not able to make them permanent and, to his disappointment, he failed to record a camera image. The first photograph was taken in 1826 or 1827 by the French physicist J. Niepce, using a pewter plate coated with a form of bitumen that hardened on exposure. His partner, Louis Daguerre and the Englishman William Fox Talbot adopted silver compounds to give light sensitivity, and the technique developed rapidly in the middle decades of the century.

▲ *Richard Trevithick, the first man to build a self-propelled locomotive that ran on rails.*

1802
STEAMING UP THE RIVER

In 1788, William Symington, son of a millwright in the north of England, began experimenting with a steamboat that was operated at 8 kph (5 mph), faster than any previous trials had accomplished. In 1801, Symington was hired by Lord Dundas, a governor of the Forth and Clyde Canal, Scotland, to build a steam tug: the Charlotte Dundas was tried out on that canal in 1802. It proved successful in pulling two 70-tonne barges the 12 km (19 1/2 miles) to the head of the canal in six hours. The governors, however, fearing bank erosion forbade its use on that route, and British experiments failed to lead further for some years; later progress was left to the Americans.

◀ *Scot Kirkpatrick Macmillan, who produced his self-propelled bicycle in 1839, after years of experimentation.*

▶ p. 181

1804
THE FIRST RAILWAYS

Railed trucks had been used for mining as early as 1550 at Leberthal, Alsace and by Ralph Allen from Combe Down to the River Avon in 1731, but the first self-propelled locomotive ever to run on rails was that built by Richard Trevithick (1771–1833) and was demonstrated over 14 km (9 miles), with a 10.2-tonne load and 70 passengers, in Penydaren, Glamorgan, on 21 February 1804. The earliest established railway to have a steam-powered locomotive was the Middleton Colliery Railway, set up by an act of 1758 running between Middleton Colliery and Leeds Bridge, Yorkshire built by Matthew Murray in 1812. The Stockton and Darlington colliery line, County Durham, which ran from Shilden through Darlington to Stockton opened on 27 September 1825.

▶ p. 178

1807
THE LAST WIND

British windmill construction was improved considerably at this time by sail refinements and by the self-correcting device of the fantail, which kept the sails pointed into the wind. Spring sails replaced the traditional canvas rig with the equivalent of a modern venetian blind, the shutters of which could be opened or closed, to let the wind pass through or to provide a surface upon which its pressure could be exerted. Sail design was further improved with the 'patent' sail in 1807. Here the shutters were controlled on all the sails simultaneously by a single lever inside the mill. With these and other modifications, British windmills adapted to the increasing demands on power technology, but the use of wind power declined sharply in the nineteenth century with the spread of steam.

▶ p. 179

1826
REAPING AND MOWING

Harvesting had always involved an army of men armed with scythes and sickles in order to reap the crops in time. In the first century AD, Pliny had described a mechanical reaper but it was left until the nineteenth century for the first commercial machines to be invented. A Scotsman, the Rev. Patrick Bell, invented the first in 1826, and Americans Obed Hussey and Cyrus McCormick followed suit in 1833 and 1834. They all used revolving horizontal blades at the front of the machine to hold the stalks vertical whilst they were cut at ground level by an upper row of toothed blades moving to and fro across a lower one. Another cutting machine, the lawn mower, was invented by Edwin Budding of Ipswich in 1830.

1830s
AN INSIGHT INTO THE FUTURE

The idea of mechanically calculating mathematical tables first came to inventor Charles Babbage in 1812 or 1813. Later he made a small calculator that could perform certain mathematical computations to eight decimals. Then in 1823 he obtained government support for the design of a machine with a 20-decimal capacity. In the 1830s Babbage developed plans for the so-called analytical engine, the forerunner of the modern digital computer. In this device he envisioned the capability of performing any arithmetical operation on the basis of instructions from punched cards, a memory unit in which to store numbers, sequential control, and most of the other basic elements of the present-day computer. The analytical engine, however, was never completed. Babbage's design was forgotten until his unpublished notebooks were discovered in 1937.

▶ p. 182

1833
THE GREAT BUILDER

The famous engineer and inventor, Isambard Kingdom Brunel, was born in 1806. He began his working life by helping his father, Sir Marc Brunel, in the construction of the first tunnel to be built under the River Thames. In 1829 he won a competition for the Clifton Suspension bridge and construction began in 1833. By then he had been appointed chief engineer to the Great Western Railway. Then, at the age of 27, he was responsible for building the new line from London to Bristol with all its bridges, tunnels and viaducts. He built in all about 2,500 km (1,553 miles) of railway track in England and Wales and was a consultant for many overseas lines. He also constructed or improved many docks.

▼ *The Clifton Suspension Bridge across the Severn Valley, built by the engineer Isambard Kingdom Brunel.*

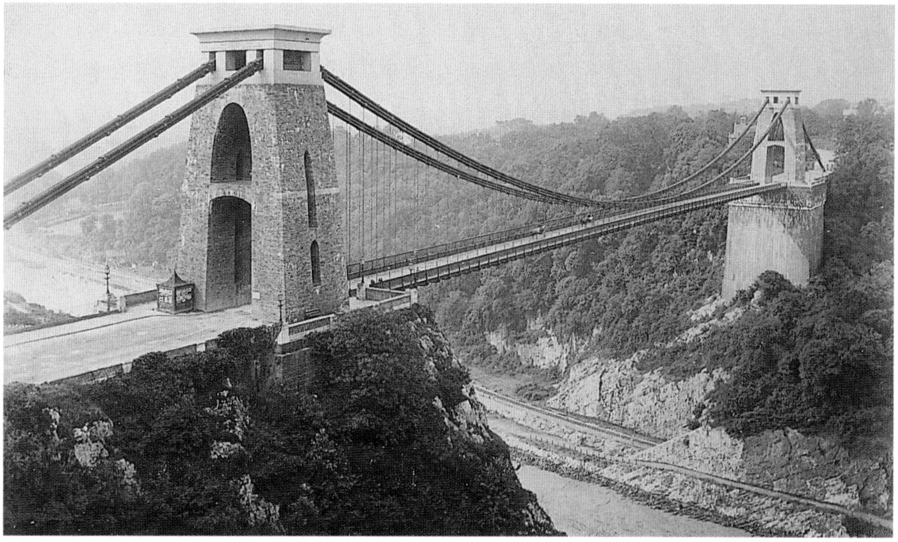

p. 175◀ **Distant Voices** ▶p. 179

Rail travel at high speed is not possible because passengers, unable to breathe, would die of asphyxia.

Professor Dionysus Lardner (1793–1859), Irish scientific writer

The Second Industrial Revolution

1831–92

THE SECOND INDUSTRIAL REVOLUTION is a term employed to describe the growth of new industries in this period. In particular there was a growth in the chemical industry along with machine tools, bicycles and cars. In addition a demand for power to generate electricity stimulated new thinking about the steam engine in the 1880s. The problem was that of achieving a sufficiently high rotational speed to make the dynamos function efficiently. Designers began to investigate the possibilities of radical modifications to the reciprocating engine to achieve the speeds desired, or of devising a steam engine working on a different principle. Many refinements were made and even today the most modern nuclear power plants use steam turbines, because of the problem of transforming nuclear energy directly into electricity.

1831
INVISIBLE POWER

The pioneering work on the use of electricity was carried out by an international collection of scientists including Benjamin Franklin of Pennsylvania, Alessandro Volta of the University of Pavia, Italy, and Michael Faraday of Britain. It was the latter who demonstrated the nature of the relationship between electricity and magnetism in 1831, and his experiments set off the development of both the mechanical generation of electric current and the utilisation of such current in electric motors. Both the generator and the motor depend on the rotation of a continuous coil of conducting wire between the poles of a strong magnet: turning the coil produces a current in it, while passing a current through the coil causes it to turn. Both generators and motors underwent substantial development in the mid-nineteenth century.

▶ p. 180

1837
OPENING UP THE WORLD

Great innovations in communications technology derived from the new knowledge of electricity. The first was the electric telegraph, invented for use on the developing railway system by two British inventors, Sir William Cooke and Sir Charles Wheatstone, who collaborated on the work and took out a joint patent in 1837. Almost simultaneously, the American inventor, Samuel Morse, devised the signalling code (1835) that was subsequently adopted all over the world. In 1843, Morse obtained financial support from the US government to build a demonstration telegraph system 60 km (35 miles) long between Washington and Baltimore. Wires were attached by glass insulators to poles alongside a railroad. By 1858 the first transatlantic telegraph cable was laid and the main political and commercial centres were finally brought into instantaneous communication.

▼ *Cigarette card depicting Macmillan's first self-propelled bicycle.*

p. 173◀ **Triumphs & Tragedies** ▶p. 184

1863
GOING UNDERGROUND

The first underground line in the world was in London and opened in 1863. The linking of two terminal stations at the West End and the City was achieved in 1884 with the opening of the Metropolitan Railway. Early development of underground railways in London was helped by the clay on which the city was built, which was easy to excavate. The soil provided raw material to make bricks for lining the tunnel walls. Improved deep tunnelling techniques after the First World War allowed a rapid expansion of the underground network, and consequently the Piccadilly, Bakerloo, Central and Northern lines opened up hundreds of square miles of rural Middlesex and Essex for suburbanisation. The London Underground is still the longest underground in the world with over 400 km (250 miles) of routes.

1839
TWO WHEELS

The first two-wheeled, rider-propelled bicycle was the *draisienne*, invented by Baron Karl de Drais de Sauerbrun and exhibited in Paris on 6 April 1818. The vehicle was made of wood and the seated rider propelled himself simply by paddling his feet against the ground. Steerable, crude

▲ *Construction work on the London Underground near King's Cross.*

and clumsy, it worked after a fashion. But it was not until Scot Kirkpatrick Macmillan completed four years of experiments in 1839 that a self-propelled bicycle appeared. Macmillan's machine had wheels rimmed with iron and, though lighter in appearance than the *draisienne*, it was still heavy. With a steerable front wheel about 75 cm (30 in) in diameter and a driven rear wheel of about 100 cm (40 in) in diameter, it could move at a brisk pace. In 1842, Macmillan's bicycle successfully challenged a post carriage.

1840
MUCK AND BRASS

The Greeks and Romans had used farm manure and vegetable waste as fertilisers to replace the chemicals extracted from the soil by growing plants. Eventually, intense cultivation led to natural resources running out. South American guano (sea bird droppings) was imported into England from 1840 to meet the need, but by then it had been learnt that nitrogen, phosphorus and potassium were the key elements required in the soil and so it became possible to replace natural by synthetic fertilisers. The widespread use of phosphate fertilisers was due to the work of Sir John Bennet Lawes, who used a bedroom in his ancestral home as a laboratory. In 1840 he patented a process for making a phosphate fertiliser and in 1843 founded the famous Rothamsted Experimental Station with Sir John Gilbert.

1856
FROM A MESS TO SUCCESS

The first dyes to be used were all naturally occurring substances such as indigo (from woad) and Tyrian purple (from sea snails). William Henry Perkins changed the colour of the world in 1856 when he made the first synthetic dye. The discovery was made by accident when he was an assistant at the Royal College of Chemistry in London. Whilst trying to make the white solid, quinine, he ended up with a blackish mess from which he extracted a purple substance which he found would dye silk. He patented the product and began manufacturing the dye. The dye was known as mauve, Queen Victoria wore a dress dyed with it and the purple penny postage stamps issued in 1881 owed their colour to it.

1866
THE BIRTH OF THE TORPEDO

The cigar-shaped underwater guided missile known as the torpedo was invented by a British engineer, Robert Whitened, in 1866. His first design was about 4.26 m (14 ft) long and 36 cm (14 in) in diameter. It carried an 8.16-kg (18-lb) warhead of dynamite, was powered by a propeller driven by a compressed air engine and was held at a set depth by a hydrostatic valve which operated horizontal rudders at the rear. Vertical rudders, controlled by a pre-set gyroscope to give lateral steering were added in 1896. The early torpedoes were launched from specially designed torpedo boats, whereas now they are also launched from submarines and aircraft. Modern torpedoes are driven by battery-operated electric motors and have full guidance systems.

▶ p. 184

1892
PICNIC AND ROCKETS

The vacuum flask was invented by the British chemist and physicist Sir James Dewar in 1892. He devised it to preserve liquefied gases by preventing the transfer of heat from the surroundings to the liquid. The evacuated space between the walls (which are ordinarily glass or steel) is practically a non-conductor of heat; radiation is reduced to a minimum by silvering the glass or steel. The idea was patented by a German glass-blower Reinhold Burger in 1904 who helped Dewar put it into practice and the proprietary name Thermos was suggested by a member of the public in a competition. The flask was used for storing liquid oxygen in rockets such as the V-2 during the Second World War and of course today for carrying hot or cold drinks.

▼ *The torpedo, an underwater guided missile, completely changed the nature of warfare at sea.*

p. 177◀ **Distant Voices** ▶p. 181

How charming it would be if it were possible to cause these natural images to imprint themselves durably.

W. H. Fox Talbot (1800–77), English scientist and photography pioneer

A New Transport Revolution
1900–17

IN THE RECENT HISTORY of industry and invention, one fact stands out clearly: despite the immense achievements that had been made by 1900, the following decades witnessed more advance over a wide range of activities than the whole of previously recorded history. A changing world, particularly the two world wars, led to a new revolution in invention, most notably in warfare and transport. The aeroplane, the rocket and interplanetary probes, electronics, atomic power, antibiotics, insecticides, and a host of new materials have all been invented and developed to create an unparalleled social situation, full of possibilities and dangers, which would have been virtually unimaginable before the twentieth century.

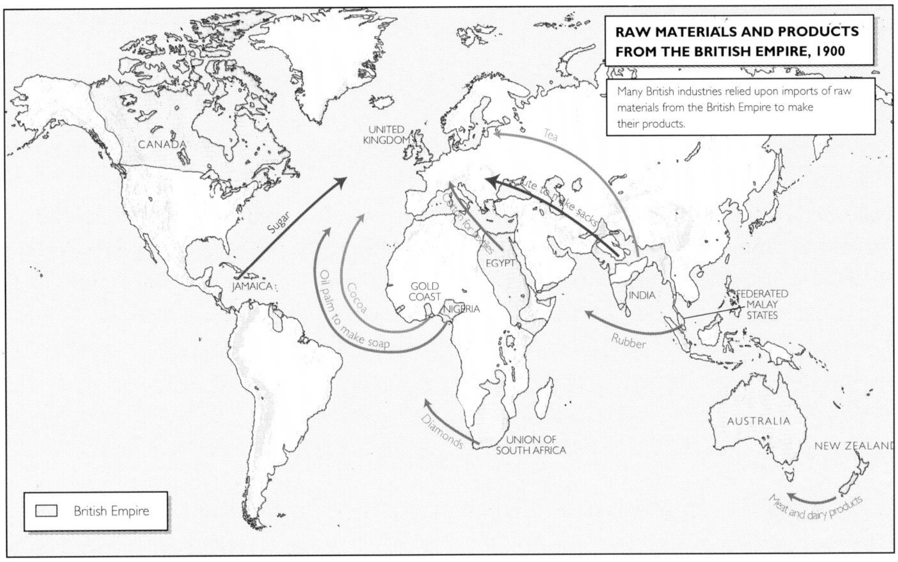

1900
LIGHTING UP TIME

The principle of the filament lamp was that a thin conductor could be made to glow by using an electric current, provided that it was sealed in a vacuum to keep it from burning out. Thomas Edison and British chemist Joseph Swan experimented with various materials for the filament around 1878 and both chose carbon. The lamp did not immediately supersede gas lighting, which remained popular for some forms of street lighting until the middle of the twentieth century. However, electric lighting became an accepted part of urban life by 1900. The tungsten filament lamp, which has become the principal form of electric lamp, was introduced during the early 1900s. More efficient fluorescent gas discharge lamps have found widespread use as well.

▶ p. 182

1901
WIRES AND WIRELESS

The electric telegraph was followed by the telephone, invented by Alexander Graham Bell in 1876, as a result of Faraday's discoveries in electromagnetism. It was adopted quickly for short-range oral communication in the cities of America and Europe. About the same time, theoretical work on the electromagnetic properties of light and other radiation was beginning to produce astonishing experimental results, and the possibilities of wireless telegraphy began to be explored. By the end of the century, the Italian Guglielmo Marconi had transmitted messages over many miles in Britain and was preparing the apparatus with which he eventually made the first transatlantic radio communication on 12 December 1901. By these means, the world was being drawn inexorably into a closer community by the spread of instantaneous communication.

1901
CLEANING UP

The first electrical vacuum cleaner was invented in 1901 by the Scot Hubert Booth. He came up with the idea when he saw how much dust was blown out of a carpet by a jet of compressed air. His system used an electric pump to remove the dust from a carpet by sucking air along a tube and through a cloth filter. The equipment was bulky and noisy and was improved on by US janitor J. Spangler. He used an electric motor to rotate a brush at the front of his portable machine and a fan behind it to suck the dirt into a collecting bag. Patented in 1907, he did not have the money to promote it and sold the rights to a relative, William Hoover, whose name is now synonymous with the invention.

1903
NEW ENGINES

The German engineer Nikolaus Otto is credited with building the first practical internal-combustion engine (1876); although Scot Sir Dugald Clerk built a gas engine (1876) and in 1881 patented his two-stroke engine. The main difference between the Clerk and Otto cycles is that Clerks' cycle generated an explosion once every two strokes of the piston, not once every four. In 1885 Gottlieb Daimler, another German engineer, modified the Otto engine to burn petrol (instead of coal powder) and built the first successful high-speed internal-combustion engine. Another type of internal-combustion engine was introduced by German Rudolf Diesel in the early 1890s. This was the gas-turbine engine, the first successful version of which was built in 1903 in France.

▶ p. 186

1903
FIRST FLIGHT

Throughout the nineteenth century, investigations into aerodynamic effects were carried out by inventors such as Sir George Cayley in England, who, by 1799 had established the basic configuration of the modern aeroplane with fixed wings, fuselage and tail unit. In 1804, Cayley flew the first of his successful model gliders and in 1853, a full-sized glider carried his coachman on the first manned glider flight. Several designers perceived that the internal-combustion engine promised to provide the light, compact power unit that was a prerequisite of powered flight, and on 17 December 1903, Wilbur and Orville Wright in their Flyer I at the Kill Devil Hills in North Carolina achieved sustained, controlled, powered flight. Flight developed so quickly that the brothers were flying across the Atlantic to Europe to give demonstrations by 1908.

▲ *The Wright brothers achieved the first successful manned flight in 1903.*

▲ *Most households in Britain now own a car, but early automobiles were primarily toys for the rich.*

1906
TOYS FOR THE RICH

In the developed world, the automobile entered the transportation market as a toy for the rich at the beginning of the twentieth century. In 1885, two Germans, Gottlieb Daimler and Karl Benz, built and ran the first petrol-driven motor car. The pattern for the modern car was set by Mercedes in 1901, with mass-production on an assembly line introduced at the Ransome Olds factory in America in the same year. From 1904–08, 241 automobile-manufacturing firms went into business in the US. One of these was the Ford Motor Company, which was organised as a corporation in June 1903 and sold its first car on 23 July. The company produced 1,700 cars during its first full year of business. In 1906 the British Rolls Royce company produced the legendary Silver Ghost.

▶ p. 184

1915
INVENTION OF THE DEPTH CHARGE

A depth charge is a canister of explosives which was first used as an anti-submarine weapon by the British navy in 1915. The canisters were originally dropped or thrown from the stern of a ship in a pattern of five. The explosive, detonated by a hydrostatic fuse set at a particular depth, caused serious damage even if it exploded at some distance from the submarine because the pressures built up by underwater explosions are much greater than those in the air. Today, computerised launching systems are used, the canisters are propelled over greater distances and can carry nuclear charges which can destroy a submarine up to 1.61 km (1 mile) away from the explosion.

1915
ARMOURED VEHICLES

Tanks were invented in the First World War for use as armour-shielded assault vehicles that could cross the muddy, uneven terrain of the trenches. Several European nations worked on ways to adapt internal-combustion gas engines to tracked vehicles, and in 1915 the British Admiralty's 'Landship Committee' became the first to adapt several tractors for military use. The first of these 'tanks' were dispatched to France the following year and on 15 August 1916, were assigned to combat at the first Battle of the Somme. These early tanks were lightly armed with machine guns and small-calibre guns. Tanks first played a decisive role in the First World War in the Battle of Cambrai (1917), when 474 British tanks broke through the German lines. They were increasingly used by the Allies after this.

p. 179◀ **Distant Voices** ▶p. 183

We can hardly realise the blissful quietude of the pre-telephone epoch.

Norman Douglas (1868–1952), Scottish essayist

War and Peace

1916–41

THE TWO WORLD WARS were the most important instruments of technological as well as political change in the twentieth century. The rapid evolution of the aeroplane is a striking illustration of this process, while the appearance of the tank in the first conflict and of the atomic bomb in the second show the same signs of response to an urgent military stimulus. The wars were thus responsible for speeding the transformation of ideas into practicalities and this period saw the beginnings of what was to be one of the greatest areas of growth in Britain; that of the communication industries. This was the period of the birth of television as well as the spur for possibly the greatest twentieth century communication advance; the computer.

▲ *Henry Ford, the automobile pioneer who introduced mass production of his tractors in 1916.*

1916–39
FORD AND FERGUSON

The very first tractors had appeared at the end of the nineteenth century. Early models invented by Hart and Parr in the USA and D. Albone in England were soon superseded by Henry Ford who began mass-production of Fordson tractors in 1916. However, competition and much patent legislation came with the invention of the Ferguson tractor in 1933. Harry Ferguson was born in Northern Ireland and worked on his father's farm from the age of 14. His tractor was designed for use on smaller farms and was much lighter and less cumbersome than the Fordson and utilised pneumatic rubber tyres. It was launched in England in 1936 and in collaboration with Ford, in the USA in 1939.

1922
ADVANCE WARNING

The development of radar can be traced to the work of German physicist Heinrich Hertz. Hertz proved the existence of radio waves and demonstrated that they can be reflected like light waves. The possibility of using the radio reflection phenomenon for detection purposes was further explored after the engineer Guglielmo Marconi elaborated its principles in 1922. During the 1930s several countries, including Great Britain, France, the USA, Germany and Japan, initiated research on radar systems capable of detecting aircraft and surface vessels at long range and under poor visibility. Before the outset of the Second World War, Britain had constructed a network of radar stations designed to provide early warning against approaching enemy aircraft. By late 1939, Germany had begun production of similar ground-based aircraft-warning units called Freya.

1926
SOUND AND VISION

In 1926, John Logie Baird demonstrated a mechanical scanner able to convert an image into a series of electronic impulses that could then be reassembled on a viewing screen as a pattern of light and shade. However, it was the ideas of fellow Brit A. Cambell-Swinton that helped to advance television further. In 1908 Cambell-Swinton pointed out that cathode-ray tubes would best effect transmission and reception and cathode-ray tubes were used experimentally in the UK from 1934. In 1932 the Radio Corporation of America demonstrated all-electronic television using a camera tube called the iconoscope (patented by Vladimir Zworykin in 1923) and a cathode-ray tube in the receiver. In 1929 the British Broadcasting Company began broadcasting experimental TV programmes using Baird's system and in 1936 they began regular broadcasting from Alexandra Palace, London.

1931
REACHING FOR THE HEAVENS

In the south of England at this time construction industries and new service

▼ *Steel production facilitated some of the most significant advances in the world of construction.*

industries such as hotels and the shops of London flourished. London grew enormously. Here, as in the rest of the world, conventional methods of building in brick and masonry had reached the limits of feasibility in buildings up to 16-storeys high, and the future lay with the skeleton frame or cage construction pioneered in the 1880s in Chicago. The Americans were using abundant cheap steel for columns, beams and trusses, and efficient passenger elevators. The Empire State Building was built in 1931, and with its total height of 381 m (1,250 ft) and 102 storeys, achieved a limit not exceeded for 40 years but setting a world-wide trend for taller structures.

1938
BIGGER STEAMBOATS

In transportation there was a switch from steam power, supreme in the previous century, to internal combustion and electricity. Steam, however, retained its superiority in marine transport. The steam turbine provided power for a new generation of large ocean liners beginning with the *Mauritania*, developing 70,000 horsepower and a speed of 27 knots (50 kph) in 1906. It continued throughout the period, culminating in the *Queen Elizabeth*, launched in 1938, with about 200,000 horsepower and a speed of 28.5 knots. Even here, however, there was increasing competition from large diesel-powered motor vessels. Most smaller ships adopted this form of propulsion, and even the steamships accepted the convenience of oil-burning boilers in place of the cumbersome coal burners with their large bunkers.

1939
JET SETTING

The theory of the gas turbine had been understood since the 1920s, and in 1929 Sir Frank Whittle, studying with the Royal Air Force, combined it with the principle of jet propulsion in the engine, and patented it in 1930. The construction of a satisfactory gas-turbine engine was delayed by lack of resources and the need to develop new metal alloys that could withstand the high temperatures generated in the engine. This problem was solved by the development of a nickel-chromium alloy, and work went on in both Germany and Britain to seize a military advantage in combat aircraft. The first jet-powered aeroplane was finally introduced in 1939 in Germany. The jet engine significantly simplified the propulsion process and allowed substantial increases in aircraft speed, size and operating altitudes.

1940
CODES AND COMPUTERS

Alan Turing was a brilliant English mathematician and logician. In 1936 he described a 'universal computing machine' that could theoretically be programmed to solve any problem capable of solution. This concept, now called the 'Turing Machine', foreshadowed the computer. During the Second World War he worked with the Government Code and Cypher School at Bletchley Park where he helped build a computer with vacuum tubes. It was known as the Colossus and was designed to decipher the German 'Enigma' codes, which it did in 1940. After the war, Turing worked in the construction of early computers and the development of programming techniques. He also championed the idea that computers would eventually be capable of human thought (Artificial Intelligence), and he suggested the Turing test to assess this capability.

1941
THE MANHATTAN PROJECT

On the 25 July 1941, a British committee chaired by G. P. Thomson and code-named Maud, issued a report that concluded that building an atom bomb was a possibility, and that it would 'lead to decisive results in the war'. Its recommendations were accepted by the British prime minister, Winston Churchill, in August. American scientists supported the findings of the Maud committee and President Franklin Roosevelt established the Manhattan Project to harness all the various activities. General L. R. Groves was put in charge and he chose Robert Oppenheimer, a professor of Science at the University of California, to direct a new central laboratory where the bomb would be built. It opened at Los Alamos in April 1943.

▲ *The first computer, known as ENIAC; early computers often filled entire rooms – a far cry from the microprocessors today.*

p. 181◀ **Distant Voices** ▶p. 185

The committee considers that the scheme for a uranium bomb is practicable and likely to lead to decisive results in the war.

The MAUD committee (24 July 1941)

The Atomic Age
1947–66

THE YEARS AFTER THE Second World War continued the twentieth century's advancements in engineering, chemical and medical technology, transport (particularly aeronautics) and communications, along with a more sinister advancement. The years after the war ended were spent in the shadow of nuclear weapons, even though they have not been used in war since that time. These weapons underwent momentous development: the fission bombs of 1945 were superseded by the more powerful fusion bombs in 1950, and before 1960 rockets were shown capable of delivering these weapons at ranges of thousands of miles. These developments in weapons of destruction also opened up the possibilities of the use of nuclear energy which has, as yet, not reached its true potential.

1947
THE SPEED OF SOUND

The gas turbine underwent substantial development since its first successful operational use at the end of the Second World War. The high power-to-weight ratio of this type of engine made it ideal for aircraft propulsion, so that in either the pure jet or turboprop form it was generally adopted for all large aircraft, both military and civil, by the 1960s. The immediate effect of the adoption of jet propulsion was a huge increase in aircraft speeds. The very first piloted aero-plane exceeding the speed of sound in level flight was the American aeroplane, Bell X-1 in 1947, and by the end of the 1960s supersonic flight was becoming a practicable proposition for civil-airline users.

1948
OBJECTS IN LIGHT

Holography is a method of producing three-dimensional images by means of laser light. The photographic recording of the image is called a hologram, which appears to be an unrecognisable pattern of stripes and whorls but which, when illuminated by coherent light, organises the light into a three-dimensional representation of the original object. Dennis Gabor, a Hungarian-born British scientist, invented holography in 1948, for which he received the Nobel Prize in physics more than 20 years later (1971). Gabor considered the possibility of improving the resolving power of the electron microscope, first by utilising the electron beam to make a hologram of the object and then by examining this hologram with a beam of coherent light.

▶ p. 186

1956
NEW ENERGY

Soon after the discovery of nuclear fission was announced in 1939, it was also determined that the fissile isotope involved in the reaction was uranium-238 and that neutrons were emitted in the process. Newspaper articles reporting the discovery mentioned the possibility that a fission chain reaction could be exploited as a source of power. After the Second World War, reactor development was placed under the supervision of the leading experimental nuclear physicist of the era, Enrico Fermi at Columbia University. On 2 December 1942, Fermi reported having produced the first self-sustaining chain reaction. His reactor was later called Chicago Pile No. 1 (CP-1). In 1956 the opening of Calder Hall in Britain seemed to herald a new age of cheap nuclear electricity.

p. 178◀ **Triumphs & Tragedies** ▶p. 190

1958
SOUNDS THROUGH SPACE

In 1945 the British author/scientist Arthur C. Clarke proposed the use of an Earth satellite for radio communication between, and radio broadcast to, points widely removed on the surface of the Earth. The station would be positioned at an altitude of about 35,900 km (22,300 miles) so that its period of revolution about the Earth would be the same as the period of the Earth's rotation. The first satellite communication experiment was the US government's Project SCORE, which launched a satellite on 18 December 1958. *Prospero* was the first of four X-3 satellites orbited by the UK. Launched with a British missile in 1971 from Australia, it was designed to test the efficiency of a new system of telemetry and solar cell assemblies.

1957
THE LARGEST RADIO TELESCOPE

After the Second World War, the British Astronomer Alfred Lovell began working at the University of Manchester's botanical site at Jodrell Bank with war-surplus radar

▼ *Modern telescopes have allowed astronomers to understand the universe beyond our planet.*

equipment. Researching into radio and radar astronomy he began to construct the Lovell telescope, a fully steerable radio telescope with a reflector that measures 76 m (250 ft) in diameter. Operation of this, the largest radio telescope, began in 1957 shortly before the launch of *Sputnik I*, and the satellite's carrier rocket was tracked at Jodrell Bank. Most operational time at Jodrell Bank is devoted to astronomy rather than tracking and communication, but the telescope has been part of the tracking network for the US programme of space exploration and monitored most of the Soviet accomplishments.

1959
CROSSING ON AIR

Perhaps the first man to research the air-cushion vehicle concept was Sir John Thornycroft, a British engineer who, in the 1870s, began to build test models to check his theory that drag on a ship's hull could be reduced if the vessel were given a concave bottom in which air could be contained between hull and water. The proper development of the hovercraft, though, was due to the Englishman Sir Christopher Cockerell. His early experiments on air cushions were carried out using tin cans but, by 1955, he had built a working model from balsa wood and taken out his first patent. The *SRN1*, capable of carrying four men at 45 kph (28 mph) was launched in 1959 and crossed the English Channel on 25 July.

▼ *Modern high-speed boats include the hovercraft and the catamaran.*

1966
LIGHT SIGNALS

Optical fibres are glass or plastic waveguides for transmitting visible or infrared signals. Their use was first suggested by Dr Charles Kao, born in China and trained and working in Britain, in 1966. Once it became possible to make the fibres of sufficiently pure glass, new optical fibres began to replace the old metal ones in the UK and the US in the late 70s. The first transatlantic optical fibre cable was laid in 1988 and an integrated services digital network (ISDN) is being installed all over Europe, which can transmit at speeds up to 64,000 bits per second. They have wonderful potential for the future of telecommunication and computer technology.

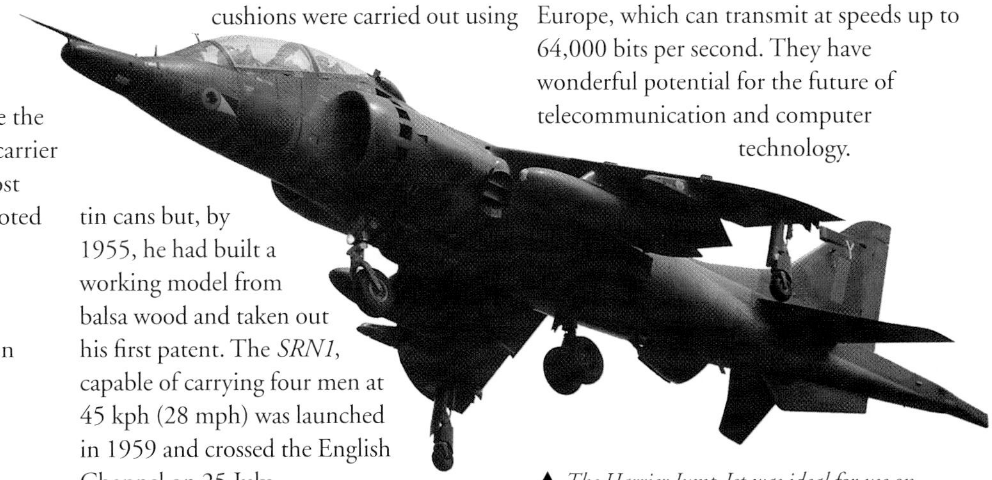

▲ *The Harrier Jump Jet was ideal for use on aircraft carriers.*

1966
VERTICAL TAKE-OFF

The Harrier jet is a single-engine, 'jump-jet' fighter-bomber designed to fly from combat areas and aircraft carriers and to support ground forces. It was made by Hawker Siddeley Aviation and first flew on 31 August 1966, after a long period of development. The several versions of the Harrier could take off straight up or with a short roll, and thus did not need conventional runways. Powered by a vectored-thrust turbofan engine, the plane diverted its engine thrust downward for vertical take off using rotatable engine exhaust ports. It could carry a combination of armaments, including air-to-air missiles, air-to-surface anti-ship missiles, rockets and bombs. The Sea Harrier saw combat in the Falkland Islands War of 1982.

p. 183◀ **Distant Voices** ▶p. 187

What was gunpowder? Trivial.
What was electricity? Meaningless.
This atomic bomb is the Second
Coming in Wrath.

Winston Churchill (1874–1965), English statesman

Electronic and Space Technology

1954–95

THE RAPID DEVELOPMENT of electronic engineering has created a new world of computer technology, remote control, miniaturisation, and instant communication. Even more expressive of the character of this period has been the leap over the threshold of extraterrestrial exploration. The techniques of rocketry, first applied in weapons, were developed to provide launch vehicles for satellites and lunar and planetary probes and eventually, in 1969, to set the first men on the Moon and to bring them home safely again. It justifies the description of this period, however, as that of 'the space age'. With advancements in communications and computer technology being made almost daily now, it seems that the future will open up newer horizons and even more spectacular innovations.

1954
TERRESTRIAL TV

A monopoly of both radio and television broadcasting was in the hands of the BBC, which had been established as an independent public corporation in 1927, until 1954, when the Independent Television Authority (ITA) was established. The ITA was intended to provide the facilities for a number of commercial television programme companies. In 1972 the ITA became the Independent Broadcasting Authority (IBA), with responsibility also for commercial radio. The BBC draws its revenue from licence fees from persons owning receiving sets, whereas the independent companies obtain their revenue from selling advertising time. The Independent Television company (ITV) was founded in 1955 and in 1982 Channel 4 was launched. Channel 5 arrived in 1997 and 1998 saw the launch of digital television for the first time in the UK.

1972
THE NEW CERAMICS

A whole new range of ceramic-like materials have been made in recent years from oxides of aluminium and zirconium, silicon carbide and nitride, and synthetic materials known as sialons, first made at the University of Newcastle-upon-Tyne in 1972. They are made by baking powders (sintering) in high-temperature kilns, under pressure if necessary, and are shaped by abrasives. The materials are extremely hard, resistant to corrosion and highly refractory. Many of them have excellent electrical, magnetic and optical properties and they have been used in making cutting tools, bearings, hip-replacement joints and heat shields for spacecraft. Cermets are composite materials containing a hard ceramic with a metal such as cobalt. These are easier to manufacture yet similar to ceramics and are used in making cutting tools.

1973
SEEING THROUGH THE BODY

Godfrey Hounsfield, the British electrical engineer, headed the team which pioneered the development of computerised axial tomography (CAT) in 1973. Inadvertently his team was working on the project at the same time as the American physicist Allan Cormack. They both shared the Nobel Prize for Medicine for the CAT scan device in 1979. The CAT scan enables detailed X-ray pictures of 'slices' of the human body to be produced and displayed as cross sections on a viewing screen. Using views taken from varying angles a three-dimensional picture of any organ or tissue irregularities in the body can be analysed and used as an aid in diagnosis without the need for surgery.

1975
EUROPE IN SPACE

The space race truly took off when the US *Apollo* program culminated in man's first lunar landing in 1969. Neil Armstrong and Edwin Aldrin exited *Apollo 11* on 20 July to become the first men to walk on the Moon. The European Space Agency, founded in 1975 by most European nations, has co-operated with the US National Aeronautics and Space Administration (NASA) on many projects and, on its own, was responsible for the *Giotto* space probe, which enabled examination of the core of Halley's Comet in 1986. The ESA also developed *Ariane* (first flight 1979), a three-stage launch vehicle using liquid fuels, and established a system of meteorological satellites known as *Meteosat.*

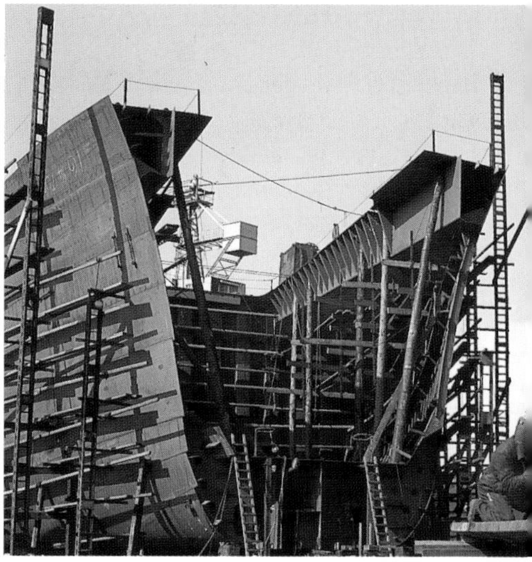

▲ *A bulk carrier in the Clydeside shipyard, Greenock.*

1980s
ENGLAND'S MANUFACTURING

The manufacturing industry as a whole has continued to shrink both in employment and in its contribution (now less than one-fourth) to the gross domestic product (GDP). This part of the economy was the major contributor to the rapid rise in unemployment in the early 1980s. Once economic growth returned there was great improvement in productivity through expansion in the manufacturing labour force. In terms of their relative importance to the GDP, the most important manufacturing industries are engineering; food, beverages (including alcoholic beverages) and tobacco; chemicals; paper, printing, and publishing; metals and minerals; and textiles, clothing, footwear and leather. The fastest-growing sectors have been metals, chemicals, man-made fibres, timber, furniture, rubber, and plastics. Within the chemical industry, pharmaceuticals and speciality products have shown the largest increases.

1980s
SCOTTISH INDUSTRY

In its industrial heyday Scotland's prosperity was based on such heavy industries as coal, steel, shipbuilding and engineering. In more recent times these industries have been exposed to foreign competition and to changes of demand. Throughout the 1980s the special facilities built to provide rigs and platforms for exploiting the North Sea oil and gas reserves experienced fluctuating demand, and some of them closed down. Severe cuts in capacity were also made in the steel industry as the state-owned British Steel Corporation strove to meet the government's financial targets as a prelude to privatisation. Though not matching the older manufacturers in terms of employment, the computer, office equipment and electronics industries have expanded, notably in the Fife, Lothian and Strathclyde regions. Much of this investment has come from overseas, particularly the United States.

1991
A LINK BETWEEN TWO NATIONS

The often-considered idea of constructing a tunnel under the English Channel was revived in 1986 by the UK and France. A rail tunnel was chosen over proposals for a suspension bridge, a bridge and tunnel link, and a combined rail and road link, and the project was privately financed by British and French corporations and banks. Digging began on both sides of the Strait of Dover in 1987–88 and was completed in 1991. The tunnel was officially opened in May 1994. The tunnel runs beneath the English Channel for 50 km (31 miles), and actually consists of three tunnels: two for rail traffic and a central tunnel for services and security. Trains can travel at speeds of 160 kph (100 mph) through the tunnel.

▲ *View of the inside of the newly constructed Channel Tunnel, providing a rail link between Britain and France.*

▶ *Nuclear power station cooling towers are now almost as familiar a sight as the factory towers of late-Victorian industries.*

1995
NUCLEAR FUTURE

The most widely used nuclear reactor is the pressurised-water reactor, which contains a sealed system of pressurised water that is heated to form steam in heat exchangers in an external circuit. It was designed in the USA and was fitted on the submarine USS *Nautilus* in 1954. The first nuclear reactor of this type built in England was Sizewell B on the Suffolk coast. It cost nearly £3 billion and has an output of 1200 MW. It first fed electricity into the national grid in February 1995. Data for 1993, released by the International Atomic Energy Agency (IAEA), showed there were 430 nuclear power units in operation in 29 countries, with a total capacity of 330,651 MW.

p. 185◀ **Distant Voices** ▶p. 191

Space isn't remote at all. It's only an hour's drive away if your car could go straight upwards.

Fred Hoyle (b. 1915), English astronomer

Culture, Arts and Leisure

LOOKING AT THE HISTORY of culture is like looking at the history of our inner life. While every generation has a history of events and important people that dominates its history, there is another story to be written about what thrilled them, moved them and inspired them. Sometimes it will have been the new English translations of the Bible, held illegally by shepherds or craftspeople. Sometimes it will have been the raucous plays of Shakespeare or Jonson. Sometimes it will have been Grace, Fry or Botham at the wicket. In each case, our ancestors will have talked about them, written about them in their diaries, maybe wept or cheered about them. We can only guess exactly what they felt at the time, but we can see this cultural story stretching back in an intricately woven strand, mixing together architecture, music, literature and sport, which inspired people to build the ideas and politics which drove history forward. In this strand we can see the big ideas like Romanticism, Enlightenment or individualism making their presence felt. Taken together, they make a distant connection between watching the great performers of today – with all their sophisticated sound effects and lights – and gathering around the fire in a Saxon hall to listen to the poetry of the bards.

KEY THEMES

- ARCHITECTURE
- MUSIC
- LITERATURE
- ART
- DRAMA
- SPORT
- POPULAR CULTURE
- POETRY
- RELIGION
- ENTERTAINMENT

KEY EVENTS

1 AD 715
BEOWULF

The author of the 3,500 lines of the epic Saxon poem *Beowulf* has long since been forgotten, but his heroic descriptions mark the early beginning of English literature. The poem is written in Old English, some centuries after it was first composed orally, but it still has the power to move people to this day.

2 1378
ON THE TRUTH OF HOLY WRIT

'Who has the authority,' asked John Wyclif: 'is it the Church and the Pope, or the written word of the Bible?' His opinions were condemned by the Pope and he and his followers were driven out of Oxford, but the desire for the right to read the Bible for oneself had now been ignited.

3 1387
THE CANTERBURY TALES

Geoffrey Chaucer's comic descriptions of the stories told by pilgrims were so successful that they were among the first books to be printed a century later. Chaucer inspired his contemporaries to write in English as well, and did more than anyone else to make English the dominant language it is today.

4 1601
HAMLET

William Shakespeare's *Hamlet*, one of his most powerful works, marked the turning point in his plays, and remains one of the most performed around the world. His rich language and extraordinary dramatic power make his writing still relevant today, and he is studied all over the world.

5 1818
FRANKENSTEIN

When the 16-year-old Mary Shelley was playing with ghost stories on holiday with the great romantic poets Shelley and Byron, she began to write the ultimate gothic novel. *Frankenstein* gave birth to a whole movement of horrifying investigations into the nature of mankind. She wrote several other novels, but none captured the imagination of the public as much as the tragic story of this monster.

6 1843
A CHRISTMAS CAROL

Charles Dickens' first Christmas story may not have been his greatest novel, or even the best piece of work in his prodigious output, but it established him as an institution – and as a part of British literary and social culture ever since.

7 1913
CHARLIE CHAPLIN

Charlie Chaplin was more than the first British film star, he was the first cinema star of the modern age. He went on to play a leading role in Hollywood. After his first film in 1913, the cinema gained a mass appeal, making it what some would say is the pre-eminent art form of the twentieth century.

8 1962
'PLEASE PLEASE ME'

'Groups with guitars are on the way out,' said an executive of the Decca recording company as he cancelled an audition with the Beatles in 1961. A year later the group had their first number one hit, and popular music was never the same: it has been one of the top earners for the British economy ever since.

TIMELINE

3400 BC Avebury Stone Circle
AD 698 The *Lindisfarne Gospels*
1 **AD 715** *Beowulf* written
AD 891 *Anglo-Saxon Chronicle* written
1079 Winchester Cathedral rebuilt
1110 First miracle play
1350 *Sir Gawain and the Green* Knight verses written
2 **1378** *On the Truth of the Holy Writ* written
3 **1387** The *Canterbury Tales* written
1539 Holbein's portrait of Anne of Cleves
1575 Tallis and Byrd given monopoly of music printing
4 **1601** *Hamlet* seen for the first time
1625 Death of musician Orlando Gibbons
1651 *Leviathan* written by Thomas Hobbes
1653 *The Compleat Angler* first published
1660 Samuel Pepys' diaries written
1675 Christopher Wren's St Paul's Cathedral built
1689 The first British opera, *Dido and Aeneas*
1740 Music for 'Rule Britannia' composed
1742 George Frederick Handel writes *Messiah*
1755 Johnson's Dictionary compiled
1777 *The School for Scandal* written
1794 'Auld Lang Syne' published
1798 *Lyrical Ballads* written by Wordsworth and Coleridge
1815 Brighton Pavilion
1816 *Emma* written by Jane Austen
5 **1818** *Frankenstein* written by Mary Shelley
1821 *The Hay Wain* painted by John Constable
1835 Madame Tussaud's waxworks shown
6 **1843** Charles Dickens writes *A Christmas Carol*
1847 The Brontë sisters begin their writing careers
1852 First music halls opened by landlord Charles Morton
1871 *Middlemarch* written by George Eliot
1880 W. G. Grace scores first-ever test century against Australia
1886 Advertising campaigns take off with 'Bubbles', the Pears Soap posters
1887 Sherlock Holmes and Dr Watson are created by Conan Doyle
1895 *Jude the Obscure* written by Thomas Hardy
7 **1913** Charlie Chaplin appears in his first film
1922 'The Waste Land' written by T. S. Eliot
1948 *1984* written by George Orwell
1954 *The Lord of the Rings* written by J. R. R. Tolkien
1958 Cliff Richard becomes Britain's most successful artist
8 **1962** Beatles get their first number one hit
1963 *That Was The Week That Was* launched by the BBC
1969 *Monty Python* hits Britain's TV screens
1976 Sex Pistols release their album *Anarchy in the UK*
1984 Torvill and Dean win the Olympic Gold Medal
1988 Salman Rushdie publishes *The Satanic Verses*
1996 The Spice Girls become the new teenage pop phenomenon

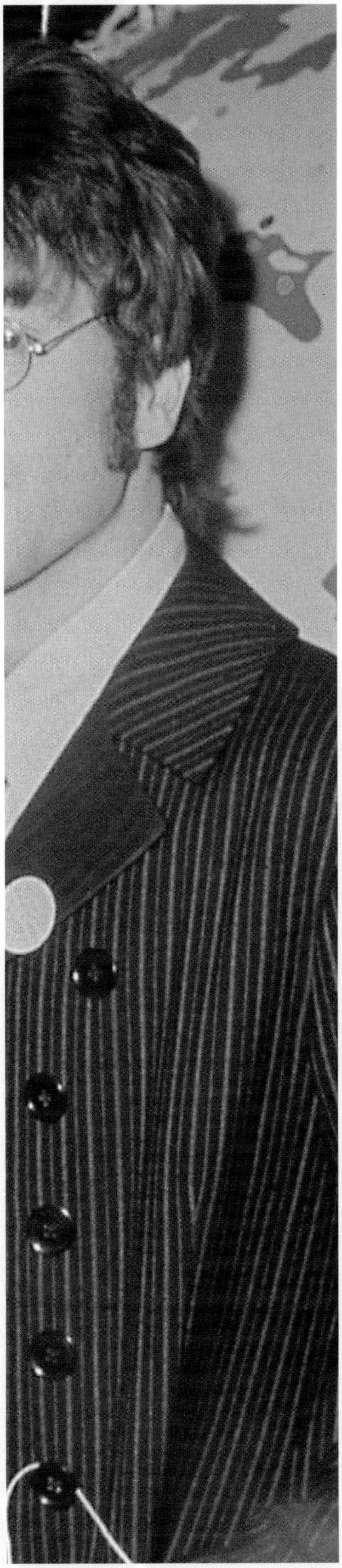

From Avebury to Abbeys

3400 BC–AD 1065

IT IS HARD TO separate the different aspects of culture – music, religion, architecture, poetry – and see exactly how each fitted into the pattern of life, as it changed between Neolithic and Saxon times. But we can be sure that prehistoric culture included a deep sense of connection with the land, through the changing seasons, and – judging by the alignments in sites like Stonehenge – to the stars and planets. Later cultures used music as a social glue, and memorised long tracts of heroic songs and poetry beyond anything that is possible today. Although there were probably no literate kings between Alfred and Henry I two centuries later, writing and learning had become considerably more widespread by the time the Normans arrived.

▲ *The stone circle at Avebury, like that at Stonehenge, continues to baffle archeologists as to its original purpose, although it is likely to have had a religious significance.*

▶ p. 194

3400 BC
AVEBURY STONE CIRCLE

'Avebury doth as much exceed Stonehenge in grandeur as a Cathedral doth an ordinary Parish Church,' said the antiquary John Aubrey, but more than 4,000 years after it was built, it is difficult to understand exactly what role the enormous stone circle played. It is surrounded by a 426-m (1,300-ft) earth bank, and each remaining stone weighs up to 40 tons, but the two avenues of stones, 2.4 km (1 ½ miles) long, which once snaked through the site, are now gone. Was it a great sun temple, or a 'moongate' – a place where heaven and earth meet – as some archeologists suggest? We will probably never know, but we can be sure that its purpose was central to people's lives.

▶ p. 196

450 BC
ARRIVAL OF THE BARDS

Historians can never be sure about the arrival of the Celts across Britain, but they were probably here by 450 BC, and they brought with them a verbal loquacity and fascination with music which has remained to a great or lesser degree ever since. Wandering bards would entertain the gathered Celts with songs and music on the lyre or harp, praising chieftains gone by in epics learned by heart. Bards and poets were a Druidic branch and learned their craft for up to 20 years, often in schools, committing a great deal of poetry to memory. The highest class of poet, or *ollam*, was equal to a minor king and would travel with a retinue of up to 24 companions, defending themselves with the magical power of satire.

AD 84
FOUNDATION OF BATH

Legend has it that Bath dates back as far as the legendary British king Bladud around 860 BC; but the construction of the Roman Baths there, known as *Aquae Sulis*, certainly began around AD 84 near the Fosse Way, and they were soon the centre of a major healing centre dedicated to the Celtic god Sulis and the Roman goddess Minerva. The baths themselves fell into disuse in the fifth century, and the town may have stayed ruined for 300 years after that. The remains of the baths stayed undiscovered until the eighteenth century, but – together with their mosaics, altars and temples – they are a monument to

p. 184◀ **Triumphs & Tragedies** ▶p. 196

AD 891
ANGLO-SAXON CHRONICLE

The *Anglo-Saxon Chronicle* is the main literary source of Saxon history. It was started in AD 891, during the reign of the learned king Alfred the Great (AD 849–99) and continued in various forms until 1154, in the case of the version in Peterborough Abbey. It provides a year-by-year digest of the main events, though there are periods when the information is very sketchy. It is particularly detailed about the triumphs of the reign of Alfred and the disasters of Ethelred the Unready (AD 966–1016). Manuscripts of the first section were widely available in the AD 890s, and now there are seven different versions still in existence. The chronicle was used by medieval historians like William of Malmesbury (*c.* 1095–1143).

Roman design which strongly influenced the fashionable people who flocked to the same springs a thousand years later.

AD 657
CAEDMON'S VISION

Caedmon (d. AD 680) was the first important English writer, and one of the central figures in the flowering of Christian culture and learning known as the Northumbrian Renaissance in the period of peace before the arrival of the Vikings. Caedmon's own story was recorded less than 60 years

▲ *A Classical illustration of the ancient Roman public baths, or* Aquae Sulis.

after his death by the Venerable Bede (*c.* 672–735), and describes how he had tended to avoid his turn on the harp at festivals, when a vision persuaded him to sing. 'Sing what?' asked Caedmon. 'Sing the beginning of created things,' said the vision. So Caedmon became a monk in Whitby and devoted his life to turning Bible stories into Old English verse. Thus he became one of those cultural figures who was clearly influential in assimilating Christian and pagan cultures.

AD 698
THE *LINDISFARNE GOSPELS*

The *Lindisfarne Gospels*, written and illustrated by a monk called Eadfrith, remain one of the most beautiful creations

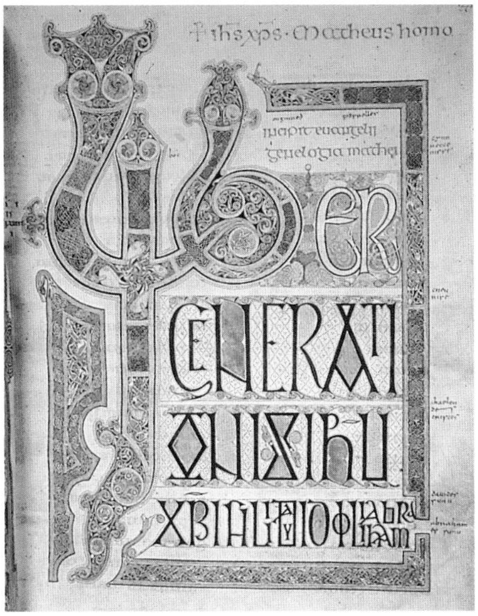

▲ *The* Lindisfarne Gospels, *written and illustrated by the monk Eadfrith.*

of Saxon England, and they can still be seen in the British Museum today. Lindisfarne was a monastery in Northumberland, which flourished under the Bishop of Lindisfarne, St Cuthbert (*c.* AD 635–687), and became the centre for Irish missionary activity in the north of England. His body is now in Durham Cathedral, but in 698 – the year the gospels were created – the first miracles were reported at his tomb in Lindisfarne, which is perhaps why the gospels are also known as the Gospels of St Cuthbert. Two years later, the Psalms were translated into Anglo-Saxon. The monastery was destroyed by the Vikings in 793.

❧ ▶ p. 204

AD 715
BEOWULF

At 3,200 lines, *Beowulf* is the longest surviving poem in Old English, written down in the tenth century in West Saxon dialect, but composed by a single poet, probably around AD 715, most likely in Mercia or Northumberland. The poem makes no reference to England at all, but is set in Scandinavia, where the hero Beowulf kills both the monster Grendel and its mother, and is fatally wounded in a battle with a dragon. The poem covers life and death, good and evil, as well as the relationship between society and the individual. Later generations have interpreted it according to the Christian tradition, but there have been a range of other mythic and allegorical interpretations as well.

1065
CONSECRATION OF WESTMINSTER ABBEY

There is evidence for a Roman settlement underneath what is now Westminster Abbey, and probably some kind of Anglo-Saxon settlement as well. But it was Edward the Confessor (1005–66) who made the abbey the important site it is today – though the current abbey is mostly the result of rebuilding under Henry III (1207–72). Edward moved his palace to Westminster from Winchester, and began extensive rebuilding work to the abbey in the 1050s. It was finished on 8 December, eight days before Edward's death, and was ready to witness two coronations in 1066, those of both Harold II (*c.* 1020–1066) and William I (*c.* 1027–87). Contemporary sources suggest that Edward's new abbey was the most sumptuous Saxon building ever built.

p. 187◀ **Distant Voices** ▶p. 193

They named the huge one Grendel:
If he had a father no-one knew him,
Or whether there'd been others before
these two,
Hidden evil before hidden evil.
They live in secret places, windy
Cliffs, wolf dens where water pours
From the ricks, then runs
underground, where mist
steams like black clouds, and the groves
of trees
Growing out over their lake are all
covered
With frozen spray, and wind down
snake-like
Roots that reach as far as the water
And help keep it dark....

From *Beowulf*, translated by Burton Raffel (AD 715)

From Tapestries to Troubadours

1077–1277

SOME TIME BETWEEN 1160 and 1207, an English priest called Layamon wrote a poem called *Brut*, which describes the beings who live in the air – some good and some bad – who will live there until the end of the world. This armageddon had been expected a thousand years after the birth of Christ, so the medieval world regarded itself as living on borrowed time, and the existence of angels and demons were generally accepted. Yet the Middle Ages was also a period of historical and scientific inquiry, the practitioners of both coming mainly from the monasteries. It was a period of authority, but where – in spite of invasion by another culture and the use of Latin across Europe – English somehow managed to survive and develop.

▲ *Romanesque arches, vaults and domes, such as those at Ely Cathedral, were built by the Normans.*

▲ *The Bayeux Tapestry, depicting the Norman conquest, is one of the most important historical documents to have survived over 900 years.*

✻ ▶ p. 199

1077 BAYEUX TAPESTRY

Everything about the Bayeux Tapestry remains controversial. It is not actually a tapestry at all, but an embroidered strip of linen. Even the depiction of the death of Harold at the Battle of Hastings (1066), and whether the knight with the arrow in his eye was actually supposed to be him, is questioned. But the 68-m (223-ft) tapestry was probably commissioned in 1077 for Odo (*c.* 1030–97), then Bishop of Bayeux, to depict his role as central to the Norman conquest. It was designed by an English artist and may have been created in a workshop at St Augustine's Abbey in Canterbury. It was almost certainly intended to be a wall-hanging, though this is the only wall-hanging of its size to have survived from before the fourteenth century.

▶ p. 196

1079 WINCHESTER CATHEDRAL

Winchester had been the capital of England under the Saxon kings, many of whom were buried there. But their cathedral was demolished under one of William I's relatives, Bishop Walkelin (d. 1098), and starting in 1079 William began to replace it with the Norman building which forms the basis for the cathedral you can still see today, with its distinctive rounded Norman arches. Similar styles – known as 'Romanesque' – can be seen in other cathedrals like those in Chichester, Durham, Ely, Hereford, Norwich, Oxford and St Albans. In fact, most remaining Norman buildings are either castles or churches. The stone for Winchester cathedral was brought from quarries on the Isle of Wight. The cathedral design was sadly flawed: the bishop's central tower fell down in 1107.

▶ p. 197

1110 THE FIRST MIRACLE PLAY

The first recorded miracle play was performed in Dunstable in Kent in 1110, and the genre flourished in England from the thirteenth to the fifteenth centuries. Miracle plays were performed, using characters from the Bible or mythology, by wandering players – often from guilds – usually on the street on a wheeled stage, or sometimes on platforms next to the road for processions. The stories were familiar and the words of some plays have been passed down to the present day. They probably developed out of liturgical processions, and were given a boost by a papal edict in 1210 forbidding the clergy to appear on stage.

Performances took place on festival days, especially Corpus Christi. Later, stories began to develop on non-biblical subjects in the same format.

▶ p. 198

1133
BARTHOLOMEW FAIR

The great fairs were central to medieval life in Britain, both for selling goods and livestock and for entertainment, with performances, juggling, acrobats, prostitutes, quacks and mummers entertaining the crowds – many of whom would go on foot or horseback for days to join in the festivities. The most famous was Bartholomew Fair, which was held annually at West Smithfield in London from 1133, and lasted over 700 years before it was finally wound up in 1855. The first charter was given to Rahere (d. 1144), who had been the jester for Henry I (1068–1135), and the fair was held every year on the festival of St Bartholomew, then 24 August; it was the main annual cloth fair in the country.

1170
STAINED GLASS

The first stained glass still in existence is in Augsberg Cathedral in Germany, made around 1080, but it was not until 90 years later that the medieval art form reached England, into the beautiful windows of York Minster. York's cathedral church had been destroyed in the Norman invasion, just as it had been during the Viking invasions, and was being rebuilt by Archbishop Roger (d. 1181). Stained glass, especially the deep reds and blues of England and northern France, was a medium that was typical of the gothic style. The colours were added using oxides of iron for red, copper for green and cobalt for blue. Stained glass windows continue to thrill visitors to the great cathedrals, as they must have done when they were first constructed.

1174
CANTERBURY CHOIR

The choir of Canterbury Cathedral was gutted by fire in 1174, just as the pilgrims were beginning to arrive at the tomb of St Thomas Becket (*c.* 1120–70). Its rebuilding that year marked the first appearance of the pointed arch. Music sung there was plainsong, consisting of a single line of song in unison, without harmonisation or musical accompaniment, standardised by Pope Gregory (d. AD 604). Plainsong derived from Jewish and Greek chants, which in turn were based on the rhythm of speech. The eleventh-century Benedictine monk, Guido d'Arrezzo, had introduced the method of recording music with the horizontal lines, and as the arches went up, plainsong was in the process of developing the idea of a second harmony sung around it.

1193
BLONDEL'S SONG

On his way back from the Third Crusade, in 1193, Richard I (1157–99) was captured by Leopold, Duke of Austria, inspiring his lover Blondel de Nestle, to wander through Germany in disguise looking for him. It is said that, when he played their love-song under the walls of Durrenstein in Austria, Richard joined in the singing from the tower – allowing Blondel to dash back to England and organise a ransom. Blondel was one of the most famous troubadours, the poet-musicians who emerged from Provence and wandered across Europe from the eleventh to the thirteenth centuries, with songs which were among the first in native language rather than Latin. Most troubadours were nobles and considered this artistic life to be a manifestation of the chivalric ideal.

▶ p. 201

1277
IMPRISONMENT OF ROGER BACON

Roger Bacon (*c.* 1220–92) is best known as one of the pioneers of science teaching, though he never succeeded in his aim of getting science recognised as part of the curriculum of Oxford University, where he lived and worked. As a Franciscan friar and a scholar in mathematics, optics, astronomy and alchemy, he was also one of the first science writers. In the end he succumbed to a cold – it is said – after an experiment to test whether snow could preserve a chicken. His interest in alchemy and his attacks on the local theologians were enough to destroy his academic career, and he was sent to prison for unorthodox teaching in 1277. Stories of his bizarre experiments made him a well-known figure in popular literature.

▼ *The scientific scholar Roger Bacon, who was imprisoned for his unorthodox teachings.*

p. 191◀ **Distant Voices** ▶p. 195

Summer has come, loudly sing cuckoo. Now is the seed growing and the meadow flowering and the forest springing to life. Sing cuckoo. The ewe bleats after the lamb, the cow lows after the calf, the bullock leaps, the buck breaks wind. Merrily sing cuckoo. Cuckoo, cuckoo, well dost thou sing cuckoo, never cease now.

A translation of the English lyric 'Sumer is icumen in' (late-thirteenth century)

The High Middle Ages
1290–1484

THE MIDDLE AGES ENDED on a colourful note, with the bright new coats of arms, new cloth-dyeing techniques, the emergence of new musical instruments like the clavichord, the soaring fan-vaulted roofs of the perpendicular style, and the triumph of the English language as written by William Langland and Geoffrey Chaucer. But a period which began when books were the learned preserve of monks and universities, ended with the start of William Caxton's new printing press in Westminster, making the work of Chaucer and the newly-translated Bibles available to people of all classes. It was those who championed a literate population, like the radical John Wyclif, whose influence would be felt most strongly in the centuries that followed.

1290
SIR GAWAIN AND THE GREEN KNIGHT

By the twelfth century, the legend of King Arthur and his knights had been appearing in literature as far south as Spain and as far north as Iceland. The stories fuelled Celtic resistance in Wales and Scotland, with the idea of Arthur's imminent return – scotched in 1191 by the discovery of his grave at Glastonbury Abbey – and were also fuelling the growing popularity of chivalry and romance in Britain. Prose romances about Arthur began appearing again in England from the second half of the thirteenth century, culminating in *Sir Gawain and the Green Knight* (*c.* 1290): 2,500 lines of alliterative verse following the knight Gawain's moral dilemmas as he clings to his chivalric values. The anonymous author probably came from the west Midlands.

▼ *The legend of King Arthur and the Knights of the Round Table has endured since the twelfth century.*

1331
THE PERPENDICULAR STYLE

Against a background of war and disorder in the fourteenth century, English architecture developed a gothic style of its own which is found nowhere else and which dominated building for the next two centuries. Known as 'perpendicular' it was flatter, more ordered and more secular than the 'decorated' style that preceded it – more suited to the sermon, which was growing in significance, rather than an attempt to build a soaring City of God on earth. It was adapted for colleges and great houses as well, but the earliest surviving example is in the choir of Gloucester cathedral, the south transept of which began to be rebuilt around 1331. Other examples include the nave of Canterbury cathedral, by the celebrated architect Henry Yevele (d. 1400).

▶ p. 199

1349
FOOTBALL FORBIDDEN

Even the Romans seem to have had a game that involved kicking a ball around a field, but it was not until the Middle Ages that football between villages – a raucous and brutal affair – reached its height of popularity. Teams sometimes included whole villages; goals could be miles apart and many places held an annual game on Shrove Tuesday. The authorities disapproved and Edward III made the first moves to ban it in 1349, followed by Henry IV in 1401; by the reign of Elizabeth, players were liable to imprisonment. The game continued, however, until the puritans made it unfashionable, and it was brought back to popularity through the efforts of the public schools in the nineteenth century.

▶ p. 196

1378
ON THE TRUTH OF HOLY WRIT

The radical theologian John Wyclif (*c.* 1330–84) was one of the first Protestants, and in the 1370s found himself questioning

▲ *An illustration of one of the* Canterbury Tales *by Geoffrey Chaucer, Britain's most famous medieval author.*

the authority of the pope, the clergy's right to property and much else besides. When his opinions were condemned by Rome in 1377, he responded with a treatise arguing that the word of God revealed in the Bible was the only true authority. *On the Truth of Holy Writ* was the beginning of the Lollard movement, the early translations of the Bible into English and the spread of literacy among all classes. Wyclif and his followers were driven out of Oxford and he lived out his final days in Lutterworth in Leicestershire, described by the early English Protestants as 'the morning star of the Reformation'.

1387
THE CANTERBURY TALES

The Canterbury Tales by Geoffrey Chaucer (*c.* 1340–1400) was an immediate success, and proved to be one of the most influential books in the language, helping to set the style of English spoken in south-east England as the main language of literature, instead of French and Latin. Chaucer had an eventful life himself, living above Aldgate as the Peasants' Revolt played out underneath his rooms in 1381 and becoming an MP. He is buried in Westminster Abbey, not as a poet – though his tomb later became the nucleus for Poet's Corner – but as a royal servant who leased a house in the Abbey precincts. The humour of the *Tales* and his other works meant that they were among the first works to be printed.

1390
THE PORTRAIT OF RICHARD II

Artists before the Renaissance were not very interested in individual people. Their pictures are idealised representations of kings and people, and it was not until the end of the fourteenth century that portraits began to appear. One of the first in existence is the picture of Richard II (1367–1400), now in Westminster Abbey, which reveals him as a forbidding character with little tenderness of feeling. The portrait was probably presented for Richard's visit to the Abbey in 1390 for the re-burial of Edward the Confessor, and may be by the same artist who painted the Wilton Diptych around 1395, a portrait now in the National Gallery. The stern, proud individual revealed in the painting of Richard may offer some explanation why he would shortly be deposed.

1451
WELSH BARDIC TRADITION

By the time of the mysterious disappearance of the Welsh independence leader Owen Glendower (*c.* 1359–1416), the Welsh bardic tradition had been almost eradicated. But by the mid-fifteenth century, there was a revitalisation of Welsh poetry under the influence of Dafydd ap Gwilym (*c.* 1320–80), writing about nature with passion and humour and using a flexible verse form known as the *cywydd*. Eisteddfods – meaning 'sitting of the learned' – had formerly been held regularly in the capitals of the Welsh princes, and were revived as well. One was held in Carmarthen in 1451, voting Dafydd ap Edmwnd (1425–1500) as its most distinguished poet. By the following century, the Bible was also being translated into Welsh.

✳ ▶ p. 201

1484
THE COLLEGE OF ARMS

The high Middle Ages was a period of spectacular aristocratic display, at the heart of which was the colourful science of heraldry – the method of identifying families using a symbolic language of pictures.

▲ *Family insignia were often embroidered as flags or embossed on shields during the Middle Ages.*

Family insignia had been embroidered on the surcoats of knights since the previous century, until the practice was restrained by Henry V (1387–1422). Heralds, meanwhile, had changed their traditional role as announcers, diplomats and tournament organisers to define heraldry, and Edward IV (1442–83) gave their profession a formal existence by setting up the College of Arms in 1484. The importance of heraldry was demonstrated later by the execution of Henry Howard, Earl of Surrey (*c.* 1516–1547), for quartering his own coat with the royal coat of arms.

p. 193◀ **Distant Voices** ▶p. 197

In the old days, men sang songs of mourning when they were in prison, in order to teach the Gospel, to put away idleness, and to be occupied in a useful way for the time. But these songs and ours do not agree, for ours invite jollity and pride, and theirs lead to mourning and to dwelling longer on the words of God's Law. When there are forty or fifty in a choir, three or four proud and lecherous rascals perform the most devout service with flourishes so that no one can hear the words, and all the others are dumb and watch them like fools.

John Wyclif, *Sermon on the Feigned Contemplative Life* (1378)

From Hampton Court to Hamlet

1485–1601

'I BOUGHT THIS BOOK when the Testament was abrogated, that shepherds might not read it,' wrote a Gloucestershire shepherd in his illegal Bible. 'I pray God amend that blindness. Writ by Robert Williams keeping sheep upon Seynbury Hill, 1546.' The growth of literacy affected all classes and, together with the Italian Renaissance, was enormously influential on art and architecture. It also laid the foundations for a flowering of English literature, which formed the basis of its astonishing creativity through the centuries. A period which began with the spectacular Duke Humphrey Library in Oxford, at the very beginning of printed books, ended with the poetry of Edmund Spenser and Sir Philip Sidney, and the plays of Marlowe and Shakespeare.

▶ p. 205

1526
HAMPTON COURT PALACE

The first whiff of the Renaissance reached the British Isles at the start of the sixteenth century with the arrival of Desiderius Erasmus (*c.* 1469–1536) for the first time in 1499, and with his translation of the Bible into Latin in 1516. The same influence is apparent in the tomb of Henry VII (1457–1509) in Westminster Abbey – built by Italian craftsmen – and the broad expanses, courtyards and terracotta busts of Roman emperors at Hampton Court Palace. The palace was built by Cardinal Thomas Wolsey (*c.* 1472–1530), appointed chancellor for life by Henry VIII (1491–1547), but forced to hand over Hampton Court to the king for his own use when it was completed in 1526. The palace was later extended by Sir Christopher Wren (1632–1723).

▲ *Hampton Court Palace, originally built by Thomas Wolsey for his own use, but soon taken over by Henry VIII.*

1539
HOLBEIN'S PORTRAIT OF ANNE OF CLEVES

Hans Holbein the Younger (*c.* 1497–1543) was another of the European humanists, one of Erasmus' wide circle of friends, who made their home in England. He arrived in 1526, and after 1532 he rarely left, building up a unique memory of Henry VIII's court with his superb portraits of the most eminent people in the land, many of which are now housed in the National Portrait Gallery in London. His portraits included some of the candidates for Henry's various marriages, and it was on one of these rare visits abroad that Henry asked him to paint Anne of Cleves (1515–57). Enchanted, Holbein 'expressed her imaige verye lyvelye' and Henry married her, although he dismissed her shortly afterwards as a 'Flanders mare'. Holbein died of the plague in 1543.

▶ p. 199

1549
BOOK OF COMMON PRAYER

Thomas Cranmer, the Archbishop of Canterbury (1489–1556), was a key figure in the English Reformation, bold enough to marry the niece of a Lutheran theologian while clerical marriage was still illegal, and eventually burned at the stake under Mary I (1516–58). He was also the main architect of the religious changes under Edward VI (1537–53), constructing the Prayer Books of 1549 and 1552, the Ordinal of 1550 and the Thirty-Nine Articles of the Anglican faith. But it was as author of the Prayer Book, the only legal liturgy in the Church of England between 1549–54 and 1559–1645, and the basis of the 1662 *Book of Common Prayer*, that Cranmer is best remembered. His genius for prose and his soaring phrases have spread throughout English literature.

p. 190◀ **Triumphs & Tragedies** ▶p. 200

1485
LE MORTE D'ARTHUR

Historians are unsure about the identity of Sir Thomas Malory (*c.* 1416–71), but he may have completed his distillation of the English and French versions of the Arthurian legends while in Newgate Prison on charges of rape and theft. But if, as some sources suggest, Malory helped the pioneer printer William Caxton (*c.* 1420–91) with the text of his book before printing in 1485, it must have been somebody other than the prisoner. *Le Morte D'Arthur* was enormously influential at a time when a Welsh king had taken the throne, naming his son and Prince of Wales Arthur (1486–1502). A century later, Arthurian enthusiast Edmund Spenser (1552–99) was able to tell Queen Elizabeth that her name, realm and race all derived from 'this renowned prince'.

▶ p. 201

1575
TALLIS AND BYRD

The so-called 'Father of English Cathedral Music', Thomas Tallis (*c.* 1505–85), was a Gentleman of the Chapel Royal and was able to write church music for the Catholic queen Mary I and her Protestant sister Elizabeth I (1533–1603), alike. In fact in 1575, Elizabeth granted Tallis and his collaborator William

Byrd (1543–1623) a monopoly of music printing and publishing in England. The same year, they produced *Cantiones Sacrae*, which included most of Tallis' choral works and included one piece for eight choirs. Byrd became organist of Lincoln Cathedral at the age of just 20, and stayed a Catholic, but together their music formed the basis of church music for the new Anglican Church, bridging the gap with the old Catholic liturgy.

▶ p. 202

1576
ENGLAND'S FIRST THEATRE

The first purpose-built theatre in England opened in Shoreditch, London in 1576, built by the actor and carpenter James Burbage, the father of Richard Burbage (*c.* 1569–1619). It became the home of the Lord Chamberlain's Men, with members including Richard and the young play-wright William Shakespeare (1564– 1616). When the lease on the land ran out in 1597, they dismantled the theatre, carried it to the south bank of the Thames and used it as building material for the famous Globe Theatre. The rowdy audience would gather in the open air, some showing off their costumes by sitting on the stage itself – which was strewn with rushes for performances – while the better-off sat in the galleries around three sides of the theatre.

▼ *Shakespeare (seated centre) with his contemporary playwrights.*

1593
THE DEATH OF MARLOWE

The playwright Christopher Marlowe (1564–93) was the son of a Canterbury shoemaker. He was only 29 years old when he met his mysterious and violent death in a Deptford tavern in 1593. It has been speculated that he was a secret agent employed by Francis Walsingham (d. *c.* 1622). Marlowe was a free-thinker, a homosexual and wildly indiscreet, and his writings led to accusations of atheism, blasphemy and subversion. They reached a climax with his play *Edward II*, the tragedy of a homosexual king undermined by his barons – which paved the way towards Shakespeare's sophisticated historical tragedies – and *Doctor Faustus*, the story of a man's pact with the devil. He spent the last months of his life in plague-ridden London, writing the narrative poems *Hero and Leander* and *The Lyrical Shepherd*.

1601
HAMLET

Shakespeare's most famous play was probably first seen in 1601, one of the first plays performed at the Globe Theatre, just before the playwright moved his lodgings from Bishopsgate to Southwark. There Shakespeare continued to write about two plays a year – struggling through a period of unpopularity for the new theatres – while he kept his financial interest at his real home in Stratford-on-Avon. *Hamlet*, the story of an anguished Danish prince, has fascinated critics and audiences ever since, but it also marked the turning point in Shakespeare's career, between the comedies and histories like *Midsummer Night's Dream* (1596) and *Henry V* (1599) and the great tragedies like *King Lear* (1605) and *Macbeth* (1606). It remains probably his most challenging play.

▲ *The new Globe Theatre on London's South Bank, reconstructed in the style of Shakepeare's original Globe Theatre.*

p. 195◀ **Distant Voices** ▶p. 199

> Cade: *There shall be in England seven halfpenny loaves sold for a penny; the three-hooped pot shall have ten hoops; and I will make it a felony to drink small beer. All the realm shall be in common, and in Cheapside shall my palfrey go to grass. And when I am king – as king I shall be – there shall be no money; all shall eat and drink on my score; and I will apparel them all in one livery, that they may agree like brothers, and worship me their lord.*
> Dick: *The first thing we do, let's kill all the lawyers.*

William Shakespeare, *Henry VI Part 2* (1592)

The Puritan Influence

1614–53

'NEVER SEND TO KNOW for whom the bell tolls,' said the poet John Donne from the pulpit in Old St Paul's cathedral, a little ashamed of his romantic youthful poems. Just as Donne was embarrassed about his youth once he became Dean of St Paul's, so English culture seemed to turn away from such fripperies. A century that began with Shakespeare, and blossomed into poets like Robert Herrick and Andrew Marvell, had within four decades plunged itself into the puritanism of the 1640s, which caused the theatres to close and public entertainment to be banned. Writing continued under the Commonwealth, however: Marvell and John Milton were exponents of the new regime, and Marvell survived to write biting satires of the returning royalist regime in the 1660s and 1670s.

▶ p. 209

1614
BARTHOLOMEW FAIR

The annual Bartholomew Fair, held in London's Smithfield every 24 August, was used as the basis of the greatest play by Ben Jonson (1572–1637), who was the son of a master bricklayer and was probably imprisoned after acting in the notorious play *The Isle of Dogs* in 1597. *Bartholomew Fair* was first performed in 1614 and depicted a range of outrageous characters, notably the hypocritical puritan Zeal-of-the-Land Busy and the Justice Adam Overdo, who is eventually engulfed in the iniquities of the fair. A partnership between Jonson and the architect Inigo Jones (1573–1652) created the spectacular masques of the Stuart court, which combined drama, music, art and dance. The masques were brought to an end when the Civil War dispersed the court in 1642.

1625
THE DEATH OF GIBBONS

By the death of Elizabeth I in 1603, English music had become the envy of Europe. Orlando Gibbons (1583–1625) upheld the tradition into the reign of James I (VI of Scotland, 1566–1625). By 1619, Gibbons had become one of the 'musicians for the virginals to attend his highness' private chamber', and in 1625 he conducted the music for James' funeral. The new king, Charles I (1600–49), invited Gibbons and the Chapel Royal to Canterbury to welcome his queen two months later, but just before she arrived, Gibbons died from an apoplectic fit. Apart from his sacred anthems, he is best remembered for his songs, notably 'Fair is the Rose', 'The Silver Swan' and 'Dainty Fine Bird That Art Encaged'.

1631
COVENT GARDEN MARKET

In an attempt to relieve London's overcrowding, the restrictions on new building were loosened under Charles I, and it was with his support that Inigo Jones, who had studied in Italy and Denmark, was able to lay out Covent Garden market in 1631, marking the introduction of mature Italian Renaissance architecture to England. Jones was also responsible for the Banqueting House in Whitehall, through the windows of which Charles would walk to his execution in 1649. Originally known as 'Convent Garden', the development was built on land belonging to the Dukes of Bedford. It was later rebuilt, but

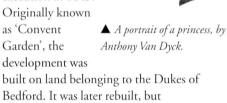

▲ *A portrait of a princess, by Anthony Van Dyck.*

▲ *Covent Garden market, originally designed and laid out by architect Inigo Jones.*

nevertheless changed the way cities looked and was followed, after the Restoration, by new suburbs in Bloomsbury and elsewhere.

▶ p. 204

1636
THE CHILDREN OF CHARLES I

Anthony Van Dyck (1599–1641) was born in Antwerp, and studied under Peter Paul Rubens (1577–1640), before arriving in England as court painter to Charles I, where he painted almost everybody connected with the court – including his famous painting of the royal children. He lived in continual penury, finding it difficult to extract the money he was owed from the king, and died broken-hearted at the outbreak of Civil War. However, he was knighted, installed in a house in Blackfriars and given a country home. His new approach to portrait-painting, adopting a poetic and graceful style – which influenced the portrait painters who followed him – meant that his pictures are now in most of the best-known galleries in the UK.

1644
THE COMMONWEALTH

Once the Civil War had broken out, after Charles I's failed attempt to arrest five MPs in the House of Commons, Parliament passed a series of proclamations against popular sports and pastimes. The king's army reached no further into London than Turnham Green, and the city came under the control of the puritanical Parliament, closing the theatres and removing the may-poles. Shakespeare's Globe was even torn down by puritan enthusiasts in 1644. Theatres remained closed for the next 18 years, though there were private theatrical performances that paved the way for the explosion of Restoration drama after 1660. To a fanfare of trumpets and guns, the period was brought to an end in 1661 with the erection of a 130-foot maypole in the Strand.

1644
'AREOPAGITICA'

Arguably the century's greatest poet, John Milton (1608–74) – later to write *Paradise Lost* (1667) – came to political prominence as the propagandist for Parliament against the royalist cause, defending the decision to execute Charles I, even drafting letters for Oliver Cromwell (1599–1658) to send to foreign rulers. His pamphlets about education and the controversy over his view that a mismatch of minds was a better reason for separation in marriage than sexual incompatibility or adultery, were over-shadowed by his great defence of freedom of speech. 'Areopagitica' (1644) was a protest against the reimposition of censorship by Parliamentarians. Almost blind, his life – endangered by his royalist loyalties – was saved after the Restoration by the payment of an enormous fine and the intervention of fellow poet Andrew Marvell (1621–78).

▶ p. 220

1651
LEVIATHAN

The life of man without law, said the philosopher and writer Thomas Hobbes (1588–1679) in *Leviathan*, is 'solitary, poor, nasty, brutish and short'. Appalled by the violence of the Civil War around him, Hobbes was searching for a more logical basis for ordering human society, following on from the humanism of his friend Sir Francis Bacon (1561–1626). In his long and well-travelled life, he also met other enlightened contemporaries, including Galileo Galilei (1565–1642) and Rene Descartes (1596–1650). The publication of the immensely influential and materialistic *Leviathan* in 1651 caused outrage among politicians and theologians, and although he was given a pension by Charles II (1630–85), he was forbidden to write by Parliament and his books were publicly burned.

▲ *Thomas Hobbes – the celebrated philosopher and author of* Leviathan.

▶ p. 204

1653
THE COMPLEAT ANGLER

The Compleat Angler is one of the most reprinted books in the English language. Subtitled 'The contemplative man's recreation', and published in 1653, Izaak Walton (1593–1683) describes a fishing trip along the River Lea from Tottenham to Ware – a fitting occupation for a staunch royalist during the Commonwealth. The book was partly an anthology of fishing writing and lore, but was also a collection of songs and verses and pastoral elegy in the tradition of Sidney and Spenser nearly a century before. Walton was a former apprentice, first to a draper and then to an ironmonger, and was later buried in Winchester Cathedral. He also wrote the biographies of his two ecclesiastical poet friends, John Donne (*c.* 1572–1631) and George Herbert (1593–1633).

p. 197 ◀ **Distant Voices** ▶ p. 201

Busi old foole, unruly Sunne,
Why dost thou thus,
Through windows and through
curtaines call on us?
Must to thy motions lovers seasons run?
Sawcy pedantique wretch, goe chide
Late schoole boyes and sowre prentices,
Goe tell Court-huntsmen that the
King will ride,
Call countrey ants to harvest offices;
Love, all alike, no season knowes, nor
clyme,
Nor houres, dayes, moneths, which are
the rags of time.

John Donne, *The Sunne Rising* (1633)

Restoration

1660–1713

THE RE-ESTABLISHMENT of the monarchy meant enormous changes in every area of life. As the theatres re-opened, and the writers found themselves adapting for or against the new regime, the first indoor performances, the first concerts and the first operas were beginning to be held. With the influence of Christopher Wren and Nicholas Hawksmoor, a new kind of classical architecture was emerging too, as befits a culture struggling to escape from the danger of religious differences. Under the influence of Charles II, a new generation of scientists – led by Isaac Newton – was changing people's views of the world. And writers like Milton and Bunyan were writing verse and prose that has survived into the present day.

▲ *During the Restoration, London played host to the resurgence of enthusiasm for theatre-going, and many new theatres opened.*

1660s
PEPYS' DIARY

The naval administrator Samuel Pepys (1633–1703) is better known as the author of the diary which has provided the model for diarists ever since. The surviving volumes record his everyday life in code, plus the ups and downs of his marriage, with endearing honesty, from 1660–69. They were left to his old college, Magdalene in Cambridge, but the code was not broken and the diaries published until 1825. In fact, it was the discovery in 1818 of the diary of his friend John Evelyn (1620–1706) that enabled Pepys' cypher to be cracked. The diary reveals Pepys as an opinionated man of his time, who dismissed a production of *A Midsummer Night's Dream* as 'the most insipid, ridiculous play that I ever saw in my life'.

p. 196◀ **Triumphs & Tragedies** ▶p. 204

1675
ST PAUL'S CATHEDRAL

The religious disputes of the previous century meant that very few churches had been built before the centre of London burned down in 1666. The ruins of Old St Paul's Cathedral stayed where they were for eight years before the site was cleared, and Sir Christopher Wren began work on his new Classical design in 1675. Wren forced through his design against great opposition from the church authorities, and the building was finished 35 years later, with one architect, one master mason and one bishop. The use of Portland stone, and Wren's classical style, changed English architecture forever. Wren was paid £200 a year. 'And for this,' said the Duchess of Marlborough, 'he was content to be dragged up in a basket three or four times a week'.

▲ *The interior of St Paul's Cathedral, rebuilt by Christopher Wren after the Great Fire of London.*

1662
THEATRE ROYAL, DRURY LANE

With the end of the restrictions of the Commonwealth, Charles II distributed the sole legal rights to arrange performances in Westminster to Thomas Killigrew (1612–83) and Sir William D'Avenant (1606–68). While D'Avenant opened the first indoor theatre in London's Dorset Gardens, Killigrew opened the Patent Theatre, later renamed the Theatre Royal, in Drury Lane in 1662. Just 12 years later it was rebuilt after the first of many fires, to boost its capacity from 700 to 2,000, and it was soon prospering showing the new Restoration dramas by William Congreve (1670–1729) and Sir John Vanbrugh (1664–1726). The Theatre Royal was rebuilt once more in 1791, burned down again in 1809 and was rebuilt in its present form in 1812.

1667
POET LAUREATE

The poet and playwright John Dryden (1631–1700) was born into a puritan family, and spent his career adapting to the prevailing political climate, ending up as a Catholic in 1686. His adaptation was all the more important, because Dryden was appointed as Poet Laureate on the death of D'Avenant, and was the first poet to hold the title officially. Dryden achieved the position with his poem 'Annus Mirabilis' in 1667, describing the Great Fire and naval war with the Dutch the year before. Towards the end of his life, dismissed as Laureate during the Protestant Revolution of 1688, he turned to the theatre and then to translating Latin classics, developing the heroic couplet, which would be adopted by poets in the next century.

✣ ▶ p. 202

1672
THE FIRST CONCERTS

Until 1672, people heard music by going to church or organising their own private performances. But that was the year when a violinist called John Bannister, sacked from the King's Musik for misappropriating money, began a series of paid concerts, 'over against the George Tavern in White Friars, near the back of the Temple'. His example was soon followed by the musical coal merchant Thomas Britton (1654–1714), above whose shop George Frederick Handel (1685–1759) later played. Other concert societies followed, taking the names from the taverns where they played, for example, the Angel and Crown in Whitechapel, which specialised in the music of Henry Purcell (1659–95). The first purpose-built concert hall was built in Oxford in 1748.

1689
THE FIRST BRITISH OPERA

While Cromwell had forbidden plays, he had never forbidden music. Even so, opera did not develop in Britain until 1689, when Henry Purcell was asked to write an entertainment for a young gentlewoman's boarding school in Chelsea. The result was *Dido and Aeneas*, which marked the introduction of this art form to England. Purcell was also involved in a series of masques, writing melodies around popular historical themes. He had been organist of Westminster Abbey, where he was later buried, and composed music for the coronations of James VII (and II) (1633–1701) and William III (1650–1702). He also composed much chamber music and many dance tunes and harpsichord suites. 'We have at length found an Englishman equal with the best abroad,' wrote his collaborator, Dryden.

✳ ▶ p. 205

1709
THE TATLER

Richard Steele (1672–1729) first met his collaborator Joseph Addison (1672–1719) at Oxford, and launched *The Tatler* in

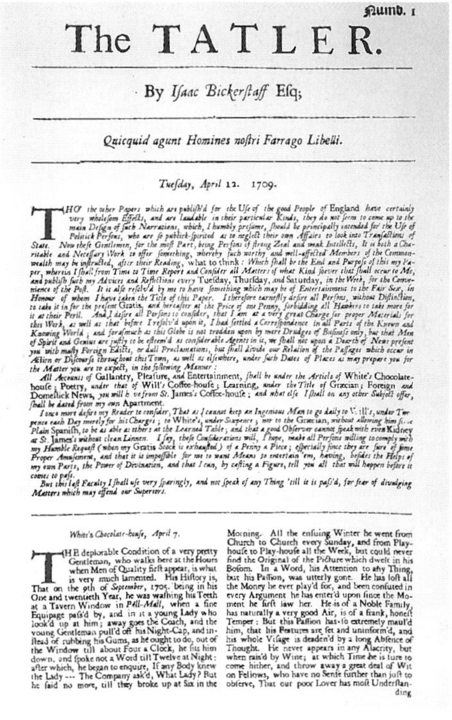

Numb. 1

The TATLER.

By *Isaac Bickerstaff* Esq;

Quicquid agunt Homines nostri Farrago Libelli.

Tuesday, April 12. 1709.

THO' the other Papers which are publish'd for the Use of the good People of England *have certainly very wholesom Effects, and are laudable in their particular Kinds, they do not seem to come up to the main Design of such Narrations, which, I humbly presume, should be principally intended for the Use of Politick Persons, who are so publick-spirited as to neglect their own Affairs to look into Transactions of State. Now these Gentlemen, for the most Part, being Persons of strong Zeal and weak Intellects, It is both a Charitable and Necessary Work to offer something, whereby such worthy and well-affected Members of the Commonwealth may be instructed, after their Reading,* what to think*: Which shall be the End and Purpose of this my Paper, wherein I shall from Time to Time Report and Consider all Matters of what Kind soever that shall occur to Me, and publish such my Advices and Reflections every* Tuesday, Thursday, *and* Saturday, *in the Week, for the Convenience of the Post. It is also resolv'd by me to have something which may be of Entertainment to the Fair Sex, in Honour of whom I have taken the Title of this Paper. I therefore earnestly desire all Persons, without Distinction, to take it in for the present* Gratis, *and hereafter at the Price of one Penny, forbidding all Hawkers to take more for it at their Peril. And I desire all Persons to consider, that I am at a very great Charge for proper Materials for this Work, as well as that before I resolv'd upon it, I had settled a Correspondence in all Parts of the Known and Knowing World; and forasmuch as this Globe is not trodden upon by mere Drudges of Business only, but that Men of Spirit and Genius are justly to be esteem'd as considerable Agents in it, we shall not upon a Dearth of News present you with musty Foreign Edicts, or dull Proclamations, but shall divide our Relation of the Passages which occur in Action or Discourse throughout this Town, as well as elsewhere, under such Dates of Places as may prepare you for the Matter you are to expect, in the following Manner:*

All Accounts of Gallantry, Pleasure, *and* Entertainment, *shall be under the Article of* White's Chocolate-house; Poetry, *under that of* Will's Coffee-house; Learning, *under the Title of* Græcian; Foreign *and* Domestick News, *you will have from St.* James's Coffee-house; *and what else I shall on any other Subject offer, shall be dated from my own* Apartment.

I once more desire my Reader to consider, That as I cannot keep an Ingenious Man to go daily to Will's, *under Twopence each Day merely for his Charges; to* White's, *under Sixpence; nor to the* Græcian, *without allowing him some* Plain Spanish, *to be as able as others at the Learned Table; and that a good Observer cannot speak with even* Kidney *at St.* James's *without clean Linnen. I say, these Considerations will, I hope, make all Persons willing to comply with my Humble Request (when my* Gratis *Stock is exhausted) of a Penny a Piece; especially since they are sure of some Proper Amusement, and that it is impossible for me to want Means to entertain 'em, having, besides the Helps of my own Parts, the Power of Divination, and that I can, by casting a Figure, tell you all that will happen before it comes to pass.*

But this last Faculty I shall use very sparingly, and not speak of any Thing 'till it is pass'd, for fear of divulging Matters which may offend our Superiors.

White's Chocolate-house, April 7.

THE deplorable Condition of a very pretty Gentleman, who walks here at the Hours when Men of Quality first appear, is what is very much lamented. His History is, That on the 9th of *September*, 1705, being in his One and twentieth Year, he was washing his Teeth at a Tavern Window in *Pall-Mall*, when a fine Equipage pass'd by, and in it a young Lady who look'd up at him; away goes the Coach, and the young Gentleman pull'd off his Night-Cap, and instead of rubbing his Gums, as he ought to do, out of the Window till about Four a Clock, he sits him down, and spoke not a Word till Twelve at Night: after which, he began to enquire, If any Body knew the Lady --- The Company ask'd, What Lady? But he said no more, till they broke up at Six in the Morning. All the ensuing Winter he went from Church to Church every Sunday, and from Play-house to Play-house all the Week, but could never find the Original of the Picture which dwelt in his Bosom. In a Word, his Attention to any Thing, but his Passion, was utterly gone. He has lost all the Money he ever play'd for, and been confuted in every Argument he has enter'd upon since the Moment he first saw her. He is of a Noble Family, has naturally a very good Air, is of a frank, honest Temper: But this Passion has so extremely maul'd him, that his Features are set and uninform'd, and his whole Visage is deaden'd by a long Absence of Thought. He never appears in any Alacrity, but when rais'd by Wine; at which Time he is sure to come hither, and throw away a great deal of Wit on Fellows, who have no Sense further than just to observe, That our poor Lover has most Understanding

▲ The Tatler *was popular amongst the literate upper classes during the early eighteenth century.*

1709, publishing three times a week for nearly two years – reporting from various new coffee and chocolate houses in London. When it unexpectedly ceased publication, he and Addison brought their high moral tone to bear through *The Spectator*, inventing a country gentleman called Sir Roger de Coverley, and giving editorial space to some of the leading writers and poets of the age. Having been prosecuted for seditious libel over a pamphlet about the Hanoverian succession, Steele devoted himself to running the Theatre Royal, Drury Lane, developing the dramatic tradition known as 'sentimental comedy' where emotion became the main object of interest.

❂ ▶ p. 206

1713
THE SCRIBLERUS CLUB

In the winter of 1713, in the last days of Queen Anne (1665–1714), a group of Tory intellectuals formed the Scriblerus Club devoted to witty repartee and the ridicule of 'all the false tastes in learning'. The satirical literature which followed was for a time given the title 'scriblerian', and among the distinguished club members were the playwright John Gay (1685–1732), the poet Alexander Pope (1688–1744) and the writer Jonathan Swift (1667–1745). They devoted themselves to writing the satirical memoirs of an imaginary Whig, called *The Memoirs of Martinus Scriblerus*, eventually published in 1741 – by which time the club had influenced the creation of Gay's *The Beggar's Opera*, Pope's *The Dunciad* and Swift's *Gulliver's Travels.*

p. 199◀ **Distant Voices** ▶p. 203

Took coach and called Mercer, and I to the Duke of York's playhouse, and there saw The Tempest, and between two acts I went out to Mr. Harris, and got him to repeat to me the words of Echo, while I write them down, having tried in the play to have wrote them; but, having done it without looking upon my paper, I found I could not read the blacklead.

Samuel Pepys' diary (11 May 1668)

From Handel to Hogarth

1725–70

'BOOKS THAT YOU MAY carry to the fire, and hold readily in your hand, are the most useful after all,' said Samuel Johnson in one of his self-deprecating moods. Actually his life was dedicated to the development of literature. The eighteenth century began with Swift and Pope and ended with Johnson's masterpiece, *A Dictionary of the English Language*. His witticisms about London, hanging and the weather, and much else besides, have passed into the culture. His contradictions also sum up a confusing age: the violence of speech, the apparent cruelty and coarseness of life – Johnson ate so fast that his whole face would swell up – somehow combined with a delicacy of expression to create one of the great periods of literature.

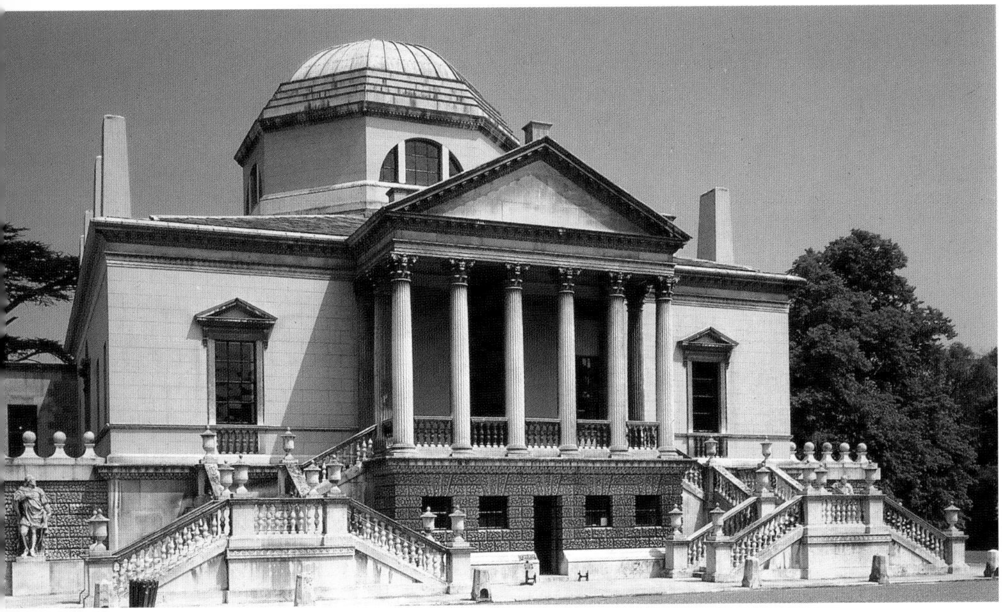

▲ *Chiswick House, modelled on Palladio's Villa Rotunda; each room in the house was designed as a perfect cube.*

1725
CHISWICK HOUSE

Palladian architecture – called after the Italian architect Andrea Palladio (1508–80) – had first been introduced to Britain by Inigo Jones, but it lost favour under the influence of Christopher Wren and others. But in the 1720s, neo-Palladianism made a comeback, increasingly associated with Whig politics against the more baroque Tories, and popularised by the architect peer Richard Boyle, Earl of Burlington (1695–1753). His Chiswick House was modelled on Palladio's Villa Rotunda and became a model for a new style of country house building. Each room was designed as a perfect cube, and it was intended primarily for entertainment. 'Too little to live in,' said Lord Hervey (1696–1743) about the rooms, 'too big to hang on a watch chain.'

✣ ▶ p. 210

1740
'RULE BRITANNIA'

The mid-eighteenth century was a period of wealth and growing national consciousness, where the growth of trade and Britain's American empire led to an increasing understanding of nationhood. So it was not surprising that the period also saw the growth of patriotic songs. 'God Save the King' appeared in almost its present form around 1744, and the music for 'Rule Britannia' by Thomas Arne (1710–78), appeared in his masque *Alfred*, performed before Frederick, Prince of Wales (1727–51) at Cliveden House in 1740. The words included the phrase 'Britons never shall be slaves', and were by the writer and author of *The Seasons*, James Thomson (1700–48). They were adapted five years later by the Jacobites as the anthem for their 1745 rising.

❣ ▶ p. 212

1741
GARRICK AS RICHARD III

The young David Garrick (1717–79) set out from his home in Lichfield in 1737 with his teacher – the great lexicographer Samuel Johnson (1709-?84) – on the journey to London. For four years he worked in the wine trade and took part in amateur theatricals, but he caused a sensation performing in Shakespeare's *Richard III*, at an unlicensed performance in Goodman's Fields in 1741. For the rest of his career, including 30 years as manager at Drury Lane, he transformed the theatre and made acting into a respectable profession, writing a large number of plays and farces – and even a musical adaptation of *The Tempest*. He was famous for his naturalness on stage and the variety and emotion of his performances.

1741
THE MESSIAH

George Frederick Handel (1685–1759) was the son of a barber-surgeon from Lower Saxony who became the

▶ *George Frederick Handel, a significant figure in the London opera scene.*

kapellmeister to the Elector of Hanover, later George I (1660–1727). He arrived in London in 1711 and went on to dominate the London opera circuit. An invitation to Dublin led to a burst of 25 days' feverish activity to write *The Messiah* in his home near Oxford Street in London in 1741; so busy was he that his meals were left uneaten outside the door. *The Messiah* was admired in Dublin in its first performance, and George II (1683–1760) rose in his seat during the London performance – overwhelmed by the 'Alleluia Chorus'. Handel later went blind, his eyes ruined by the same surgeon who had tried to save the eyesight of Johann Sebastian Bach (1685–1750).

▲ *The parklands of Blenheim Palace, laid out in the style of 'Capability' Brown.*

1743–45
MARRIAGE Á LA MODE

Our view of the mid-eighteenth century is coloured by the moral engravings of William Hogarth (1697–1764), the first British artist of the century to win an international reputation for himself. His pictures like *Gin Lane* and *Chairing the Candidate* provided a raucous and brutal view of ordinary life, but it was his moral series, like *Rake's Progress* (1733–35) and *Marriage á la Mode* (1743–45), which made him famous. He had an unsuccessful and miserable foray into politics in the 1750s, though it was his lobbying which produced the Engravers' Copyright Act of 1735. He ended his career with a theoretical work on aesthetics, *The Analysis of Beauty* (1753), which was ridiculed in Britain but welcomed on the Continent.

1749
TOM JONES

Henry Fielding (1707–54) was a pioneering magistrate, starting the Bow Street Runners as a team of 'thief-takers' in Westminster with his blind half-brother John. He was also a prolific comedy writer and satirist, parodying the enormously successful *Pamela* by Samuel Richardson (1689–1761) with his own *Shamela*, and then writing what has been claimed as the first great English novel, *Tom Jones*, in 1749. The story describes the adventures of a 'foundling' who redeems himself, and one which established a narrative voice that involved the reader in a way that had never been done before. Fielding was also a successful dramatist, and opened himself to ridicule by marrying his dead wife's former maid.

1755
JOHNSON'S DICTIONARY

The great dictionary of Dr Samuel Johnson, published in 1755, remains one of the milestones in the development of the English language, and it marked the turning point in his own career. For eight years he struggled with the project, working with a team of editors at his London home, and justifying his dictionary definition of lexicographer as 'a harmless drudge'. By 1762, he had been given an annual pension by George III (1738–1820) and had met the Scots lawyer James Boswell (1740–95) who would write his biography (1791), make his name and popularise his eccentric development of the art of conversation. Moralist, journalist, critic, novelist and poet, Johnson knew all the most famous men of his age.

1770
BLENHEIM PARK

A grateful nation had bestowed Blenheim Palace on the Duke of Marlborough (1650--1722). The palace was designed by the playwright and architect Sir John Vanbrugh, but the grounds were laid out in the new style – with 1,094 ha (2,700 acres) of natural parks and lakes instead of formal gardens – associated with Lancelot 'Capability' Brown (1716–83). The trees are said to have been planted, not in formal lines, but in accordance with the troop dispositions at one of Marlborough's victories. Brown won his nickname by telling clients their gardens had 'capabilities for improvement', and by the end of a successful career, starting with experience under the great landscape architect William Kent (1686–1748), he had designed more than 140 estates.

p. 201◀ **Distant Voices** ▶p. 205

Is not a Patron, my Lord, one who looks with unconcern on a man struggling for life in the water, and, when he has reached ground, encumbers him with help? The notice which you have been pleased to take of my labours, had it been early, had been kind; but it has been delayed till I am indifferent, and cannot enjoy it; till I am solitary, and cannot impart it; till I am known, and do not want it.

Samuel Johnson's letter to Lord Chesterfield (7 February 1755)

Age of Jerusalem

1774–1815

BLISS WAS IT IN THAT dawn to be alive,' wrote William Wordsworth, remembering his feelings about the French Revolution in 1789, 'but to be young was very heaven!' The Lakes poet changed his radical views in the years that followed, but there was a sense of excitement at the end of the eighteenth century, stirring new romantic poets like Burns, Coleridge, Blake and Byron. The first purpose-built art gallery, the Dulwich Picture Gallery, opened in London in 1814, and romantic pictures of landscapes by Turner and Constable, were appearing on the walls of other galleries. The new, shockingly intimate dance, the waltz, had also arrived in England in 1791. With the revolutionaries in control across the English Channel, everything seemed possible.

❈ ▶ p. 206

1774
THE ARRIVAL OF GAINSBOROUGH

The great landscape and portrait artist Thomas Gainsborough (1727–88) had moved his practice to fashionable Bath in 1759, and he developed a distinctive style of painting in the grand tradition of Van Dyck. But it was not until his arrival in London in 1774, where he set up in Pall Mall, that he became the most successful portrait painter of the century, with his fluid and impressionistic style portraying country gentlemen posing in front of their land. He was the only rival to Sir Joshua Reynolds (1723–92), the first president of the Royal Academy and the embodiment of the artistic establishment. Gainsborough caught a chill listening to the trial of Warren Hastings (1732–1818) in Westminster Hall in 1788 and died shortly afterwards.

▲ *Thomas Gainsborough became as renowned for his portraits as for his landscapes.*

p. 200◀ **Triumphs & Tragedies** ▶p. 212

1804
'JERUSALEM'

The engraver, poet and artist William Blake (1757–1827) was an enigmatic and unrecognised genius, ending his life in an unmarked grave in a public cemetery. He claimed to see angels, developed his own complex mythology and at the low-point of his life was arrested on trumped-up charges of sedition. The pictures he painted were of a kind never seen before and his verses were stark and complex, and grow more influential with each century that passes. But it is his poem 'Jerusalem' (1804) which is best known, part of a cycle of poems about Milton written and engraved between 1803–08. The famous tune was finally added to turn it into a patriotic song during the First World War.

1777
THE SCHOOL FOR SCANDAL

Playwright Richard Brinsley Sheridan (1751–1816) had bought a share in the Theatre Royal, Drury Lane on impulse after the success of his first play *The Rivals* in 1775. By 1777, he was the leading partner and wrote *The School for Scandal* at great speed. The result was the most successful comedy of manners of the century. Within three years he had been elected to Parliament, and his theatrical career was put aside, though he kept an interest in his theatre until the building was burned down again in 1809. One actress not in the 1777 cast was the tragic genius Sarah Siddons (1755–1831), whose first appearance at Drury Lane in 1775 had fallen so flat that she had been exiled to the theatrical provinces.

▶ p. 210

1787
MARYLEBONE CRICKET CLUB

The word 'cricket' was recorded as long ago as 1300, and the game had clearly existed in various forms for centuries, but it was not until 1774 that a committee of the well-to-do met in the Star and Garter pub in London's Pall Mall to formally draw up the rules. In those early days there were only two stumps, and no limit to the size of the curved bat, which gave an enormous advantage to the batsman. Games used to take place on White Conduit Fields, and when the club there was dissolved in 1787, the Marylebone Cricket Club (MCC) took its place. The new club, destined to control the game, started in Dorset Square and moved to its present site at Lords in St John's Wood Road in 1814.

▶ p. 209

1794
'AULD LANG SYNE'

Robert Burns (1759–96) was born William Burnes, the son of a Calvinist small farmer, and his verse – often in Scottish dialect – was published only in the last 10 years of his life, before he died of rheumatic heart disease at the age of 37. He was lionised as an untutored rustic genius with striking good looks, whose life was constantly beset

▲ *The popularity of cricket as a 'gentleman's sport' grew in the eighteenth century.*

by poverty. Scots people around the world still celebrate his birthday, on 25 January, known as Burns' night. His songs include 'O My Love's Like a Red, Red Rose', 'Ye Banks and Braes' and 'Auld Lang Syne' – the reworking of an older song by Sir Robert Ayton (1570–1638) of the same name, which was published in 1794 in a collection called *The Scots Musical Museum*.

1798
LYRICAL BALLADS

When two political radicals, William Wordsworth (1770–1850) and Samuel Taylor Coleridge (1772–1834), met in the Quantock Hills in 1797, their conversation changed the direction of literature. They agreed with each other's sense that eighteenth century poetry was emotionally artificial, and their *Lyrical Ballads* the following year pointed in another direction. Only four of the anonymous poems in the original edition were by Coleridge – although one was 'The Rime of the Ancient Mariner', it was described by one contemporary critic as 'the strangest story of cock and bull that we ever saw on paper'. *Lyrical Ballads*, however, founded the Romantic Movement in poetry, which became so important in the early years of the next century.

✳ ▶ p. 207

1806
NURSERY RHYMES

Nursery rhymes are often very ancient, but 1806 – the year after the Battle of Trafalgar – saw one of the first attempts to collect them for children. This was the book *Rhymes for the Nursery*, by Jane Taylor (1783–1824) and her sister Ann (1782–1866), the daughters of an engraver. These included 'Twinkle, Twinkle Little Star', by Jane, author also of 'The Way to be Happy' ('How pleasant it is, at the end of the day, No follies to have to repent; But reflect on the past, and be able to say, That my time has been properly spent'). Ann continued the work for four decades after here sister's death. Their verses marked the beginning of the recognition of childhood as a separate state.

▶ p. 208

1815
BRIGHTON PAVILION

While George III (1738–1820) remained insane, his profligate son George (1762–1830) acted as Prince Regent, stamping his style on the architecture of London, Brighton and Bath. His friend the architect John Nash (1752–1835), who was working in partnership with the landscape gardener Humphrey Repton (1752–1818), was probably the most influential, eventually laying out Regents Park, Regent Street, Carlton House Terrace and the surrounding streets. In 1815, he began what would be eight years' work re-modelling the Prince's notorious Pavilion in Brighton, mixing neo-classical style with Gothic, Chinese, Egyptian and Indian influences. It was designed for a flamboyant prince who left £10,000 in small change in his various suits after his death in 1830.

p. 203 ◀ **Distant Voices** ▶ p. 207

He who doubts from what he sees
Will ne'er believe, do what you please.
If the Sun and Moon should doubt,
They'd immediately go out.
To be in a passion you good may do,
But no good if a passion is in you.
The whore and gambler, by the state
Licensed, build that nation's fate.
The harlot's cry from street to street
Shall weave old England's winding
sheet.

William Blake, from *Auguries of Innocence* (1802)

▲ *The Brighton Pavilion, built in a curious mixture of styles for the decadent Prince Regent.*

From Constable to Carlyle

1816–39

WHETHER BY CHOICE OR NOT, British artists and writers found themselves reacting to the revolutionary changes happening around them in society, as the end of the Napoleonic wars put enormous economic pressures on the nation. This could be seen in Walter Scott harking back to a lost medieval age, Jane Austen attacking those who reduced everything to money, the romantic painters and poets who communicated the nobility of nature, and in the commentary of social critics like Thomas Carlyle, who communicated the nobility of man. While they were doing so, William Cobbett was riding about the countryside describing the plight of people that lived there, and Charles Dickens was exploring London describing the depths of poverty it was possible to find in the cities as well.

1816
EMMA

Few novelists can have had quite such an uneventful life as Jane Austen (1775–1817) did, living with her mother and sisters throughout her relatively short life. As she wrote in 1814, however: 'Three or four families in a country village is the very thing to work on'. Her tomb in Winchester Cathedral includes no mention of the novels, though her genius was recognised before her death – notably by Sir Walter Scott (1771–1832) and the Prince Regent. Along with *Pride and Prejudice* (1813), *Emma* (1816) is probably her most enduring novel, but it is one where she deliberately moved away from the comedy of manners to create a dangerously high-spirited heroine whom she feared nobody would like but herself.

▲ *Mary Shelley's* Frankenstein, *a gothic tale of horror that has retained its popularity.*

✪ ▶ p. 209

1818
FRANKENSTEIN

Apart from being the wife of the great romantic poet Percy Bysshe Shelley, Mary Shelley (1797–1851) was the daughter of two radicals: the pioneer feminist Mary Wollstonecraft (1759–97) and the writer William Godwin (1756–1836). Her important gothic novel *Frankenstein, or The Modern Prometheus* was started when she was 16, when she, Byron and Shelley were writing ghost stories to pass the time during a summer in Switzerland. She wrote several other novels after two miscarriages and the death of her husband and two children. However, none caught the imagination of the public like the story of the monster who creates horror in anyone who sees it, but desperately needs to be loved.

1819
IVANHOE

Two events shaped the enormously successful novel-writing career of the barrister, Sir Walter Scott. One was the publication in 1810 of *Childe Harold's Pilgimage* by Lord Byron (1788–1824), which completely overshadowed the kind of romantic narrative verse Scott had been known for. The other was a debt of £130,000 in 1826, which he was determined to pay off, and hoped to do so by means of his prodigious output. He was a major cultural influence for well over a century, and his novels were enormously popular. *Rob Roy* (1817) helped rebuild Scottish self-esteem after the defeat of the 1745 rebellion, and *Ivanhoe* (1819) entrenched a fascination for medieval chivalry which was to dominate the nineteenth century, and provide the gentlemanly code of the Victorians.

❋ ▶ p. 209

1821
THE HAY WAIN

John Constable (1776–1837) was one of the most popular English artists. The son of a Suffolk miller, he specialised in rural landscapes, documenting the simplicity of nature just as Wordsworth was doing in poetry. His impressionistic method of portraying light caused a sensation when his most famous picture – *The Hay Wain* (1821), originally called *Landscape, Noon* – was exhibited at the Salon in 1824, although it probably had more of an influence in France than it did in Britain. His pictures, such as *Flatford Mill* (1817) – the first large painting he sent to the Royal Academy – and *Dedham Vale* (1828) remain etched on the national consciousness. His favourite area around the River Stour is still known as 'Constable Country'.

1821
DEATH OF KEATS

The Romantic poet John Keats (1795–1821) died in Rome of turberculosis at the age of only 25. He had given up his work as an apprentice to an apothecary-surgeon five years previously in order to concentrate on poetry, and his worked marked the full flowering of the Romantic movement – in fact most of his great poems, like 'The Eve of St Agnes' and 'Ode to a Nightingale', were written in two years of productivity in 1818 and 1819. It was a difficult time for Romantic poets. Keats struggled with money, as well as his love for Fanny Brawne; Percy Bysshe Shelley (1792–1822) was drowned in the Bay of Spezia in 1822 and the other great Romantic poet, Lord Byron, died of fever caught while fighting for the Greek nationalists in 1824.

✳ ▶ p. 211

1835
MADAME TUSSAUD'S

Waxworks existed in London, notably at Westminster Abbey – where the unkempt representations of royalty were known as the 'ragged regiment' – before Madame Tussaud (Marie Grosholtz, 1760–1850) set herself up in England in 1802. She had been imprisoned for three months in Paris during the French Revolution, and had even modelled some of the revolutionary leaders from their heads after they had been taken from the scaffold. Her collection of 300 wax figures was first seen at the Lyceum in the Strand, but moved to a permanent home in London's Baker Street in 1835. The Chamber of Horrors was opened there, and included the knife from the Paris guillotine which had executed 22,000 people in the revolution.

▲ *Marie Grosholtz, better known today as Madame Tussaud, who began creating wax figures during her imprisonment in Paris.*

1836
THOMAS CARLYLE

The social theorist, historian and writer Thomas Carlyle (1795–1881) brought himself to the attention of the country with his 1836 study *The French Revolution* – 'itself a kind of revolution', he wrote later. In this and later works, he attacked unfettered industrial capitalism, affirming moral certainties at a time of revolutionary change, and insisting on the importance of the individual. He was fascinated by heroism, and his lectures *On Heroes, Hero-Worship and the Heroic in History* (1841) marked the beginning of his search for strong leaders that was so influential on the Victorians who came after him. Those deeply influenced by him included the novelist Charles Dickens (1812–1870) and the critic John Ruskin (1819–1900).

1839
THE GRAND NATIONAL

Although the Derby had ushered in a new kind of sporting event in 1780, attracting all classes – with a combination of high breeding and betting adding to the social mix of horse-racing culture – it was not until 1839 that the classic British steeplechase began. The Grand National has been held every year in March at the Aintree track near Liverpool. It is still regarded as the most difficult steeplechase in the world, with 15 jumps – so dangerous that it took nearly 30 years for the National Hunt Committee to recognise it. Thoroughbred horses, all descendants of three Arab stallions imported into Britain between 1689 and 1724, made race days an exciting classless pastime. The range of activities at Victorian racetracks was captured in the celebrated painting *Derby Day* in 1858.

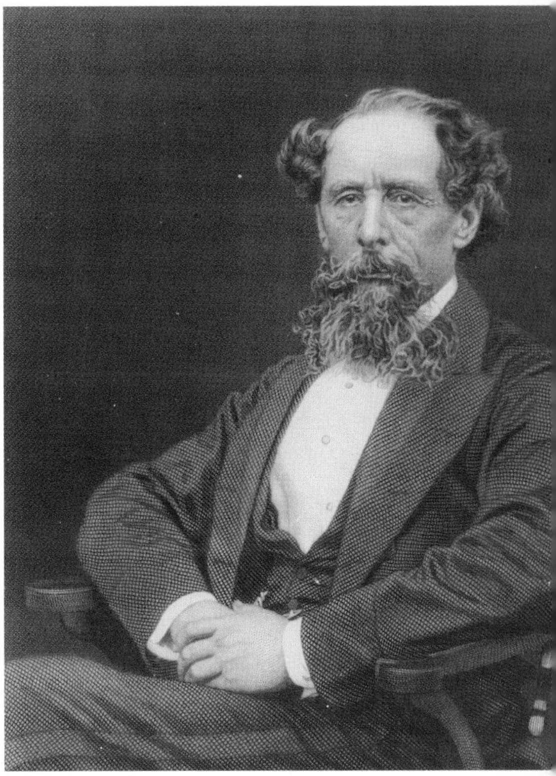

▲ *Charles Dickens, who drew much inspiration from the works of the social theorist Thomas Carlyle.*

p. 205◀ **Distant Voices** ▶p. 209

'And what are you reading, Miss –?' 'Oh! It is only a novel!' replies the young lady: while she lays down her book with affected indifference, or momentary shame. – 'It is only Cecilia, or Camilla, or Belinda:' or, in short, only some work in which the most thorough knowledge of human nature, the happiest delineation of its varieties, the liveliest effusions of wit and humour are conveyed to the world in the best chosen language.

Jane Austen, *Northanger Abbey* (1818)

From Westminster to Wonderland

1840–68

THE NAMES OF DICKENS and Tennyson stride through the middle years of the nineteenth century, but these were years of other great names as well. Anthony Trollope, Benjamin Disraeli, W. M. Thackeray and the Brontës were writing novels, while the gothic revival was a growing force in architecture and in the art of the Pre-Raphaelites. The Great Exhibition of 1851 gave Britain a new sense of design and importance – though the over-wrought Victoriana inside it made the young William Morris physically sick. The Halle Orchestra began playing in 1857, and the artist William Powell Frith exhibited his painting *Derby Day* – the painting equivalent of Dickens' novels, representing the whole range of society. For the Victorians, it was the height of creativity.

▲ *The impressive façade of London's Houses of Parliament as they look today.*

▶ p. 220

1840
HOUSES OF PARLIAMENT

When Parliament burned down in 1834, as many as 97 architects entered the competition to replace it. The winner was Charles Barry (1795–1860), with his design which incorporated Elizabethan and medieval styles to blend in with Westminster Hall and Westminster Abbey next door. Barry actually preferred designing Classical buildings, such as the Reform Club in London (1837–41), but was also responsible for one of the first gothic revival buildings in Britain, St Peter's Church in Brighton (1823–26). He was helped in the design for Parliament by the great gothic revivalist Augustus Pugin (1812–52), who was later driven mad by his own eccentricities. The Victoria Tower, at the opposite end from Big Ben, was then the tallest building in the world.

1843
A CHRISTMAS CAROL

The reputation of the great novelist and social reformer Charles Dickens (1812–70), had been made by the publication of *The Pickwick Papers* in 1836–37, but it was his novella, *A Christmas Carol* (1843), that first made the link between Dickens and Christmas. His Christmas stories were collected together later and published in 1852. Most of them ended – like the first – in a glowing sense of *bonhomie.* His voluminous novels, stories and magazines changed the way we live, and the monthly publication of his stories held mass audiences enthralled on both sides of the Atlantic. Large crowds gathered at American ports to read the latest installments – or later to hear him read from his own works. He died, exhausted, at the young age of 58.

1847
THE BRONTË SISTERS

When the Brontë sisters, Charlotte (1816–55), Emily (1818–48) and Anne (1820–49), published their first poems in 1846, they used the androgynous pseudonyms Currer, Ellis and Acton Bell. They used the same names the following year when all three published novels. Charlotte's *Jane Eyre* and Emily's *Wuthering Heights* were both immediate successes, and Anne's *Agnes Grey* remains in print a century and a half later. Within two years, all had revealed their real names – causing astonishment that a woman could have written a novel as brutal as *Wuthering Heights* – but Emily, Anne and their alcoholic brother Branwell (1817–48) were dead. Charlotte survived until 1855, when she succumbed to complications in pregnancy.

▲ *Charlotte Brontë, author of* Jane Eyre.

✳ ▶ p. 219

1848
THE PRE-RAPHAELITES

What Keats and Scott had done for literature, the Pre-Raphaelite Brotherhood was doing for painting. The original members of the brotherhood, including John Everett Millais (1829–96), William Holman Hunt (1827–1910) and Dante Gabriel Rossetti (1828–82), were admirers of fifteenth-century Italy and set about illustrating medieval life, or other high moral subjects, with their strong colours and detailed illustrations. The brotherhood began in 1848 and dissolved during the 1850s, but its members continued to react against the ugliness of modern life. They were a formative influence on the poet, designer and philosopher William Morris (1834–96) – whose wife Jane was a regular model for Pre-Raphaelite portraits – as well as the Arts and Crafts movement and utopian socialism that he inspired.

▶ p. 214

1850
'IN MEMORIAM'

Occasionally a poet is able to capture the mood of a generation, and Alfred Tennyson (1809–92) managed this in his elegy about his friend Arthur Hallam (1811–33), who died in 1833. 'In Memoriam' was published in 1850 – the same year Tennyson became Poet Laureate – and describes his grief, but also his doubt about faith: 'This I believe but could not prove,' he repeated. It became an important Victorian theme, echoed by Matthew Arnold (1822–88) in his poem 'Dover Beach' in 1867, and by scientists and theologians after the 1859 publication of *The Origin of Species* by Charles Darwin (1809–82). Tennyson's greatest poems were still to come, including 'The Charge of the Light Brigade' (1854) and 'The Idylls of the King' (1859).

Λ ▶ p. 213

1852
MUSIC HALLS

When pub landlord Charles Morton (1819–1905) took over the Canterbury Arms in Lambeth in 1849, he added popular musical evenings to the food and drink available. The formula was so successful that, in 1852, he opened the first music hall – the Canterbury – offering sing-songs and variety entertainment for the working classes. Morton was given the title 'Father of the Halls', though a rival contender to the Canterbury was the Evans Music-and-Supper Rooms in King Street, Covent Garden, where the entertainment was considered so shocking that women could only watch from behind a screen. Music halls, with names like 'Palladium', 'Alhambra', 'Empire' or 'Hippodrome' were soon more numerous than theatres, but were superseded by cinema and radio after 1914.

▼ *Dante Gabriel Rossetti, one of the best-known members of the artistic movement known as the Pre-Raphaelite Brotherhood.*

1865
ALICE'S ADVENTURES IN WONDERLAND

Lewis Carroll was the pen-name of the reclusive Oxford mathematics don and photography enthusiast Charles Lutwidge Dodgson (1832–98). Both he and his friends were astonished when the story he told on a children's picnic in 1862, and published as *Alice's Adventures Under Ground* in 1865, became an immediate bestseller. The illustrations, by the political cartoonist Sir John Tenniel (1820–1914), became almost as famous as the story. In fact the book, and its sequel *Through the Looking Glass and What Alice Found There* (1871), revolutionised children's literature. After Carroll and Edward Lear's *A Book of Nonsense* (1845), the way was open for children's literature which did not have to preach, but which could entertain for its own sake.

✪ ▶ p. 214

1868
THE MOONSTONE

The detective story, where one intelligent outsider is able to see through the mists of confusion, was the invention of the American writer Edgar Allan Poe (1809–49) in the 1840s, but it was Wilkie Collins (1824–89) – the son of a landscape painter – who made the idea British. His novel *The Moonstone*, written in 1868, introduced the character of Sergeant Cuff, and was serialised in Dickens' magazine *All the Year Round.* Along with his other great success, *The Woman in White* (1860), Collins used his own advice to himself: 'Make 'em laugh, make 'em cry, make 'em wait'. His career petered out as he experienced ill-health and private confusion: at one point he was sharing his home with two of his mistresses simultaneously.

p. 207◀ **Distant Voices** ▶p. 211

It was the best of times, it was the worst of times, it was the age of wisdom, it was the age of foolishness, it was the epoch of belief, it was the epoch of incredulity, it was the season of Light, it was the season of Darkness, it was the spring of hope, it was the winter of despair, we had everything before us, we had nothing before us, we were all going direct to Heaven, we were all going direct the other way.'

Charles Dickens, *A Tale of Two Cities* (1859)

From Middlemarch to Morris

1871–95

THE TWO DECADES from 1870 saw Queen Victoria's Golden Jubilee and a taming and regulating of popular culture. The laws of cricket were being set down and the first football league emerged in the north and Midlands in 1888. Even the music halls were now too profitable to risk a brush with the censors, replacing social comment with a mixture of sentimentality and 'jingoism' – a word coined during the Turkish crisis of 1878. The rest of the world was impinging on British culture through greater awareness of the empire, whether it was Stanley tracking down Livingstone in the jungle in 1871 or Sir James Frazer's monumental of world mythologies *The Golden Bough* in 1890. Even words from empire languages, like 'pyjamas' or 'shampoo', were coming into common use.

1871
MIDDLEMARCH

Mary Ann Evans (1819–80) was, like the Brontës, a powerful women writer who chose not to publish under a woman's name. This was partly because she was living with the philosopher George Henry Lewes (1817–78), who was separated from his wife – a fact that would undoubtedly have had a negative influence on public reception if it had been known. It was as George Eliot that she created powerful women characters for novels like *Silas Marner* (1861) and *Daniel Deronda* (1876). *Middlemarch: A Study of Provincial Life* describes country life in the 1820s, but its concerns are about ardent and more modern characters, like her heroine Dorothea Brooke. To Virginia Woolf (1882–1941), half a century later, it was 'one of the few English novels to be written for grown-up people'.

▲ *The celebrated cricketer W. G. Grace, whose career spanned more than 30 years.*

1877
WHISTLER VS RUSKIN

An American by birth, Whistler settled in London in the 1860s under the influence of the Pre-Raphaelite group. His almost abstract and atmospheric paintings, often with musical names like his series of *Nocturnes*, changed the direction of British art – but also infuriated the great critic John Ruskin. In fact, the disagreement between them ended up in court after Ruskin visited Whistler's 1877 exhibition at the Grosvenor Gallery and accused him of 'throwing a pot of paint in the public's face'. Ruskin was having one of his periodic breakdowns, and was unable to defend the libel action in person, but Whistler was awarded damages of only a halfpenny. Despite the setback, Ruskin's resistance to industrial culture remains a major influence a century later.

▶ p. 213

1880
W. G. GRACE

When Dr William Gilbert Grace (1848–1915) began his career in first class cricket at the age of 16, the game was still rough and ready. By the time he retired at the age of 50, the rules were set and – partly through his influence – cricket was established as England's national summer game. His heavy frame and large black beard made him the most famous cricketer in history, winning a total of 54,904 runs in his first class career – including 126 centuries and 877 catches. He captained England 13 times, but the pinnacle of his career came when he scored the first ever test century, against Australia in 1880. In 1903, he also became the first president of the English Bowling Association.

✣ ▶ p. 221

1880
THE PIRATES OF PENZANCE

No matter how much he struggled for recognition as a serious composer, it was light operas that kept Arthur Sullivan (1842–1900) in the public eye. Starting with the now-lost *Thespis* (1871), his partnership with the light-verse writer W. S. Gilbert (1836–1911) produced a string of successes, including *The Pirates of Penzance* (1880). Their backer, the impressario Richard D'Oyly-Carte (1844–1901), opened the Savoy Theatre in London entirely for their production. It was a petty squabble over a new carpet in the theatre, during the production of *The Gondoliers* (1889), that led to a long rift between them. Gilbert was also a playwright, but his profoundly cynical view of human nature was more easily swallowed together with Sullivan's jaunty music.

1887
SHERLOCK HOLMES

The great detective Sherlock Holmes is probably the most imitated and parodied character in literature. He and Dr Watson

▲ *Sherlock Holmes and Dr Watson survived attempts to kill them off by their creator.*

appeared for the first time from the pen of the doctor-turned writer Arthur Conan Doyle (1859–1930) in the novel *A Study in Scarlet*, published in *Beeton's Christmas Annual* for 1887. But it was not until the short stories began for *The Strand Magazine* in 1891 that Holmes acquired a mass audience. Doyle borrowed some of the literary method from Poe, and Holmes' scientific method from one of his teachers at Edinburgh University. He tried to kill Holmes off in *The Memoirs of Sherlock Holmes* (1894), however, popular demand brought him back from the dead and by 1927 Conan Doyle had written four novels and 56 short stories.

✳ ▶ p. 212

1889
BUBBLES

When Sir John Millais painted a little boy blowing soap bubbles, the sentimental painting was enormously popular – but it received a new life of its own as a popular icon when the painting was bought by Pears Soap. The 1880s were a time when the new advertising industry expanded enormously, starting to experiment with using pictures as well, instead of only their bland slogans. The sector that resorted to advertising more than any other in the late Victorian period was the soap industry. By 1889, Pears was spending what was at the time an enormous sum of £100,000 year on advertising. The little boy chosen by Millais for the painting grew up to be Admiral Sir William James (1881–1973), known throughout his naval career as 'Bubbles'.

1890
NEWS FROM NOWHERE

The influence of William Morris on poetry, furniture, printing, interior decor and politics has been immense. His horrified reaction to over-wrought Victorian design, led to a fascination with the simplicity of the Middle Ages. He was also influenced by the Pre-Raphaelites, was converted into poetry – including reading long translations from Icelandic – and political tracts, like *The Dream of John Ball* (1886–87). His utopian socialist novel *News from Nowhere* (1890) imagined waking up a century after his time, and travelling down the Thames from his homes in Hammersmith and Oxfordshire, finding London transformed into a pastoral idyll of his own Arts and Crafts movement. His wallpaper company made a fortune, and he died at the relatively young age of 63 – according to his doctor 'of being William Morris'.

▲ *A tapestry by the designer, poet, artist and social commentator William Morris.*

1895
JUDE THE OBSCURE

When the former architect's apprentice, Thomas Hardy (1840–1928) reached the pinnacle of his career as a novelist with *Tess of the D'Urbervilles* in 1891, he faced a campaign of outrage about the novel's 'indecency' led by his wife – and he promised to give up novels altogether if he ever faced such a reception again. But the clamour was even stronger about *Jude the Obscure* (1895), a novel that reflected some of the tensions in his own marriage, and it was the last one he ever wrote. His Wessex novels had been written over a period of 25 years, since *Desperate Remedies* (1871), painting a romantic portrait of country life. In the years that followed, he devoted himself to poetry and became the Grand Old Man of English letters.

p. 209◀ **Distant Voices** ▶p. 213

Harris said he felt such extraordinary fits of giddiness come over him at times, that he hardly knew what he was doing; and then George said that he had fits of giddiness too, and hardly knew what he was doing. With me, it was my liver that was out of order. I knew it was my liver that was out of order because I had just been reading a patent liver-pill circular, in which were detailed various symptoms by which a man could tell whether his liver was out of order. I had them all.

Jerome K. Jerome, from *Three Men in a Boat* (1889)

Fin de Siècle

1895–1913

IMPERIAL CULTURE REACHED its zenith with Queen Victoria's Diamond Jubilee in 1897, a much more sumptuous affair than her Golden Jubilee a decade before, and the nation was puffed up with its own importance. There were social critics, however, such as George Bernard Shaw and H. G. Wells, to worry the nation, and children's writers to help them escape: the turn of the century was also the great age of children's literature – E. Nesbit, Kenneth Grahame, Rudyard Kipling and Beatrix Potter were all writing at this time. The Edwardian years were also the great age of football, with 100,000 spectators turning out for the FA Cup final at Crystal Palace in London in 1901 – a similar number now owned telephones: the modern age of communications was beginning.

1899
THE ENIGMA VARIATIONS

The composer Edward Elgar (1857–1934) began his musical career as bandmaster at the Worcester county lunatic asylum, but by the 1890s he had won himself an international reputation. A 1899 performance of his best-loved orchestral portraits of his friends was called *The Enigma Variations.* This was followed a year later by his celebrated oratorio, *The Dream of Gerontius.* In 1901, he was asked to write something for the coronation of Edward VII (1840–1910), and his *Pomp and Circumstance* marches – including the tune which became known as *Land of Hope and Glory* – was given its premiere in Liverpool. This was followed by a double encore at the annual Promenade concerts in London, and it has been played there ever since.

p. 204◀ **Triumphs & Tragedies** ▶p. 216

1895
THE IMPRISONMENT OF OSCAR WILDE

Oscar Wilde (1854–1900) was the best-known and one of the most outrageous members of the Aesthetic movement, which espoused art for art's sake. The year 1895 was also the most important of his life: not only was his brilliant comedy *The Importance of Being Earnest* an enormous success, but he also ended up in Reading Gaol. Although his homosexuality was an open secret, he made the mistake of suing for libel the Marquis of Queensberry (1844–1900), the father of his lover, over a note accusing him of 'posing as a sodomite [sic]'. He lost the case and became the first person prosecuted under the new homosexuality laws. He died in Paris five years later, a tragic and broken figure.

▲ *Oscar Wilde, brilliant playwright and novelist, as well as one of the most outrageous members of the aesthetic movement.*

1904
TINKERBELL

J. M. Barrie (1860–1937) was the ninth of 10 children of a Scottish handloom weaver, and was already a successful playwright before he met the Llewelyn-Davies family in Kensington Gardens. His friendship with their children inspired the enormous success of *Peter Pan*, first performed in London in 1904, where he urged the audience to clap to save the life of the fairy Tinkerbell. It was a popular period for fairies, though it was a much more material variety which took centre stage in *Puck of Pook's Hill* (1906), by the journalist and poet Rudyard Kipling (1865–1936). Kipling's reputation as the 'Poet of Empire' was so high, that he was the first English writer to win the Nobel Prize for Literature.

▶ p. 215

1904
ABBEY THEATRE

When Cecil Sharp (1859–1924) overheard a Somerset gardener singing a local folk song, it set him off on a lifetime's quest collecting the remaining songs still remembered in rural villages. While Sharp was collecting folk songs, the Irish nationalist poet W. B. Yeats (1865–1939) was also collecting folk stories, which were published in his collection *The Celtic Twilight* (1893) – an important milestone in the so-called Celtic Revival. Yeats's Irish National Theatre Society opened its headquarters at the Abbey Theatre in Dublin in 1904, dedicated to providing Ireland with its own dramatic literature, and employing some of the actors from Yeats' most successful play *Cathleen Ni Houlihan* two years before. Yeats shunned violence but knew many of those executed in the Easter Rising in 1916.

▶ p. 215

1904
FRY'S MAGAZINE

C. B. Fry (1872–1956) was the pre-eminent amateur sportsman of his generation. He played soccer for Southampton and England, captained the England cricket side – scoring six centuries in succession in 1901 – and played first class rugby too. As well as all this, he found time to be an Oxford scholar and a successful athlete, equalling the world long jump record. His popularity was such that his own publication, *Fry's Magazine*, had a wide circulation from its launch in 1904 until the war. Fry was so famous that, in addition to representing India at the League of Nations after the First World War, he was even offered – and refused – the throne of Albania. He devoted his retirement to sail training for boy's clubs.

▼ *The bowler hat, cane and moustache – and the funny walk – soon became Chaplin's trademarks.*

1912
TIPPERARY

The years before the First World War were the great years of the music hall, with their stages frequented by comedians like Dan Leno (1861–1904) and performers such as Marie Lloyd (1870–1922) dominating their profession – with songs like 'A Little of What You Fancy Does You Good'. Crowds lined the three-mile route of Leno's funeral route after his death. One of the most enduring music hall songs was 'It's a Long Way to Tipperary' (1912) – now inextricably linked to the war which followed – which was written by Harry J. Williams (1874–1924) and composed by Jack Judge (1878–1938), both from near Birmingham. The words 'Goodbye Piccadilly/Farewell Leicester Square' caught the imagination of the troops who sailed off to war two years later.

1913
PYGMALION

Fabian pamphleteer, theatre critic, Labour councillor and playwright, George Bernard Shaw (1856–1950) reinvented himself many times during his long life. But he also reinvented the British theatre, transforming it from the bowlderised Shakespeare and romantic melodramas that were all one could see around the turn of the century to provocative and intelligent plays inspired by those of Henrik Ibsen (1828–1906). Shaw's fascination with class dominated his greatest success, *Pygmalion*, where a flower girl is taught the language of the upper classes – only to give herself away with the phrase 'Not bloody likely!'. The play was first produced in German in Vienna in 1913, opening in London the following year.

▲ ▶ p. 216

1913
CHARLIE CHAPLIN

London's first specially-built cinema opened in 1912, but the first international movie star did not make his first appearance until the following year – and he was British. Charlie Chaplin (1889–1977) was on a tour of the US when his talent was recognised by the Keystone Studios; he made his first film with them in 1913, soon gaining his trademark bowler hat, moustache and walking stick. By 1918, Chaplin was internationally famous and instantly recognisable, and he was able to command a fee of $1 million for his performance in *Shoulder Arms*. He went on to be co-founder of United Artists. 'Chaplin means more to me than the than the idea of God,' said the French director François Truffaut (1932–84).

p. 211◀ **Distant Voices** ▶p. 215

The sand of the desert is sodden red, -
Red with the wreck of a square
that broke; -
The Gatling's jammed and the
Colonel dead,
And the regiment blind with dust
and smoke.
The river of death has brimmed
its banks,
And England's far, and Honour a
name,
But the voice of a schoolboy rallies
the ranks:
'Play up! play up! and play the game!'

Henry Newbolt, 'Vitai Lampada' (1892)

From Brooke to Body Line

1915–34

THE TERRIBLE LOSSES of the Great War led to a law-abiding weariness in Britain. At the so-called White Horse Final of the FA Cup in 1923, a single mounted policeman was able to control the enormous crowds when they spilled onto the pitch at Wembley Stadium. Culture reacted to the war in different ways. Some preferred the realism of Robert Graves' *Goodbye to All That.* Some read the new detective stories of Agatha Christie. Some concentrated on flippant comedies and escapism, and comic creations like P. G. Wodehouse's Jeeves, while others in a new search for truth followed the new modernist artists and writers who were determined that art, literature and truthful design would protect the world from another conflagration.

▲ *PC George Scorey and his horse Billy controlling the crowds at the 1923 FA Cup Final, henceforth known as the 'White Horse Final'.*

► p. 216

1915
RUPERT BROOKE

The outbreak of the First World War had a strange effect on writers, and none more than on the romantic socialist poet Rupert Brooke (1887–1915), who described going to fight as 'swimmers into cleanness leaping'. His poem *The Soldier* had an enormous impact when it was published in 1915, just before Brooke died of blood poisoning on the way to the Dardanelles. But the war will be remembered more for the poets who recorded its horrors, like Wilfred Owen (1893–1918), Siegfried Sassoon (1886–1967) and Isaac Rosenberg (1890–1918). Their work had a profound effect on the years afterwards: 'My subject is War, and the pity of War,' wrote Owen just before his death – a week before the armistice.

▲ *The poet Wilfred Owen, who was killed just two weeks before the armistice was signed at the end of the First World War.*

1923
FAÇADE

The Sitwell family, Edith (1887–1964), Osbert (1892–1969), and Sacheverell (1897–1988), declared war on philistinism in the name of modern art and writing, and in doing so, they faced reactions ranging from ridicule to outright rage. All had a strong sense of irony and a genius for publicity, and their campaign reached a climax in 1923 with the performance of Edith's cycle of poems known as *Façade* – which she described as 'patterns in sound'. The sounds were delivered to the audience through a megaphone in a painted screen, accompanied by music written by the young composer William Walton (1902–83), later famous for writing the score for the 1944 film *Henry V*. The public was duly shocked.

1926
WINNIE-THE-POOH

The playwright A. A. Milne (1882–1956) was a former assistant editor of *Punch* magazine who became known for his successful light comedies – and then he published the verses written for his young son Christopher Robin, starting with *When We Were Very Young* (1924). But it was the stories about Christopher Robin's toys which, to his frustration, made him internationally famous. *Winnie-the-Pooh* (1926) and *The House at Pooh Corner* (1928) were enhanced by the illustrations by E. H. Shepard (1879–1976) – who did the same service for *The Wind in the Willows* – and concerned Pooh and Piglet's minor adventures involving birthdays and the weather. Milne's verses about his son's nanny were set to music and have been lampooned ever since.

1928
ORLANDO

When a group of writers, artists and intellectuals, known as the Bloomsbury Group, began meeting in Gordon Square, London before the First World War, they launched an artistic movement which lasted nearly 40 years – and changed the way people thought. The house was the home of the sisters Vanessa (1879–1961) and Virginia Stephen (1882–1941, later Virginia Woolf) and the group including the economist J. M. Keynes (1883–1946), the critic Lytton Strachey (1880–1932), the artist Duncan Grant (1885–1978) and the philosopher Bertrand Russell (1972–1970) became extremely influential among the *avant garde.* Virginia Woolf's most famous novel is *Orlando* (1928), and is a celebration of her friend Vita Sackville-West (1892–1962), written as an imaginary biography over four centuries, where the hero wakes up half way through as a woman.

1929
THE LAWRENCE EXHIBITION

The novelist D. H. Lawrence (1885–1930), who shocked the public by eloping with the wife of a German baron, was prosecuted for indecency for his novel *The Rainbow* (1915); two others, *Women in Love* (1920) and *Lady Chatterley's Lover* (1928), proved too shocking for British publishers. *Lady Chatterley* stayed unpublished in the UK until Penguin Books won a famous 1960 court battle. Lawrence lived in Mexico during the early-1920s, but died in France of tuberculosis at the age of only 44. Even his paintings offended the establishment: although 12,000 people visited an exhibition of them in London in 1929, 13 pictures were seized by the puritanical home secretary, Sir William Joynson-Hicks (1865–1932). An 82-year-old judge refused to sign the order for their destruction though.

1930
PRIVATE LIVES

The actor and playwright Noel Coward (1899–1973) began his career by shocking his audiences with a play about drug addiction, *The Vortex* (1924), but made his reputation with patriotic set-pieces, comic songs and stylish comedies. His song 'Mad Dogs and Englishmen' caught the public mood, though his wartime 'Don't Let's be Beastly to the Germans' caused a public furore and forced him to leave the country to perform to troops instead. But it was his comedy, *Private Lives,* first performed in London in 1930, which was the pinnacle of his career. The play concerns a divorced couple who meet by accident on their respective honeymoons; the cast of four included Coward, Gertrude Lawrence (1898–1952) and Laurence Olivier (1907–89).

1932
BODY LINE BOWLING

During the 1930 cricket test series between England and Australia, the young Australian batsman Don Bradman (b. 1908) scored a total of 974 runs. For the England team, national pride was at stake, and – under their uncompromising captain Douglas Jardine (1900–58) – they developed a bowling theory which involved aiming directly at the batsman. This leg theory, or 'body line' bowling, was first put into practice by Harold Larwood (1904–1995) during the next test series in Australia in 1932–33. He took 33 wickets, injuring a number of batsmen in the process, and caused a serious diplomatic incident between Britain and Australia. Larwood was one of the fastest bowlers in history, but he resigned from test cricket afterwards, settling eventually in Australia.

1934
RALPH VAUGHAN WILLIAMS

'What we want in England is real music,' said the composer Ralph Vaughan Williams (1872–1948), 'which possesses real feelings and real life.' When he first overheard the folk-song 'Bushes and Briars' in an Essex village in 1903, he felt he had known it all his life, and went on to weave traditional songs into his music. His *Fantasia on Greensleeves* in 1934 knits together the traditional song 'Greensleeves', said to have been written by Henry VIII, and 'Lovely Joan', a folk-song he discovered in Norfolk in 1908. His songs, such as 'Linden Lea' (1903) and 'On Wenlock Edge' (1908) – using the poems of A. E. Housman (1859–1936) – have become part of a true sense of the English.

▼ *The composer Ralph Vaughan Williams.*

p. 213 ◀ **Distant Voices** ▶ p. 217

Come friendly bombs, and fall on Slough
It isn't fit for humans now,
There isn't grass to graze a cow
Swarm over, Death!
Come, bombs, and blow to smithereens
Those air-conditioned, bright canteens,
Tinned fruit, tinned meat, tinned milk, tinned beans,
Tinned minds, tinned breath.
Mess up that place they call a town –
A house for ninety-seven down
And once a week for half-a-crown
For twenty years.

John Betjeman, 'Slough' (1937)

From Eliot to Ealing Comedies

1939–59

THE SECOND WORLD WAR, like the First, created a new generation determined to build a better world – a hope frustrated by Britain's disastrous economic position and the cynicism of the Cold War. But the 1948 Olympic Games in London, the Festival of Britain in 1951 and the coronation in 1953 all gave a sense of the beginning of a new age. Cities were changing, with new modernist buildings springing up, like Basil Spence's replacement for the blitzed Coventry Cathedral. It took 10 years to build and was finally opened in 1961 with a performance of Benjamin Britten's *War Requiem*, based on the poems of Wilfred Owen. By 1960, British culture included television, Angry Young Men and rock 'n' roll and looked very different to the way it had before the war.

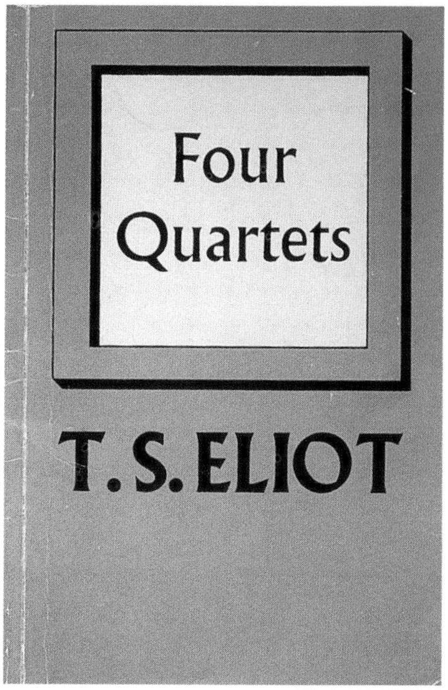

▲ *T. S. Eliots 'Four Quartets', first published in 1943, epitomised the new modernist style.*

▶ p. 216

1939
LUNCHTIME RECITALS

'There is no such thing as culture in wartime,' said the *Daily Express* in 1940, complaining about a government grant to CEMA, the forerunner of the Arts Council. In fact, the upsurge of creativity, theatre, film, music and dance was already proving them wrong, even in a blacked-out and half-empty London. Within weeks of the outbreak of war, the pianist Myra Hess (1890–1965) began her famous lunchtime recitals, which became a symbol of cultural resistance. They took place in the National Gallery, with its walls bare because its pictures had been hidden in a Welsh quarry, and continued throughout the war. The audience moved to basement shelters during air-raids and the pianists often played through the noise of falling bombs.

p. 212◀ **Triumphs & Tragedies** ▶p. 218

1954
THE FOUR-MINUTE MILE

Running a mile in under four minutes was a symbolic, but apparently unreachable, goal for athletes, and the world record – set by Gunther Hargg (b. 1918) – had been unchallenged for eight years before 1953 when Christopher Chataway (b. 1931) ran two miles in a world record time of 8 minutes 49.6 seconds, just a week before the coronation. Middle-distance runner Roger Bannister (b. 1929) finally passed the magic four-minute mark in 1954 on the Iffley Road running track in Oxford, with a time of 3 minutes 59.4 seconds. His achievement was crucial to the development of British athletics, inspiring the next generation of Olympic athletes such as David Hemery (b. 1944) and Sebastian Coe (b. 1956).

1943
'THE FOUR QUARTETS'

The poet and playwright T. S. Eliot (1888–1965) was born in America but came to London in 1915 and worked as a clerk in Lloyds Bank. His poem cycle 'The Waste Land' (1922) was one of the most influential examples of modernist writing, edited by the poet Ezra Pound (1885–1972) – who was later discredited for broadcasting from fascist Italy during the war. Eliot became increasingly religious during the 1920s, a trend which culminated in 'The Four Quartets', which were first published together in 1943. Eliot demonstrated a whole new way of writing poetry, obscure and spiritual, but it was his *Old Possum's Book of Practical Cats* (1939) which became his greatest success after his death. It was turned into the musical *Cats* by Andrew Lloyd Webber (b. 1948).

▲ *Roger Bannister breaking the four-minute mile for the first time on the Iffley Road track in 1954; his time was 3 minutes, 59.4 seconds.*

1948
THE ALDEBURGH FESTIVAL

'If wind and water could write music, it would sound like Ben's,' wrote the violinist Yehudi Menuhin (b. 1916), about the composer Benjamin Britten (1913–76). Britten revolutionised British opera in 1945 with *Peter Grimes*, based in an East Anglian fishing village, and followed it up with a string of songs designed for the voice of his lover and collaborator Peter Pears

▶ *A still from the film* Nineteen Eighty-Four, *starring John Hurt and based on George Orwell's spine-chilling book.*

(1910–86). Both Britten and Pears founded the Aldeburgh festival in 1948, in another East Anglian fishing village, and it grew into one of the top concert halls in Europe, the Maltings at nearby Snape. Britten dominated British music in the middle years of the century, and became the first composer to be given a peerage, just six months before his death.

1949
NINETEEN EIGHTY-FOUR

George Orwell was once a policeman in Imperial Burma called Eric Blair (1903–50), but he became well-known as a powerful social prophet – lambasting unemployment in his book *The Road to Wigan Pier* (1937). He became increasingly disillusioned with Soviet-style totalitarianism, however, which he ridiculed in his novel *Animal Farm* (1945). *Nineteen Eighty-Four* is an ironic commentary on the world in 1948 when he was writing it, where Britain has been transformed into Airstrip One in a superstate called Oceania, ruled by the image of Big Brother. The hero commits thought crimes by keeping a diary and falling in love. It became one of the most important texts of the Cold War.

1954
THE LORD OF THE RINGS

A select group of academics met every Tuesday in the Eagle and Child pub in Oxford throughout the war. The result, among other writings, were the children's classics by C. S. Lewis (1898–1963), starting with *The Lion, the Witch and the Wardrobe* (1950), and the fantasy epic *The Lord of the Rings* by the Anglo-Saxon scholar J. R. R. Tolkien (1892–1973). Tolkien invented a whole new mythology for his imaginary land 'Middle Earth', and the whole conception of Shire hobbits fighting the evil enemy in the East owes a great deal to the experience of the war. But *The Lord of the Rings* (1954) also began a whole new style, and gave birth to a new genre of fantasy and science fantasy, culminating in the Hollywood epic *Star Wars* in 1978.

1955
THE SALE OF EALING STUDIOS

The late 1940s and early 1950s were the years of a string of successful British comedy films, made in the Ealing Studios in west London under Michael Balcon (1896–1977). Critics have hailed them since as the high point of the British film industry, brought to an end with the sale of the studios to the BBC in 1955. Ealing Studio's films were gutsy, intelligent comedies and they made stars out of their leading actors, like Stanley Holloway (1890–1982) and Alec Guinness (b. 1914) in films like *Passport to Pimlico* (1949) and *The Lavender Hill Mob* (1951). More serious films like *The Blue Lamp* (1948), with Jack Warner (1895–1981) were resurrected for television six years later for the long-running police series *Dixon of Dock Green.*

1959
CLIFF RICHARD

Across the Atlantic, the record companies and the emerging teenage market had discovered rock 'n' roll as created by Bill Haley (1927–81) and Elvis Presley (1935–77). It took longer in the UK, where the number one album throughout 1959 was the sound track of the film *South Pacific*, but by then Britain had its answer – an 18-year-old called Cliff Richard (b. 1940). He had been born in India as Harry Webb, and produced his first chart success – *Move It* – in 1958, which sent him on his way to being Britain's most successful recording artist. He and his group, the Drifters, met in a London coffee bar called 21s. Their first number one single and gold disc came the following year with 'Livin' Doll', and by 1960 they had changed their name to the Shadows.

p. 215◀ **Distant Voices** ▶p. 219

Jimmy: ... *The old Edwardian brigade do make their brief little world look pretty tempting. All home-made cakes and croquet, bright ideas, bright uniforms. Always the same picture: high summer, the long days in the sun, slim volumes of verse, crisp linen, the smell of starch. What a romantic picture. Phoney too, of course.... Still, even I regret it somehow, phoney or not. If you've no world of your own, it's rather pleasant to regret the passing of someone else's. I must be getting sentimental. But I must say it's pretty dreary living in the American Age – unless you're American of course....*

John Osborne, from *Look Back in Anger* (1956)

From McCartney to Monty Python
1962–76

WHEN A BRITISH COURT finally ruled that D. H. Lawrence's classic *Lady Chatterley's Lover* was not obscene, it was the signal for a breath of fresh air through British culture. Censorship ended in the theatre. Television, under Sir Hugh Greene's permissive director-generalship of the BBC, became bolder – launching a new brand of fierce satire known as *TW3*. In books, art and music, British culture became increasingly important in the world, led by the phenomenal success of the Beatles and other British bands like the Rolling Stones and the Who. Televised sport meant that football and cricket gained new enthusiasts from all classes; British television comedy became popular across the globe. Only the British film industry lagged behind.

▲ *The National Theatre, at its current site on London's South Bank.*

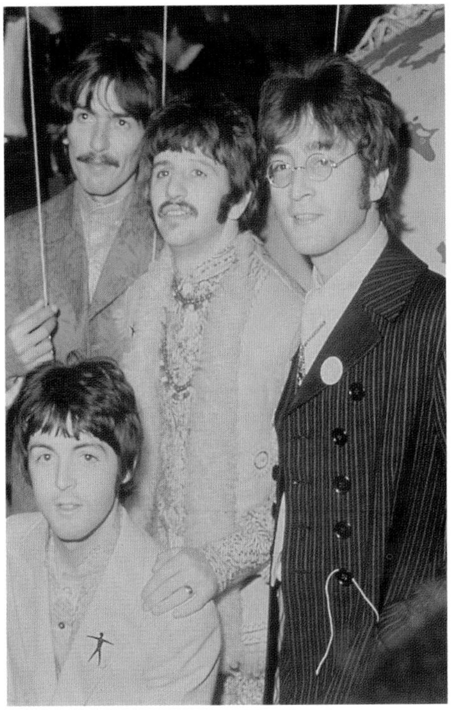

▲ *The Beatles, who became the most successful pop group of the 1960s.*

1962
'PLEASE PLEASE ME'

The Beatles achieved their first number one hit with 'Please Please Me' in 1962, but it had been a long slog since John Lennon (1940–80) first met Paul McCartney (b. 1942) in a Liverpool band called The Quarrymen in 1957. Their success fixed Liverpool as the capital city of the so-called beat generation, stamped their mark on the 1960s, and they became the ultimate international pop success. The Beatles' story culminated in the universal popularity of *Sergeant Pepper's Lonely Hearts' Club Band* in 1967, just in time for the explosion of the hippy culture the following year. Legal wrangles over their company, Apple, meant that by 1970 they could no longer bear to be in the same room. Hopes that they might one day reunite ended when Lennon was shot in New York a decade later.

1962
NATIONAL THEATRE

The foundation stone for a national theatre had been laid three times, twice by the Queen Mother, when the institution finally became a reality. 'Why don't they put it on castors?' she had asked on the last occasion. Actors and critics since David Garrick had been calling for one, but not until 1962 – when the National Theatre opened at the Old Vic theatre in London under Laurence Olivier – did the idea become real. Its first production, of *Hamlet*, was a success, and the director Peter Hall (b. 1930) took over in 1973, moving it to its present site on the South Bank in 1976. Together with the Royal Shakespeare Company, the Royal National Theatre is one of the best-known and most successful subsidised theatre companies in the world.

p. 216◀ **Triumphs & Tragedies** ▶p. 224

1966
THE WORLD CUP

The World Cup Final took place at Wembley Stadium in 1966 in front of the queen and the world's television cameras, and brought football to the forefront of British culture. The architect of success for the England team was Alf Ramsey (1920–99), who had made his reputation by taking Ipswich from the third division to the league championship between 1955 and 1962. His reign as England manager meant reconnecting the game in the UK to the new techniques in the rest of the world, and he stayed in the job until 1974. The Final itself was secured by West Ham's Geoff Hurst (b. 1941), who scored three goals against West Germany. The final score was 4–2, and Hurst finally received a knighthood for his efforts in 1998.

1963
THAT WAS THE WEEK THAT WAS

Until 1963, the BBC had remained deferential to politicians, banning humorous references to a whole range of public figures. But *That Was The Week That Was* – also known as *TW3* – changed all that. Produced by Ned Sherrin (b. 1931), *TW3* made a star of the presenter David Frost (b. 1939) and unleashed a tide of satire on Britain. A new generation of humorists, also represented in the new satirical magazine *Private Eye*, had an enormous influence on Britain and the USA – which developed its own version of satirical TV. *TW3* could be devastatingly critical of the powerful and pompous, but it also included softer items, like the famous review of the budget by comedian Frankie Howerd (1917–92).

1967
THE DEATH OF ORTON

The actor Joe Orton (1933–67) was briefly the *enfant terrible* of British theatre, specialising in exuberant and extravagently irreverent black farces, starting with *Entertaining Mr Sloane* (1964). He was influenced by the playwright Harold Pinter (b. 1930) and the French writer Jean Genet (1910–86), but he increasingly developed his own style which took the plays into taboo areas of sex, incest and violence, culminating in *Loot* in 1966. His plays thrived in the permissive period after the end of theatrical censorship, part of a cultural revolution which affected most areas of British life. His last play, *What the Butler Saw*, was produced in 1969, two years after Orton had been murdered by his lover, who then committed suicide himself.

✳ 1967
A BIGGER SPLASH

The British artist David Hockney (b. 1937) was trained in Bradford, but has spent most of his career in California. He was a key figure in the British contribution to the Pop Art movement in the 1960s and early 1970s, which was youthful, witty and drew on images of consumerism, comics and pop culture. Teaching in Los Angeles inspired him to create his series of swimming pool paintings, the most famous of which was *A Bigger Splash* in 1967, now on show in the Tate Gallery. It was even turned into a film in 1974. Hockney also became famous for his portraits, like *Mr and Mrs Clark and Percy* (1970–71), for illustrating Grimm's *Fairy Tales* (1969) and for his opera designs at Covent Garden and the Metropolitan Opera in New York.

1969
MONTY PYTHON

Anarchic comedy of the type represented by the BBC series *Monty Python's Flying Circus* had never been seen before, when it hit Britain's TV screens in 1969. Its bizarre characters sometimes spilled out between scenes, or even between episodes, but the series became famous all over the world – as did its catch phrases, like 'Now for something completely different' and its most memorable sketches, like the Dead Parrot or the Ministry of Silly Walks. It made the careers of its leading members, like John Cleese (b. 1939) as a film actor, Michael Palin (b. 1943) as a documentary-maker, transport campaigner and film actor and Terry Gilliam (b. 1940) as an international film director. Python films followed, including *Monty Python's Life of Brian* (1979).

▲ *The* Monty Python *team, demonstrating the Ministry of Silly Walks.*

1976
'ANARCHY IN THE UK'

The Sex Pistols, the creation of Kings Road clothes shop-owner Malcolm McLaren (b. 1946), shot to notoriety after swearing during a TV interview at the end of 1976. The Damned made the first punk single, but it was the Sex Pistols' 'Anarchy in the UK' which really launched the Punk phenomenon in Britain, characterised by its spiky hair and anarchic bondage-style fashion created by designer Vivienne Westwood (b. 1941) and turning the conventional rock industry upside down in the process. Their first album, *Never Mind the Bollocks, Here's the Sex Pistols* was banned from TV and shop windows because of the word 'bollocks'. They disbanded in 1978 after the suicide of band member Sid Vicious (1957–79).

p. 217◀ **Distant Voices** ▶p. 221

Adam was simultaneously reminded that he was twenty-five years of age, and would soon be twenty-six, that he was a postgraduate student preparing a thesis which he was unlikely to complete in this the third and final year of his scholarship, that the latter was hugely overdrawn, that he was married with three very young children, that one of them had manifested an alarming rash the previous evening, that his name was ridiculous, that his leg hurt, that his decrepit scooter had failed to start the previous morning and would no doubt fail to start this morning....

David Lodge, from *The British Museum is Falling Down* (1965)

From Torvill to Teletubbies

1981–97

HOW DO YOU SUMMARISE a period which included films such as *Chariots of Fire* and *Trainspotting*, buildings like Canary Wharf and the Millennium Dome, sculptures like the Angel of the North, poets such as Benjamin Zephaniah and Sophie Hannah, the novelists Iain Banks and Martin Amis, comedians like Lenny Henry and Ben Elton, artists like Damien Hurst, grand spectacles like Riverdance, sports stars like Paul Gascoigne, Steve Ovett and Ian Botham? It is hard enough to explain the culture of your own time, but even harder now that the people and cultures of the UK are so diverse and varied, and now that there are more than 70 television channels to choose from. Later generations will judge us better than we can.

1981
CATS

The composer Andrew Lloyd Webber (b. 1948) achieved his first West End musical success in partnership with lyricist Tim Rice (b. 1944), with *Jesus Christ Superstar* in 1973. For *Cats* (1981), he used the children's poems of the poet T. S. Eliot and the result was the most successful stage musical of all time, leading to the domination by British musicals of both the West End and Broadway throughout the 1980s. Its success was also due in part to director Trevor Nunn (b. 1940) from the Royal Shakespeare Company. The main song, 'Memory', was first sung by Lloyd Webber's future wife Sarah Brightman (b. 1961): within 10 years, it had been recorded as many as 150 times around the world.

1984
TORVILL AND DEAN

British ice skaters had performed well in the late 1970s and early 1980s, but it was the partnership of Jayne Torvill (b. 1957) and Christopher Dean (b. 1958) that took the world by storm. They were British champions from 1978 to 1983, staging a surprise come-back after a period as professionals, in 1994 – the same year they repeated their Olympic success to win a bronze medal. But it was in 1984 that they thrilled Olympic viewers with the performance that won them the gold medal, and at the same time popularised their chosen accompanying music, Ravel's *Bolero.* As a result, ice skating enjoyed a burst of popularity in Britain, with new rinks opening in Oxford and open air in the new Broadgate development in London.

1986
LLOYD'S BUILDING

The mid-1980s property boom, and the development of dock areas in London, Merseyside and Glasgow, brought the future of architecture into the forefront of debate. Prince Charles (b. 1948) led the assault on modernist architects with his attack on a

▲ *The Lloyd's Building in London, with its distinctive glass and tube exterior.*

design for the National Gallery extension, describing it as 'a monstrous carbuncle on the face of a much-loved friend'. Together with James Stirling (1926–92) and Norman Foster (b. 1935), architect Richard Rogers (b. 1933) was the most public of the modernist architects, and was particularly celebrated for his design of the Pompidou Centre in Paris. His Lloyd's Building, with its big atrium of light in the centre, and its mixture of glass and colourful tubes, became the most famous new building in London.

1988
THE SATANIC VERSES

The writer Salman Rushdie (b. 1947) arrived in Britain in 1965, from India where he was born. His novel *Midnight's Children* was based in his native Bombay and won the Booker Prize in 1981, reflecting the increasingly diverse culture which now made up the UK. But the diverse culture began to pose a serious threat to him after his 1988 novel *The Satanic Verses.* What some of the Muslim community around the world saw as an attack on Islam led to the book being banned in India. It also led to book-burnings around the world and a death sentence – or *fatwa* – announced against him by the Ayatollah Khomeini (1900–89) of Iran. Rushdie was forced into hiding, from which he seldom emerged until the *fatwa* was lifted in 1998.

1989
RAVE CULTURE

The attack by the police on a convoy of hippies and new age travellers at Stonehenge, before the 1985 summer solstice, put the spotlight on a new kind of youth culture. The Stone Roses, for example, were almost unknown outside Manchester, but were able to fill secret warehouse parties and large venues by word of mouth. By 1989, they were nationally known, and other groups like them were entertaining a new kind of clientele taking the designer drug ecstasy. Thousands of young people were driving to secret locations for rave parties, the site of venues being passed by word of mouth just ahead of the police. But the Stone Roses' attempt to redefine pop festivals came to nothing, and they disbanded in 1996.

1996
THE SPICE GIRLS

1996 saw the rise of a new pop phenomenon in the form of the all-girl group the Spice Girls. The five girls had been sharing a house together in Maidenhead, Berkshire, back in 1993 before they shot to international fame with their first hit single *Wannabe*. The marketing mix was an enormous success, partly because of the concept of 'girl power' – which meant that, although the five could be attractive to men, their heady female aggression made them enormously popular among teenage girls and young women as well. They hit the political headlines in 1997 in an interview for the *Spectator* magazine when they claimed they supported the Conservatives and that former prime minister Margaret Thatcher (b. 1925) was the first spice girl.

▲ *The Spice Girls shot to fame as they spread their concept of 'Girl Power' to audiences worldwide.*

1997
TELETUBBIES

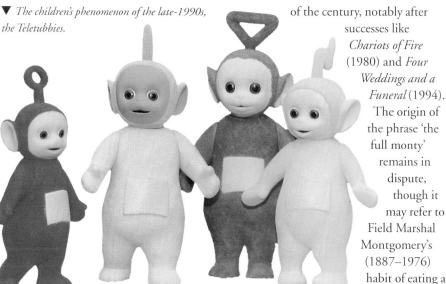

The BBC's attempt to tailor a regular television series directly at children aged two to five years old gave birth to the *Teletubbies.* The series involved four brightly coloured characters of indeterminate sex: Tinky Winky, Dipsy, Laa Laa and Po, who were created after months of research to find out how very young children respond to TV, and how best to prepare them for pre-school education. The programme often repeats whole sections as young children like, but adults found they enjoyed it as well and the series gained a worldwide cult status, with the Teletubby dolls selling out in the shops before Christmas 1997. Po's special song turned out to mean 'quickly, quickly, quickly' or 'slowly, slowly, slowly' in Cantonese.

▼ *The children's phenomenon of the late-1990s, the Teletubbies.*

1997
THE FULL MONTY

The revival of the British film industry was often hailed in the last two decades of the century, notably after successes like *Chariots of Fire* (1980) and *Four Weddings and a Funeral* (1994). The origin of the phrase 'the full monty' remains in dispute, though it may refer to Field Marshal Montgomery's (1887–1976) habit of eating a hearty breakfast before battle. Either way, it provided the title to the most successful British film ever made: *The Full Monty* (1997) was set in Sheffield, and covered two major social phenomenons of the 1990s – the collapse of British industry and shifting gender roles, showing how unemployed steel workers became male strippers to provide themselves with work.

p. 219◀ **Distant Voices** ▶p. 225

I am here today my friends to tell you
there is hope.
As high as that mountain may seem
I must tell you
I have a dream
And my friend There is a tunnel at the
end of the light.
And behind that tunnel I see a future
I see a time
When angry white men
Will sit down with angry black women
And talk about the weather,
Black employers will display notice-
boards proclaiming,
'Me nu care wea you come from yu
know
So long as you can do a good day's work,
dat cool wid me.

Benjamin Zephaniah, 'I Have a Scheme', from *Propa Propaganda* (1996)

Religions, Belief and Thought

THE INFLUENCE OF THE Judaic-Christian heritage in the West has provided a broad framework into which religion is normally placed. Occasionally it is a tight fit because some ideas and radical thinkers break the mould. Even classic definitions of orthodoxy can find it difficult to accept new or old ideas. The religion of Britain pre-Roman times can only be presumed through burial mounds and structures which may, or may not, have had religious significance. After the coming of Christianity it is relatively easy to trace the slow spread of the new religion, its interaction with the old religion and its growing political influence. Once it took centre stage internal struggles commenced and much of the history of religious thought in the West is of Christian verses Christian. It does, however, include the methodical rise of humanism and secularism, at first within the Christian context and then outside it. The Enlightenment, the rise of scientific enquiry and the effect of two world wars in the twentieth century have set religious thinkers on the defensive, and the traditional model of the Christian religion struggles for recognition and relevance.

KEY THEMES

- ☆ BEGINNINGS
- ◩ ART & ARCHITECTURE
- ✶ VISIONARIES
- ↗ BREAKING THE MOULD
- ✕ SAINTS
- PHILOSOPHERS
- RELIGIOUS ORDERS
- FOUNDERS
- ◉ SEEKERS & SCHOLARS
- TENSIONS

KEY EVENTS

① 3000 BC
PRE-CHRISTIAN RELIGION

There is evidence in Stonehenge, Avebury and other sites that Britain was populated with thinkers who studied the movements of the sun, moon and stars. They buried their dead with possessions for a journey – an acknowledgement that the end of one life may not be the end. The body curled up foetus-like in death is, maybe, awaiting a new birth.

② AD 597
CHRISTIANITY ARRIVES IN BRITAIN

First recognised in symbols on plates and scratched on buildings, Christianity flourished among the Celts – those not conquered by the Romans. The advent Roman Christianity in AD 597 changed the religious face of Britain, for there was a strong political link with chiefs and kings and with Rome.

③ 1066
THE NORMAN PERIOD

There was a flowering of Christianity expressed in the building of cathedrals, the intellectual acumen of some of the bishops and the arrival of the great monastic houses. Scholarship began to flourish and the first signs of real tension between secular and religious power emerged in Norman times.

④ 1400s
THE GROWTH OF LEARNING

The authoritarianism of the Church had been challenged by monarchs and religious thinkers. The growth of individualism and the challenge to traditional authority led to scholars and kings being excommunicated, but it was ineffectual. The wealth of the church was always an attraction for kings and it was inevitable that protest would have a political and a religious dimension.

⑤ 1500–1700
REFORMATION IN BRITAIN

Catholic Scotland became Presbyterian and then those in England and Wales who were Catholic, became Protestant. Ireland remained Catholic. People were burned, religion was formed and reformed, kings were executed and exiled. Still the innumerable rise of individualism and secular thinking continued, albeit within a broadly theistic point of view.

⑥ 1600–1820
PHILOSOPHERS AND THINKERS

The Christian assumptions of society made it difficult for philosophers to stray far from Christian assumptions. The rise of individualism, however, continued unchecked and while this found some expression in religious divisions and sectarianism, the age was to challenge the relevance of the Church to everyday people.

⑦ 1800–1900
THE VICTORIAN AGE

The influence of scientific discoveries caused the Christians much consternation. While some scientists remained Christian, the discoveries and influence of Darwin revealed the theological intellectual inadequacy of the Churches. There was no defence and the pace of secularism and the influence of ethical humanism spread rapidly.

⑧ 1900–2000
THE TWENTIETH CENTURY

Two world wars, increasing urbanisation and the lack of interest in religious matters caused the Churches to work together more effectively. Humanism was attractive because it offered ethical goals without the encumbrances of beliefs and archaic practices. The arrival in Britain of many people from non-Christian religions created a real plurality of beliefs in the country for the first time.

TIMELINE

3100 BC Stonehenge
(1) **3000 BC** Early beliefs in an afterlife
2750 BC Long Barrows built
2500 BC Woodhenge built
1400 BC Cremation begins
AD 51 Irish and Welsh Christianity develops
AD 400 Patrick preaches in Ireland
(2) **AD 597** Columba founds monastery on Iona
AD 598 Augustine of Canterbury brings Latin Christianity to Britain
AD 664 Hilda and the Synod of Whitby
AD 673 Venerable Bede records early history
AD 871 King Alfred encourages learning
(3) **1066** Normans begin building cathedrals
1093 Durham Cathedral begun
1200 Dominican and Franciscan monasteries established
1308 Scholar Duns Scotus teaches
1349 William of Ockham, radical scholar
1383 Lollards established
(4) **1400s** Individualism challenges the authority of the Church
(5) **1500** Beginnings of the Reformation in the British Isles
1534 Act of Supremacy denies supremacy of the pope
(6) **1600s** Rise of philosophy and sectarian thinking
1611 'Authorised' version of the Bible published
1620 Puritans sail to Massachusetts, where they set up a religious community
1650 Rise of the Quakers
1698 Society for the Promotion of Christian Knowledge established
1738 Conversion of the Wesleys
1797 Wilberforce publishes *A Practical View of Christianity*
(7) **1800s** Scientific discoveries lead to questioning of Christianity
1833 The Oxford movement
1843 John Stuart Mill publishes works on social issues
1859 *The Origin of Species* written by Charles Darwin
1879 Vicar of Oxford, John Henry Newman, becomes a Cardinal
1881 Francis Galton writes *Human Improvement Programme*
(8) **1900s** Rise of humanism
1946 Bertrand Russell writes *History of Western Philosophy*
1950 Hindus form 20 per cent of Leicester's population
1998 First Muslim school opened in England

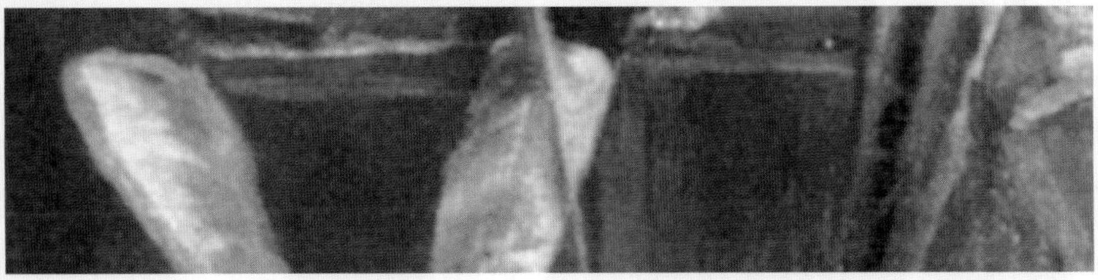

Mists of Time

3400–600 BC

THE BRITAIN OF THE pre-Roman era is shrouded in mystery. There are obvious signs of a coherent strain of thinking which could be called 'religious' stretching almost as far back as the evidence for *Homo sapiens* itself. In the twentieth century, however, the view held of religion in the West is of a structured and ordered community with an agreed set of beliefs and practices and of people to organise it, participate in it and 'run it'. This is not so in many other parts of the world where religious belief relies less upon literacy and the written revelation of a book (or books) but upon stories, drama, rites and practices. Such would have been the situation in Britain before the Romans, their gods, literacy and the Christian religion.

3400 BC
AVEBURY

The huge circle of stones at Avebury would comfortably fit three Stonehenges across its diameter. The stones are not dressed and provide a coarse contrast to the stones of Stonehenge. Only 76 stones of its original 600 or so survive today. While Stonehenge has gathered a greater popular currency, Avebury predates the stone circles of Stonehenge by several centuries. Like other such ancient relics, is not clear why it was built and probably never will be. Was Avebury a place where human beings were trying to live in harmony with the natural world? We may never know.

2750 BC
LONG BARROWS

Near to Avebury and overlooking the earth work and mysterious mound of Silbury Hill (built about 2750 BC), is the Long Barrow at West Kennet. Barrows served as burial places and West Kennet is one of the most significant memorials to the dead. The small areas inside the barrow are now empty but there is the smell of death about the place, not a chilling fear, but the simplicity of a resting place of lives well spent. To bury the dead, perhaps with some possessions or some protection, and/or food for the future, implies some sort of belief in a journey beyond this life. Is the need to bury the dead, the creation of ritual, and the gifts for an (unknown) future life the bedrock from which religious thinking emerges?

▲ *The huge monoliths at Stonehenge appear to be orientated towards the midsummer solstice, and are a huge attraction on this day every year.*

2500 BC
WOODHENGE

Situated two miles from Stonehenge, Woodhenge was a huge wooden hut laid out, like Stonehenge, with considerable expertise and oriented towards the summer solstice. In the centre of the wooden circle was a grave with a skeleton, axe and a

p. 218◀ **Triumphs & Tragedies** ▶p. 228

3100 BC
THE RELIGIOUS MEANING OF STONEHENGE

A feature of the twentieth-century Stonehenge is its size: it is a surprisingly small construction. It continues, however, to hold a fascination in the history of British culture. Probably begun in about 3100 BC, it developed in a number of stages and may have been in use until about 1100 BC. Stonehenge is likely to have been the focus for religious and ritual functions but beyond that it is difficult to be sure. What Stonehenge does is draw attention to the sophistication of those who planned and built it. The calculations necessary to order the stones, to understand the movement of the earth, sun and moon would have required careful observation of the skies. This suggests a thinking and sophisticated people, exploring fundamental religious and philosophical questions and reflecting on their place in the universe.

beaker, facing east. As with other sites, it is not clear how Woodhenge was used but, like Stonehenge and Avebury, it indicates the importance of social activity and intercourse. One aspect of religion that is common to all societies, is the urge to meet together at key times and share common concerns. It is possible that the Henges indicate the concern people had for fertility and/or for survival. They may act as a focal point for the worship of gods or nature, even an acknowledgement that people had to live in sympathy with the greater powers of nature.

1500 BC
BRYN CELLI DHU

The chambered cairn of Bryn Celli Dhu in Anglesey is a variation on the model of pre-historic burial monuments. It appears to be constructed as a series of circles. This may be significant for it would create a link with the circles, spirals, images and labyrinths common across Europe that act as a motif of eternal pilgrimage. The chamber is clearly a burial monument but it seems to link the

▲ *The stone circle at Avebury possesses an ancient and mysterious air.*

symbol of circles with that of the barrow. If the first signs of human culture are linked with burial rituals (going back 4–500,000 years BC) then there is a long history of belief in some form of existence after death. The placing of many bodies in a foetal position suggests a return to the 'birth state'; a preparation for a new birth place, perhaps.

1400 BC
BURIAL RITES

There appears to have been a change in burial rites in Northern Europe from about the thirteenth century BC. A change took place from burial (or placing the body in a barrow or tomb) to cremation. This may suggest a more sophisticated understanding of what awaited one after life on earth. The body would be burned and the ashes placed in a pot. A Bronze Age etching on a piece of pottery shows a chariot being used in a funeral. It is drawn by two horses and preceded by a horse being led by a handler. The chariot bears the ashes of the dead person in a container. The analogy to some forms of modern state funerals is clear. It is likely the horse would have belonged to the dead person and have been sacrificed.

↗ ▶ p. 234

600 BC
CELTIC SOCIETY AND THE DRUIDS

The Celts became a powerful influence across parts of Europe around 600 BC. A society was created in which people were bound to each other by obligations, duties and responsibilities. There was a priesthood, the members of which, owing to the pre-literate nature of the society, were probably story tellers and organisers of ritual and tradition. The religion, Druidism, was probably the religion of the Celts in Britain but it appears to have been linked with the sun and moon worship of previous ages as well. Old faiths were adapted to meet new needs and newer religions. 'They [the Gaulish nation] employ the Druids as ministers for such sacrifices [human] because they think that, unless the life of man be repaid for the life of man, the will of the immortal gods cannot be appeased,' wrote Caesar in his *De Bello Gallico BK VI.*

✶ ▶ p. 229

600 BC
SPREAD OF IDEAS

The Celts adapted many of their ideas from their contemporaries in the south of Europe. The archeology of earlier periods shows there was considerable movement of peoples exchanging new ideas and new practices. It is not possible to know much of

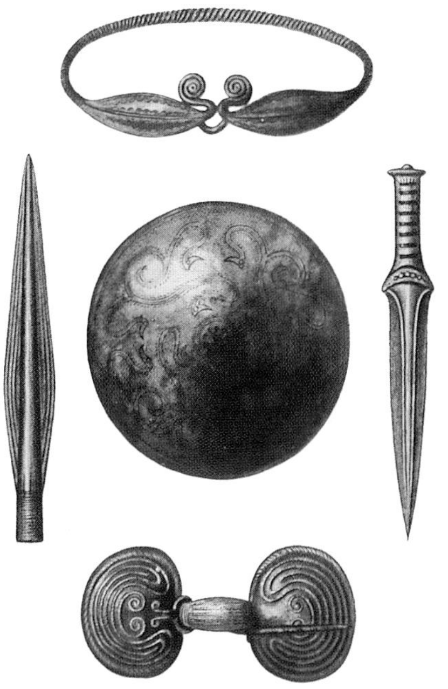

▲ *The engravings on relics from the Bronze Age are often well-preserved enough to tell their own story.*

the religious beliefs of Neolithic, Bronze and Iron Age peoples; we can only draw inferences from their creation of quoits, henges and barrows and how they buried their dead. Movements in the skies, tides and seasons affected them. Human sacrifice was not unknown as a feature of some rituals and that sacrifice would have been for, or to, something. Religion in a pre-literate society was a social tool, welding together through story and ritual the diverse needs of society. This is most potent in the ritual surrounding death.

p. 221 ◀ **Distant Voices** ▶ p. 227

The first major step in laying bare the moon's secrets was the realisation that it works to a cycle of 18.61 years. The Greeks had discovered that by the fifth century BC; ... the intellectual miracle of Stonehenge is the evidence that its first builders had discovered it two thousand years earlier.'

The Enigma of Stonehenge, by John Fowles and Barry Bruboge

The Advent of Christianity

AD 300–500s

IT IS NOT KNOWN when Christianity first came to Britain. The first mention of Christians in Britain is in the writings of Tertullian (*c.* AD 200). Origen, another early Church leader, writing 40 years later, says that Christianity can be found in Britain, but there is little evidence until the fourth century AD. Certainly by AD 314 three bishops, of York, London and probably Colchester, attended a council at Arles, but none went to the great Council of Nicaea in AD 325. Symbols indicating a Christian presence have been discovered in various archeological investigations and it is certain that there were a number of wealthy Christians in Britain by the middle of the fourth century. It was a scattered presence lacking in charismatic leadership of the type found in other parts of Europe.

▶ p. 230 **AD 300s**

EVIDENCE FOR CHRISTIANITY

Christians have left little evidence of their presence in Britain during these years. The Chi-Rho symbol appears on some mosaics and silverware, though it is occasionally found in the midst of pagan or pre-Christian symbols. The Chi-Rho sign was used as a symbol by Christians because the Chi and the Rho are the first two letters of 'Christ' in Greek. The great monuments to Romano-Christian religion are found in the mosaics of Frampton and Hinton St Mary and the wall paintings of Lullingstone; but otherwise the evidence is patchy. One cemetery in Dorset suggests a large wealthy Christian community – but other cemeteries revealed nothing.

▶ p. 227 **AD 304**

THE MARTYRDOM OF ST ALBAN

The first Christian known to have been martyred in Britain is recorded as Alban. The Venerable Bede, writing hundreds of years later, says he was a layman from the city of Verulamium and had given shelter to a Christian priest fleeing from persecution, but the first reference to the 'blessed martyr Alban' occurs in about AD 480. While he hid the priest, they talked and Alban was converted to Christianity. The story tells that when the soldiers came to arrest the priest Alban wrapped the priest's cloak around himself and was martyred in his place. Legend says his death (probably in AD 304) took place on the hill where St Alban's abbey church now stands. Bede also refers to the martyrdoms of Aaron and Julius at Caerleon in Gwent and of many more.

▲ *The Venerable Bede, whose writings provide some of the earliest records of religion in Britain's ancient times.*

▶ p. 233 **AD 312**

THE EDICT OF MILAN

The Edict of Milan was the obvious consequence of the Constantine's succession to the title of Emperor and his conversion to Christianity. For three hundred years Christianity had been an illicit religion and had suffered severe persecution. Like all 'new religions' it had also suffered periods of unpopularity. Now, for the first time, Christians could be open about their commitment and rapid advances could be made. The evidence for such advance, while rich in other European countries, is thin in Britain. In AD 359 British bishops attended the Council of Rimini but could not pay their own expenses. This suggests the Church in Britain was poor and not well organised, with members drawn from the less wealthy members of the community.

AD 397

NINIAN

'Nynia, a most venerable and holy man, of the nation of the Britons, who had been instructed properly in the faith and the mysteries of the truth at Rome,' so Bede describes the first bishop to live among the Picts in Cumberland and southern Scotland. He studied in Rome and may have returned to Britain as early as AD 397. What is known of him is found in Bede's work more that 300 years later and the twelfth-century writings of Ailred of Rievaulx so it is difficult to be certain about the details of his teaching and history. He did found a monastery at Whithorn in Galloway, which came to be known as the 'White House'. This became the base for Ninian and his monks' evangelistic mission up into the east coastal area of Scotland.

▶ p. 240 **AD 400s**

PELAGIUS

Pelagius is the only Briton, apart from Alban, of this early period who has a discernible personality. His name is associated with the heresy of Pelagianism: Pelagius objected to the emphasis put on the complete sinfulness of human beings so their only chance of salvation was through the grace and forgiveness of God. He had a strong faith in the inherent possibility of each person to reach perfection without the intervention of God's grace. He left Britain as a young man and never returned, but his message was brought to his homeland by

▲ *St Patrick, who was made Bishop of Ireland in* AD *430.*

Agricola early in the fifth century. Pelagius was condemned and excommunicated by the pope. Though an unorthodox Christian he foreshadowed the rise of ethical humanism, albeit in a Christian context, and the struggle of the British with the Christian doctrine of Original Sin.

AD 429
AFTER PELAGIUS

So concerned were the authorities in Gaul that two bishops, Germanus Bishop of Auxerre (AD 418–48) and Lupus, Bishop of Troyes (AD 427–79) were asked to go to Britain to introduce some discipline into the Romano-British church. They arrived in 429 and, among other things, visited the shrine of St Alban. They preached against the liberal teachings of Pelagius 'not only in the churches but also at the cross roads and in the fields and lanes'. Germanus had been a fighting man and obviously had great strength of character. He appears to have found the British timid and lacking in self-confidence, although the implications of Pelagius' teaching suggests a people at peace with itself and able to take a relaxed view of human nature.

▶ p. 228

AD 430
PATRICK

Patrick's family, who lived near the sea in Bannavern, were attacked one day and Patrick was taken to Ireland by pirates. His birth place isn't known though there are various English and Welsh claimants. He looked after cattle before escaping to Gaul. He received a vision asking him to return to Ireland and in about AD 430 he was made a bishop for the Irish. He seems to have travelled over most of northern and central Ireland during the next 30 years. He tried to introduce a diocesan form of government but the rural nature of the country defeated him. Although the hymn the 'Breastplate of St Patrick' has long been popular, the earliest known version was three centuries after Patrick's death.

▶ p. 228

AD 500S
IRISH AND WELSH CHRISTIANITY

The Celts adopted the Christian faith with enthusiasm. In spite of Christianity having been carried to them by the Roman invasion, the Celts rejected neither the Latin language nor the importance of the Bishop of Rome. The period began a flowering of Celtic civilisation which lasted for hundreds of years, often characterised in England as the 'Dark Ages'. In Wales and Ireland monks were the custodians of the Bible, copying manuscripts and serving as the base for missionary activity. As far as is known, the Irish monks played a prominent role in the conversion of England. In Wales, David (*c.* AD 520–588) was an abbot-bishop and was supported by Deiniol and Illtyd. But the energy of Christians in Wales did not match the missionary zeal of the Irish during this period.

▼ *Simple wooden crosses and crucifixes adorned the churches built across the British Isles in ancient times.*

p. 225◀ **Distant Voices** ▶p. 229

Christ shield me this day:
Christ be with me,
Christ before me,
Christ behind me,
Christ in me,
Christ beneath me.

From 'The Breastplate of St Patrick'

The Conversion of England

AD 597–710

POPE GREGORY, apparently moved by the sight of British slaves in Rome, asked Augustine to go to Britain. He led an expedition to evangelise the nation. The mission would have enormous consequences for the history of Britain for the reverberations of Augustine's landing echo down the centuries. The nature of Christianity in Britain would change and there would be a more organised and coherent church, which would both support and criticise the leadership be it chieftain or king. The very different organisational style of the Celtic church would be muted and never be fully absorbed into the dominant power of Roman Christianity. The conversion of Britain began in AD 597, which was as a pebble tossed into a pool from which ripples continued for well over a thousand years.

▶ p. 230 **AD 597**

AUGUSTINE OF CANTERBURY

A monk of Whitby writing between AD 704 and 714 tells us in his life of Pope Gregory that when the saint-to-be saw two Angles (from Britain) he thought they looked like angels. True or not, it was a turning point, for Latin Christianity was to come to Britain in 597 in the person of Augustine. On Augustine's arrival he was met by King Ethelbert who had a Christian wife and some sympathy for the Christian faith. The king was baptised and other conversions followed rapidly. Gregory wrote in July 598 that 10,000 English had been baptised on Christmas Day. Augustine was made a Bishop. Such enthusiasm for the faith may have been encouraged by weariness with the Teutonic gods but more certainly by a keen interest to link with mainland Europe.

p. 224◀ **Triumphs & Tragedies** ▶p. 232

AD 635

AIDAN AND THE MISSION TO THE NORTH

Aidan came from Iona and set up a monastery on the island of Lindisfarne in around AD 635. He travelled widely, often with King Oswald who was happy to act as his interpreter. Fervent and enthusiastic, he was rarely in his monastery until the fusion of church and state ceased when Oswald was killed in battle in 642. Aidan died in 651 and his monastery continued and perhaps flowered under Cuthbert (634–687). A shepherd boy, Cuthbert became Bishop of Lindisfarne. He loved to fast and lived an austere life, and behaving more like a monk than a bishop. He knew the church in England would have to fall into line with the rest of western Christianity but he was a true Celt, worthy of its tradition.

▲ *The ruins of the monastery on the holy island of Lindisfarne, built by St Aidan.*

▶ p. 232 **AD 597**

THE INFLUENCE OF COLUMBA

'A typical Irishman, vehement, irresistible, hear him curse the niggardly rich man or bless the heifers of a poor peasant'. Colum (or Columba) was a powerful, irresistible force. His name means 'dove' but there was more of the lion about him. Of princely birth, he later chose to become a monk. His involvement in a battle over the ownership of a manuscript caused him to leave Ireland and sail to Iona, where he was out of sight of Ireland and less tempted to return home. Life was austere in the monastery he founded but it became a stepping stone for missionary work in Scotland and the Isles. He met the Druids and 'Christ is my Druid' was his weapon against them. He died just after Augustine landed in Kent in AD 597 and the 'conversion of England' was to begin.

▶ p. 230 **AD 601**

EARLY PROBLEMS

Augustine wrote to Pope Gregory, in about AD 601, regarding a number of ecclesiastical problems. Pope Gregory wanted to lay down the principle that church income should be divided into four: to the bishop, to the priest, to the poor and to the upkeep of the church. Gregory also wanted to divide England into two provinces, each with an archbishop and 12 suffragans. Gregory's mistake was to affirm Augustine's authority over the other British bishops, who had battled hard to keep England Christian during the heathen days, and were consequently not amused to be ruled by an outsider. There was resentment with papal imposition and a refusal to co-operate with Rome over various issues. Augustine's success has been questioned, for much of Kent appears to have remained vigorously pagan, as indeed much of England did before the eighth to ninth centuries.

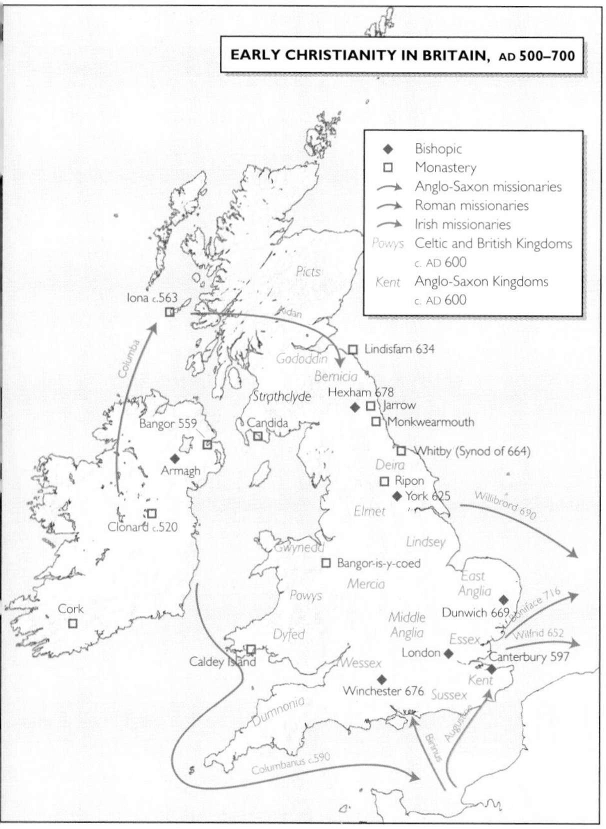

AD 625
THE NEW RELIGION SPREADS

The spread of Roman Christianity was closely associated with politics: Ethelbert persuaded Redwald, king of the East Angles, to be baptised but, according to Bede, on his return his wife told him to ignore his conversion; he was simply to set up a Christian altar alongside the pagan one in his temple. This semi-Christian attitude is important. The discovery of a major burial site at Sutton Hoo in Suffolk, probably dated AD 625, may well be that of Redwald. It is a magnificent pagan burial site but not obviously, or even apparently, Christian. Did Redwald forgo his Christian conversion? Was he a pagan king who happened to become, for whatever reason, in part a Christian? Paganism continued to exist beside and in the midst of the 'new' religion.

AD 625
MISSIONS MOVE OUT

Augustine had been joined by another Italian monk, Paulinus, in around AD 601. He became a bishop in 625 and went north with Ethelburga when she married Edwin, king of Numbria. Edwin was not a Christian but prepared to show a willing concern for the faith of his new bride, and was later converted in 627 at York. Paulinus travelled widely. His preaching and teaching were so successful he was made archbishop in 634. However, then the situation changed: Edwin was killed, a new political alliance was forged and Paulinus fled south. Only James the Deacon carried on. Obviously royal patronage was the key to evangelism. If the king was not in sympathy, the missionaries' lives were forfeited and conversions quickly evaporated.

✶ ▶ p. 238 **AD 664**
HILDA AND THE SYNOD OF WHITBY

The issue of Celtic and Roman Christianity was brought to the fore in AD 663 when Oswy, king of Northumbria, became aware he would be celebrating Easter when his wife, who was a Roman Christian, would be keeping her Lent fast. A Synod was called at Whitby under the supervision of its abbess, Hilda, in 644. When Oswy came down in favour of the Roman Christians 'with a smile', it was clear Christianity in Britain would be allied to Rome. This would remain the case for nearly 900 years. Hilda, who ruled over the double monastery (male and female) at Hartlepool and Whitby, until her death in 680, showed how devotion to the new religion could capture powerful, outstanding women. She promoted education, and social welfare for the young, old and destitute.

AD 710
THE END OF THE ANGLO-SAXON PERIOD

The period of the mid-660s was a turning point in Christian belief and practice in Britain. Although the Celts returned to their lands and continued with their enthusiasm and zeal, the church was now organised under one primate in Rome and a more forceful, coherent pattern of government could begin. In 672, a Synod at Hertford established the first canons for church government. Wilfred was bishop for 40 years and although he had championed the Roman cause at Whitby, he was not a prelate to sit quietly after his victory. He built churches at Hexham and Ripon, with monks living under the austere rule of St Benedict. When he died in 710 he had symbolised the new, young energetic and aristocratic church that was to develop.

▲ *Hilda at the Synod of Whitby, where issues of Celtic and Roman Christianity were discussed.*

p. 227◀ **Distant Voices** ▶p. 231

Thus was fulfilled the prophecy of the holy Bishop Augustine that those perfidious men (the Welsh) should be punished by temporal death because they had despised the offer of eternal salvation.

An astonishing verdict on the Celtic tradition, which had maintained Christianity in Britain for almost 400 years, from Bede's *Ecclesiastical History* (*c.* AD 730)

Consolidation

AD 650–943

THE WORKS OF THE great saints resulted in the evangelisation of parts of northern Europe and in the monasteries, particularly in the Celtic monasteries, there was a flowering of art and poetry. This is no doubt, however, that the conversion of England did not happen overnight and the mixing of Christian beliefs and practices with pre-Christian rites and rituals was common. Augustine brought a new perspective to Christian thinking but in practice the link between politics and religion would remain as strong as it has ever been. In England the figure of a Christian King Alfred would be of enormous importance for the self-confidence of the country.

▶ p. 232 **AD 650–850**

ART AND ARCHITECTURE

The *Lindisfarne Gospels* (late seventh to early eighth century), now in the British Museum, are thought to have been written in Lindisfarne in honour of St Cuthbert. Illuminated in red, blue, green, yellow and purple, the document is a spectacular tribute to the skill of Eadfrith and provides an insight into the links between Celtic and Christian imagery. Other remarkable manuscripts are the *Codex Anniatinus* (from Jarrow or Wearmouth early eighth century) and the *Book of Kells* (eighth century). The latter has links with the monks from Iona who fled to Kells from their island because of Viking raids in the early eighth century. Great churches were built in the late seventh century but probably the most remarkable example in southern Britain is at Brixworth, 'perhaps the most imposing architectural memorial of the seventh century yet surviving north of the Alps'.

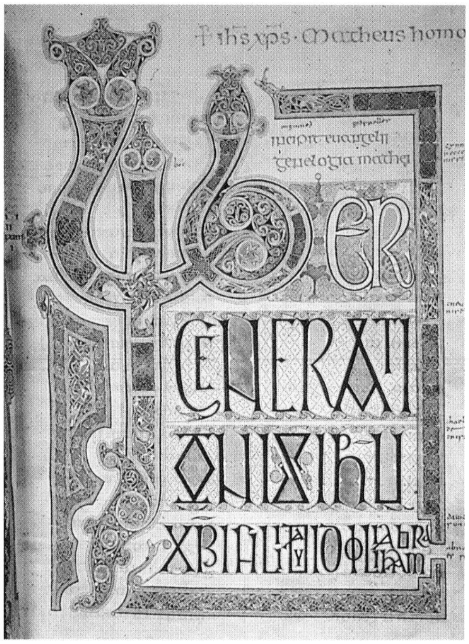

▲ *The* Lindisfarne Gospels, *which demonstrate an important link between Celtic and Christian imagery.*

▶ p. 238 **AD 669**

THEODORE

Theodore (AD 603–690) was born in Tarsus and came to England in AD 669 at the age of 66. As Archbishop of Canterbury he set about organising the church and through the use of various synods, brought an unusual unity to the Church in England. He was, Bede says, the first Archbishop whom the whole Church obeyed. He was a man of profound wisdom and tireless energy and in *Penitentiale* he handed down judgement on varied but common, moral problems such as drunkenness, fornication, matrimonial questions etc. Theodore presided over part of what has been regarded as one of the most brilliant centuries of the Church. He left the church self-confident and well organised, very different from the confused and drifting church of the mid-seventh century.

AD 670–850

POETRY, SONGS AND HYMNS

'The Dream of the Rood' (early eighth century) is one of the first Anglo-Saxon poems. The image of the cross is central to the dream and it is, as it is in all Christian theology, the symbol of triumph. Caedmon (AD 670), a monk of Whitby, was the first Englishman to compose religious poems and managed to link secular poetry based on the war-lords with praise to God's creation. His tradition was carried on by Cynewolf (*c.* AD 750). But while later poems are more sophisticated than Caedmon's, most are anonymous and draw on Teutonic heroic paganism. Popularly Christian images, visual and verbal, were often clothed in pagan language. Assimilation and synectism may have made the Christian missionary monk less threatening than he might at first have seemed.

▶ p. 233 **AD 678**

EVANGELISATION

The Synod of Whitby encouraged the exchange between Britain and parts of southern Europe. Wilfred (AD 678–9) went to the Frisians and Willibrord from Ripon built a cathedral in Utrecht and became Archbishop in 695. He was followed by Wepefred from Devon, better known as Boniface. He sailed away in 718, when not yet 40, and never returned. He was martyred in 754 in Dokkum Germany having become Archbishop of Mainz in 745. 'On every hand is struggle and grief' he wrote,' fighting without a fear within. Worst of all, the treachery of the false brethren surpasses the malice of unbelieving pagans'. Two hundred years later, English missionaries shared in expeditions to Scandinavia.

AD 720

THE VENERABLE BEDE

'A candle of the church, lit by the Holy Spirit' and 'the father of English historians' are two tributes to the work of the Venerable Bede (AD 673–735). He entered Wearmouth monastery at the age of seven, but in a year or two was transferred to Jarrow which, apart from visits to Lindisfarne or York, he never left. He was renowned as a scholar, a theologian, historian, scientist and poet. His book *Ecclesiastical History of the English People* (AD 720) is extremely important for knowledge of the history of the Church in England during and before his time. He believed passionately in unity and while he travelled little he was concerned that although political unity did not exist, there should be Catholic uniformity in the church.

▲ *The scholar, theologian, historian and scientist, the Venerable Bede.*

◉ ▶ p. 232

AD 804

THE INFLUENCE OF ALCUIN

Relations were not always easy between church and state. Tensions existed between leaders spiritual and temporal and some saw the growing wealth of the church as a temptation. One outstanding scholar of the period was Alcuin (*c.* AD 735–804). He was a pupil then a teacher at the cathedral school in York but never became a priest. He travelled widely and impressed Emperor Charlemagne who appointed him to run his Palace school in Aachen. Later he became Abbot of Tours and died in AD 804. His influence on the development of the Christian liturgy was enormous. Alcuin brought uniformity to the services of the church indeed his influence is till felt in the churches today. He was the dominant intellectual of late-eighth century Europe. 'My name was Alcuin, and wisdom was always dear to me' is his epitaph.

▲ *King Alfred the Great, dividing up the kingdom into separate provinces.*

AD 871

ALFRED AND AFTER

Alfred was born in AD 848 and came to the throne in 871. While 'England' did not exist as such at this time, Alfred fought through his difficulties and by his death in 899 peace was established, learning was on the increase and religious life was being re-built. He came to literacy late in life but founded a Palace school and encouraged the nobles to educate their sons. He learned Latin and translated Pope Gregory's book of advice on pastoral care and various other ecclesiastical works including Bede's *Ecclesiastical History.* He insisted that priests had to have a good Latin education if they were to hold high office. It is not easy to evaluate the success of Alfred's work but he was the leader who met the needs of the time. He, as a Christian king, gave hope to the nation.

AD 943

DUNSTAN

Dunstan was born in AD 909 and became a powerful archbishop. Educated by Irish monks in Glastonbury, he became Abbot in *c.* 943 – this has been seen as 'a turning point in the history of religion in England'. He set about establishing other monasteries based on the Rule of St Benedict. In about 970 a meeting was held to modify the Benedictine Rule to the English situation. Dunstan became Archbishop of Canterbury from 960–88 and revitalised monasteries. Many monks became bishops and he created a framework of monastic and church government which remained in place until the Reformation. Another powerful prelate, Wulfstan, Bishop of London then of York and Worcester, in 1002 wrote 'The Institutes of Policy' idealising the king as 'Christ's substitute'.

p. 229◀ **Distant Voices** ▶p. 233

If anyone who is a bishop or an ordained man shall be a habitual drunkard, let him either cease to be so or deposed. If a monk make himself sick through drinking let him do penance for thirty days.

Opening of *Peniteniale*, Archbishop Theodore (AD 670)

The Norman Influence

1070–1221

WILLIAM I WISHED the English Church to be brought more into line with church life in Europe. As the Norman period developed, however, the seeds of discontent were sown: there were struggles for power; the wealth of the church was attractive to the state; and the English Church began to produce thinkers and bishops of considerable intellect. The building of cathedrals testify to the wealth of their sponsors but they are also theological statements of power and authority. The *Domesday Book* indicates the village priest was usually of peasant stock and very unlikely to be celibate but by the late thirteenth century married clergy were the exception. There certainly was a rise in education during the twelfth and thirteenth centuries and by the end of this period there had been a huge diversification of religious orders catering for every need.

◉ ▶ p. 234

1070
LANFRANC

Lafranc (*c.* 1010–89) became Archbishop of Canterbury in 1070 and had been well known to William as Abbot of Caen. His first task was to ensure the primacy of Canterbury over the archbishop of York. Having done this he set out to reform the church. The English Church was not as keen on celibacy as the Pope would have liked and Lanfranc recognised this. Over the next century or so celibate (or at least unmarried) clergy became the norm. Lanfranc re-organised the Episcopal sees to be centred in larger towns and separated ecclesiastical justice (Canon Law) from civil justice. On William's death in 1087 the church was strong, enjoying good relationships with bishops in Scotland, Ireland and Normandy.

▲ *The murder of Thomas Becket in Canterbury Cathedral where he was seeking sanctuary; a shrine to the saint still stands where he was killed.*

p. 228◀ **Triumphs & Tragedies** ▶p. 236

1170
BECKET AND HENRY II

'Will no one rid me of this turbulent priest?' This question is dramatically associated with the death of Thomas Becket (*c.* 1118–1170). A Londoner of Norman stock, he had been Archdeacon of Canterbury when Henry II made him chancellor of England in 1155. When the post of Archbishop of Canterbury fell vacant, Henry insisted Becket be consecrated and he was made Archbishop on 3 June 1162. Not long after, Becket became an opponent of the king, yielding nothing to him; even the Pope warned him to take a more conciliatory tone. Becket eventually fled in fear of his life and spent five years in exile, but he returned in 1170 to face his enemies at court. On 29 December 1170 Becket was murdered in his own cathedral.

⚔ ▶ p. 237

1093
ANSELM

Anselm (1034–1109) was an Italian-born theologian, with little experience of practical affairs and seemed an unlikely choice as Archbishop of Canterbury in 1093. He was, however, a true revolutionary and the first great theologian of medieval Europe. His most famous, *Cur Deus Homo*, written in exile in 1098, asks 'why did God become man?' and the answer 'Because it was necessary'. If God's honour was not satisfied then man's soul would be left to the devils. Only by God becoming human and sacrificing himself could mankind be saved. On a more practical level, Anselm believed the pope as head of the church on earth had to take precedence over every earthly ruler. He won his argument with Henry I but the price was growing papal control, and more trouble ahead.

◩ ▶ p. 237

1100s
BUILDING CATHEDRALS

In medieval England there were 19 cathedrals, often containing holy relics or the remains of saints. Cathedrals like St Paul's that were not linked to monasteries, frequently used the nave for all sorts of secular purposes. The cathedral, however, was where the bishop's throne was and therefore had status over perhaps grander churches in the same diocese. Durham Cathedral, built in the early twelfth century, had Romanesque pillars and arches. What the cathedrals provided was undoubtedly great art and they helped to unify the nation but, most importantly perhaps, these massive beautiful buildings reminded mere mortals of their frailty and the power and authority of the church.

1100s
THE INTELLECTUAL ADVANCE

Probably the most distinguished scholar of the twelfth century was John of Salisbury

▲ *The interior of St Paul's; since the cathedral was not directly associated with the monastery, it may have been used for secular purposes.*

(*c.* 1120–80), who had a wide knowledge of literature. He reflected his humanism in his book, *Policratious*; here he tried to form a picture of the ideal state, in which spiritual and temporal power were held in perfect union. Robert Grosseteste (*c.* 1168) was a scientist and a Christian, later to become Bishop of Lincoln. Grosseteste has been called the first great English scientist and philosopher. Roger Bacon (*c.* 1215–92) was not a systematic thinker, but argued for the possibility of submarines, self-propelling boats and flying machines. He was a symbol of new thinking in the Church. Even people who could not read were aware they were living in a world of growing literacy, new ideas and new visions.

☆ ▶ p. 239

1208
TIMES OF TENSION

The thirteenth century had witnessed the Church in England becoming locked into a formal organisation. In the following century, while the popes had been able to develop a very effective form of central government, almost a state within a state, the clergy and the nobility drifted apart. When King John was excommunicated for six years (1208–14) the clergy responded. The church doors were closed, there was no sacrament, marriages were not solemnised and no-one was buried in consecrated ground. When Edward I became king in 1272 he sought to reduce the power of the Church and legislate against it. Edward wanted money for his battles, the clergy refused to pay and consequently the king outlawed them in 1297.

▶ p. 233

1220s
THE FRIARS

The origins of the friars are probably rooted in the new interest in learning and the consequences of the Crusades. Men were returning from the Holy Land with ideas, beliefs and ways of living which challenged the existing orthodoxy. First the Order of Preachers was formed by St Dominic, then soon after, the Friars Minor or Franciscans by St Francis. They arrived in Britain in the 1220s and were supported by the king. They suffered hardships in the early days but were, generally accepted by the townspeople. The Dominicans established a footing in the academic world and gathered a group of scholars around them. The Franciscans, too, built up a famous school of theologians including Duns Scotus and William of Ockham.

1221
GROWTH OF MONASTICISM

By the early fourteenth century there were 900 monastic houses and about 17,500 monks and nuns. In the eleventh century all houses were Benedictine; by the thirteenth century there were a variety of houses to choose from. Now people took monastic vows because they wished to and they could choose which type of life they preferred, teacher, ascetic, contemplative etc. In the twelfth century, a new form of religious life came into being. Mendicant friars, not responsible to diocese or bishop, could cross boundaries of parish, diocese and country. The first mendicants to arrive were the Dominicans in 1221 to be followed in 1224 by the Franciscans, then the Carmelites. The liberty of the friars and religious orders was, in part, forged in the conflict to give the pope supremacy over kings and princes.

▲ *St Francis, the founder of the Friars Minor, or Franciscan order of monks.*

p. 231◀ **Distant Voices** ▶p. 235

Archbishops, bishops, and persons of the realm are not allowed to depart from the Kingdom without leave of the Lord the King; and if they do depart, they shall, if the King so please, give security [they will not] seek the ill or damage of the Lord the King or realm.

Constitutions of Clarendon, Article 4 (1164)

The Growth of Learning

1300–1516

THE FOURTEENTH CENTURY was not an easy century for the British. Added to weaknesses in government and church and a general lack of leadership, was the Black Death (1348–50). There was, however, an emerging intellectual tradition. People like Wyclif, Ockham and later Thomas More, showed that the tide of questioning and new learning was not left on the shores of the English Channel. Christians throughout Europe were deeply influenced by the work of Thomas Aquinas (1225–74), 'the Angelic Doctor'. Aquinas knew that ultimately the truth would lie in the Catholic faith; not all agreed but his influence was, and is, enormous. The fourteenth century also produced mystical writers of distinction to guide English-reading Christians.

↗ ▶ p. 241

1300s
CIVIC UNREST

Wars had created a financial vacuum: the money had run out. Over-population was a menace, there was famine; and in the middle of the century, the hand of the Black Death lay on the land. Hundreds of thousands died. The fascination with death, a characteristic of the Middle Ages, was rooted in the plague. How could the exchequer be fed? Create a poll tax of a shilling a head and make the poor pay as much as the rich! Church and state were attacked and the monks who controlled civic life were pressed to allow more freedom. Unusually, the revolt found support in the teaching and person of John Wyclif (*c.* 1328–84). The pressure that had built up in society found an expression in Wyclif and a release in the growing body of literature of the century.

1300s
WRITERS AND MYSTICS

The fourteenth century marked the appearance of mystical writings. Richard Rolle (*c.* 1300–49) was a hermit, considered mad by his friends and close relatives. His most famous work *The Fire of Love* (1343) encouraged delight in private prayer. *The Cloud of Unknowing* appeared about 1350; this was an anonymous work, absorbed with the transcendence of God living in a 'dark cloud of unknowing'. If Walter Hilton's (d. 1396) *The Ladder of Perfection* reminded the reader of the performance of everyday duties in honour of God, the *Revelations of Divine Love* by Lady Julian of Norwich (*c.* 1343–1413) represented all the best elements of English mysticism. The book is based on 'showings' or revelations. Her work expresses her all-enquiring faith in the message of Christ.

◉ ▶ p. 245

1308
THE INFLUENCE OF DUNS SCOTUS

Duns Scotus (*c.* 1270–1308), known as the 'Subtle Doctor', is probably best remembered for giving us the 'Dunce's cap', which is a most unworthy epitaph. He was born in Scotland and became a Franciscan. His genius lies in his meticulous dissection of arguments and the novelty of his mind. Though influenced by the great Thomas Aquinas, he rarely mentions him and attacks less eminent opponents. He was a Pelagian, believing in free will and the essential goodness of human kind. Scotus was interested in evidence, for example, the kinds of things that can be known without proof. There were, he said, three kinds: principles by themselves; things known by experience; and our own actions; but without divine illumination we can know nothing. Most Franciscans followed Duns Scotus's teaching rather than that of Aquinas who was a Dominican.

1349
THE INFLUENCE OF WILLIAM OF OCKHAM

After Thomas Aquinas, William of Ockham (*c.* 1290–1349) was the most important of the schoolmen. The phrase 'Entities are not to be multiplied without necessity' is not found in his works but captures the spirit of his philosophy. i.e. 'if everything in some science can be interpreted without assuming this or that hypothetical entity, there is no ground for assuming it.' By insisting the possibility of studying logic and human knowledge without reference to metaphysics or theology, Ockham's work encouraged scientific research. Aquinas, the Great Teacher, may have been a theologian but Ockham, as far as logic was concerned, was a secular philosopher. He was the last of the scholastics and the forerunner of a theological revolution. He probably died in the plague epidemic of 1349.

▲ *John Wyclif, condemned by the pope following his accusation that he was the anti-Christ.*

1377
JOHN WYCLIF

The life of Wyclif (*c.* 1328–84) illustrates the diminished authority of the pope; so much so that Wyclif has been called the 'morning star of the Reformation'. He taught in Oxford and until the mid-1370s was quite orthodox, being driven to 'heresy' eventually through his concern for the poor and a horror of worldly ecclesiastics. He was condemned by the pope (1377) who was deeply wounded by Wyclif's claim that the pope was the 'anti-christ'. The Bible was translated in the last few years of his life and he appealed to it over the heads of ecclesiastical authority. He did not condemn the Great Revolt of 1381 and was perhaps the only university intellectual to inspire a popular movement against the Church – the Lollards. After the Council of Constance (1414–17) his bones were dug up and burned.

▶ p. 236

1430 THE LOLLARDS

When Wyclif died he left behind a group of followers who were ready to face martyrdom in the propagation of their faith. The Lollards, the name is probably taken from Lollaer which means ' to mumble (prayers)', consisted of educated laymen and some disgruntled clergy who were very critical of the Church and the unworthiness of many of its clergy. Henry IV ascended the throne and supported those pursuing heresy; almost immediately William Sawtre, a leading Lollard, was burned to death. The movement was strongest in the Welsh borders and the industrial towns of the Midlands. They insisted on the Bible being available to the laity, and biblical preaching as well as objecting to ecclesiastical authority. In that sense they prefigured Reformation and English Protestantism.

▲ *Prisoners in the Lollards Tower.*

1499 JOHN COLET AND DESIDERIUS ERASMUS

John Colet (1466–1519) tended to be critical of the state of morality in the country but still managed to be popular and well-liked. He founded St Paul's school for 153 poor boys in 1509. His emphasis on the unity of divine truth, concern for historical context and his literal approach to texts excited Desiderius Erasmus and, no doubt, influenced Thomas More. Erasmus (1466–1536) was born in Rotterdam, became a monk in his childhood and regretted it! He became friends with More and Colet on his arrival in England in 1499. His best known work *In Praise of Folly* (1514), was written in More's house and is a witty satire on lay and ecclesiastical society. His studies on the text of the Bible influenced scholars for many generations but, surprisingly, he did not welcome the Protestant Reformation.

▲ *Desiderius Erasmus, whose works were satires on both secular and ecclesiastical society.*

1516 THOMAS MORE'S *UTOPIA*

Thomas More's (1478–1535) book *Utopia* (1516) was an astonishingly liberal response to the world in which More lived. In the book, a group of pagans live on a remote island, following the principles of natural virtue. There is an implied preaching of the virtues of community, support for religious toleration and for a mild criminal law. More is often characterised as the ideal 'Renaissance Man', but he was a traditionalist in many ways. He attended Mass daily, sang in his local church choir and used a wooden block as a pillow. He was 'the king's good servant but God's first' and was opposed to the divorce of Henry VIII from Catherine of Aragon. When he would not take the oath acknowledging Henry's supremacy over the pope, he was executed in 1535.

p. 233◀ **Distant Voices** ▶p. 237

Give me, good Lord, a humble, lowly, quiet, peaceable, patient, charitable, kind, tender and pitiful mind; with all my works and words and all my thoughts to have a taste of the holy blessed spirit!

Thomas More (1478–1535)

The English Reformation
1515–1603

THE SIXTEENTH CENTURY was one of brutality and heroism. Martyrdom was not just of the great and the good but ordinary village folk. The religious beliefs in England, Scotland, Wales and Ireland were deeply affected by the religious turmoil in mainland Europe. The three great personalities of the Reformation and the Counter-Reformation were Martin Luther (1483–1546), John Calvin (1509–64) and Ignatius Loyala (1491–1556). The success of Luther and Calvin had unintentionally been prepared for by both Christian humanists and the political situation in Europe. Ireland rejected Protestantism, Scotland received it and England and Wales emerged with a form of bridge between the two. While no great philosophers emerged during the sixteenth century there was a flowering of creativity: William Byrd, Edmund Spencer and, of course, William Shakespeare.

1515
HENRY VIII AND THOMAS WOLSEY

Henry VIII (1401–1547) appointed Thomas Wolsey (1475–1530) as lord chancellor and chief councillor in 1515, and the pope made Wolsey legate for life. There were, however, signs of dissent in England: frustrated with excesses of the clergy, the rise of Christian humanism, anti-clericalism (smouldering in western Europe for centuries) and the ban on the availability of the Bible in English. To this was added the king's divorce. Henry, therefore, passed laws so that all temporal and ecclesiastical authority lay with him, the 'Supreme Head of the Church of England', for purely political reasons. Wolsey co-operated with all the king's wishes but when he was not able to secure the king's divorce from the queen, he was deprived of his chancellorship and arrested on a charge of high treason. He died on his way to the trial.

▲ *Cardinal Thomas Wolsey, Lord Chancellor and chief councillor to Henry VIII; Wolsey soon fell from favour with the king.*

p. 232◀ **Triumphs & Tragedies** ▶p. 242

1535
THE DISSOLUTION OF THE MONASTERIES

Thomas Cromwell (1485–1540) had been an aide to Wolsey and became Henry' s vice-regent in 1532, although he remained wholly subordinate to the king. He put into effect the dissolution of the monasteries after 1535. Nothing could save them because they owed allegiance to powers outside England and Wales, because the king was bankrupt and had to use the monastic estates to buy support against Rome. By 1537 the task was complete and by 1539, 560 monastic institutions had been closed. One consequence of their closure was the destruction of great buildings, libraries and works of art. Henry remained a Catholic all his life – albeit Catholic without a pope. Cromwell did promote an enlightened puritanism following the example of Erasmus but his reward was execution.

1536
WILLIAM TYNDALE

In order to make the Bible more accessible to the people, William Tyndale (d. 1536) set about translating it from the original Hebrew. Printing had revolutionised the spread of knowledge across Europe. Tyndale left England in 1524 and after his departure, copies of his translations – deemed to be heretical – were smuggled into England. Tyndale believed that a translation from the original tongue would clarify interpretation; it would be purged 'of false glosses'. His glosses, however, were too Protestant and he was executed. Henry VIII did have an eye for such things, however, and Miles Coverdale, produced a Bible translation in 1536. In 1538 the Great Bible based on Tyndale and Coverdale was produced and placed in every parish; from 1538 onwards it was possible to study the Bible in English without punishment.

▶ p. 238

1554
REUNITED WITH ROME

Mary's (r. 1553–58) real goal as queen, was reunion with Rome. In 1554 Cardinal Pole arrived in England and absolved the country from sin, establishing this reunion. In practice, the persecutions and martyrdoms of Catholics and opponents of the monarchy witnessed under Henry and Edward were now carried out on Protestants. Mary's willingness to allow about 800 Protestants to leave the country, however, indicates that she came under the influence of anti-Catholic propaganda from other European countries. The savagery of persecutions affected public opinion. Some Clergy had married and objected to the reversal back to celibacy.

▲ *During the reign of Queen Mary, Protestants experienced the same persecution previously suffered by the Catholics.*

1556
THE DEATH OF THOMAS CRANMER

Thomas Cranmer (1489–1556) became Archbishop of Canterbury in 1532; he encouraged contacts with European Protestant scholars and, by 1549, he was able to publish the first Prayer Book in English, superseding the Roman service books. Use of the new book was enforced by the threat of imprisonment. This was followed by the Prayer Book of 1552 and the Act of Uniformity, which included compulsory church attendance. The 1552 Prayer Book was much more Protestant in tone. In 1553, 42 articles were drawn up intended to provide a doctrinal platform for the Church of England. This was the first attempt to set up the *via media* of the Church of England between Rome on the one side and Anabaptists on the other. On Mary's accession to the throne, Cranmer was imprisoned, excommunicated and eventually executed in 1556.

1558
THE ELIZABETHAN YEARS

In 1563, during the reign of Elizabeth I (1558–1603), 39 Articles were approved as defining the Anglican Church's doctrine and in 1571 clergy were to subscribe to these or resign their livings. The church was clearly Protestant, and although it retained altars and vestments, toleration was not granted to Catholics. The main threat to Elizabeth, particularly after her excommunication by the pope, was a league of Catholic nations. This eased when, in the early 1560s, John Knox returned from exile to Scotland and preached the Calvinist way of reform. Soon Scotland was Calvinist, having dramatically changed from its Catholic heritage under the forceful teachings of John Knox. However, both sides were persecuted and in 1584–85 it became treason to be a Catholic priest in England.

1558
THE PURITANS UNDER ELIZABETH

The Puritans, named because of their desire to 'purify' the Christian faith, wished particularly to rid the country of 'popish rituals', to ensure preaching was undertaken by properly educated ministers, and to accept 'godly discipline' not Episcopal authority. Other things, like wedding rings, celebrating Christmas, kneeling at Holy Communion being voluntary, taking one's hat off in church (if male), were also deplored. Some churches were set up outside the framework of the Elizabethan church. The queen took a hard line against them and manipulated the confrontation with considerable political skill. The Puritans were an irritant to the queen but not a challenge to the throne – yet. The Puritans, in turn, decided to await the 'godly' success or successor James VI of Scotland. They would then be able to 'revive religion'.

▶ p. 241

1603
RELIGIOUS THOUGHT IN TUDOR LITERATURE AND MUSIC

Desiderius Erasmus and Thomas More expressed, in satirical form, the intellectual literature of pre-Renaissance Europe. The Tudor monarchs generally, with Wolsey, were patrons of sacred music. Under Mary, the music from Catholic Europe was encouraged. In Elizabeth's time, the careers of Thomas Tallis, and William Byrd flourished. There were others – Walter Raleigh, Edmund Spenser and Christopher Marlowe are three of the most notable – but they pale into insignificance under the influence of William Shakespeare. In his greatest plays, the Calvinist influence of subjectivity and self-expression can be discerned, for so inflexible is God's word that grace only comes through self-scrutiny. Chivalry was dead and in its place arose the spiritual warfare of the Elite against the World.

▲ *Elizabeth I tolerated the Puritans, although she did not completely approve of them.*

p. 235◀ **Distant Voices** ▶p. 239

Albeit her Grace's conscience is stayed in matters of religion, yet she meaneth graciously not to compel or constrain other men's consciences, otherwise than god shall [she trusteth] put into their hearts a persuasion of the truth that she is in.

Council of Mary Tudor (12 August 1553)

Philosophers and Puritans

1600–84

IF THE SIXTEENTH CENTURY had offered little in the field of philosophy, the seventeenth century offered riches without parallel. The invention of printing meant the works of Copernius, Galileo, Kepler and Newton were more easily available. Religious orthodoxy was challenged in a manner previously unknown in the western world. England was in the throes of Civil War, the execution of its king, the imposition of puritanism and, finally, the Restoration. This century affected the intellectual values of the elite and there grew up a disillusionment with the old ideals: 'all men are naturally in a state of perfect freedom to order their actions and dispose of their possessions and persons as they think fit without asking the leave or depending upon the will of any man' (John Locke *Treatise of Government*, 1690).

▶ p. 240

1600s
NEW VISIONS

John Donne (1572–1631), Dean of St Paul's, had been brought up as a Catholic, although he had enjoyed a passionate lifestyle as a young man. In 1612 he resolved to become a priest and was ordained in 1615. His poetry lives on today, but it was as preacher that he came alive to the people of his day. Another poet of the same era, George Herbert (1593–1633) was, unlike Donne, a natural believer. Herbert looked for the 'mean' between the 'painted shrines' of Rome and extreme Protestantism. Mary Ward (d. 1645) was a devoted Catholic, and taking the Jesuits as a model, founded the Institute of the Blessed Virgin Mary in 1609. On seeking approval in Rome in 1629, she was excommunicated. She founded communities in London and Yorkshire but these did not receive papal approval until 1703.

▲ *James I chaired the Hampton Court Conference of Bishops and Puritans.*

1603–40
THE MONARCHY AND PURITAN EXPECTATION

'I will hurry them out of the land,' James I is reputed to have said when met with Puritan expectations. They, in their turn, would have been disappointed with the response they received from the king of a Presbyterian country. Some Puritans expressed their concern by sailing away aboard the *Mayflower* in 1620 to Massachusetts, where they set up a strict religious community. In 1611 the authorised version of the Bible was published, after the Hampton Court Conference of bishops and Puritans under James I's chairmanship. In general, until the Civil War, Britain's monarchs remained in a tense stand-off with the Puritans. Catholics were regarded as the main target. The Puritans had to deal with Archbishop Laud and perhaps thousands left England for the New World.

▶ p. 245

1645
THE EXECUTION OF WILLIAM LAUD

William Laud (1573–1645) became Archbishop of Canterbury in 1633 and was a bitter opponent of Puritanism; equally, the Puritans disliked him. He required strict uniformity in the churches and obedience to the bishops and the Prayer Book. He became closely associated with Charles I's views and this alliance with the monarchy was not in the long term interests of the Anglican Church. Hatred of the monarch was easily transferred to hatred of the archbishop. Laud wished to re-instate the surplice, to have the altar separated off in the church, and for heads to bow at the name of Jesus; all offensive to the Puritans and Calvinists. At his execution in 1645 he said, 'I was born and baptised in the Church of England established by Law. In that profession I have lived, and in that I come now to die'.

1649
EFFECTS OF THE CIVIL WAR

It is not easy to say how much the Civil War (1642–49) was a religious war. Certainly the Anglican Church (represented by the Bishops and the Prayer Book) sided with the king while on the Parliamentary side were Puritans. During the war there was much destruction, churches were burned, works of art broken and destroyed, books torn up, and vestments cut to pieces. Parliament abolished the episcopacy. Puritan leaders drew up the Solemn League and Covenant (it became law in 1644), many clergy signed it and continued as Presbyterian ministers. Other clergy could not sign and about 25 per cent of them lost their livings. Bishops fled and became a rare species; with the bishops went the Book of Common Prayer, replaced by the Directory of Public Worship. But all was not harmonious in the Puritan camp.

▶ p. 240

1650s
SCHISMS AND INDEPENDENTS

There were strong theological differences between the Puritans: the Baptists, strong in the country before 1640, were a powerful

▲ *A Quaker meeting; the Quaker movement was established by George Fox.*

influence in the army; the Congregationalists were despised by the Presbyterians; but perhaps the largest group of all was the Quakers. George Fox (1624–91) gathered together a number of smaller visionary independent churches and acquired thousands of followers in the 1650s. Their creed of the Holy Spirit coming directly without mediation of Church or scripture, and their passive disobedience, made the Quakers greatly unpopular. Fox's remarkable energy and vision continued and the term 'Quaker',- which started as a term of abuse, lost its pejorative meaning and remains a common name for the Religious Society of Friends.

1651
THOMAS HOBBES'S *LEVIATHAN*

Thomas Hobbes (1588–1679) published *Leviathan* in 1651 and it continued to provoke debate long after his death. Hobbes secularised political thought; he sought to strip the sovereignty of its moral base. The work was a response to the damage done by kingdoms ruled by priests and preachers. He was suspected of atheism and, after the mid-1660s, could find no one to publish his works. John Locke's (1632–1704) book *Essay in Human Understanding* (1687) is his most famous work and his influence on the philosophy of politics has been enormous. His religious views revolved around the requirement to reduce Christianity to the New Testament. Moral rules are laid down by God and are in the Bible, he says, men should follow them otherwise they will be punished.

✯ ▶ p. 248

1662
THE CHURCH AFTER THE RESTORATION

A new Prayer Book was published in 1662 (it is still in use today) and inaugurated on St Bartholomew's Day 1662. Bishops resumed their seats in the House of Lords and many Presbyterian clergy were ordained and became Anglicans. The Puritan period had removed many religious and cultural celebrations from ordinary life. The Church was initially unforgiving and introduced largely unsuccessful measures which sought to destroy the Baptists, Quakers etc. The Toleration Act of 1689 was the first formal recognition of religious pluralism. Such toleration would not extend to Catholics and Unitarians but it was a step forward. The century ended with Christianity being picked over by scientists and humanists and there was a growing humanitarian concern – the poor are always present even if the eternal verities had been demolished.

▲ *An example of the public humiliation suffered by the Quakers at the hands of other religious groups.*

1667–84
JOHN MILTON AND JOHN BUNYAN

Paradise Lost (1667) and its sequel *Paradise Regained* (1671) reflect Milton's (1608–74) life experience. The former looks at the Creator who lets man fail, the latter at Christ in the wilderness and the false ways the Gospel can be proclaimed. Milton admired Cromwell, but it may be that *Samson Agonistes* (1671) expressed his concern that the republicans had taken the wrong path. More typical of puritanism is John Bunyan's *Pilgrim's Progress* (1678–84), for it is primarily concerned with the search of an individual for peace and salvation. Bunyan (1628–88) does not appear to have been a strict Calvinist. He spent 12 years in Bedford Gaol (1660–72) so had much time to reflect on his allegory of religious life.

p. 237◀ **Distant Voices** ▶p. 241

It is at least a surer and shorter way to the apprehension of the vulgar and mass of mankind, that one manifestly sent from God, and coming with visible authority from him, should, as King and law-maker, tell them their duties and require their obedience, than leave it to the long and sometimes intricate deductions of reason to be made out to them.

John Locke, *Treatise on the Reasonableness of Christianity* (1695)

Revolution and its Consequences

1650–1804

THE TOLERATION ACT, while limited in scope, had brought a certain security to the Dissenters. There were signs that the Church in England had been touched by the Enlightenment and the early eighteenth century was marked with questions about the authority of Scripture and the Church. The century was the witness to the most important religious movements for a considerable time: the rise of Methodism and the formation of Christian missionary organisations as a response to the political expansion of British influence across the world. Education for the masses was becoming a priority by the end of the period but the intellectual elite were moving on apace. The work of Kant (1724–1804) was spreading across Europe as was the influence of Rousseau (1712–78); and in England Berkeley, Hume and Bentham were increasing pressure on Church and State.

▶ p. 242

1650s
HITTING THE OLD MYSTERIES

The mid-seventeenth century had given hope that disease would be eradicated, and that agriculture would banish famine and want. Francis Bacon's (1587–1657) work had created a more accurate study of plant and animal life, and the discovery of the circulation of the blood by Harvey (1578–1657) led to advances in physiology and anatomy. Isaac Newton's (1642–1717) great work in 1687 became the basis of physical laws for 200 years and Boyle (1627–91) and Hooke (1635–1703) created new disciplines in chemistry and geology. Newton and Halley, though, still tried to interpret their advances within the context of God' s creation. Later, Thomas Paine's (1737–1809) books *The Rights of Man* and *The Age of Reason* (1790s) illustrated the inability of the Christian churches to keep abreast of radical scientific discoveries and new philosophical thinking.

▲ *Isaac Newton established some of the first laws of physics that still form the basis of that branch of science today.*

✶ ▶ p. 244

1700s
WILLIAM LAW AND THE DEISTS

Deism struck at the heart of the Christian faith. It stated that, while there was a creator who established the world and its process, there was no response to human prayer or need; this was a 'religion of nature', unencumbered by creeds and formulae. This fitted easily into the thinking of many intellectuals. John Toland's book *Christianity not Mysterious* (1696) really began the controversy and Tindal's work *Christianity as Old as Creation* (1730) intensified the debate. It was the ultimate argument for natural reason – there was no need for the incarnation. William Law (1686–1760), who abandoned a Cambridge career because he would not swear allegiance to George I, responded by a series of quiet, mystical publications outlining the importance of living a practical Christian life based on an imitation of Jesus.

1737
WALES AND IRELAND

Wales had been a conservative part of Britain, overwhelmingly Anglican and strongly royalist. The Welsh language, spoken by 80–90 per cent of the population, meant the news from England was distant and remote. The use of Welsh in religious practice was controversial. Griffith Jones (1683–1761) was denounced as a secret spreader of Methodism when he used Welsh as the medium of a literacy campaign and catechised in it. He opened 37 schools in 1737 alone and helped with the Welsh Bible and Prayer Book in 1746. In Ireland, Catholics had held 59 per cent of the land in 1641, but only five per cent in 1778. Catholics were persecuted: they could not acquire or bequeath land, they could not vote and they were barred from Parliament and military and legal offices.

▶ p. 246

1738
THE CONVERSION OF THE WESLEYS

'By the humane endeavours of him and his brother Charles a sense of decency in morals and religion was introduced into the lower classes of mankind'. John and Charles Wesley were two of 19 children, born into a High Church family. It was not considered surprising that John (1703–91) was ordained with two of his brothers, Charles (1707–88) and Samuel (who never became a Methodist). They became friendly with a fervent preacher, George Whitefield (1714–70), and accompanied him on one of his many trips to America. But the Wesleys' trip was a disaster and in 1738 they were back in Britain exhausted and near collapse. Within three days of each other in May 1738 they both received separate revelations of the power of their faith. It was this experience which was to change their lives.

1740s
THE RISE AND INFLUENCE OF METHODISM

John Wesley undertook a travelling ministry which he sustained for 52 years, travelling well over 322,000 km (200,000 miles) and preaching 40,000 sermons. By his death in

1791 over 72,000 people in Britain were 'in association' with him, and two centuries later there were 18 million Methodists in the world. He lived an austere and demanding life with a clear message: 'holiness must be perfect love'. The term 'Methodist' came into common usage in the 1740s; it referred to the methodical order of life – fasting two days a week and two services on Sundays (before and after the services in the parish church). The formation of the Methodist Preachers' Conference and their acceptance of Wesley's rights and responsibilities (1784) made separation from the Church of England inevitable.

▶ p. 245

1797
WILLIAM WILBERFORCE

William Wilberforce's (1759–1833) book, *A Practical View of the Prevailing Religious Systems of Professed Christians in the Higher and Middle Classes in this Country contrasted with Real Christianity* (1797) was surprisingly popular among evangelicals because of its call for order and acknowledgement of authority. Wilberforce emerged from an evangelical Christian group formed in Clapham in London. He was an MP and used that position as a platform to lead the anti-slavery movement. He was a saintly man and his personal charisma gathered support for his causes. He campaigned for schools for the poor, civil rights for Catholics and prison reform. What is most remarkable about the campaign against the slave trade (finally successful in 1833), was the way in which a variety of groups – religious and non-religious – put aside their differences and joined forces.

▲ *William Wordsworth – the poet who originally intended to be an Anglican clergyman.*

▲ *William Wilberforce, politican and evangelical Christian, was a key figure in the anti-slavery movement.*

1800s
BLAKE, WORDSWORTH AND COLERIDGE

William Blake (1757–1827) rebelled against all authority, but he was a visionary of incomparable genius. Blake was not a philosopher but a creative poet; he said his business was 'to create'. William Wordsworth (1770–1850) almost became an Anglican clergyman, but instead turned to writing. His poetry is full of longing – for an understanding of nature – but he is ambiguous about what constitutes nature, for it seems he felt too much to philosophise. His poetry, as Blake's, reflects the spirit of the age. Coleridge (1772–1834) had a powerful Christian faith, but not in a conventional sense – his faith came from within; if a person acted as if they believed, then faith would follow. He called on the Church to apply the principles found in the Bible to all aspects of life.

1804
EDUCATION: HOME AND AWAY

In 1698, the Society for the Promotion of Christian Knowledge was established and set up a number of charity schools in the early eighteenth century. Education had to be paid for privately, though in Scotland an act of 1496 had made education compulsory for the eldest son of the gentry. In 1804, an interdenominational body – the British and Foreign Bible Society – was founded to provide Bibles where Protestant missionaries were at work. For Christians, education was linked with evangelism at home and abroad. When the National Society for Promoting the Education of the Poor in the Principles of Established Church was founded in 1811, it was clear the Church of England would carry the burden of education for many years. By 1831 nearly a million children were in National Society schools.

p. 239◀ **Distant Voices** ▶p. 243

And did those feet in ancient time
walk upon England's mountains
green? And was the holy Lamb of God
on England's pleasant pastures seen?
And did the countenance divine, shine
forth upon our clouded hills?
And was Jerusalem builded here,
among those dark satanic mills.

William Blake (1757–1827)

Philosophers and Thinkers

1723–1859

THE TERM 'PHILOSOPHY OF RELIGION' was coined towards the end of the eighteenth century. However, the term has come to have different meanings for different philosophers. For over 1,000 years, philosophy had largely been about questions pertaining to God. Up to the early part of the nineteenth century the majority of philosophers affirmed the existence of God, though some of their notions probably hastened the demise of intellectual questions about religion. The most obviously anti-theist philosopher was David Hume (1711–76), but the atheism may have derived from his personal life rather than any philosophical reasoning. Kant (1724–1804) and Hegel (1770–1831) did not exclude religious topics, but after them Marx (1818–93), Nietzsche (1844–1900) and Schopenhaeur (1788–1860) were firmly anti-religious and anti-theistic.

▲ *Mary Wollstonecraft, whose* A Vindication of the Rights of Women *was the first publication to address the issues of women's emancipation.*

1723
GEORGE BERKELEY

Born and educated in Ireland, George Berkeley (1685–1753) first visited England in 1723 and became Bishop of Cloyne in 1734. The works on which his reputation was built were published when he was a young man, and the chief target of his criticism was John Locke. Berkeley held that the consequence of Locke's theories would lead to atheism and therefore the submersion of all morality. Locke presented God as the Creator and Designer (the starter of the great machine). Berkeley detested this metaphor, believing it denied the evidence of man's senses. It was Berkeley's misfortune – and perhaps a comment on the Christian response to the world of his time – that he opposed the 'scientific world-view' when it was in the first flush of ascendancy.

▶ p. 252

1739
DAVID HUME'S *A TREATISE OF HUMAN NATURE*

David Hume's (1711–76) best known work *A Treatise of Human Nature* (1739) disappointed him on publication. He was a sceptic and a free thinker. His emphasis lay on the value of custom and instinct as guides to life. If reason was taken as fundamental, this would lead to confusion, so custom was a better guide. To early readers Hume appeared to argue against the existence of God and the truth of religion, and in his *Dialogues Concerning Natural Religion* (published posthumously), he demolished the principal arguments for the existence of God. His purpose was to halt the pretensions of reason and put instinct in its place. His belief about an after-life was that to think of it was absurd.

▲ *David Hume, sceptic and free thinker, author of* A Treatise of Human Nature.

p. 236◀ **Triumphs & Tragedies** ▶p. 248

1792
EARLY FEMINISM

Mary Wollstonecraft's (1759–97) work *A Vindication of the Rights of Women* (1792) was a follow-up to her response to Edmund Burke's *Reflections on the French Revolution* (1790). Wollstonecraft travelled to France, eventually marrying William Godwin in 1797. Wollstonecraft died just two weeks after the birth of their daughter, Mary. Her beliefs were based on three assumptions: reason is the same in men and women; reason is a necessary condition of women's virtue; the emancipation of women demands the domination of rational feelings over love. Women deprived of education are taught to defer to men and see themselves as objects of desire. This means they have been held back from exercising genuine judgement or attaining genuine virtue. She longed for a social order in which every individual was free from the shackles of superstition and false authority.

1776
JEREMY BENTHAM'S *FRAGMENT ON GOVERNMENT*

Born in the City of London, Bentham (1748–1832) began training for the law, but was influenced by Hume (1711–76) and produced *Fragment on Government* in 1776. Bentham took the optimistic spirit of the time and gave it philosophical expression. His basic premise was: 'nature has placed mankind under the governance of two sovereign masters, pain and pleasure.... They govern us in all we do, in all we say, in all we think.' From this it was a small step to the principle of utility, which stated that the greatest happiness of all those whose interest is in question, is 'the only right and proper and universally desirable end of human conduct'. A consequence of Bentham's hypothesis was that punishment, for example, should not be a retribution for past action, but rather the prevention of future harms.

1781
IMMANUEL KANT

Kant's (1724–1804) philosophy was unique in its methods and aims, emphasising knowledge as a means of reaching philosophical conclusions. This led to the assertion that only mind existed, resulting in a rejection of utilitarian ethics in favour of systems that could be demonstrated by abstract philosophical arguments. In *The Critique of Pure Reason* (1781) he showed that all arguments (such as for the existence of God) were grounded in contradiction and paradox. Existence is not a predicate; one cannot argue from the concept of God to the existence of God: a concept cannot imply existence. His own argument for the existence of God was that moral law demanded justice and this was not assured in life, therefore a god and a future life must exist.

1790
EDMUND BURKE'S *REFLECTIONS*

In his *Reflections on the French Revolution* (1790) Edmund Burke (1729–97) affirmed that the glory of Europe would be gone for ever if the alliance between Church orthodoxy and the monarchical State were destroyed by mob forces. He was renowned as a boring speaker, but his causes – freedom for the American states; freedom for Ireland; freedom for India from the East India Company; freedom of Parliament from the influence of the king; and opposition to the atheism indicative of the French Revolution – gathered support. He saw political power as a trust, and politicians had to maintain the tradition of hierarchical, social and political order. His opinions touched the hearts of many, especially George III.

1791–92
THOMAS PAINE'S *THE RIGHTS OF MAN*

Thomas Paine (1737–1809) wrote a pamphlet in support of the American Colonialists – *Common Sense* – in 1776, and at the outbreak of the French Revolution, he produced his most influential work in its defence: *The Rights of Man* (1791–92). So supportive was it of the Revolution that Paine had to flee to France. In the second part of his book he argued that governments should recognise the natural rights of all citizens to receive education, old age pensions and other benefits of social welfare. While Paine's opponent Edmund Burke's pamphlet sold 19,000 copies in six months, *The Rights of Man* sold 200,000. He died in New York, having alarmed governments and offended the Church by promoting an argument for Deism in *The Age of Reason* (1794–97).

1859
JOHN STUART MILL

John Stuart Mill (1806–73) was probably the greatest philosopher of the eighteenth century. His two best-known works were *On Liberty* (1859) and *Utilitarianism* (1861). One of his radical causes was support for women's rights in *The Subjection of Women* (1869). A leading element in Mill's thought was to weave together the insights of enlightenment and romanticism. He held that there was no knowledge independent of experience and attitudes, and that beliefs were the result of psychological association. He believed that human nature was the seat of autonomy and individuality, and these were capable of being brought to a wholeness in the human being. Although Mill was accused of being naïve, his views, with their blend of romanticism, ethical individualism and social reform, were attractive to thinkers in the universities.

▲ *Thomas Paine's most influential work,* The Rights of Man, *expounded his support for the French Revolution.*

p. 241◀ **Distant Voices** ▶p. 245

I believe in one God, and no more; and I hope for happiness beyond this life. I believe in the equality of man, and I believe that religious duties consist in doing justice, loving mercy and endeavouring to make our fellow-creatures happy.

Thomas Paine, *The Age of Reason* (1790s)

The Victorian Era

1800–79

THERE WERE GREAT CHANGES during the Victorian era: the Empire was at its height; Christians of different denominations stopped persecuting each other unmercifully and tried to begin to co-operate; provisions for education improved; a strain of Christian socialism began to emerge; and various Christians took to the stage in the amelioration of social issues. The legacy of a religious England was still present, but the pace of life had changed; cities grew bigger and the influences of Darwin, Marx and Freud would provide a challenge the Christians would find difficult to meet. Knowledge of other countries and cultures flooded in, and even in the imperial heart of the country, seeds of uncertainty were being sown. 'Socialism' had appeared in about 1830 in opposition to the *laissez-faire* approach of the times.

▲ *The social reformer Elizabeth Fry on one of her prison visits in her campaign to improve conditions for prisoners.*

1800s
PUBLIC EDUCATION AND THE CHURCH

The evangelical Hannah More (1745–1833) believed that in order to educate and maintain order, children should be taught to read but not write. The BFSS (1808) and the National Society (1811) created some denominational tensions as they established schools. In the public schools the influence of Thomas Arnold (1795–1842) at Rugby was significant. 'Public' schools were mainly Anglican and suffered less from religious antagonism; they provided entry into the professions, Oxford and Cambridge, and served to preserve a status quo; Anglican patronage was thus much resented by others. In 1870, 'board' or state schools were created. Grants had been given to church schools since 1833, but the non-conformists objected to religious teaching being given in schools. The Catholics received grants to set up their schools in the early 1850s.

✶ 1800s
VICTORIAN REFORMERS

In 1832 the Quaker Elizabeth Fry (1786–1843) visited Newgate Prison; what she found there appalled her. She began a crusade to improve the prisoners' situation and eventually the government established minimum standards. Florence Nightingale (1820–1910) also had a burning sense of personal mission, and has become famous for the work she did in the Crimean War (1854). She founded schools for nurses and, in 1870, was involved in what later became the Red Cross. The philanthropist Thomas Barnardo (1845–1905) set up a foundation to help destitute children and, by the time of his death, had assumed responsibility for almost 60,000 lives.

1833
THE OXFORD MOVEMENT

John Keble (1792–1866) preached a sermon called 'National Apostasy' in July 1833, which raised the question of reform within the church. From Oxford the same year emerged *Tracts for the Times*, a series of pamphlets that were distributed to clergy. They advocated a *via media* between Protestantism and Catholicism – some people were thrilled, others disgusted. In the first Tract, its author John Henry Newman (1804–90) said 'choose your side', for it was very difficult to remain neutral. *Tract 90*, in 1841, was the final straw: Newman's words brought cries of 'popery' and 'antichrist at the door'; various clergy objected and extracted a promise that no more Tracts would be written. Newman felt the ever-growing attraction of Rome and in 1845 he joined the Roman Catholic Church.

1850s
DENOMINATIONS: RISE AND FALL

By 1850, Methodism was a powerful influence in the country, even though the Primitive Methodists had separated in 1812 – soon to be followed by the Bible Christians. By 1853, there were seven different Methodist Churches. Out of the Methodist movement came William Booth: originally the 'Gospel of Salvation', he and his colleagues became known as the Salvation Army and challenged Christians to work with the drunk and destitute. After the Methodists came the Congregationalists – noted for their social conscience – and then the Baptists, who were strong believers in adult or 'believers' baptism'. This sectarianism reflected the growth of individualism that marked much of the later-nineteenth century and would come to the fore in the twentieth century.

▶ p. 251

1851
DIVERSITY IN RELIGIONS

By the middle of the century, the industrialisation of Britain was well underway; agriculture was the largest industry, but there was a steady movement towards the towns. The census of 1851 caught the attention of the Churches, particularly the Church of England. It was the only census to try and establish religious attendance. The evidence was indisputable and shocking: Church of England, 5,292,551; Roman Catholics, 383,630; Protestant Dissenters, 4,536,265; Total Population, 17,927,609. Over five million people stayed at home. It was a triumph for non-Anglicans. By the end of the century in London only about 20 per cent went to church, although the Catholics attracted significant working-class attendance largely because of immigration from Ireland. Not to attend an Anglican church was a sign of protest and indifference.

▶ p. 248

1857
WOMEN

Urban society served women little better than rural society. The notion of equality was related to separate functions: women's role was home and family. The Divorce Act of 1857 was significant because divorce, although costly, did not require an Act of Parliament. It was the first step to register divorce as a secular event. The Act implied the end of the religious sub-culture's influence. The repeal of the Contagious Diseases Act (1886) can be regarded as reflecting the concern of men to protect themselves. It has been suggested that the violence of the suffragettes was in retaliation for the violence inflicted on women through compulsory medical examinations. In industry, women workers generally worked in low-pay, low-skill areas. The Victorian era also witnessed the slow progress of women to civic and legal equality.

▲ *The streets of London, and particularly the East End, became the home of the most destitute.*

1859
THE EVANGELICALS

The evangelical experience was closely bound up with conversion and showed less interest in ecclesiastical authority or the sacraments. They acquired a sense of responsibility to the weak and exploited and, as we have seen, found a cause in the slave trade. Later in the century (*c.* 1859) a second evangelical resurgence arrived from America. The hymn 'Stand up, stand up for Jesus' is one that remains from that era but the zeal and enthusiasm of the visiting evangelicals caused some staid English evangelicals to hold back. By 1850, evangelical teaching had been accepted in the Church of England but it followed a quieter path. Lord Shaftesbury (1801–85) was one of the leading evangelicals of this period. He was, like his co-evangelicals, committed to the poor and, unwittingly, laid the foundations of the twentieth century welfare state.

◉ ▶ p. 250

1879
JOHN HENRY NEWMAN

Originally an evangelical, John Henry Newman (1801–90) became vicar of the university church in Oxford, at which time he turned away from his Calvinist beliefs and became a Catholic. While working with Keble, he edited 66 Tracts in two years. His Protestant friends and admirers were amazed that so articulate and intelligent a man should affirm dogmas and miracles they believed to be nonsense. Newman, a liberal, had submitted to an authoritarian church, but it was not until Leo XIII became pope that the official attitude to him eased. In 1879 he was made a cardinal; for him it was a symbol that he was recognised and accepted by the Church he had joined.

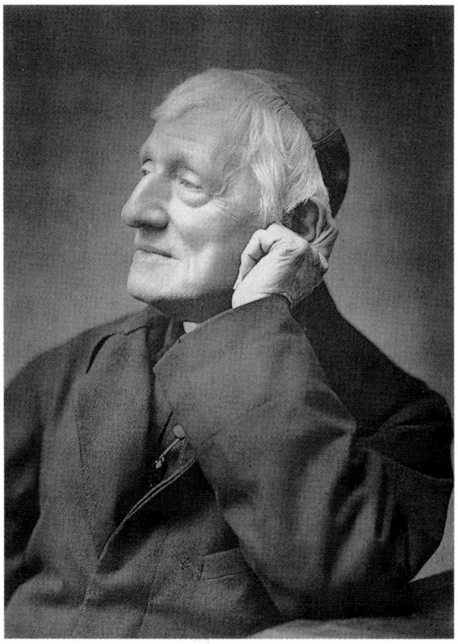

▲ *John Henry Newman was made cardinal in 1879; for him this proved he had finally been accepted by the faith he had adopted.*

p. 243◀ **Distant Voices** ▶p. 247

The creed which accepts as the foundation of morals, utility, or the Greatest Happiness Principle, holds that actions are right in proportion as they tend to promote happiness, wrong as they tend to produce the reverse of happiness. By happiness is intended pleasure and the absence of pain; by unhappiness, pain and the privation of pleasure.

John Stuart Mill, *Utilitarianism* (1863)

The Imperial Heritage
1785–1900

WHY SHOULD THE churches have been so keen to evangelise overseas when there was much to be done at home? Yet that latter work in itself was 'missionary'. The opening of Oxford and Cambridge universities to non-Anglicans in 1854 and 1856, the disestablishment of the Church of Ireland in 1869, the re-emergence of Catholicism (1850–51) and huge Irish immigration, did not weaken the British self-belief in the right to rule. The Primrose League (1883) enjoyed support in the 1850s and 1890s for its defence of Crown, Church, social structure and empire – shades of Edmund Burke. The tenor of the century was one of self-righteousness, complacency and superiority. Victorian Britain had a strong sense of national identity, nationalistic self-confidence and xenophobic contempt for foreigners. This had a direct effect on the nature of missionary activity.

▶ p. 249

1785
WILLIAM CAREY

In 1785 Carey (1762–1834) was given permission to preach as a Baptist and soon he was challenging his fellow ministers with the Great Commission – 'Go forth and teach all nations'. He formed the Baptist Missionary Society in 1792 and a year later he decided to go to India. He had been in India for seven years before he baptised a native, but he translated the Bible into six Indian languages and he proved to be a model of the fortitude of the early British missionaries. He founded schools and colleges at a time when Britain was doing precious little at home. Carey inspired many others but none really possessed the depth of his obsessive drive and evangelical zeal.

1837
CHRISTIAN SOCIALISM

The exploitation of the working class was rife in the mid-nineteenth century. The People's Charter, with its demands for more equable treatment and, among other things, manhood suffrage, lasted from 1838–42. F. D. Maurice, founder of Christian Socialism (1805–72), was a Tory paternalist with a Christian duty to help the poor. Christian Socialists saw the Christian ideal of co-operation being applied to economic life. Each act of co-operation was a gesture to defy capitalism, but this was doomed as a form of nineteenth century idealism. Maurice's book *The Kingdom of Christ* (1837) envisaged Christ's kingdom, in which there were no class distinctions, no rich or poor, oppressor or oppressed. The Christian Socialists were overtaken by the un-Christian Socialist thinking of Karl Marx and much later swept aside by popular evangelism of the later nineteenth century and the formation of the Salvation Army.

▲ *Missionaries in India; missionaries travelled around the globe spreading the word of Christianity.*

1840
AUSTRALIA AND THE ANTIPODES

By 1840, about 150,000 men and women had been deported to Australia and while Christianity was exported too, the Australian country was largely secular. When the colony of South Australia was founded in 1836, English non-conformists were among its leading lights, but it soon fell back into the prevailing secular ethos. It was difficult to persuade the Aboriginals that Christianity had anything to offer. As in other countries, the advent of a white civilisation was usually followed by death through violence or disease. In both Australia and New Zealand, church life was built on a European model of Christianity; there was no scope for the development of indigenous Christian expression.

▲ *Christian convicts were exported in large numbers to Australia in the late-nineteenth century.*

1844
WILLIAM GLADSTONE

William Ewart Gladstone (1809-98) was strongly Anglican, although he acquired non-conformist aspirations towards the end of his life. During his life, or at least until 1844, he claimed to see himself as an Anglican who happened to be a politician. In truth, regardless of his political creed, he was devoted to Christian charitable concerns, but the ambiguity of his Christianity revealed itself in his approach to slavery (his father had been a slave owner). He recognised the validity for the disestablishment of the Anglican Church in Wales and presided over the disestablishment of the Church in Ireland in 1871. He was a true missionary, in that he sought to live out Christian principles in a political context.

▲ *Matthew Arnold described London's East End as 'miserable, unmanageable masses of sunken people'.*

1860s
VICTORIAN COUNTRYMEN: MISSIONARIES AT HOME

Matthew Arnold (1822–88) believed the 'peace of God' was the Christian phrase for civilisation. In *Culture and Anarchy* (1869) he described London's East End as containing 'these vast, miserable, unmanageable masses of sunken people'. In reality, he battled with belief and un-belief and gave up orthodox Christianity as a 'fond but beautiful dream'. Charles Dickens (1812–70) was less influenced, if at all, by institutional religion. His 'mission' was to draw attention to the hypocrisy and exploitation in society. Dickens was a prophet; his novels personified social evils and revealed him to be an analyst of society. He was religious, but attacked the narrowness of Christian interpretations of the New Testament. He was intent on revealing the devils at home rather than the devils overseas.

1897
VIEWS OF 'OTHER FAITHS'

By the end of the nineteenth century, many of those responsible for directing missionary activity overseas recognised that a change of attitude was due. Its failure was accompanied by a rise in awareness of what other faiths and cultures might have to offer. The xenophobic approach of Rudyard Kipling (1865–1936) and earlier Bishop Heber (*c.* 1820s), might have caught the public imagination but scholars were attracted by the richness of Indian and Islamic civilisations. Even the visit of Vivekananda to Britain at the turn of the century revealed an increasing interest in the integrity of the different religions. Vivekananda was on his way to the first 'Parliament of Religions' held in Chicago in 1897. The approach was patronising and Christians of the late-eighteenth and early nineteenth centuries were slow to respond to the changes that were sweeping the world.

1900s
INDIA

In India, Christian missionaries failed completely to understand the depth of wisdom of the Hindu religion; they destroyed the Indian cultural framework, but replaced it with nothing. Various Christian denominations agreed to 'carve up' India between them to avoid acting against each other and they founded schools in India which continue to influence the articulate, intellectual elite. As elsewhere, the activities of Christian missionaries were littered with good intentions: they combated infanticide and the execution of widows, provided education, hospitals and raised the dignity of women, but it was 'British religion', the religion of power and might.

1900
AFRICA

Sir Harry Johnston addressed the Basagra people in 1900, saying 'we were like you, going about naked ... with our war paint on, but when we learned Christianity from the Romans we changed and became great. We want you to learn Christianity and follow our steps and you too will be great'. Although a black bishop, Samuel Growther, had been consecrated in 1864, he was later forced to resign. David Livingstone (1815–73) travelled throughout Africa for many years, failing to convert any natives to Christianity before dying penniless in 1873. The missionaries failed to recognise the huge size of Africa and its immense diversity. Christianity did take hold in parts of central and southern Africa – but this was only on the back of imperial power.

p. 245◀ **Distant Voices** ▶p. 249

Women are everywhere in this deplorable state; for, in order to preserve their innocence, as ignorance is courteously termed, truth is hidden from them, and they are made to assume an artificial character before their faculties have acquired any strength.

Mary Wollstonecraft (1792)

The Radical Challenge

1848–1930s

THE MOST FAMOUS NAME associated with social change in the nineteenth century is Karl Marx (1818–83) but Marx's influence was but one among many. It was the century when the formal religious structure of society broke down. By 1870, the future was literate and secular minded; the intellectual ferment and advance in the period brought challenge to new and old ideas. People's lives began to improve, and there was an advance in materialism. Science, in its rich variety, provided many discoveries and people were aware that medical advances were taking place, that there were more and better machines and that electricity, among other things, was changing their lives. The old (and false) security of religious teaching no longer appeared so attractive and science was ready to move in with its own myths and authoritarianism.

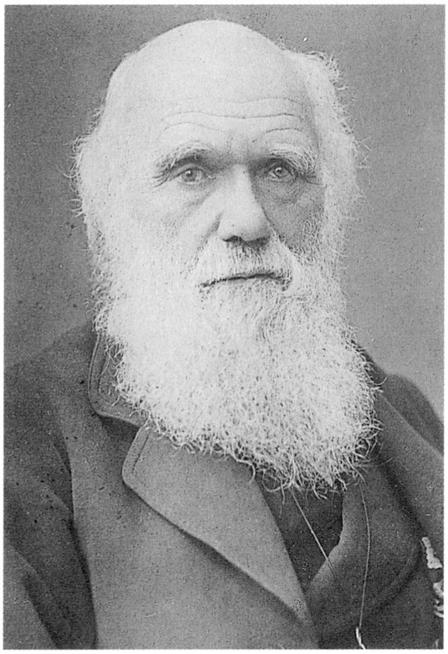

▲ *Darwin challenged the beliefs at the very foundations of the Christian faith.*

↗ ▶ p. 253

1850s
SCIENTIFIC AND CULTURAL CHANGE

Individual determinism and *laissez-faire* was very different from the Christian ideas that lay behind the Enlightenment or the free-thinking individuals envisaged by Renaissance ideals. From the 1850s, science struck its heaviest blows at religious belief in the West by undermining the authority of Scripture. The authority of the Roman Catholic Church and the emphasis on Scripture by the Protestants inhibited any possible critique of biblical revelation. The acceptance of the literal truth of Scripture essential to the nineteenth century, had, ironically not been part of the teaching of the early church. What happened next was that the scientists replaced the priests as the key holders to the future and a better life. The power of individualism was to stay and become the root of post-modern thinking in the late-twentieth century.

p. 242◀ **Triumphs & Tragedies** ▶p. 254

1848
KARL MARX – THE EARLY YEARS

The word 'socialism' first appeared in France in the 1830s to describe ideas and people opposed to a market economy that benefited the rich and powerful. Some socialists advocated the abolition of property and were called 'communists'. It was in this context that *The Communist Manifesto* appeared in 1848 (though it had yet to acquire that title). Marx (1818–83) appeared to believe that revolution would sweep away capitalist society and create a new economic order. This included its own mythology, its Chosen People (the working class) whose entry into the Promised Land of a just society would be reward for their pilgrimage. He argued that passive contemplation was an unreal abstraction. Russell (1872–1970) believed Marx had too many short-comings, he was 'too practical, too much wrapped up in the problems of his time'.

▲ *The communist Karl Marx, who strived to find a way to meet the needs of the working class, first outlined in his* The Communist Manifesto.

☆ ▶ p. 254

1859
THE MAKING OF MAN: *THE ORIGIN OF SPECIES*

Charles Darwin's (1809–92) book *The Origin of Species* (1859) set out his theory of evolution, although he did not use this word in the early editions of his book. In 1871 *The Descent of Man* made explicit his theories of natural selection as they applied to humans. This idea went against all Christian and Jewish teachings, which accepted the literal truth of the Bible. A turning point came at a debate where a colleague of Darwin, Thomas Huxley, criticised the Bishop of Oxford, Samuel Wilberforce. Darwin became a reverent agnostic, he could 'hardly see how anyone ought to wish Christianity to be true; for if it be so, the plain language of the text seems to show that the men who do not believe ... would be everlastingly punished. And this is a damnable doctrine'.

1860s
THE CHURCH'S RESPONSE

The word 'agnostic' was coined by Aldous Huxley to describe Darwin. The shock waves from Darwin's work shook the Church to its foundations, partly because other scientists had remained Christian. It characterised the low ebb which theology had reached. The response from the church was in vain. Biblical scholars had already thrown doubt on the historical authenticity of the text, and certainly the early Church fathers were never agreed on a literal interpretation. The centre of this Biblical criticism was in Germany, but the work was closely followed in England. When *Essays and Reviews* (1860) was published, 11,000 clergy and 137,000 laity signed a protest. It was condemned in 1864 because it argued that the scriptures should 'be read like any other book'.

1860
REACTION IN BRITAIN

When *Essays and Reviews* (1860) was published, the storm of controversy was remarkable. Some of the main themes of the essays would, no doubt, cause a storm today: Christian truth is not tied to the literal truth of scripture; faith reveals God's actions as miracles and prophecy; God's revelation cannot be proved. That same year came a publication from Bishop Colenso (1814–83). He denied the Mosaic authorship of the Pentateuch and argued the Ten Commandments were a product of Jewish priests. The Privy Council refused to dispose him from his see but what next? To Scotland where Robertson-Smith (1846–94) was removed from his Chair at Aberdeen Free Church College because his work impugned the authority and inspiration of the Bible. It was the authoritative work of J. B. Lightfoot (1828–89) that provided help for Christians to accept modern scholarship.

1867
THE LATER MARX

Russell may have been correct in his evaluation of Marx for he appeared to follow his theories more cautiously than some of his followers. Like many great teachers, he failed to recognise his disciples; he later protested that he was not a Marxist. His definitive work was *Das Kapital* (1867), and its posthumous volumes (1884 and 1893). His major concern was not simply to meet the needs of the 'working class' but to deal fundamentally with the conditions under which human beings can develop their essential powers. He did not believe that future society would be unchanging perfection, rather he believed it would herald the beginning of human history consciously directed by human beings.

▲ *The founder of psychoanalysis, Sigmund Freud.*

▶ p. 251

1920s
UNCONSCIOUS PROBLEMS: SIGMUND FREUD

Freud (1865–1939) was the founder of psychoanalysis and, like Darwin, he influenced education, literature and politics. His fundamental publications came before 1914, but *The Ego and the Id* was published in 1923. His views on religion were encapsulated in *The Future of an Illusion* (1927). Freud's theory stated that children both love and hate their parents; each wishes to kill the parent of the same sex: the Oedipus Complex (men) and the Electra Complex (women). Society would not allow this, so these illicit desires are repressed. Religion is therefore a projection of the father-figure, which is identified with a totem that cannot be killed, save on ceremonial occasions, when the identification of the totem with the father figure is renewed. Religion is therefore, crudely, an illusion.

1930s
ARCHETYPES AND IMAGES: CARL JUNG

The work of Darwin, Newton, Freud and others had created a post-Christian world in which people still attended churches but to which the physical removal of the institutions and symbols of religion would have made little difference. This may account for the popularity in Christian circles of Carl Gustav Jung (1875–1961). For Jung, religion was not an illusion. He came to the conclusion that humans have a natural religious function. In the 'collective unconscious' are 'archetypes' which are shared by all humans and may appear in our dreams. These archetypes are the equivalent of religious dogmas and parallel all known (to him) religious ideas. He believed religion had practical value and attributed the lack of balance in the mental state of Europeans in the 1930s to the decline of religious life.

p. 247◀ **Distant Voices** ▶p. 251

With respect to the theological view of the question. This is always painful to me. I am bewildered. I had no intention to write atheistically.... There seems to be so much misery in the world. I cannot persuade myself that a beneficent and omnipotent God would have designedly created the Ichneumonidae with the express intention of feeding within the living bodies of Caterpillars, or that a cat should play with mice....

Charles Darwin to Asa Gray (22 May 1860)

The World Wars: Pressures and Strains

1900–1944

IN 1900, MANY EUROPEANS had access to material things undreamed of in many other parts of the world. Two major wars in the next 50 years, however, would change Europe and Britain's place in it. The Churches would continue to lose influence; and there would be a rise of interest in humanism and secularism. Religion continued to be largely irrelevant, most people were neither committed nor anti-religious. Only at death did the church come into its own. As the century developed there would be a continuing tension between science and religion. The success of Hitler and the Nazi movement had a parallel voice in Britain through the activities of Oswald Mosley; and the development of Eugenics would cast a long shadow across the medical ethics of the century.

▲ *Many felt that the changing role of women after the First World War was a challenge to the long-established theology of the Virgin Mary.*

1900s
FEMINISM AND THE ROLE OF WOMEN

The enlightenment tradition was probably more prominent than evangelism in the establishment of feminism. The theology of the Virgin Mary, emphasising her obedience and making her a symbol of motherhood rather than woman, was irreconcilable with radical feminism. Three issues undermined the traditional role of women in the twentieth century. The first was the growth of the industrial economy, the second was contraception and the third was technology. The latter allowed household needs to be met and gave women opportunities to use their time for other things. Congregationalists had had female ministers since 1919; the Church of Scotland from the late 1960s, but it was not until 1994 that the Church of England ordained its first women priests.

1900s
A HUMAN IMPROVEMENT PROGRAMME

Francis Galton's work *Hereditary Genius* (1869) proposed arranged marriages between men of distinction and women of wealth. He coined the term 'eugenics' in 1881. Like most scientific theories, there would be good and less good consequences. Because some diseases are genetically transmitted, couples can be screened to see if they will pass on defective genes. Genetic surgery can, in some cases, alter harmful genes by manipulation. Programmes which range from creating sperm banks for the genetically superior to potential clonings of human beings have met with vigorous resistance. The opportunities for abuse by authoritarian regimes are obvious. The eugenists were criticised in the 1930s, when the Nazis used the theory to support the extermination of Jews, blacks and homosexuals.

1900
THE CHURCHES: DOUBTS AND FEARS

If there ever had been a concept of 'Christendom', it had disappeared by the twentieth century. When Neitzsche (1844–1900) took as his starting point 'God is Dead', he was saying, in effect, that religious conviction was not an option for the intelligent human being. Certainly, the elite still challenged traditional belief, while following basic Judaic-Christian moral values. All the Churches, except possibly the Salvation Army, appeared to have inadequate ecclesiastical machines, which could not cope with the world of the late-nineteenth century onwards. They became secularised – there were no longer absolute values and the individuality of the past. The horror of war caused deep reflection on the meaning of God, and if there were a God, what justification was there for such violent behaviour?

◉ 1909
ARCHBISHOP WILLIAM TEMPLE

The most influential clergyman of the inter-war years was William Temple (1881–1944), Archbishop of York (1929–42) and of Canterbury (1942–44). For he tried to reverse the decline in organised religion and to make England an Anglican nation again. He failed and the Church became a voice of social criticism which led it to be seen in a much more secular light. Temple was 'The People's Archbishop'. He had presided over meetings, written books, formulated statements yet he was still immensely popular with people who never read his books or heard him preach. It may have been his commitment to education and his presidency of the Workers' Educational Association from 1909 which endeared him to so many people.

1916
PACIFISM

The Conscription Act of 1916 created the term 'conscientious objector', most of whom were non-conformists. Some were not willing to play a part in war at all, while others would take non-combatant roles. The 16,500 recorded as conscientious objectors were treated very badly, and when the government finally acknowledged them, it was largely because of the work of the free churches and humanists. The distinction between 'pacificism' – the attempt to prevent war by political means – and 'pacifism' which is the refusal to take part in any war whatever the reasons and consequences, was never coherently resolved. The pacifist came to sound like an appeaser or even a sympathiser. Many individuals remained true to their pacifist faith – it was personal, spiritual and humanitarian.

► p. 255

1918
THE STATE OF THE CHURCHES

There was a crisis of authority in the Churches after the First World War, with the possible exception of the Catholic Church. Non-conformism was in decline, even in Wales and Scotland. The Church of England spoke of cohesion and discipline, but appeared ineffective. Britain was still a Christian country, the monarch was the supreme governor of the Church of England, shops closed on Sundays. The 1928 Anglican Prayer Book caused furious debate among those who were interested and the Anglo-Catholic and evangelical arms of the Church resumed their vigorous battle. The Churches were still there, in the Scouts and the Church Brigade, but the war had created a form of secular religiosity whereby the formal trappings reminded people of their inheritance and their past.

▲ *The Church suffered both physical and mental destruction after the two World Wars.*

1930
OSWALD MOSLEY AND FASCISM

In 1930 Sir Oswald Mosley (1896–1980) founded the British Union of Fascists. Mosley had been a Conservative, Independent, then a Labour MP, and believed that a dictatorial approach to government would solve economic and political problems. Mosley was an outstanding orator, with great personal charisma and, for a few years, the movement was successful. Then in 1934 the violence, extremism and anti-Semitism at a meeting caused some supporters to leave. From this time, anti-Semitism became a feature of the campaign. In May 1940, Mosley was arrested and imprisoned. Despite his outspoken xenohobia, he was an ambitious man and his radicalism touched a chord, but the British people became suspicious of his radical views. Probably the most successful radicals were the suffragettes.

1944
THE EDUCATION ACT

The Education Act of 1902 had greatly antagonised the non-conformists. Church schools, Anglican and Catholic, were to be subsidised from the public purse. The Established Church would be strengthened, the non-conformists undermined. Some Baptists went to prison rather than pay their rates. The 1944 act was a seminal piece of legislation for the religious life of the country. The Anglicans could not afford to keep all their schools and the non-conformists wanted to get rid of denominational teaching. The eventual agreement, whereby each local education authority would have its own religious education syllabus determined by an ecumenical conference, was successful. The view taken was that the Anglicans had lost control of education; they were still a part but a small part.

▲ *Lord Butler, one of the key supporters of the Education Act of 1944.*

p. 249◄ **Distant Voices** ►p. 253

O Jesus Christ!' one fellow sighed. And kneeled, and bowed, tho' not in prayer, and died.
And the Bullets sang 'In Vain',
Machine Guns chuckled 'Vain',
Big Guns guffawed 'In Vain'.
'Father and mother!' one boy said.
Then smiled – at nothing, like a small child; being dead.
And the Shrapnel cloud
Slowly gestured 'Vain',
The falling splinters muttered 'Vain'.
'My love!' another cried, 'My love, my bud!'
Then, gently lowered, his whole face kissed the mud.
And the Flares gesticulated, 'Vain'.
The Shells hooted, 'In Vain'.
The Gas hissed, 'In Vain'.

'Last Words', by Wilfred Owen (1918)

A Century of 'Isms': Ecumenism and Humanism

1902–99

NINETEENTH-CENTURY MISSIONARY activity across the world had taught the churches that working together would be more effective than pulling against each other. The International Missionary council was formed and other conferences followed, until the World Council of Churches was formally constituted in Amsterdam in 1948. Catholic participation, initially at a distance, has grown since the 1960s. In practice, the Churches work well together at local levels on practical issues; full co-operation and recognition of each other becomes more difficult as whole church administration becomes involved. Many in the churches would claim to be 'humanitarian' but would not take the name of 'humanist'. Generally, a 'humanist' in Britain would declare a need for human beings to sort out their problems, personal and social, without reference to religion.

▲ *Ludwig Wittgenstein, as open to challenging established scientific and religious thought as he was to philosophy.*

1902
WILLIAM JAMES

William James (1842–1910) was an American with a huge range of interests. He was both philosopher and psychologist and his work *The Varieties of Religious Experience* (1902), among others, has had a lasting effect. He was concerned with religious issues throughout his life and the above work studies the phenomena of mysticism and religious experience with an assessment of their validity. His work still retains its seminal significance. He developed a theory of a 'mother sea of consciousness' which plays some of the roles of an infinite God or Absolute, while leaving humans with an independence and integrity based on personal choice.

1911
SISTER CHURCHES

Inter-dominational issues are the focus for rejoicing and pain. In 1911 the Bishop of Hereford invited non-conformists to make their communion in the cathedral on Coronation Day. When attacked he denounced the protesters as 'sacerdotalists and medievalists'. But the Wars were to change the Churches' attitudes to each other. The First World War drew Orthodox and Anglican churches closer together and the Anglican Lambeth Conference of 1920 called for unity. The Edinburgh Conference of 1910 was followed by conferences in Jerusalem (1928), Madras (1938), Whitby (1947), Willengen (1952) and Ghana (1958). In 1942, the British Council of Churches was formed and then, in the 1980s, two organisations reinforced the growing sense of unity: the Council of Churches of Britain and Ireland, and Churches Together in England, marking a growing sympathy and understanding between Christian denominations.

1920s
LUDWIG WITTGENSTEIN

Ludwig Wittgenstein (1889–1951) is the leading analytical philosopher of the twentieth century, and his influence has moulded philosophy since the 1920s. He spent many years teaching in Cambridge, though born in Vienna, and having fought in the Austrian army during the First World War. Two of his most influential works were *Tractatus Logico Philosophius* (1921) and *Philosophical Investigations* (1953). He was a dissolver of orthodoxies. 'I am not a religious man but I cannot help seeing every problem from a religious point of view', he is reported to have said. He revealed that philosophical theories were as open to challenge as religious ones. His agnosticism left the door open to religious faith which influenced the balance of the debate between religion, science and philosophy.

1946
BERTRAND RUSSELL

As with many philosophers and mathematicians Russell (1875–1970) is considered to have produced his best work when he was young. *Principia Mathematica* (1910–13), written jointly with Alfred North Whitehead (1861–1947), was a magisterial work, but his best known publication is probably *History of Western Philosophy* (1946), which reveals an enormous breath of knowledge and understanding. In the public's imagination, however, he is probably best known for being a pacifist. He was imprisoned during the First World War and in his later years worked tirelessly for the Campaign for Nuclear Disarmament. He won the Nobel Prize for Literature in 1950. In *Why I am Not a Christian* (1957) he stated 'all the great religions of the world are both untrue and harmful' (and he included communism among the great religions).

1968
H. J. BLACKHAM AND THE BRITISH HUMANIST ASSOCIATION

'A humanist movement ... is pledged to work for a particular view of human advancement. Therefore it is universal in politics.... Humanism is a concern to understand and to change the world so that human life is more valuable to more people.' (H. J. Blackham, *Humanism*, 1968). Blackham (b. 1903) believes in an 'open mind' and 'open society' which Christians and communists both deny. An open society must be a plural society in which no one set of values prevails, except those of tolerance, respect for the liberty of others and humanity. Humanism is, therefore, an attitude of mind with emphasis on intellectual humility and tolerance. It is clear how this view is derived from the humanism of the Enlightenment, in fact, it is the natural corollary of Enlightenment thinking.

▲ *The queen remains the supreme governor of the Church of England.*

1999
CHURCH AND STATE: COMPLEX RELATIONS

Much liberal Protestantism in the West has become a blend of biblically oriented Christianity and democratic liberalism. In Europe, the principle of *Cuiius Regio Eius Religio* ('of whom the government, of them the ideology') has been applied. It is true that a country generates loyalty in a similar fashion to traditional religion; but is Britain a 'Christian country'? The answer, technically, is 'yes', for the monarch is the supreme governor of the Church of England, with Church and State being intertwined, but does this mean Jews, Muslims, atheists etc., are not fully British? The statement of the Prince of Wales that he wished to be the 'Defender of Faith' rather than 'the Faith' made it clear the future monarch was trying to be inclusive.

1999
HUMANISM: A STANCE FOR LIVING

Humanism is explicitly naturalistic; it denies any supernatural reality and seeks to pursue a bettering of the human condition. Human beings must decide to achieve a good life, decide what they mean by 'good' and contribute to a just society. Values are the means to resolving particular issues and are, therefore, relative to particular situations. There are different emphases within humanism – for example, secular and ethical humanism, but both are firmly based on the Enlightenment's 'rule of reason'. One of the best-known and influential humanists was John Dewey (1859–1952), but perhaps Comte's (1798–1857) words sum up the humanist position succinctly: 'man has his highest being, his 'God', in himself'.

↗ 1999
NUMBER CRUNCHING

About 27 million people (out of a 58 million population) are baptised members of the Church of England, with just over one million attending church. Even if the Catholic figure of nearly two million who attend Mass during the year is added, the statistics do not compare like with like. Membership means different things to different churches. There are, for example, over one million Presbyterians, a figure which includes – as does the figure for the Catholics – Scotland and Ireland. Perhaps the most accurate agreed statistic is that about 11 per cent of the population of the United Kingdom has membership of, or regular contact with, a Christian church. A much larger percentage will use the churches for baptisms, marriages and funerals though for the first time in 1998 secular places for the marriage ceremony were more popular than marriage in church.

▲ *Jean-Paul Sartre, one of the leaders of the Existentialist movement in the twentieth century.*

p. 251 ◀ **Distant Voices** ▶ p. 255

> *A good world needs knowledge, kindliness, and courage; it does not need a regretful hankering after the past, or a futhering of the free intelligence by the words uttered long ago by ignorant men. It needs a fearless outlook and a free intelligence.*
>
> Bertrand Russell, *Why I am Not a Christian* (1957)

Multi-faith Britain?

1940–99

IS BRITAIN A MULTI-FAITH SOCIETY? On the one hand immigration into Britain since the 1950s has seen numbers of Muslims, Sikhs and Hindus joining the Jews who have been there for centuries. On the other, the numbers of members of non-Christian religions form only about 5 per cent of the population. Perhaps it is a multi-faith world where the access offered by television and the media generally brings inter-faith issues into our houses. There have been waves of immigration into Britain, refugees from Eastern Europe, from Uganda and elsewhere; but there has been an economic immigration of people seeking a better life. All bring with them their own religions and cultures. The irony of the late twentieth century is that there are so few members of non-Christian religions that Britain is barely a multi-faith society.

1940s
LIVING AND WORKING TOGETHER

'Dialogue' became an important word in the latter half of the twentieth century. The Standing Conference on Inter-Faith Dialogue was created, as was the World Congress of Faiths and other organisations, to support inter-faith relations. In the 1980s, the Church of England produced *Guidelines on Inter-Faith Dialogue* and the Council of Christians and Jews continued to work for better relations between these two faiths. The Commonwealth Service in Westminster Abbey, however, continued to draw objections because of the presence of non-Christian religions. Teaching about World Religions blossomed in schools and universities and the Calendar of Religious Festivals produced by The Shap Working Party on World Religions in Education found its way into prisons, chain stores, hospitals and industry as the plural nature of British society was recognised as a reality.

p. 248◀ **Triumphs & Tragedies**

1999
BUDDHIST APPEAL IN THE WEST

Buddhism has a lack of dogmatism and an emphasis on free enquiry, personal experiences and development. This in itself is an attraction to those who believe institutional religion has lost its relevance and moral authority. In many ways the Buddhist ideal is a natural progression from the humanism of the Enlightenment and it has an appeal to intellectuals in the West. The flexibility of Buddhist thought and practice has enabled it to clothe itself with the cultural garb of the countries in which it rests. There are certainly many forms of Buddhism in Britain today and there are probably 50,000 active Buddhists in the country. Buddhism does not disassociate itself from other thought-systems, rather it associates with them in order to bring about the realisation of a Buddhist system.

▲ *The popularity of Buddhism and other Eastern religions has increased in the West.*

1950s
THE BRITISH SIKH COMMUNITY

Although there were Sikhs in Britain before the First World War, the major influx of Sikhs came in the 1950s, to be joined by their families in the 1960s. The number of Sikhs in Britain is uncertain, it is probably between 350,000–400,000. They are one of the most distinctive groups in Britain thanks to the males wearing turbans and having a beard. These are the normal signs of male Sikhism, though some men do shave and cut their hair. Essentially, Sikhs continue to live in the same way as in India: marriages are 'assisted', co-education is accepted but not entirely welcome, though as a group they appear to have assimilated into British culture, while still retaining their own religious identity.

✯ 1988
HOPE FOR THE FUTURE: THE EDUCATION REFORM ACT

Forty-four years after the Education Act of 1944, a new Act transformed education in England and Wales. Among its many features was the requirement that religious education in school should take account of the fact that the principal religion in Britain was Christianity, while taking account of the country's other religions. The old religious education syllabuses for schools after 1944 had been largely lists of Bible stories but towards the end of the century, the plurality of Britain was recognised in law. Pupils would not now learn only about Christianity, but would have to be taught about other religious beliefs, thoughts and practices. The shelves of classrooms were filled with religious education textbooks including a variety of religions. Not all teachers and parents approved of the change.

▲ *Muslim communities have been assimilated into the myriad faiths that can now be found in Britain.*

1998
MUSLIM COMMUNITIES IN BRITAIN

In 1998, the first state-supported Muslim school opened. This was a landmark for the Muslim community in Britain which, for many years, had sought to be placed on the same footing as Christians and Jews. It was an important decision, for it was an issue on which Muslims had protested for years. Today there are about one million Muslims in the United Kingdom. The first purpose-built mosque is over 100 years old and stands in Woking in Surrey, but the rapid increase in numbers of Muslims means there are now hundreds of mosques in Britain. The major single group of Muslims comes from South Asia but before the Second World War, the majority of Muslims in the country were Arabs.

1999
JEWS IN BRITAIN

Most of the structures of Anglo-Jewish community were in place over 100 years ago, before the Jewish population grew in size during the twentieth century. There are about 300,000 Jews in the United Kingdom. About 80 per cent of religious Jews belong to one of the orthodox groupings; the remaining 20 per cent is divided into Reform and Liberal Judaism. One of the dominant themes of the Jewish tradition is the goal of freedom from oppression and Jews, of whatever persuasion, have been deeply involved in all aspects of social concern and social welfare. The long dark shadow of the Holocaust lies over the Jewish people, yet it was only many years after the Second World War that the survivors felt able to tell their story.

1999
HINDUS AND LIFE IN BRITAIN

'Hinduism' is the name given to the religious beliefs and practices of Indians who are not members of mainstream religious groups, such as Christians or Muslims. Indians have been coming to Britain for hundreds of years – the most influential being Vivekananda at the end of the nineteenth century. His teaching of the philosophy of *Vedanta* influenced many in the West. The population of Leicester is about 20 per cent Hindu and there are over 300,000 Hindus across the country as a whole, mostly from Gujerat. The most potent symbol of Hinduism presence in Britain today is the spectacular temple (or Mandir) at Neasden. For the average Briton, however, the familiar face of 'Hinduism' is the Hari Krishna monks in their robes chanting and dancing in the street.

1999
TOLERANCE, DISCRIMINATION AND RESPECT

The paradox of religious affiliation in Britain is that while most people do not practice religion, do not pay attention to the internal arguments of the faiths, and manage their lives successfully without resource to bell, book or candle, they can experience an intolerance of what is 'foreign'. By this is usually meant an 'overseas religion'. The imperial legacy of Britain provided an unconscious assumption of superiority that applied equally to religion. The violence and rapacity apparent in the history of Christianity (internal and external) is forgotten and the 'new' religion (or 'new religion' to these shores) is subject to vilification and abuse. Many of the members of the new religious movements which have arrived since 1950 continue to be subject to discrimination and bigotry, notably the Moonies, Scientologists and Krishna-followers.

▲ *Hare Krishna followers worship at their temple in Bloomsbury in central London.*

p. 253◄ **Distant Voices**

My devotion to Truth has drawn me into the field of politics; and I can say without the slightest hesitation, and yet in all humility, that those who say that religion has nothing to do with politics do not know what religion means.

M. K. Gandhi, *An Autobiography or The Story of My Experiments with Truth* (1927)

Glossary

Aesthetic Movement
Movement dating from around 1880, based on the belief that idealised beauty and art were the pinnacle of human existence; followers included Oscar Wilde.

Agnosticism
Belief that the existence of God is indeterminable, but one which does not exclude belief in other spiritual existence.

Anabaptists
Members of Protestant movements, generally from the sixteenth century, who rejected child baptism in favour of adult baptism.

Anglicanism
Belief in the Christian teachings and doctrine of the Church of England, as opposed to that of the Roman Catholic Church.

Anglo-Saxon
Germanic Angle, Saxon or Jute tribes that settled in England from the fifth century, taking advantage of Roman withdrawal to set up individually ruled kingdoms or provinces.

Anti-Semitism
Practice of persecution or discrimination against members of the Jewish faith; anti-Semites may deny the Jews their right to a homeland.

Apartheid
Afrikaans word to describe the former segregation of races in South Africa, based on a belief in white superiority.

Atheism
Tendency to preclude the existence of a Christian God, unlike agnostics, who are sceptical about such existence.

Benedictine Rule
Sixth-century document composed by St Benedict of Nursia that serves to rule and organise life in monasteries.

Bronze Age
Period dating from around 3000–2000 BC, when people began using metal-making technology based on copper and its alloys.

Buddhism
Eastern religion based on the teachings of the sixth-century Buddha; these are founded in the destruction of mortal desires, and thus unhappiness, which can be attained by following virtuous paths.

Byzantium
Ancient Greek city, the capital of a Mediterranean empire, with a distinctive architecture and orthodox religious art.

Calvinism
Strict sixteenth-century Protestant theology, founded by John Calvin, which placed biblical authority above the Church's traditions; it strongly influenced the Puritans.

Capitalism
Economic system of private rather than state ownership, as a means to employ people and produce food and goods.

Carolingian Era
Term relating to the Frankish royal dynasty which ruled France from the eighth to tenth centuries, during which time it became Europe's most powerful Christian kingdom.

Celtic
Ancient European people, their art and languages, who were marginalised to Wales, Scotland, Ireland and Brittany by the Romans and successive invaders.

Chartism
British movement of the 1840s that campaigned for better industrial labour conditions and democratic representation for the working classes.

Civil War, the
Periodic war in the 1640s between royalist supporters of the king, Charles I, who had ruled without Parliament until 1640, and republicans under the leadership of Oliver Cromwell.

Cold War
Phoney war marked by military tension and nuclear threats between western alliances and the Soviet Union after 1945.

Commonwealth, the
Oliver Cromwell's seventeenth-century republican parliamentary protectorate; also used to describe Britain's post-1945 association of independent ex-colonies.

Communism
Classless economic system of public ownership, where producing goods and food is a communal activity for the general good; made popular in the nineteenth century by theorists such as Karl Marx and Friedrich Engels.

Constitution
Fundamental principles on which a state is governed; may be written or based on precedent, but should embody the rights of the individual.

Cro-Magnon
Early type of Stone Age *Homo sapien* who lived in Europe during Paleolithic times.

Crusades
Series of wars from the eleventh to thirteenth centuries, ostensibly to recover Palestine, the Holy City, from Muslim control, but generally acknowledged as imperialist in foundation.

Dark Ages
Period in Europe from the fifth to eleventh centuries, noted for its lack of enlightenment in thought or government, law and order.

Devolution
Process whereby certain powers are passed, or devolved, from central government to regional governments, such as Scotland or Wales.

Disestablishment
Situation in which the Church of England is denied constitutional involvement in Parliament and no longer holds the position of a national institution.

Dissenters
Christian believers who refused to conform to the established Church of England; dissenters could be Catholic or non-conformist Protestants.

Druidism
Pre-Christian pagan religion of the Celtic people in which priests were learned, artistic and significant members of the social order.

East Angles
Eastern English kingdom of the Angles – Germanic invaders who settled in the fifth and sixth centuries; now known as East Anglia.

Easter Rising
Battle resulting from continued British denial of home rule for the Irish; took place in Dublin, Easter 1916.

Ecumenicism
Thinking that argues for the unity of Christian Churches of all denominations from around the world.

Enlightenment, the
Seventeenth-century intellectual movement in which rational thought and science came to bear over the irrationality and superstition characteristic of earlier periods.

Episcopalian
Churches that are governed by the rule of bishops and are in full communion with the Church of England.

European Union
Originally termed the Common Market; it is an organisation whose aim is to maximise Europe's economic power and potential through financial collaboration.

Fascism
Authoritarian political movement, particularly powerful in the 1930s–40s, where democracy and liberalism were abandoned in favour of nationalistic ideology; fascist regimes often fell under the leadership of a dictator.

Feminism
Intellectual and political philosophy and movement which argues women's rights to equality in education, law and the workplace.

Festival of Britain
1950s celebration of British and Commonwealth post-war optimism, marked by building the South Bank arts centre in London.

Feudalism
Social and legal system, whereby peasant farmers worked a lord's land in exchange for small pecuniary rewards, protection and service in battle.

Fin de Siècle
Prevailing artistic mood at the close of the nineteenth century – one both of optimism and decadence.

French Revolution
Eighteenth-century popular uprising that saw a decadent, incompetent monarchy overthrown and its aristocracy stripped of land and power.

Gaul
Area of Europe during Roman times, covering what is now France and stretching to northern Italy and the Netherlands.

Glorious Revolution
Replacement of the king, James II, with William of Orange and his wife Mary in 1688; it led to the Bill of Rights and constitutional power for Parliament.

Guilds
Trade associations in which members share the same skill, such as silvermaking, in order to maintain craft standards and protect business.

Heretics
Those who held beliefs contrary to the teachings of the established church; heretics were frequently burnt at the stake if they would not recant.

Hinduism
Dominant religion of India; Hinduism is characterised by a complex system of customs and beliefs, including reincarnation and a caste system, as well as numerous gods.

Huguenots
French Calvinist Protestants, who were involved in the French Wars of Religion against Catholics (1562–98); they co-existed for a time, then fled to England as the persecution increased.

Imperialism
Policy and practice of a state to influence or conquer others in order to expand its wealth, power and influence.

Industrial Revolution
Process by which Britain and other countries were transformed into industrial powers during the eighteenth and nineteenth centuries, by means of technological advance and invention.

Iron Age
Period dating from around 1000–500 BC during which barbarian tribes, which were contemporaries of classical Mediterranean and African civilisations, began to use iron rather than bronze.

Islam
Religion founded in the seventh century AD by the prophet Muhammad, messenger of Allah; Islam emphasises God's omnipotence and inscrutability.

Jacobite
Follower of James II or his descendants, wishing to restore the Stuarts to the throne after the Glorious Revolution.

Judaism
Religion and cultural tradition of the Jewish people; Judaism follows one God and is based on the *Pentateuch.*

Liberalism
Thinking which attaches importance to the civil and political rights of individuals, and their freedoms of speech and expression.

Lollards
Fourteenth-century movement under the leadership of John Wyclif; Lollards challenged Church corruption and emphasised personal not clerical interpretations of the Bible.

Materialism
Philosophical idea that the world is made of tangible matter and what we see or feel is created by our minds.

Maypoles
Poles painted with spiral stripes and decked with flowers; danced around on May Day to celebrate the coming Spring.

Medieval
Cultures and beliefs of the Middle Ages, dating from the Roman Empire's fifth-century decline to the fifteenth-century Renaissance.

Mercia
Most powerful Anglo-Saxon kingdom encroached upon by Viking settlers and the Danelaw before disappearing after the Norman conquest.

Mesolithic
Middle era of the Stone Age, when the final Ice Age disappeared to produce present-day climates 10,000 years ago.

Mesopotamia
Land between the Rivers Tigris and Euphrates, now Iraq, where Sumer and Babylon flourished from around 3500 BC.

Modernism
Early twentieth-century approach to the arts that explored Freud's ideas on human consciousness through abstract artistic techniques.

Muslim
Followers of Islam, whose sacred book is the Qur'an; membership falls into sects – the main two are Sunni or Shi'ite.

Napoleonic Wars
Series of battles fought between 1803–15; they brought much of Europe under Napoleon's dictatorship until France's final defeat by the British.

Nazism
German fascist regime of the National Socialist Party, led by Adolf Hitler from 1933, who desired an empire for what he called his 'Aryan' race; characterised by persecution of minorities.

Neanderthal
Type of primitive Stone Age man, who hunted and gathered thoughout Europe in late Paleolithic times.

Neolithic
Final part of the Stone Age period, marked by the development of agriculture and forest clearance, dating from around 8000–3000 BC.

Nobel Prize
Prizes established by Alfred Nobel, awarded for outstanding contributions in various fields.

Normans
Viking 'Northmen' who settled in France, then expanded and took control of what is now Normandy, then conquered England under King William I.

Old English
Earliest English, spoken by Anglo-Saxons from their first settlements in the fifth to twelfth centuries.

Paganism
From the fourteenth century, worshippers following any other religion other than Christianity; for a while pagan rituals and beliefs were tolerated, then pagans began to suffer persecution.

Paleolithic
Stone Age period, divided into lower, middle and upper eras, dating from approximately one million years ago to around 10,000 BC, the start of the Mesolithic Stone Age; Paleolithic times saw modern man develop from earlier types.

Paternalism
When a male ruling class or politicians believe that they act parentally, in the interests of women and the lower classes.

Patriotism
Historically a devotion to and desire to defend one's nation and way of life; patriotism can now have nationalistic connotations.

Pelagianism
Fifth-century version of Christianity, received as heretical; it was formulated by Pelagius, who rejected the idea of mankind's original sin.

Persia
Now called Iran; Persia headed an Asian and Mediterranean empire from 550 BC until defeated by Alexander the Great.

Phoenician
Mediterranean civilisation of explorers and traders that flourished from 1200 BC until conquered by Alexander the Great in 332 BC.

Picts
Roman name given to Scottish tribes inhabiting Britain before the Celts; the Picts united with Scotland's Celts in AD 844.

Prehistoric
Period that covers from the beginning of life on earth, 3.5 billion years ago, to approximately 3500 BC, when humans began to keep records.

Pre-Raphaelites
Mid-nineteenth-century naturalistic movement that shunned the artistic conventions used since Raphael, and focused on biblical and literary subjects.

Presbyterian
Sixteenth-century Protestant puritans, who followed Calvinism; Presbyterians set up non-conformist churches eliminating Catholic rituals and organ music.

Protestantism
Christian religious faith that takes its name from Martin Luther's protest against Roman Catholic corruption in 1529, which precipitated major splits in European Christianity.

Puritanism
Extreme following of Protestantism; puritanism was characterised by austerity, opposition to sexual freedom and belief in the Divine Right of Kings.

Racism
Belief in the superiority of one race over another, often manifesting itself in social and civil discrimination or violence.

Reformation
Sixteenth-century European movement to reform the Catholic Church, used by Henry VIII to separate the Church of England from Rome.

Renaissance
Fourteenth to seventeenth century European intellectual and artistic movement, ending the Middle Ages with its emphasis on science and exploration.

Republicanism
Support for a system where heads of state are not monarchs; only once realised in England under Oliver Cromwell, who was named 'Lord Protector'.

Restoration
Period when the English monarch (Charles II) was restored after the seventeenth-century civil war and Cromwell's republic.

Romanticism
Late eighteenth to early nineteenth-century Classical artistic movement in Europe, emphasising individual imagination, inspired by revolution and social changes.

Saxons
German tribes that responded to fifth-century Roman decline by expanding west until absorbed into the Frankish Empire.

Secularism
Belief that rejects religion, particularly in political or civil matters, and embraces worldly and material rather than sacred things.

Sikhism
Belief in the religion founded as a Hindu sect in the sixteenth century by Guru Nanak, teaching the belief in one god.

Solstice
Longest and shortest days in the year; celebrated in pagan ceremonies by Druids at sites such as Stonehenge.

Stone Age
The earliest period of human culture, marked by the use of stone implements and covering Paleolithic, Mesolithic and Neolithic times.

Stuart Period
Era covering the reigns of the Stuart kings: James I (VI of Scotland), Charles I and II; it ended Tudor rule and saw unity with Scotland and Ireland, autocratic governance and civil war.

Suffragism
Belief in the extension of suffrage, generally to women and the working classes, who were traditionally denied the right to vote.

Teutonic
Named after fifth century invaders of Bavaria, Teutonic Knights were medieval aristocratic German crusaders carrying Roman Catholicism to eastern Europe.

Toryism
Political ideology of Conservative values, from 1680 to modern day Conservatives, traditionally supported by landed classes and latterly the middle classes.

Utilitarianism
Ethical thinking outlined by Jeremy Bentham and John Stuart Mill maintaining that actions are morally right if leading to happiness.

Utopianism
Idea that an ideal society is possible where systems are set in place for humans to live in co-operative communities.

Wars of the Roses
English civil wars fought from 1455–85 between the houses of Lancaster and York, over Henry Tudor's claim to the throne.

Whigs
Predecessors of the Liberals who opposed the Tories; Whigs enjoyed much power in the eighteenth century, advocating commercialism and tolerance.

Bibliography

The authors and publishers readily acknowledge the work of a large number of scholars and published works on which they have drawn in the preparation of this book. Artwork and text references have been drawn from a wide variety of sources. Among them are the following books which can provide a good source of further information:

Alford, B. W. E., *Britain in the World Economy Since 1880*, Harlow, 1996

Arnold, C. J. *An Archeology of the early Anglo-Saxon Kingdoms*, London, 1998

Banks, A., *A Military Atlas of the First World War*, London, 1975

Bennett, M., *The Civil Wars In Britain and Ireland, 1638-1651,* Oxford, 1997

Blair, P. H., *Roman Britain and Early England, 55 BC–AD 871*, 1963

Brailsford, Dennis, *British Sport: a Social History*, Cambridge, 1997

Brownstone, D. and Franck, I., *Timelines of War*, USA, 1996

Bruce, George, *Collins Dictionary of Wars*, London, 1995

Carruth, Gordon, *The Encyclopedia of World Facts and Dates*, New York, 1993

Chandler, David, *The Dictionary of Battles*, London, 1987

Chapman, Stanley, *Merchant Enterprise in Britain from the Industrial Revolution to World War One*, Cambridge, 1992

Cootes, R. J. *Britain Since 1700*, London, 1968

Corrie, L. W., *Life in Britain*, London, 1980

Cunliffe, Barry (Foreword), *The Cassell Atlas of World History*, London, 1997

Dalton, P., *Conquest, Anarchy & Lordship, Yorkshire, 1066–1154*, Cambridge, 1994

Darby H. C. (ed.), *A New Historical Geography of England*, Cambridge, 1973

Darvill, T., *Prehistoric Britain*, London, 1987

Daunton, M. J., *Progress and Poverty: An Economic and Social History of Britain, 1700–1850*, Oxford, 1995

Deane, P., *The First Industrial Revolution*, Cambridge, 1965

Delaney, Frank, *A Walk in the Dark Ages*, London, 1994

Du Boulery, F. R. H., *An Age of Reason*, London, 1970

Edmund, G. E., *Land and Society*, London, 1994

Eliade, Mircea, *A History of Religious Ideas*, Chicago, 1982

Evans, Eric, *The Complete A-Z Nineteenth and Twentieth Century British History Handbook*, London, 1998

Fieldhouse, D. K., *The Colonial Empires*, London, 1966

Foreman-Peck, James and Millward, Robert, *Public and Private Ownership of British Industry 1820–1990*, Oxford, 1994

Friend, W. H. C., *The Rise of Christianity*, London, 1984

Fussell, P., *The Great War and Modern Memory* , London, 1975

Gilbert, Martin, *The Dent Atlas of British History*, London, 1993

Goodman, A. *The Wars of the Roses, Military Activity and English Society, 1452–1497*, London, 1981

Graham-Campbell, J. (ed.), *Atlas of the Viking World*, Oxford, 1994

Greene, D. M., *Greene's Biographical Encyclopedia of Composers*, London, 1996

Haigh, Christopher (ed.), *The Cambridge Historical Encyclopedia of Great Britain and Ireland*, Cambridge, 1996

Hayes, M. and Smalley, K. (eds), *Work, Employment & Development*, London, 1990

Herrin, J., *The Formation of Christendom*, 1987

Hobsbawm, E. J., *The Penguin Economic History of Britain, Volume 3: Industry and Empire*, London, 1990

Janson, H .W., *History of Art*, London, 1991

Jones, B. & Mattingly, D., *An Atlas of Roman Britain*, Oxford, 1990

Keen, M., *The Pelican History of Medieval Europe*, London, 1968

Kenny, Anthony, *The Oxford History of Western Philosophy*, Oxford, 1994

Kinder, Hermann & Hilgemann, W., *The Penguin Atlas of World History Vols 1 & 2*, Penguin

Knowles, D., *The Monastic Order in England 940–1216*, Cambridge, 1963

Kussmaul, A. *A General View of the Rural Economy of England, 1538–1840*, Cambridge, 1990

Lanfton, J. & Morris, R. J. (eds), *Atlas of Industrialising Britain, 1780–1914*, London, 1986

Larkin, Colin, *The Virgin Encyclopedia of Popular Music*, London, 1997

Laybourn, Keith, *Britain on the Breadline*, Surrey, 1990

Lloyd, T. O., *The British Empire, 1558–1995*, Oxford, 1996

Marshall, P. J. (ed.), *The Eighteenth Century: Oxford History of the British Empire, Vol. II*, Oxford, 1998

Mathias, Hefin, *Wales and Britain in the Early Medieval World c. 1000–c. 1500*, London, 1996

Mayr-Harting, H., *The Coming of Christianity to Anglo-Saxon England*, London, 1972

McManners, John, *The Oxford History of Christianity*, Oxford, 1993

Messenger, Charles, *The Century of Warfare: Worldwide Conflict from 1900 to the Present Day*, London, 1995

Morgan, Kenneth O. (ed.), *The Oxford Illustrated History of Britain*, Oxford, 1997

Morillo, S., *Warfare Under the Anglo-Norman Kings, 1066–1135*, Woodbridge, 1994

Newman, P., *A Companion to the English Civil Wars*, Oxford, 1990

Parker, G. (Ed.) *The Times Atlas of World History* (4th ed.), London, 1996

Pollard, A. J. *The Wars of the Roses*, London, 1988

Pope, R. (ed.), *Atlas of British Social and Economic History Since c. 1700*, London, 1990

Pugh, Martin, *The Making of Modern British Politics*, Oxford, 1982

Quennell, Q. and C. H. B., *A History of Everyday Things 1066–1799*, London, 1931

Radway, R. *Britain, 1900-1951*, London, 1997

Reay, Barry, *Popular Cultures in England 1550–1750*, London, 1998

Rolleston, T. W., *Celtic*, London, 1995

Ross, Josephine, *Kings and Queens of Britain*, London, 1982

Salway, P., *Roman Britain*, Oxford, 1981

Sauvain, Philip A., *British Economic and Social History*, 1987

Savage, A. (trans.), *The Anglo-Saxon Chronicles*, London, 1982

Smout, T. C., *A History of the Scottish Peoples*, London, 1969

Solomon, R. C. and Higgins, K. M., *A Short History of Philosophy*, New York, 1996

Taylor, A. J. P., *English History, 1914–1945*, Oxford, 1965

Taylor, David, *Mastering Economic and Social History*, London, 1988

The Cambridge Guide to the Arts in Britain, Cambridge, 1989

The Hutchinson Illustrated Encyclopedia of British History, Oxford, 1998

Treasure, Geoffrey, *Who's Who in British History*, London, 1997

Walsh, B., *British Economic & Social History*, London, 1997

Wood, Jack, *Union for Recovery the Failure and Rise of British Industry*, Wembley, 1986

Young, John, W., *Britain and the World in the Twentieth Century*, London, 1997

Author Biographies and Picture Credits

PROFESSOR E. J. EVANS
General Editor
Eric Evans is a Professor of Social History at Lancaster University. He has contributed to numerous historical studies as well as writing many of his own titles.

DAVID BOYLE
Ordinary Lives; Culture, Arts and Leisure
David Boyle is an experienced journalist and editor of *Liberal Democrat News*. He has written on a range of subjects, from money to the arts.

ALAN BROWN
Religions, Belief and Thought
Alan Brown is an educationalist at The National Society. He has contributed to a number of works on all aspects of religion and belief.

MALCOLM CHANDLER
Britain in the World
Malcolm Chandler is a historian and author, who has written widely on all manner of historical subjects, particularly for schools.

DAVID HARDING
Politics and Power
David Harding is an experienced journalist, who writes on a wide range of subjects. He has contributed to numerous books and magazines and his specialist subjects are as diverse as sport and political history.

BRENDA RALPH LEWIS
The Peoples of Britain
Brenda Ralph Lewis has been writing on historical subjects for 35 years. She has published 85 history books, and has contributed to many others, as well as to numerous magazines and BBC programmes.

JON SUTHERLAND
Industry and Invention
Jon Sutherland is an experienced writer and a lecturer in Business Studies. His specialist interests include economics and science, and he has written over 50 books.

Allsport: 214 (r).

Christie's Images: 23 (t), 26, 75 (t), 88, 89 (b), 167 (l), 197 (b), 198 (t), 238.

Foundry Arts: Claire Dashwood 130.

Image Select: 28, 31 (b), 36 (t), 37, 39, 46 (r), 47, 48 (l), 51 (l), 52 (r), 69 (b), 80 (r), 81, 82 (r), 85 (r), 86 (l), 89 (t), 93, 96, 98 (b), 104, 105 (r), 107, 108 (t), 109, 118 (l), 122, 124 (l), 131 (l), 132 (l), 138 (b), 145 (l), 156 (r), 165 (t), 167 (r), 170 (l), 176 (r), 183, 184, 192 (r), 194, 198 (b), 200 (t), 202 (l), 204, 216 (t), 217, 222, 224, 235 (b), 237 (l), 239 (t), 249. **Image Select/CFCL:** 75 (b). **Image Select/Ann Ronan:** 62, 103 (r), 135, 141, 63 (t), 169 (b), 173, 211 (t), 240. **Image Select/Giraudon:** 20 (l), 24, 31 (t), 33, 36 (b), 52 (l), 56 (l), 58, 123 (b), 133, 142, 168, 172, 191 (l), 192 (l), 233 (r), 235 (t). **Image Select/FPG:** 25, 32 (l), 51 (r), 73 (l), 91, 151, 160 (t), 170 (r).

Mary Evans Picture Library: 18, 20 (r), 22, 29, 34, 35, 38, 44, 46 (l), 48 (r), 50, 54, 59, 61, 63, 64, 66 (r), 69 (t), 71, 78, 80 (l), 82 (l), 83, 85 (t), 86 (r), 87, 90 (r), 92, 95, 97, 98 (t), 99, 100, 101, 103 (l), 105 (l), 106, 108 (b), 111, 116, 118 (r), 119, 120 (r), 121, 124 (r), 125, 126 (r), 127, 128, 131 (r), 132 (r), 134 (r), 136 (b), 137, 138 (t), 140 (r), 143 (r), 146, 148, 149, 150, 153 (t), 154, 156 (l), 158 (l), 159, 164, 166, 169 (t), 171, 174, 175, 176 (l), 177, 178, 179, 181 (l), 182 (l), 193, 195 (l), 199, 201, 205 (t), 206, 207 (l), 208 (r), 210, 212, 213, 214 (l), 215, 225 (r), 226, 229, 231 (l), 234, 236, 241, 242, 243, 244, 245, 246 (r), 247, 248.

Topham: 21, 23 (b), 27, 32 (r), 42, Associated Press 41, 43 (l), Press Association 43 (r), 53, 56, 57, 60, 66 (l), 67, 70, 72, 73 (r), 74, 76, Press Association 77 (l), 77 (r), 84, 90 (l), 110, 11 (l), 112, 113, Press Association 114, 115, 120 (l), 123 (t), 126 (l), 129, 134 (l), 136 (t), 139, 140 (l), 143 (l), Press Association 145 (r), 152, Associated Press 153 (b), 158 (r), 160 (b), 161, 162, 163 (b), 165 (b), 181 (r), 182 (r), 185, 186, 187, 188, 190, 191 (r), 195 (r), 196, 197 (r), 200 (l), 202 (r), 203, 205 (b), 207 (r), 208 (l), 209, 211 (b), 216 (b), 218, 219, 220, 221, 225 (l), 227, 228, 230, 231 (r), 232, 233 (l), 237 (r), 239 (b), 246 (l), 250, 251 (l), Press Association 251 (r), 252, 253, 254, 255.

Visual Arts Library: 55.

Every effort has been made to contact copyright holders of pictures used in this book. In the event of an oversight, the publishers will be pleased to rectify any omissions in future editions of the book.

Index